LIVE FROM THE
MISSISSIPPI
DELTA

LIVE FROM THE MISSISSIPPI DELTA

PANNY FLAUTT MAYFIELD

University Press of Mississippi / Jackson

www.upress.state.ms.us

The University Press of Mississippi is a member
of the Association of American University Presses.

Copyright © 2017 by University Press of Mississippi
All photographs © copyright Panny Flautt Mayfield

First printing 2017
∞

Library of Congress Cataloging-in-Publication Data

Names: Mayfield, Panny Flautt.
Title: Live from the Mississippi Delta / Panny Flautt Mayfield.
Description: Jackson : University Press of Mississippi, [2017] | Includes index.
Identifiers: LCCN 2017003568 (print) | LCCN 2017008296 (ebook) | ISBN
9781496813749 (cloth : alk. paper) | ISBN 9781496813756 (epub single) |
ISBN 9781496813763 (epub institutional) | ISBN 9781496813770 (pdf single)
| ISBN 9781496813787 (pdf institutional)
Subjects: LCSH: Blues (Music)—Mississippi—Delta (Region)—History and
criticism.
Classification: LCC ML3521 .M4 2017 (print) | LCC ML3521 (ebook) | DDC
781.64309753—dc23
LC record available at https://lccn.loc.gov/2017003568

British Library Cataloging-in-Publication Data available

CONTENTS

ACKNOWLEDGMENTS

This manuscript documenting decades of blues events and musicians I have been privileged to know would not have come together without the encouragement of Molly Porter and her confidence in the importance of its stories. A talented artist and landscape painter from Vermont who fell in love with the Delta and its magic in the 1990s, Molly lived here, captured its aura in her own artistic collections, and experienced its blues culture. Although she now lives and paints in her studio on the Porter family's farm, she remains our New England daughter, staying in close touch and visiting the Delta at least once a year. Molly scanned hundreds of my photographs, continually critiques my work, and offers sane, impartial opinions. Her parents and other family members are talented published writers and have been supportive of this project for years.

PANNY MAYFIELD

A journalist, documentarian, collector of stories and fables—

"knower" of families and dynasties . . . "capturer" of the moment,
then, now, and beyond . . .

Charming and erudite she crosses the unspoken divide . . . the social
and emotional negotiations everyone must make in the Delta . . .

Her photographs and ledgers are a testimony to the care and love
of her peoples, their histories, and their mysterious homeland.

—ROBERT PLANT

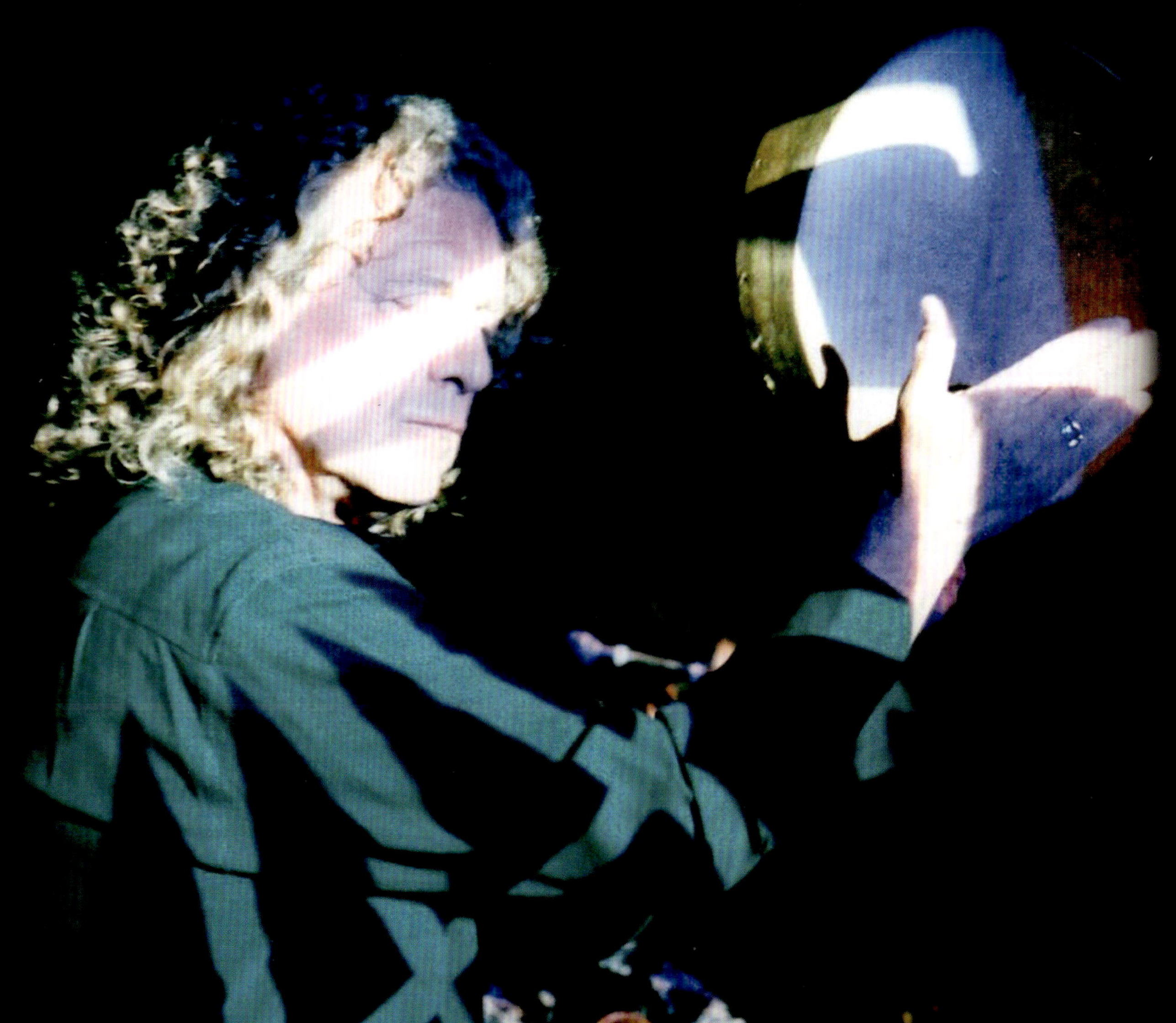

LIVE FROM THE MISSISSIPPI DELTA

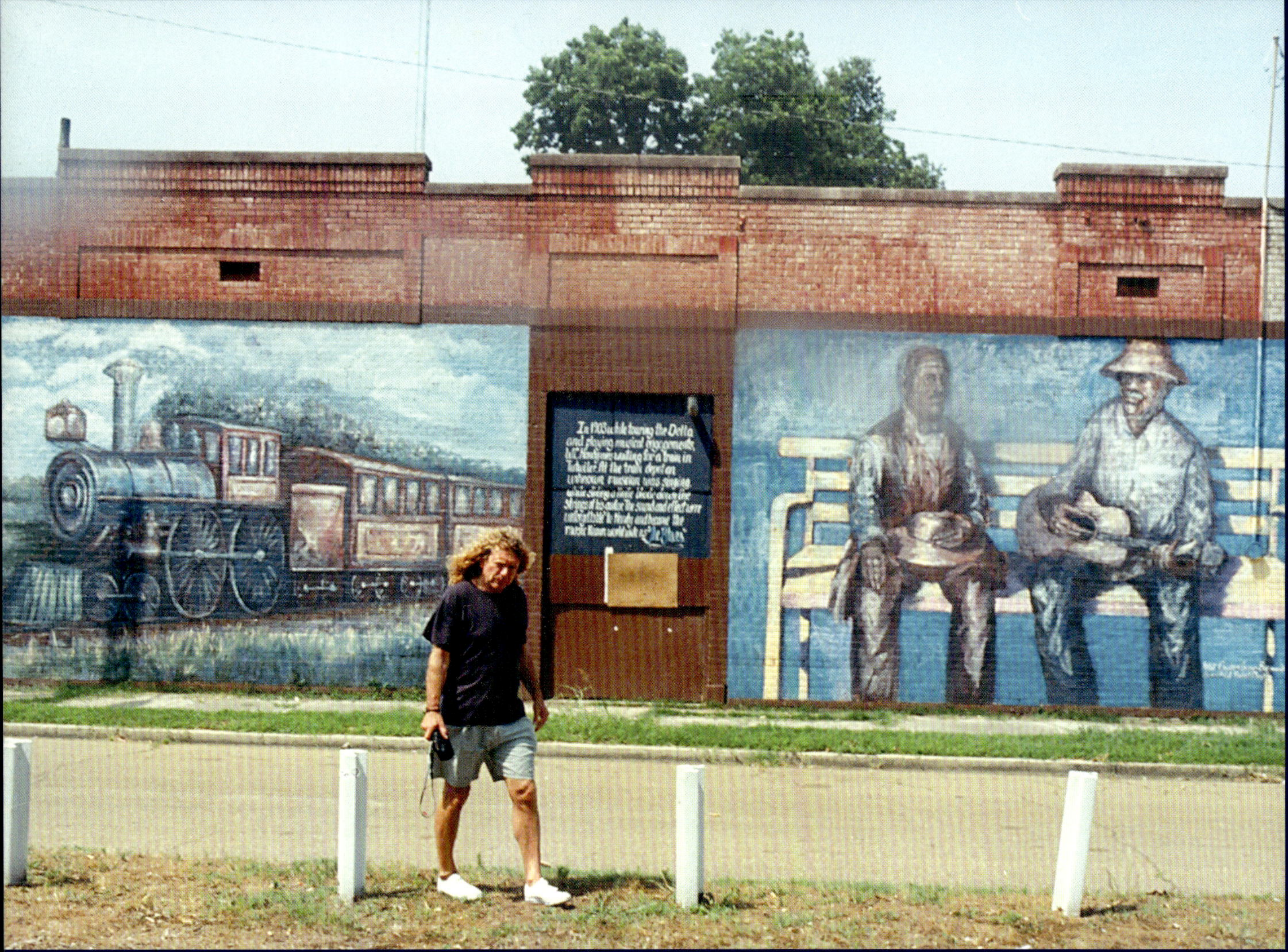

Outlawing advance publicity about his coming to Tutwiler,
quintessential rock star Robert Plant faces a small crowd of
Senior Citizens Club members in Railroad Park. Although
they knew he was responsible for a historic marker being
unveiled, they were clueless about his identity. At a reception
afterward, in the Tutwiler Community Education Center, he
receives a T-shirt and crafts from the center's cottage industry
quilters from Tutwiler mayor Genether Miller-Spurlock, and Sr.
Maureen Delaney, center director.

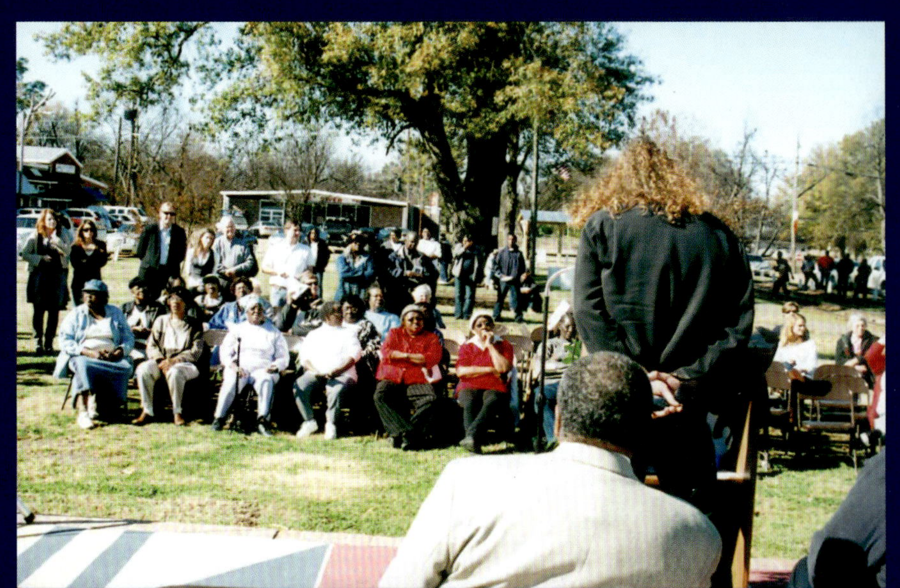

1

ROBERT PLANT COMES TO TUTWILER

Although shadows of the devil and Robert Johnson may mark its flatlands, the Mississippi Delta is God's Country to those of us who live here and would be miserable anywhere else. Leaving could never be in May, with its clusters of privet hedge, honeysuckle, and magnolia overwhelming the senses, and pale primroses, purple vetch, and thistles spilling over the roadside and ditch banks. Summer is lay-by time for cotton, followed by fall's fast pace of excitement, and the barebones vastness of a brown winter landscape interrupted only by cypress brakes.

Growing up in Tutwiler, a busy railroad town fifteen miles south of Clarksdale, I was aware of

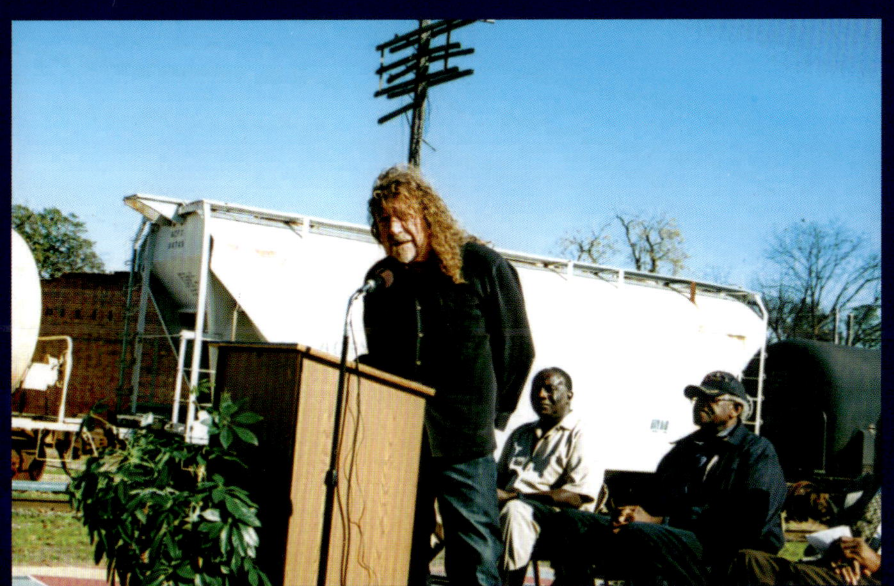

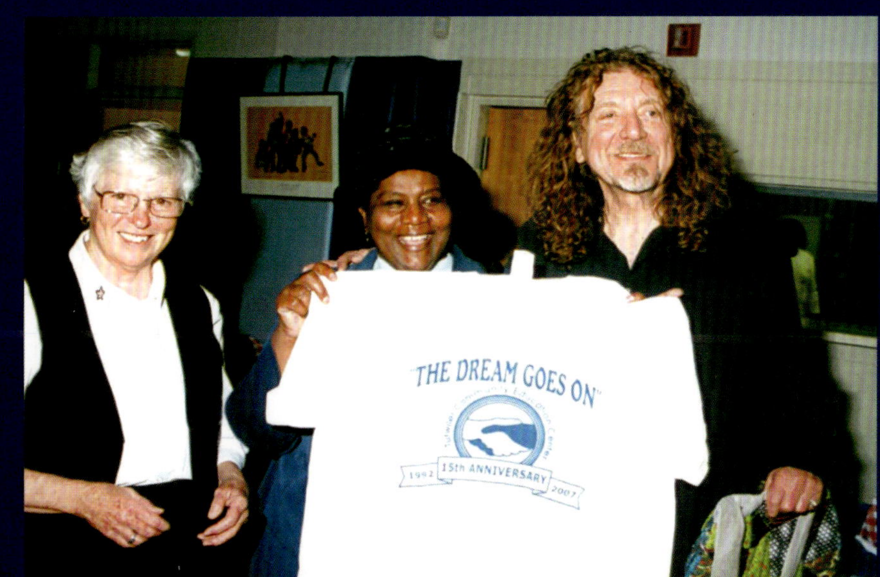

places like Lula Mae's Sunrise Café. Located not far from the depot and Foster's Shoe Repair Shop, it angled across the street from Lomenick's Meat Market. At the time it also was so off-limits to me, I never dreamed of stepping inside to hear infectious music. On weekends I was probably inside the Tutrovansum Theatre (named for Tutwiler and neighboring towns of Rome, Vance, and Sumner) watching Randolph Scott movies, running through backyards playing "kick the can," or experimenting with a Brownie camera. Ora Lee and Jack Mahan, who ran the picture show, once interrupted the movie to enlist cars to light up Strange Flying Service's airstrip with their headlights so the local crop duster could make a night landing. When he touched down, all returned to the movie.

Decades later, on Thanksgiving Eve 2009, I am downtown again in Tutwiler's Railroad Park, to introduce one of the world's most famous voices describing my hometown as the birthplace of blues. Standing behind a podium before a small crowd, Led Zeppelin superstar Robert Plant is principal speaker for a Mississippi Blues Trail marker defining the depot as a historic landmark in American music.

One night in 1903 while waiting on a train to Clarksdale, W. C. Handy first heard soulful chords from a slide guitar being played with a kitchen knife. Later he took this sound to Memphis, St. Louis, and the world, where it impacted millions, including Led Zeppelin's quintessential voice. The centennial of this event was celebrated when Congress proclaimed 2003 Year of the Blues. One October Sunday following King Biscuit, a group of important bluesmen observed this 100th anniversary on the railroad tracks in Tutwiler.

In 2009 Robert Plant was emphatic about no advance publicity of his coming to this small town where Dixie Haven's terrier routinely crossed the same railroad tracks each day with a quarter in his mouth to buy wieners from Henry Wing's Grocery. Although most of the audience—members of the Community Center's Senior Citizens Club—knew that the curly-haired visitor was responsible for the marker being unveiled, they were clueless about his identity. Delaying their

Following his address honoring the Tutwiler depot site as an important influence as the birthplace of blues music, where W. C. Handy first heard it being played in 1903, the Led Zeppelin superstar joins other dedication dignitaries, including (from left) Mayor Genether Miller-Spurlock; Jim O'Neal, Blues Trail research director; former Tutwiler mayor Robert Grayson; and state senator David Jordan.

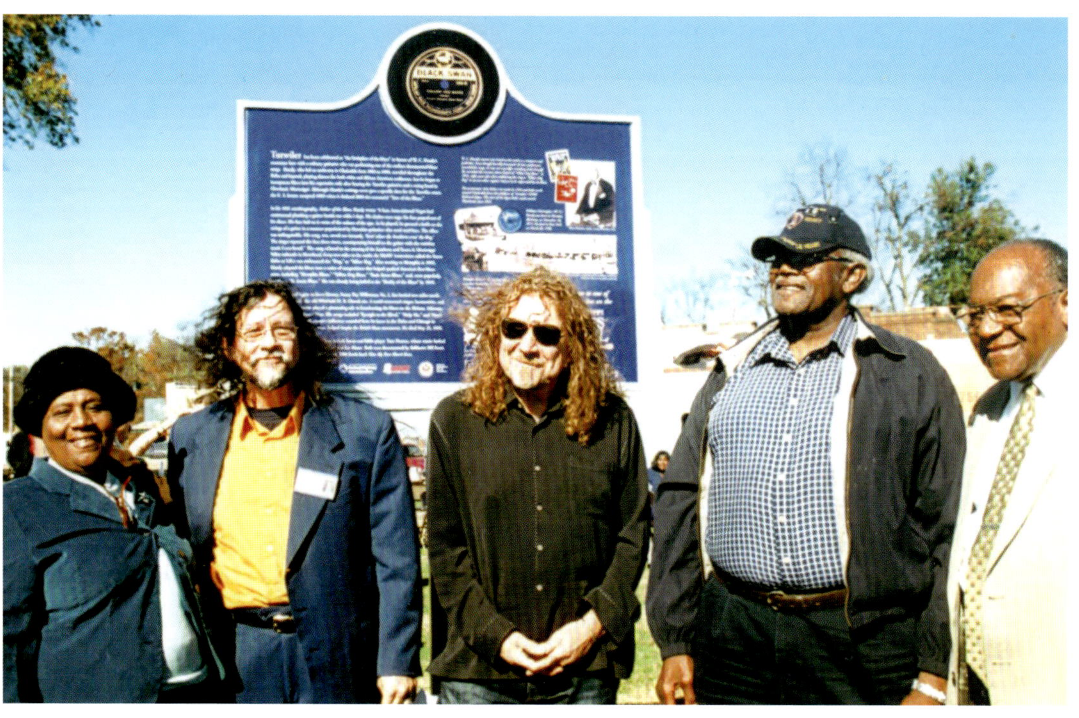

Celebrating the Year of the Blues Centennial on the railroad tracks in Tutwiler in October 2003 following Helena's King Biscuit Blues Festival is a large group of musicians, including (seated from left) Sam Carr, Robert Junior Lockwood, Charlie Musselwhite, Pinetop Perkins, Willie King, Mr. Johnnie Billington, Foster "Tater" Wiley, Jim O'Neal, Layla Musselwhite, Henrietta Musselwhite, and dozens of others.

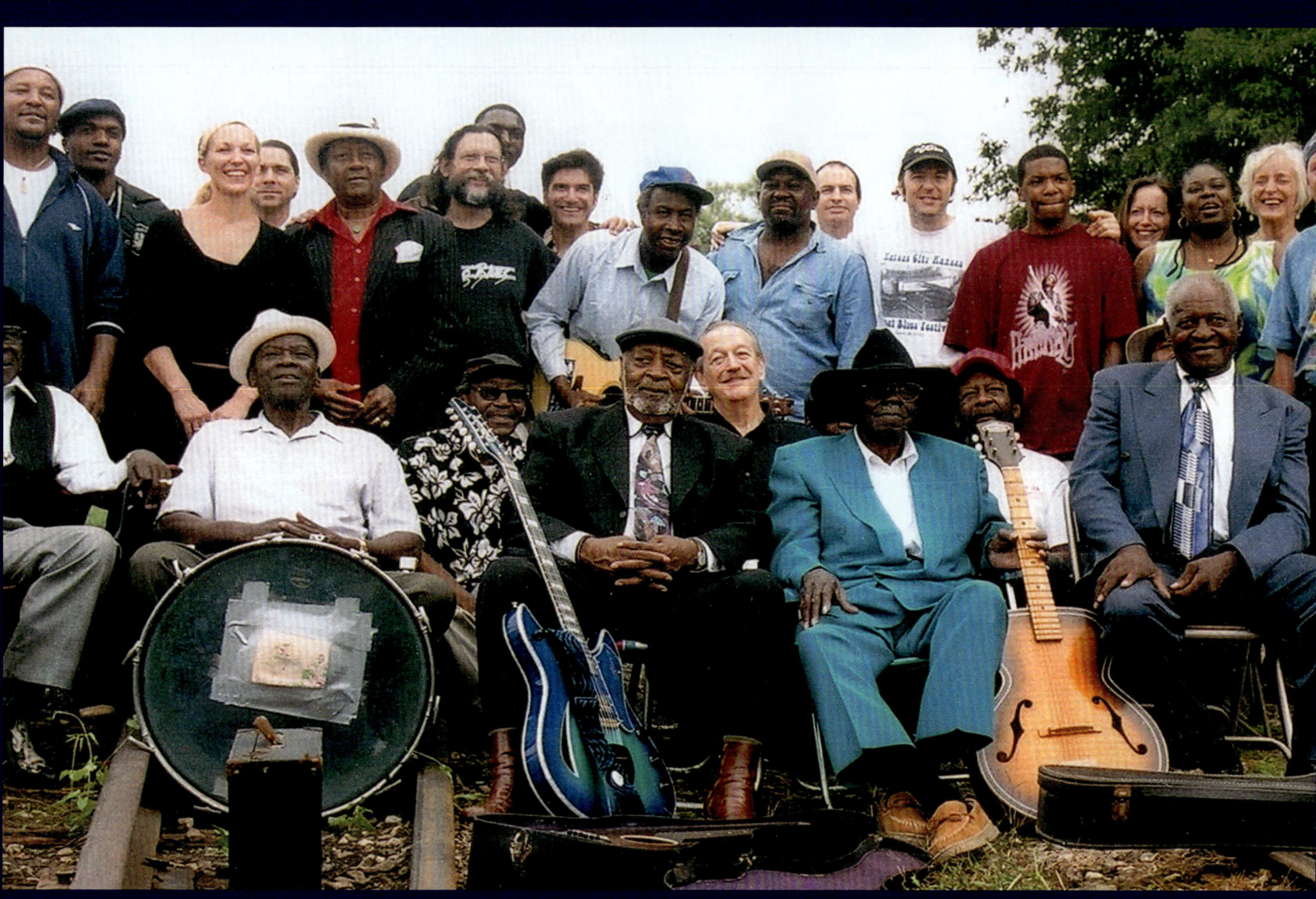

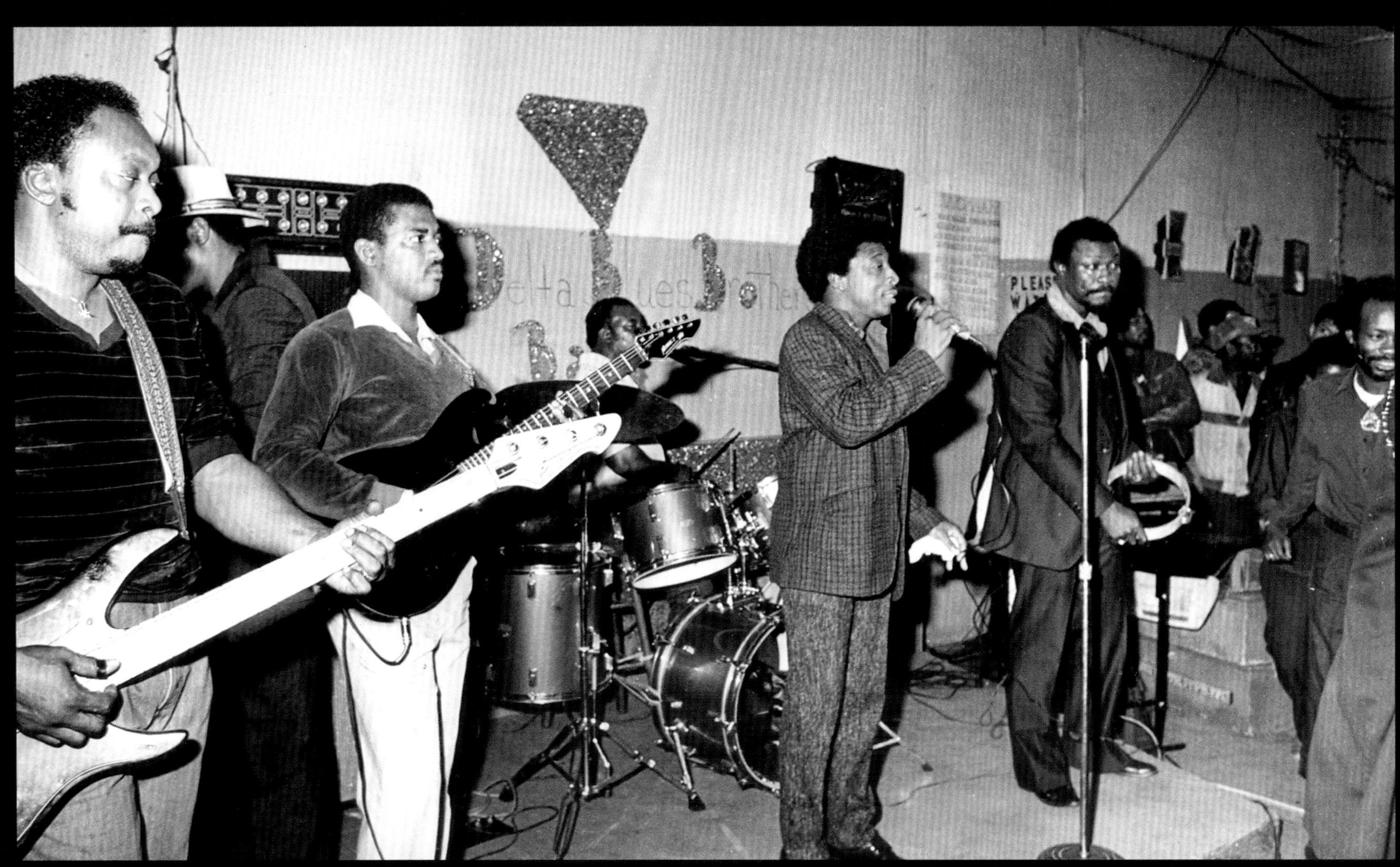
Delta Blues Brothers
PLEASE

usual 10 A.M. Wednesday meeting till noon to coincide with a marker reception, they had prepared pimento cheese sandwiches and fruit punch. Alice and Sally Chow's two-layer cake was decorated with brown sugar railroad tracks and "Birthplace of the Blues" written across the top in blue icing.

Robert was given a quilted "man's shoulder bag" and other crafts from the town's cottage-industry quilters directed by Sister Maureen Delaney and other Catholic sisters of the Holy Names of Jesus and Mary. Later all were thanked internationally on the official Robert Plant website and named in the liner notes of his album *Robert Plant and the Band of Joy*. Since Tutwiler has no Chamber of Commerce or tourism commission—entities that collaborate with state tourism officials on marker dedications—Robert underwrote expenses for the Town of Tutwiler. He also cheerfully acquiesced to video interviews with tourism officials that have been broadcast globally. Afterward we drove down Highway 49 to Money Road near Greenwood to visit the third gravesite of Robert Johnson.

Getting back to my own Delta growing-up days, I was as intrigued with journalism and photography as my harmonica virtuoso friend Charlie Musselwhite was with blues music in his lyric "The blues overtook me when I was just a little child." While editing high school and college newspapers, I also danced in school gyms across the Delta to the fabulous Red Tops till their "Danny Boy" finale, and I never stopped writing and taking photographs. This obsession was fine-tuned one intense summer without air conditioning in the Ole Miss Journalism Department's small darkroom. I developed and printed film under the scrutiny of Dr. Gerald Forbes, journalism department chairman. My so-called eye for photography was influenced by Dr. Forbes and my admiration of images taken by the great French photographer Henri Cartier-Bresson. My own attempts at capturing special moments and personalities in thousands of photographs, however, fall woefully short of the magic he created. But that is the direction I have followed, especially in the vibrant world of blues music and its rock offspring.

I don't remember when I first started going down to Smitty's Red Top Lounge by myself on weekends. It was after Mae, Michael James's lady, began teaching me to dance to blues in her kitchen without moving my feet around. It definitely was not the Memphis Shuffle I had danced at Christmas in Rosedale's Court House or Greenwood's Elks Club. My body wouldn't move the way hers did, but I was working on it. About the same time, Wesley Jefferson asked me to take publicity photos of his Southern Soul Band at Margaret's Blue Diamond on the railroad tracks. This was my first time to work on a music portfolio. Later I organized a folder for Super Chikan Johnson, who needed to

◀

Wesley Jefferson invited me to photograph his Southern Soul Band for a music portfolio. This image from the early 1980s was taken inside Margaret's Blue Diamond Blues Club in Clarksdale and includes (from left) bassist/vocalist Rip Butler, guitarist Michael James, vocalist Patrick Murphy, and band leader Wesley Jefferson.

get serious booking gigs after the tax man took his money and left him with only a lawn mower in his garage.

Decades later I am still working on my dancing . . . sharing the drama of volatile relationships, emotional outbursts, jealousies, joys, intrigues, and the passionate music flourishing in juke joints, clubs, churches, and festivals. This experience changed my life and became a catalyst to my understanding the world of Mississippi Delta blues. As a journalist, I have made occasional excursions to the outside world, but have never stayed away very long. This book pays homage to these rare musicians, performers, families and friends who allowed me into their lives. This is not a quiet, gentle story. It can be raucous, rough, competitive, and at times even dangerous, but never boring—often humorous, always vibrant, exciting, and creative.

Among the pilgrims I have escorted to Tutwiler's depot site and Sonny Boy Williamson's lonely grave several miles away in Whiteside Chapel Cemetery are Paul Oliver, Robert Plant, Jimmy Page, and scores of music professionals from Tokyo, London, Oslo, and Paris. Some leave behind coins, harmonicas, and whiskey that locals probably recycle before dust settles behind our car. I rode there once on the back of a Harley behind a Tokyo pilgrim/photographer in black leather.

He showed up for festivals occasionally and once introduced me and several of my Norwegian friends to the mystique of good luck beads from Senegal. Buying a necklace from a West African street vendor at Helena's King Biscuit, he snipped its cord and passed out one bead to each of us. To this day, we never go anywhere without our bead. Except . . . once, at Othar Turner's goat roast.

I had driven through the hill country near Como alone, parked hurriedly, rushing not to miss anything. Two hours later, when I felt for the bead on a leather cord around my neck, it was not there. It was not on the ground where I photographed the procession of Othar, his granddaughter Sharde, and the drummers or around the concession stand or around my parked car. Next, I could not find my car key, and it was dark.

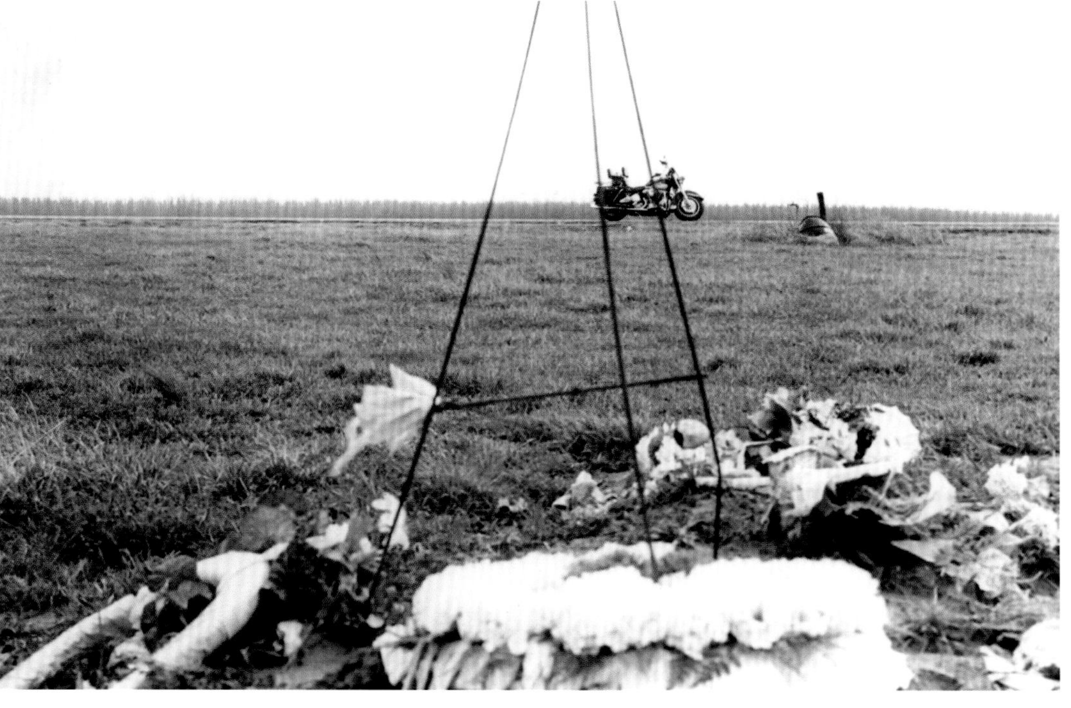

Although I drove many pilgrims to Tutwiler's depot site and Sonny Boy Williamson's grave several miles away, I rode once on the back of a Harley with a pilgrim/photographer from Tokyo. He introduced several of us later to Senegal's good luck beads.

This photo defines the vitality of Delta Blues: guitarist Michael James on his knees before his lady, Mae, with vocalist Rip Butler singing, "You're Gonna Make Me Cry" in Shelby's Dew Drop Inn. The Wesley Jefferson Band played there every summer Sunday in the late 1980s. We were welcomed by owners Mama Rene, Big E, Super Chikan's sister Christine, and a large gathering of blues fan regulars from Shelby.

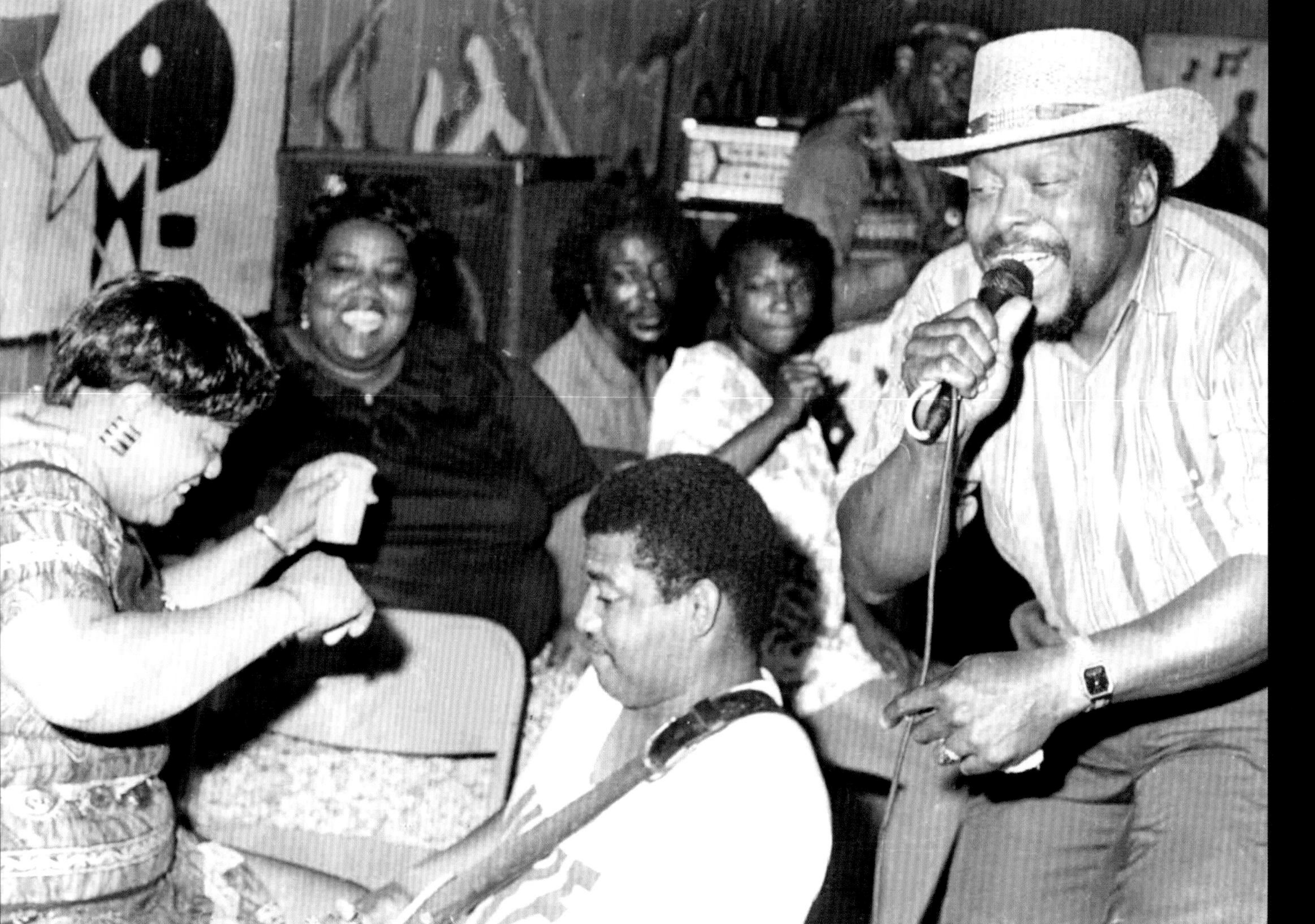

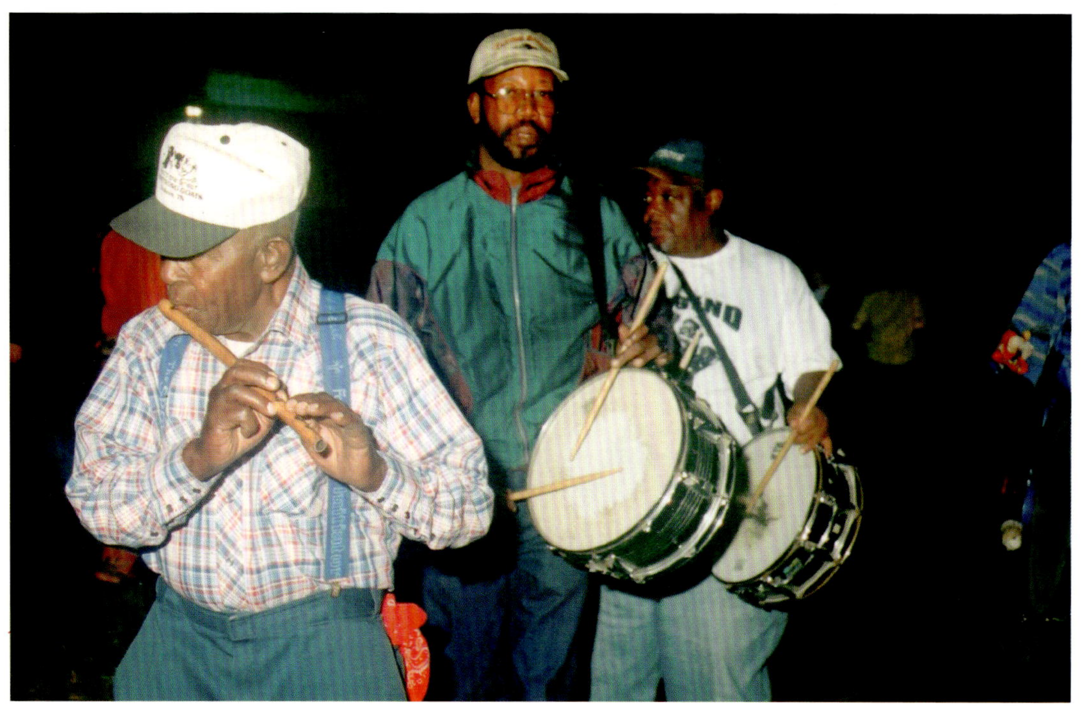

While photographing Othar Turner and drummers in procession at his annual Hill Country goat roast, I lost my West African bead and my good luck.

Fortunately, the Cooper brothers—Sherman and Tom—came to the rescue. And Sherman's pal Romeo, who owned a wrecker service, agreed to tow my car to Sherman's yard in Como for $60. I had $15. Tom loaned me the rest and took me back to Clarksdale, where he and his family also lived. The next day a friend agreed to drive me and my spare car key back to Como. Waiting for her, I sat down on my front porch swing, crushing a pair of $400 glasses. "Help!" I telephoned my friend, who fortunately had not returned to Japan. We met at the Greenville Blues Festival, and he brought me another bead, which I am still wearing.

Robert Plant returned to Sonny Boy's grave many times with family and friends. He touches base with the dandy harp master he was so excited to meet as a schoolboy in England despite being "blown off" as a worrisome kid. Speaking informally and with humor following the official Tutwiler marker unveiling that also honored Williamson, Robert described meeting the strutting harmonica virtuoso, a big star in Europe in the 1960s and something of an idol for this young kid in the UK. The incident took place following Sonny Boy's concert when by chance both happened to be in the men's restroom at the same time. When Robert began praising the star and saying how much his music meant to his career, Sonny Boy unceremoniously cut him off and directed him to get lost.

► Robert Plant has returned to Sonny Boy Williamson's grave many times with family and friends, including Jimmy Page, and touches base with the dandy harp master he was so excited to meet as a schoolboy in the UK.

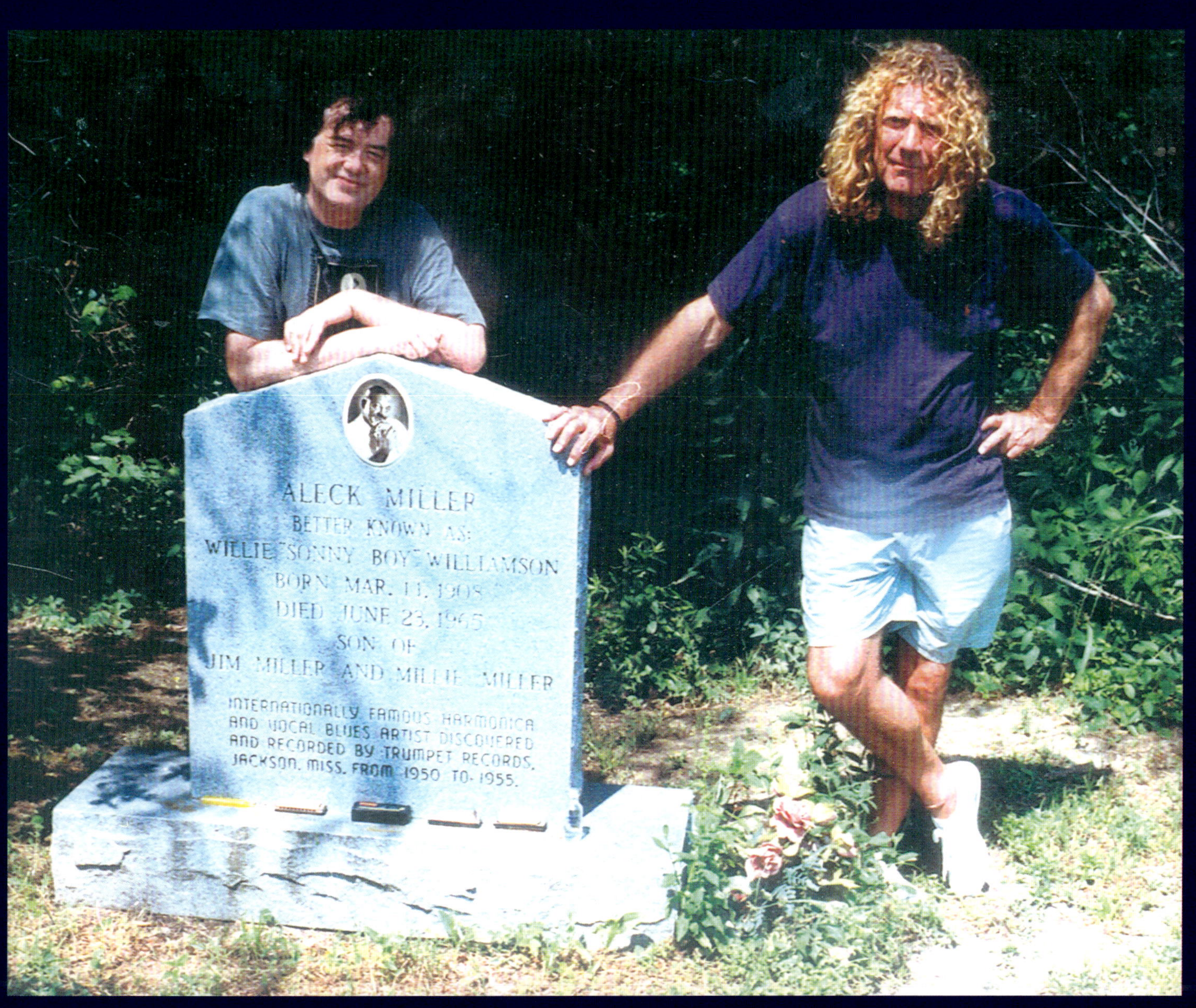

ALECK MILLER
BETTER KNOWN AS:
WILLIE "SONNY BOY" WILLIAMSON
BORN MAR. 11, 1908
DIED JUNE 23, 1965
SON OF
JIM MILLER AND MILLIE MILLER
INTERNATIONALLY FAMOUS HARMONICA
AND VOCAL BLUES ARTIST DISCOVERED
AND RECORDED BY TRUMPET RECORDS,
JACKSON, MISS. FROM 1950 TO 1955.

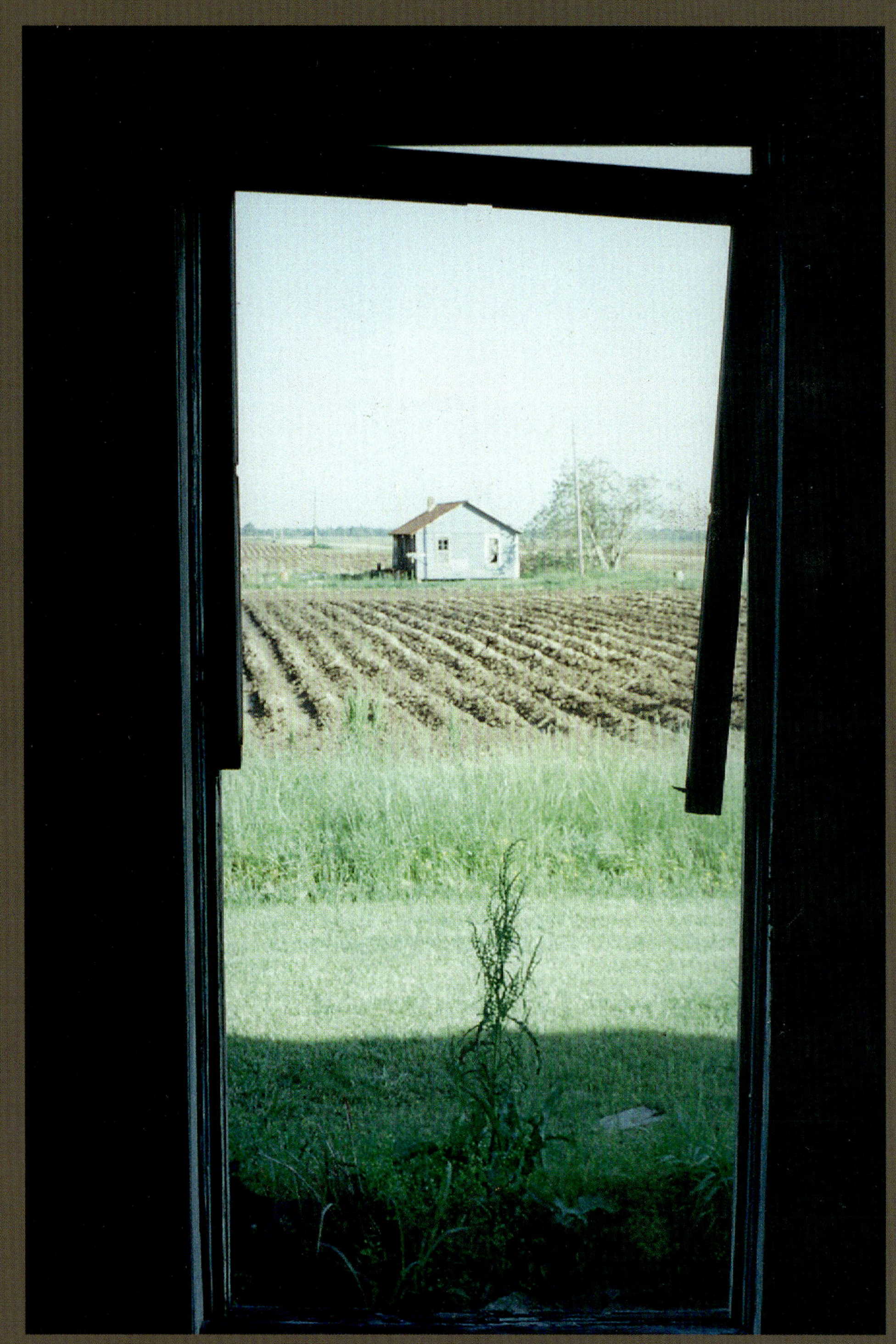

2

DELTA LANDSCAPES

When the eminent folklorist Alan Lomax quietly came to Clarksdale in 1994 more than fifty years after his initial search for Robert Johnson, he compared Delta plantations to the African kingdoms of Senegal. A hostile reception had greeted him and his father, John Lomax, back in 1939. He said shots were fired through the roof of their car, and the FBI warned them not to visit plantations without permission from the landowners.

In *The Land Where the Blues Began*, published in 1993 by Pantheon Books, a division of Random House, he describes great difficulties visiting isolated plantations to record musicians for the Library of Congress:

> At a memorable meeting with young Anderson and his overseers, they had first flatly refused to allow us on their plantation. "President Roosevelt himself couldn't come on our place," they assured us. Then perhaps recalling Fort Sumter and its unhappy consequences and thinking they had

Framing a Tallahatchie County farm scene overlooking Sonny Boy's grave, this picture taken from inside Whitfield Chapel reflects the isolation of many in the Delta.

gone a little too far, they decided to give us a temporary visiting permit:

KING AND ANDERSON PLANTATIONS
Alan Lomax and members of his party can
visit tenants on this place, providing this
Does not interfere with work
GOOD FOR TWO WEEKS
Signed by the plantation manager

Lomax says this "pass" was stuck in their windshield as they drove down the public county road that ran through the plantation. He continued, "Some of these plantations are enormous—three, four thousand acres. The biggest is fifteen thousand acre—takes eight hundred families to farm." Although this era passed with the mechanization of farming, and thousands of farm workers migrated to Chicago and other locations, many Delta residents continue to live on farms with few close neighbors.

America's great playwright Tennessee Williams spent his childhood in Clarksdale living in St. George's Episcopal Rectory, where his grandfather, the Reverend Walter Dakin, was the very popular church rector for sixteen years. Young Tom Williams was not only very familiar with the Delta's landscape but later recreated local settings and characters in many of his great Delta plays, from *Cat on a Hot Tin Roof, Orpheus Descending, Summer and Smoke,* and *Baby Doll* to *This Property Is Condemned.* In *Tennessee Williams and the South,* a book coauthored by Kenneth Holditch and Richard Freeman Leavitt and published in 1992 by the University Press of Mississippi, Dr. Holditch cites Tennessee's remarks about the Delta's "immeasurable dimensions." The playwright refers to the Delta as "this extraordinary country," and "the mysterious landscape" in his poem "The Couple," which is included in *The Collected Poems of Tennessee Williams*, edited by David Roessel and Nicholas Moschovakis and published by New Directions in 2002. Tennessee Williams writes:

It's all so wide in the Delta, and so level! / The seasons could walk
across it four-abreast! / and still avoid the hidden cypress knees. . . .

The Delta's vast unbroken landscapes are reflected in many of my photographs. For early African American farm workers living on plantations decades ago, this meant isolation, except for Saturday nights on Issaquena and Fourth Street in Clarksdale's New World District if a

▶   Eminent folklorist Alan Lomax returns to Clarksdale in 1994 more than fifty years after his search for Robert Johnson and compares Delta plantations to African kingdoms.

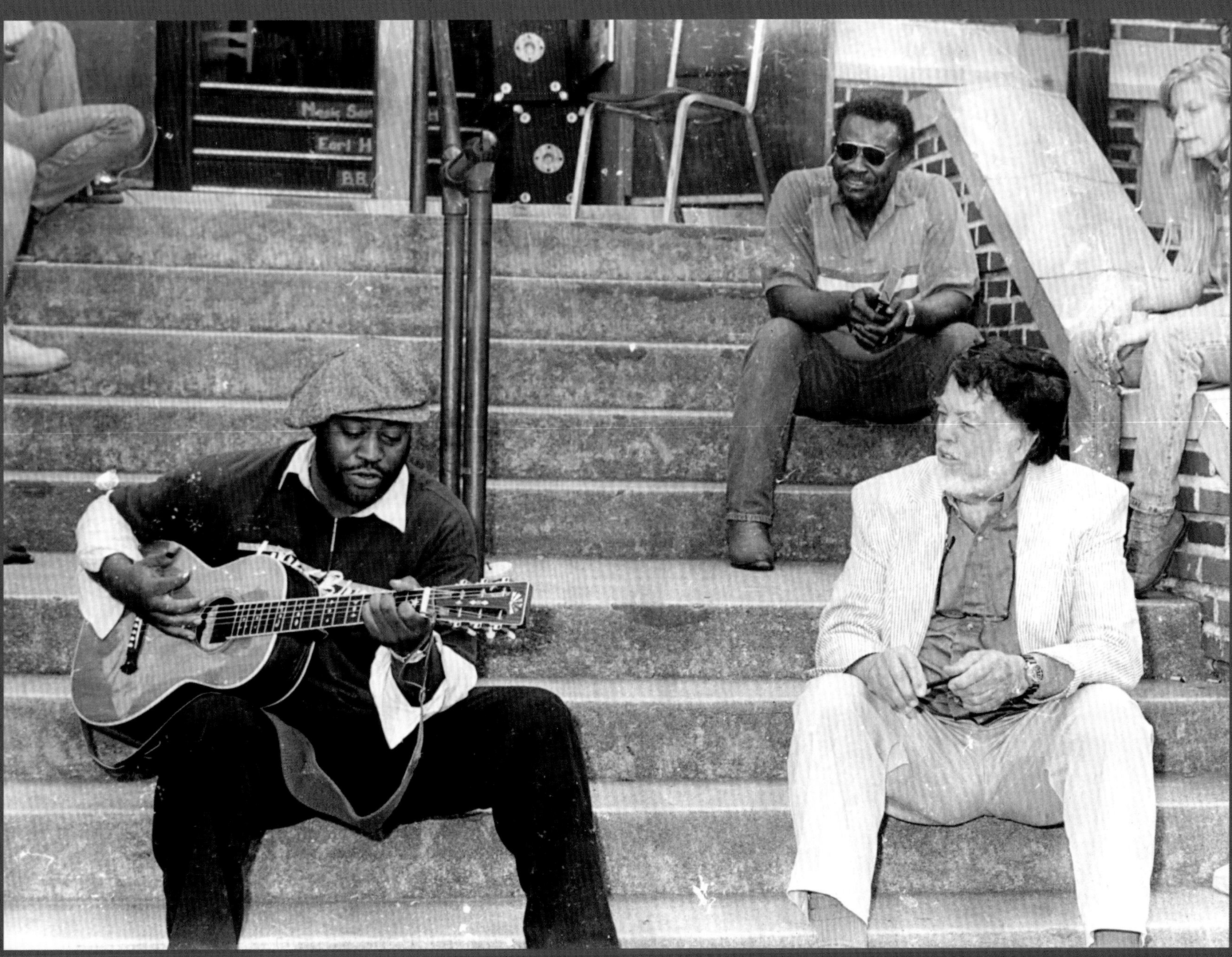

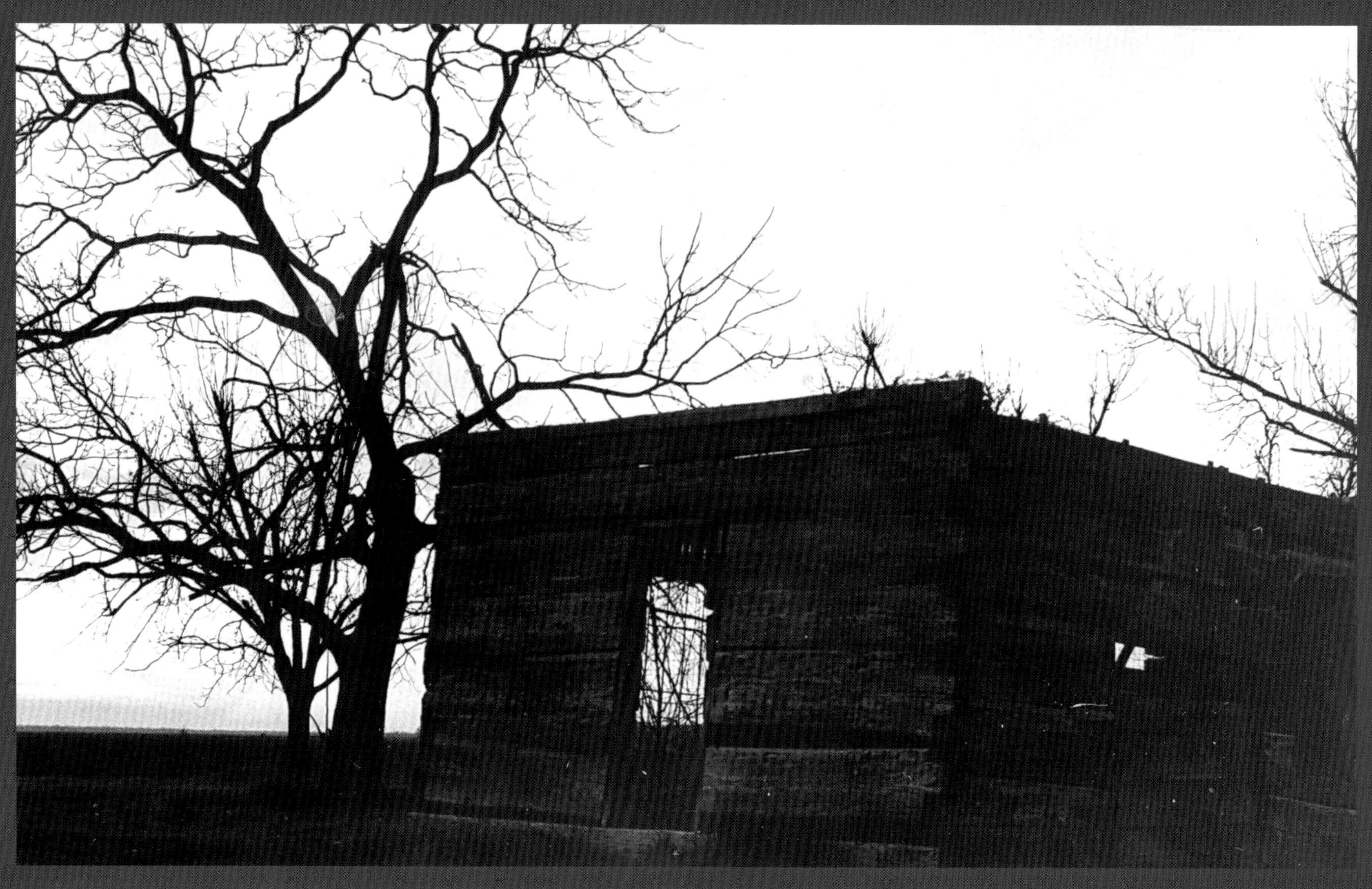

person could catch a ride to town. Blues music, dancing, and socializing flourished there on street corners and in clubs like the Dipsie Doodle, the Red Wagon, and the Chicken Roost. A local resident once told me Issaquena Avenue was "so crowded on Saturday night, you had to walk sideways to get down the street." Sundays were spent back on the farms inside plantation churches that doubled as schoolhouses.

Wearing a slightly rumpled seersucker jacket on this 1994 visit to Clarksdale, Lomax plopped down on the concrete steps of the Delta Blues Museum and joined Fruteland Jackson in singing "Midnight Special." Scattered across the grassy lawn, the audience was hushed and respectful. Lomax spoke informally and played African work songs he had taped in Senegal, followed by another of field shouts and hollers from Coahoma County.

"This link to Mississippi is distinctive," he said. "It does not exist in Texas or Georgia, but emanates from thousands of homeless people working in labor camps and on the levees in Mississippi. These people had no homes and no women; blues came out of that: music always comes with sorrow." In Africa, he said, similar sounds evolved from oppressed people in kingdoms—not tribes. "They had kings . . . it goes with tyranny and can be traced in the Middle East and Egypt," he continued.

Although Lomax never found Robert Johnson, he recorded Muddy Waters on Stovall Plantation for the Library of Congress. My own theory about blues germinating in the isolation of winter landscapes informally borrows its seeds from his fieldwork. I was also very pleased Alan Lomax liked the photos I took of him that day; he wrote back later asking me for copies.

Although many of my photographs address isolation, none speaks stronger to me than the cabin scenes I took one late-winter afternoon where Muddy grew up with his grandmother.

The stark landscape speaks volumes. Facing sameness over and over and over, his creative talents and a "diddley bow" on the front porch could have conjured up the life of a rolling stone.

Through the years, many "overseas" visitors came to visit the Muddy Waters cabin. One serious pilgrim walked the eight-mile round trip from Clarksdale; on January 15, 1996, I photographed the wedding of Anne Marie Donovan and Phillip Zeller of New Orleans, married there by justice court judge Kenneth Bush; others took away more than memories—a few souvenirs, which gradually began to erode the structure . . . and led the Stovall family to consider having it moved. Rumors about the cabin being leased to the House of Blues circulated

Although many of my photographs address isolation, none speak stronger to me than the cabin scenes I took one late winter afternoon on Stovall Plantation, where Muddy Waters grew up with his grandmother.

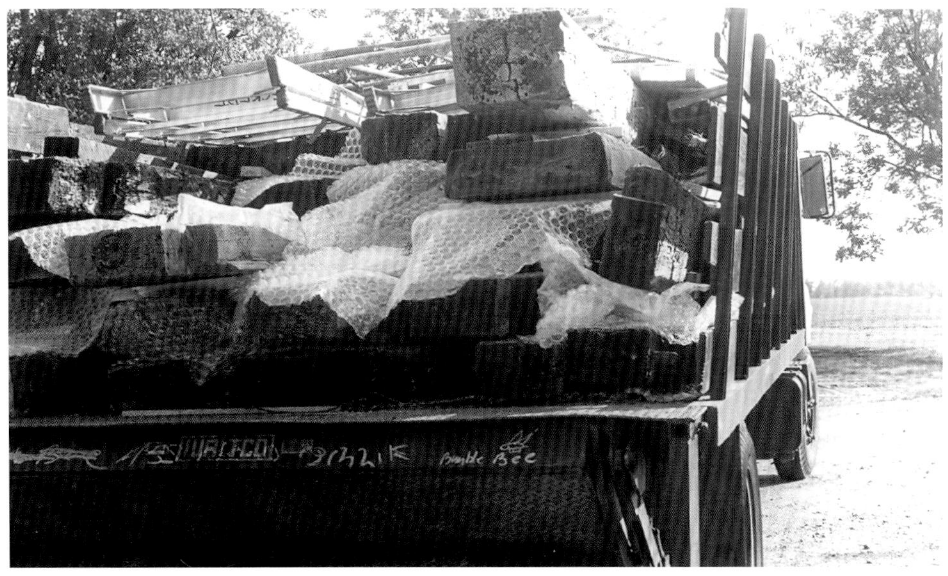

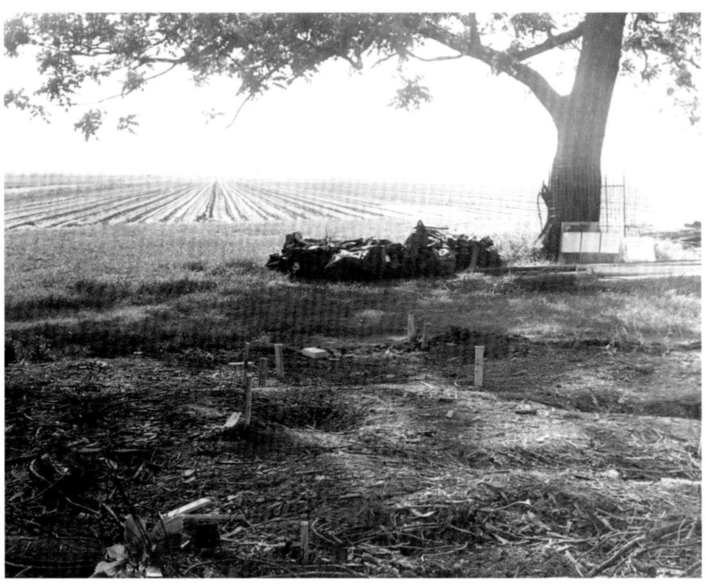

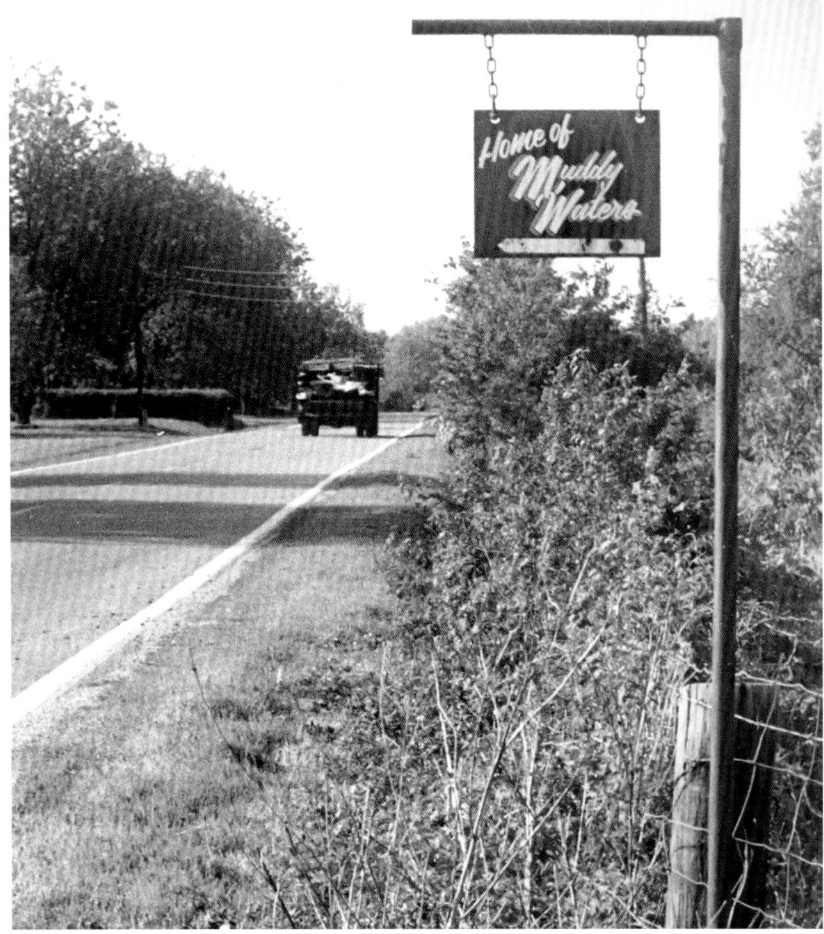

◄ Although rumors about the Muddy Waters cabin being leased to the House of Blues initially were denied, I received a call one day in May that workers were dismantling the cabin. Driving there immediately, I photographed the action in progress and the numbered cypress logs leaving Stovall Road.

and were denounced by purists who viewed such an action as commercial, the conversion of a historic structure into a traveling sideshow. Others simply hoped the cabin could remain in its natural setting. Although these rumors were denied to me as a journalist, I received a call May 7, 1996, that workers were dismantling the cabin. Driving there immediately, I photographed the action in progress and the truck loaded with numbered cypress logs leaving Stovall Road. Later I was told that family members were being interviewed at home at the same time.

Afterward, a few of us would gather occasionally at the empty site with a bottle of wine to mourn the loss of a shrine. The pain was assuaged to some extent by the Stovall family donating part of its annual House of Blues lease money to keep the Sunflower River Blues and Gospel Festival free and accessible to all true blues lovers. Unfortunately, this did not last long. Five years later, the reconstructed cabin—scrubbed spiffy and adorned with plaques—following outings at the Chicago Blues Festival, the Atlanta Olympics and House of Blues events, was returned to Coahoma County, housed inside the Delta Blues Museum. Today it is visited by thousands, including historian/architect Paul Oliver, who first wrote about early blues sites in the 1950s.

When I consider many Delta landscapes I have photographed and the remarkable individuals who shared their stories with me, Mrs. Elma McCoy and Elma's Place immediately come to mind. Driving to Greenwood, I had passed her small country store on Highway 49 near Minter City many times. Fortunately, one day I stopped to explore and to meet the owner sitting on the front porch. I call her story "Waiting for Amos."

Inside, the almost-bare grocery shelves repeat a story begun on the porch: a few bags of potato chips hanging above the counter, old-fashioned glass jars filled with peanuts . . . soft drinks in the cooler and a few sweet potatoes in a cardboard box on the floor. For years, Elma said, she sold produce from her garden, but heavy rains had kept her from planting one this spring. She had a theory about the flooding. "It comes from people taking water from the land to irrigate crops and dig those catfish ponds," she said. "Sometimes I can feel the candy jars and the store rattle, the earth shaking."

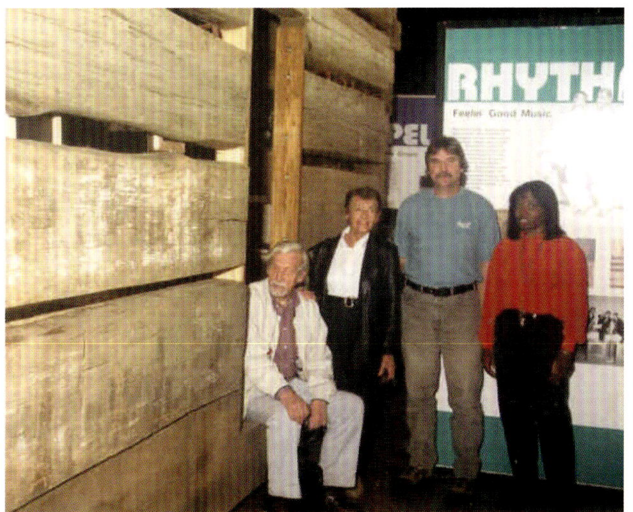

▶

Five years later, following outings at the Atlanta Olympics and House of Blues events, the reconstructed cabin was returned to Coahoma County and installed inside the Delta Blues Museum. It is visited by thousands, including distinguished historian/architect Paul Oliver from the United Kingdom, who wrote about Delta blues in the 1950s, pictured with his wife and Tony Czech, former DBM director, and Maie Smith, DBM tour director.

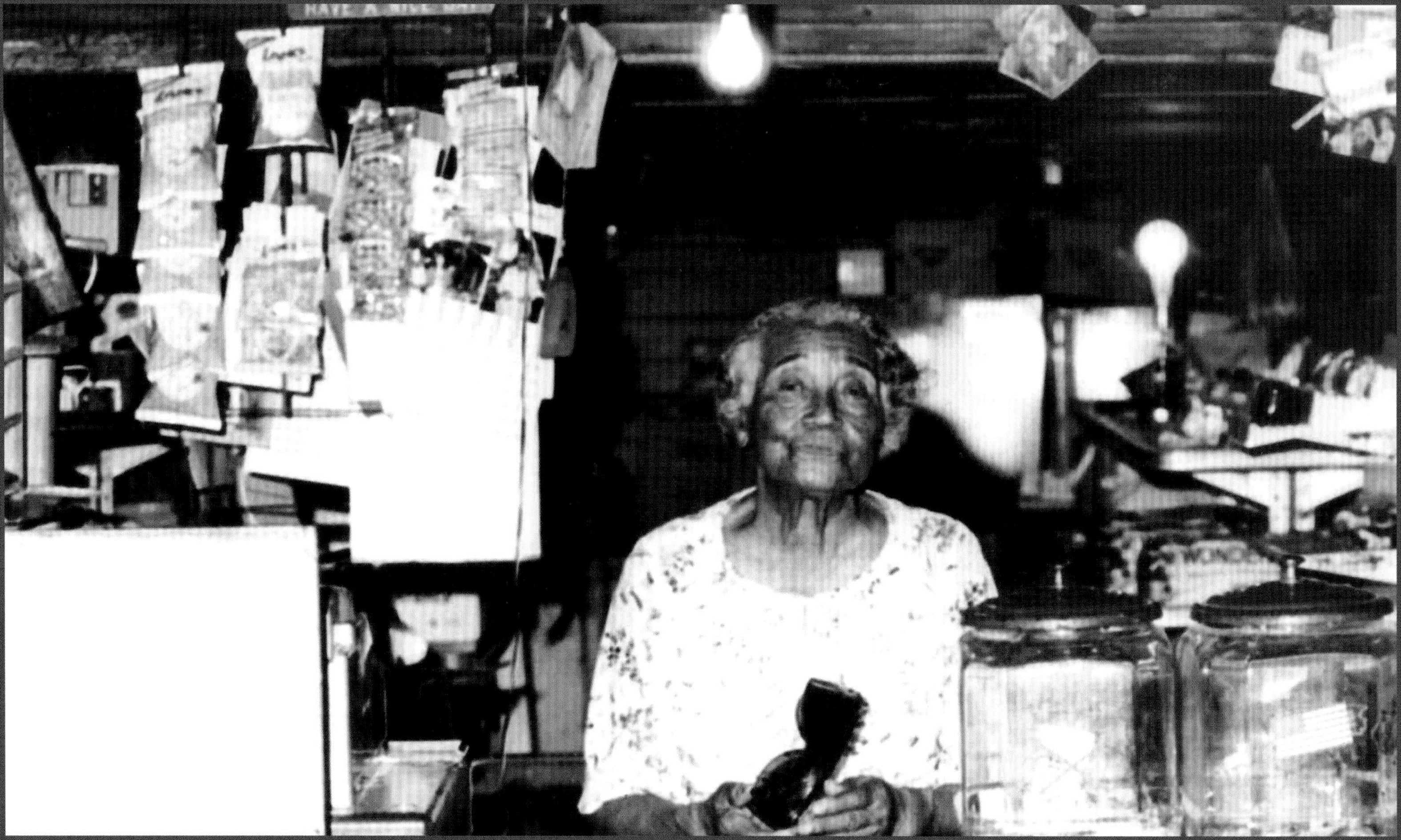

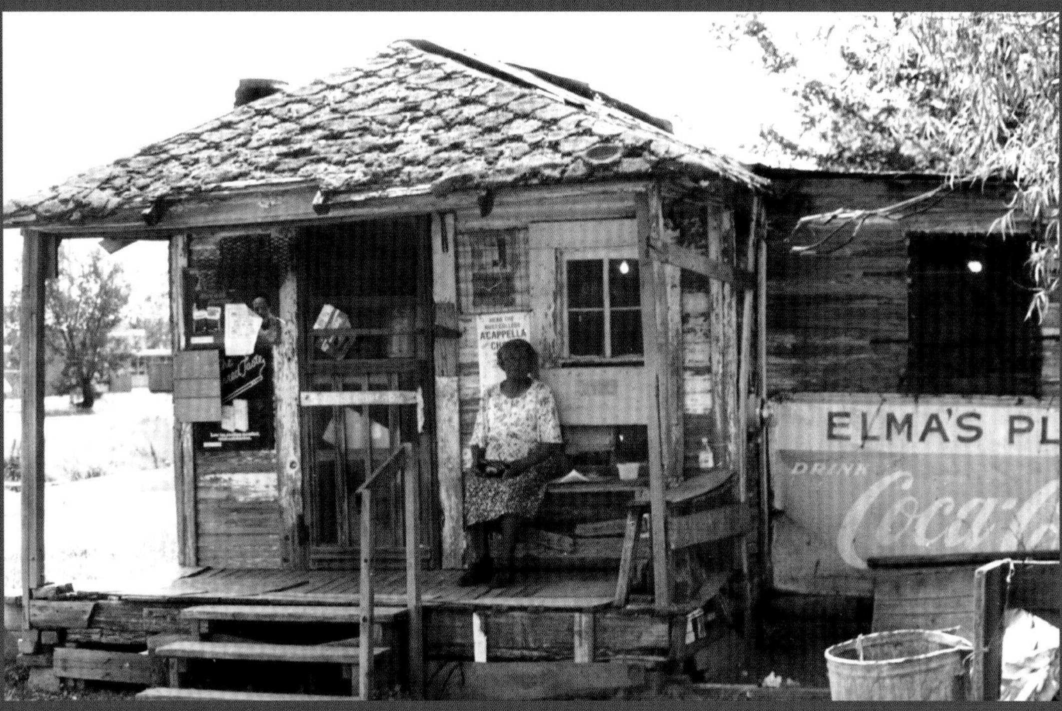

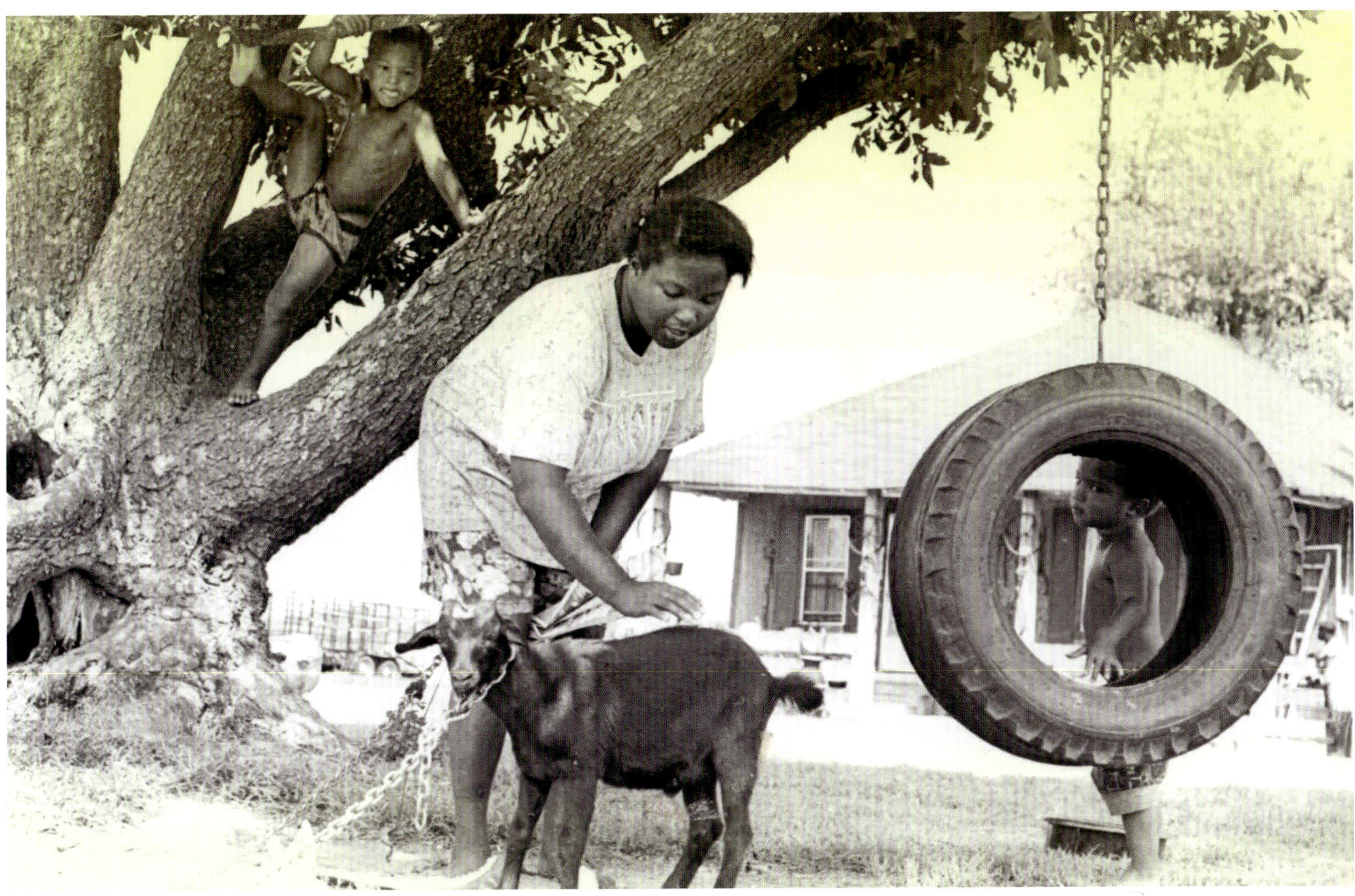

▲

On the way home from Parchman's printing facility, I glanced outside the front window of my car: a mother and her children were in the yard petting a billy goat munching watermelon rinds, and my brain registered "Stop." The stop became *Summertime*.

◄

The almost-bare grocery shelves of Elma's Place repeat a story begun on the porch that I title "Waiting for Amos."

Business was slow, she said. But life had slowed down too for Mrs. Elma McCoy, who came to Minter City years earlier from Houston, Mississippi, to marry Amos McCoy. He died in 1968, and Elma told me: "I miss him so much. Sometimes I feel him put his hand on my shoulder, and I say, 'Is that you, Amos? Are you coming for me?'"

Since her cataract operation, Elma wears dark glasses outside. "I don't drive anymore. I sold my car," she said. Mostly she sits on the porch and visits with people who stop by.

The store is gone now; so are Elma's house and garden.

Summertime is a joyous Delta scene. It was taken one afternoon while I was traveling on another lonely stretch of Highway 49 near Parchman Penitentiary. I had been editing my order of postcards featuring images of Delta musicians. It seemed fitting that "Printed by Mississippi Prison Industries" would appear in the liner notes, since early bluesmen had "done time" there.

Decades later members of the Norwegian Blues Union were relentless about visiting the prison for the same reason. I assured

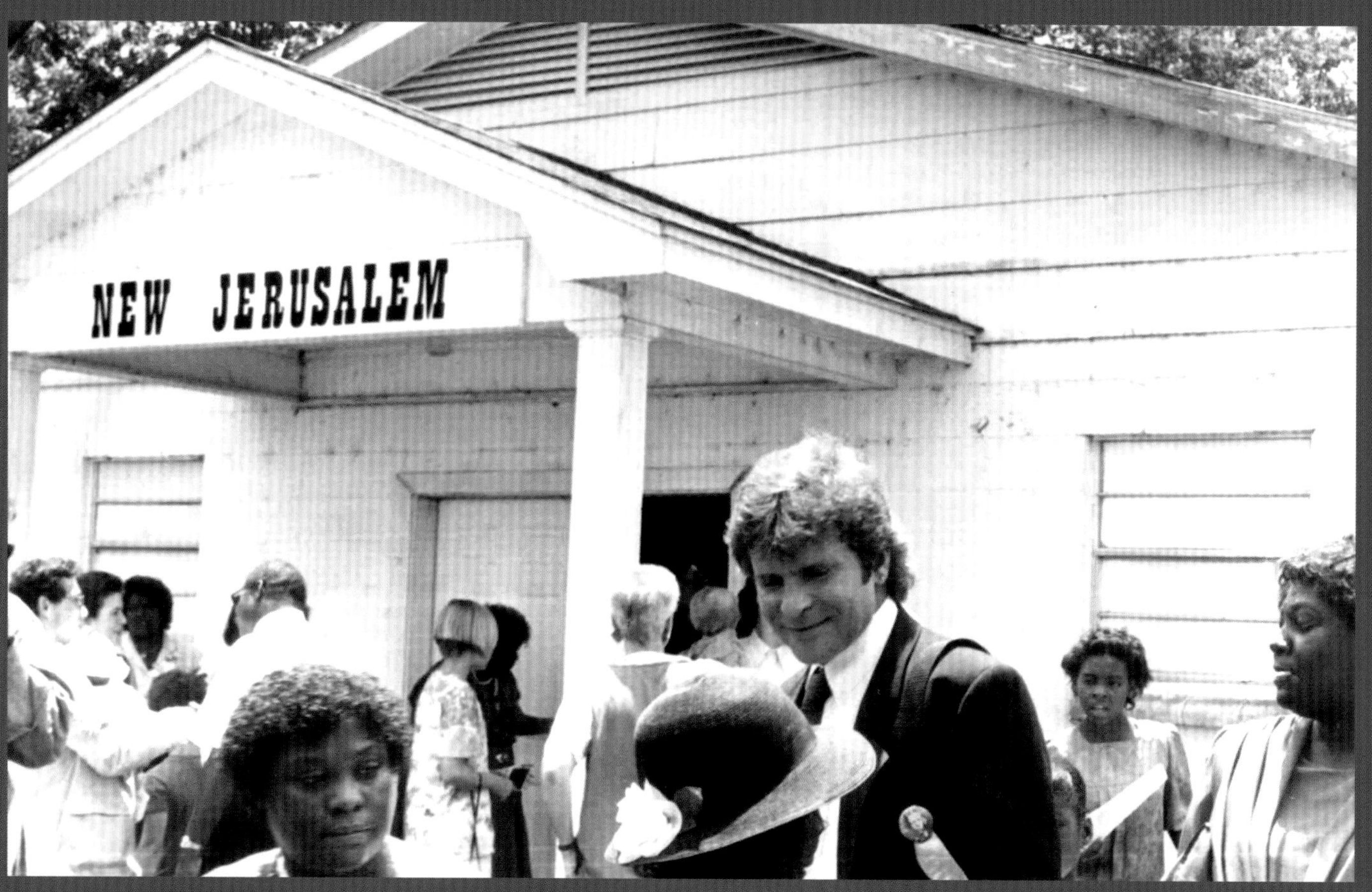
NEW JERUSALEM

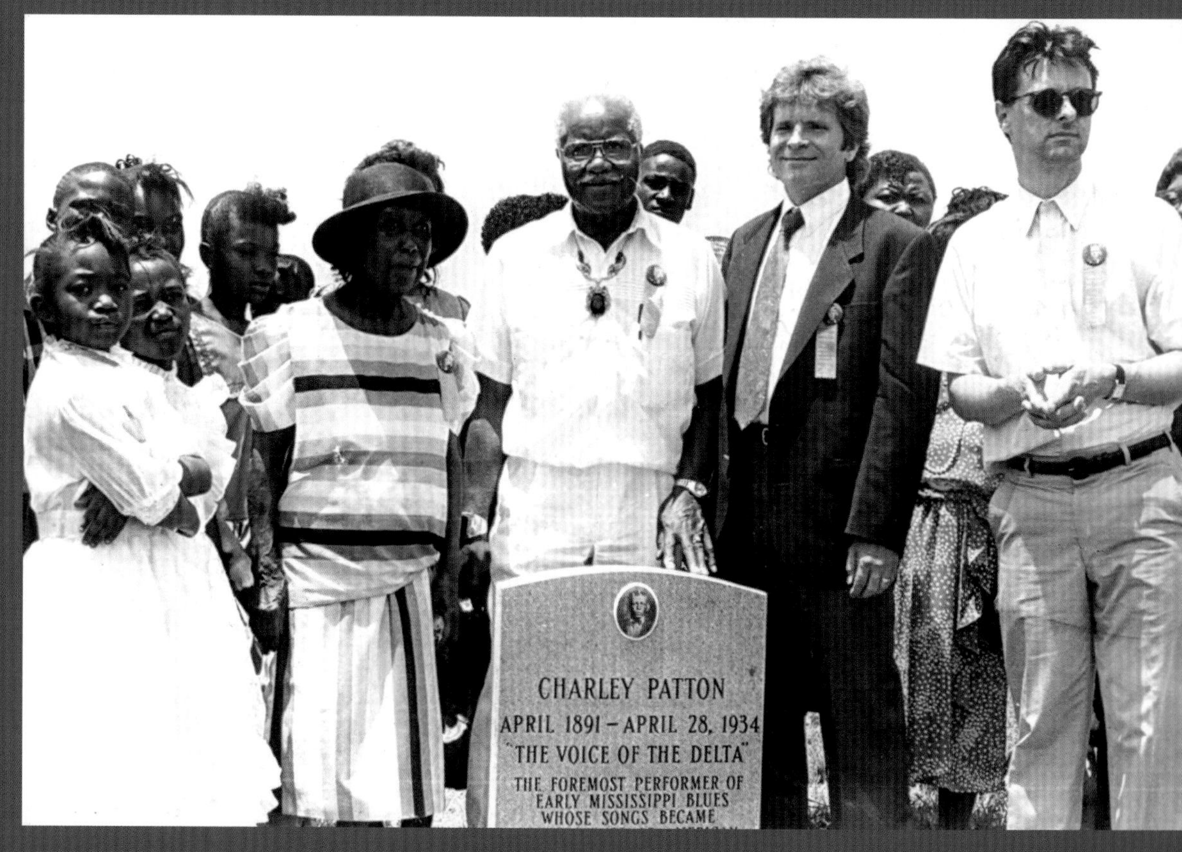
CHARLEY PATTON
APRIL 1891 – APRIL 28, 1934
"THE VOICE OF THE DELTA"
THE FOREMOST PERFORMER OF
EARLY MISSISSIPPI BLUES
WHOSE SONGS BECAME

them it was not a tourism destination. However, they persisted until I begged one of the wardens to consider the visit educational and a move forward in international diplomacy. One Sunday morning he called my house and said to bring them on down, and the prison gates opened wide for the busload of eager Scandinavians.

Enjoying the warden's informative introduction, a viewing of confiscated handmade weapons, and an excellent lunch served by prisoners, the visitors were eager to tour the large prison. An officer came on board to give directions and answer questions. The first stop was a security check of our possessions outside one of the housing units. Later, peering down from an elevated level above the dormitory-style beds with prisoners walking below us like animals in a zoo was the first clue this was not a folksy institution.

Back on the bus after observing guards/trustees on horseback supervising other convicts at work in a field, the Norwegians became reflective. When the officer on board pointed in the direction of the maximum security unit and asked what they would like to see next, their English-speaking Norwegian leader, journalist Tore Hvaal, translated: "They say they've seen enough." In silence we left, thoroughly depressed and with absolutely no inclination to return.

At the time of my *Summertime* picture, the prison's printing facility was not far from Clarksdale. Despite the in-and-out hassle of guards searching my car at the prison gates, it was easier traveling to Parchman than to Jackson or Memphis. On the way home when I glanced outside the front window of my car, a mother and her children were in the yard petting a billy goat munching watermelon rinds. My brain registered: "Stop." Which I did at the next turnrow; I photographed the scene with no hesitation and visited afterward with the family. After the film was developed, and I printed *Summertime*, it became a favorite.

Some of the most isolated Delta landscapes I've photographed are burial sites of early blues musicians. They are recognized today with handsome monuments placed there years ago by the Mt. Zion Fund founded by Skip Henderson: Charley Patton at Holly Ridge; Joe Callicott near Nesbit; and Memphis Minnie out from Walls.

Spreading the word about the man named Charley Patton was the gospel in 1991 at New Jerusalem Baptist Church, according to pastor Ernest Ward and veteran musicians Pop Staples of Chicago and John Fogerty. The gospel choir sang "You Gave Me One More Sunny Day" and "Amazing Grace," and the preacher likened Patton to Paul, "who was a bad man who started out to do wrong" until "God blinded him" and Paul "pressed toward the mark of high calling. When Charley Patton was playing blues, he was pressing the mark. Let the mark be

Some of the most isolated Delta landscapes I've photographed are burial sites of early musicians recognized today with handsome monuments placed by the Mt. Zion Fund founded by Skip Henderson. Celebrity musicians Pop Staples and John Fogerty pay tribute to Charley Patton, along with Henderson, (far right), pictured with Patton's daughter, Rosetta Patton Brown (in hat), and her family in Holly Ridge and her great-granddaughter Keisha Brown (arms crossed), who years later accepted a Mississippi Musicians Hall of Fame plaque for Patton. Outside New Jerusalem Baptist Church where pastor Ernest Ward preached a sermon, John Fogerty visits with Rosetta Patton Brown.

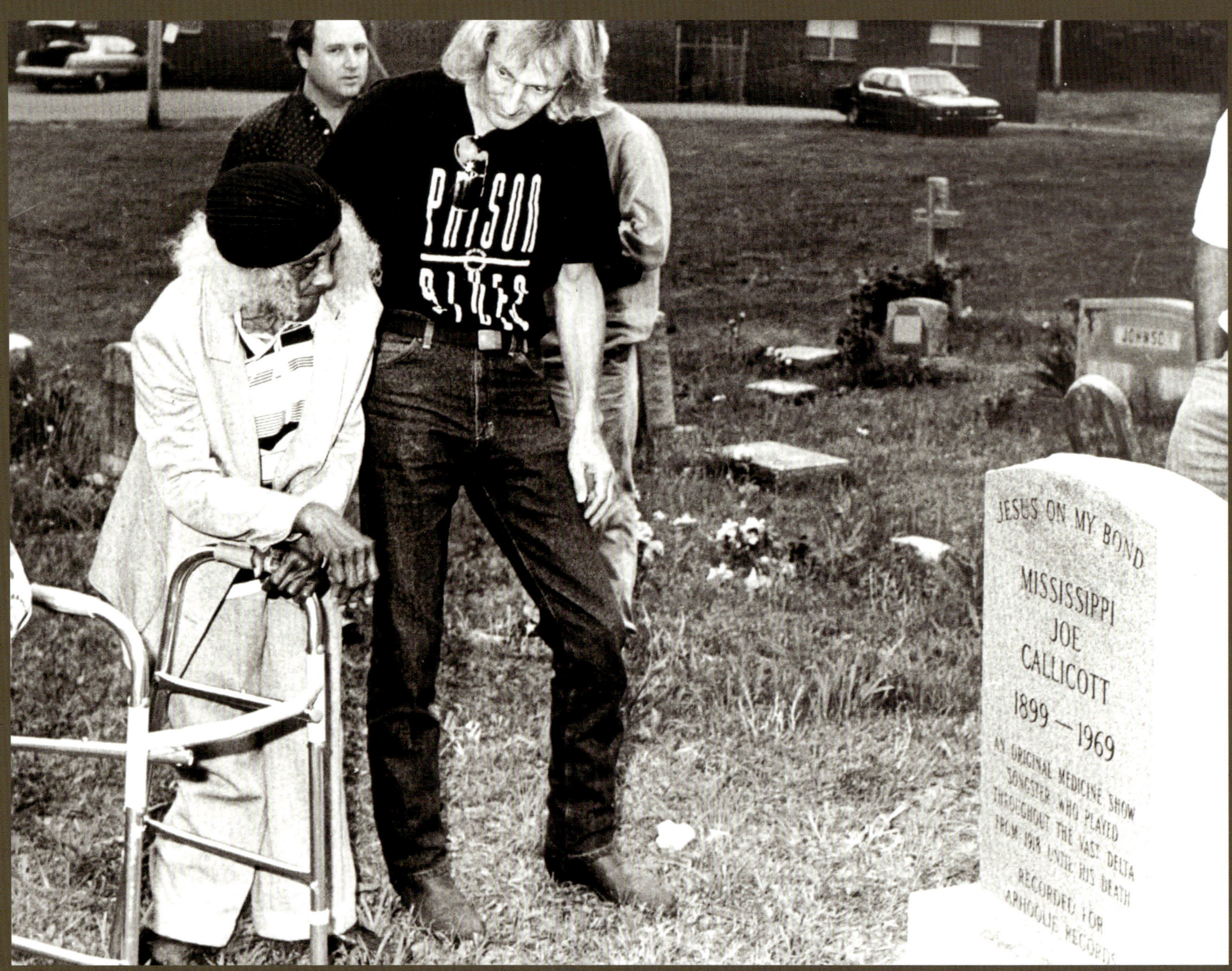

Near Nesbit, ninety-two-year-old "Doll" Callicott beams with each step she takes up the slopes of Mt. Olive Baptist Church cemetery to visit the grave of her husband, Mississippi Joe Callicott, and the marker honoring his career. She is gently assisted by bluesman Kenny Brown, who viewed Joe as a mentor and father figure.

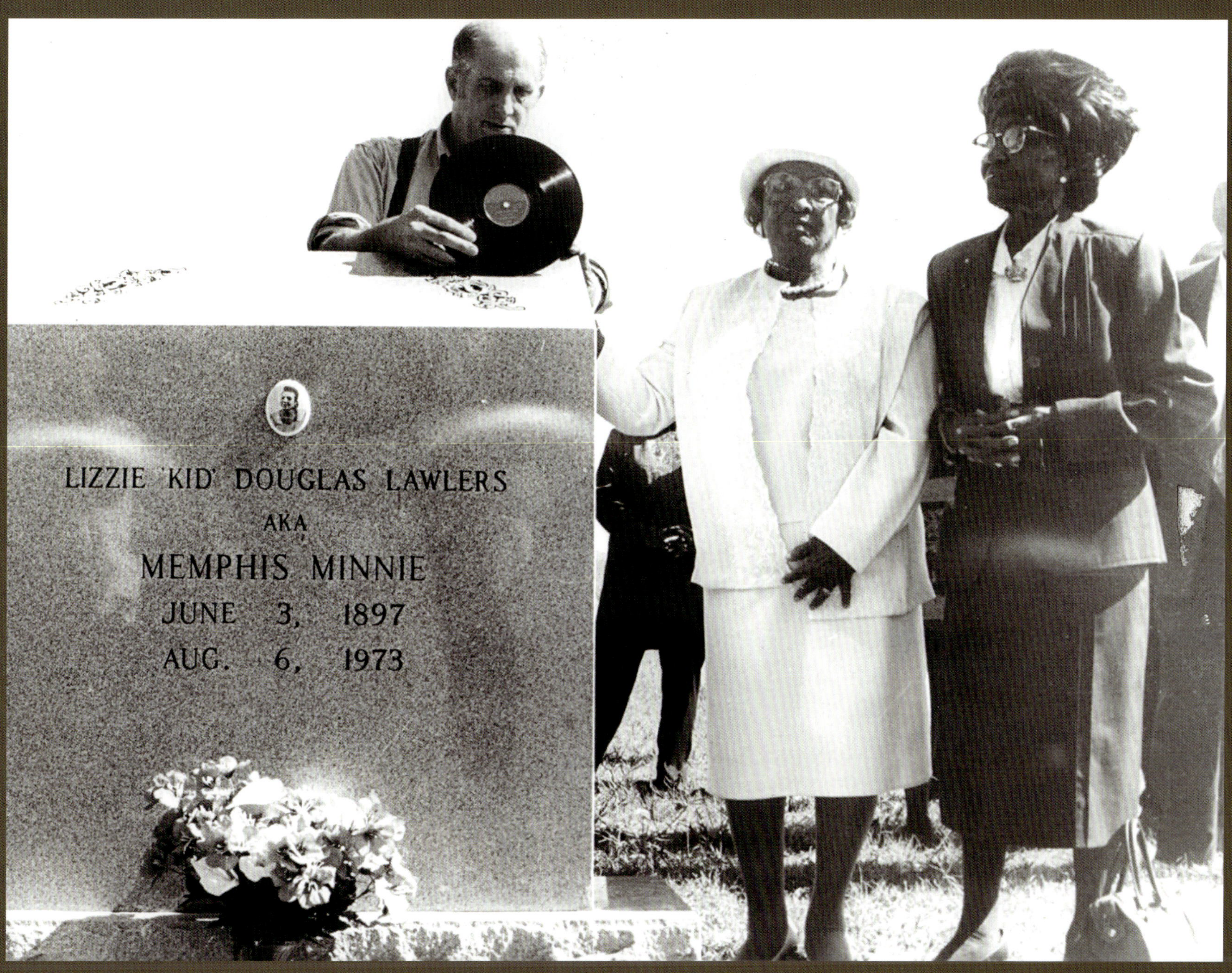

Down a meandering blacktop road near Walls, where dusty soybeans were being cut, Lizzie "Kid" Douglas Lawlers—Memphis Minnie—is celebrated outside New Hope Baptist Church by pastor Roger Brown, her biographer Paul Garon, and family members.

Jesus Christ," said the minister at this sermon's conclusion. Fogerty and Staples both paid tribute to the Mississippi Delta bluesman as an important influence in their careers.

In 1995 near Nesbit, ninety-two-year-old "Doll" Callicott beams with each deliberate step she takes up the slopes of Mt. Olive Baptist Church cemetery. She is going uphill to visit the grave of her husband, dead over twenty-five years, and to view the tall granite headstone marking his importance in music. Supported by tall, fair-haired Kenny Brown, "Doll" reaches the summit and gazes for the first time at the words inscribed deep in stone: "Jesus on My Bond, Mississippi Joe Callicott 1899–1969. Recorded for Arhoolie Records." It is a moment charged with emotion for "Doll" and for Kenny, who viewed Joe as a mentor and father figure.

Although eulogizing blues musicians inside churches where their lifestyles were rarely admired presented a diplomatic stretch for preachers and kinfolk, there have been many numerous dedications attracting celebrities, music fans, and Sunday-morning churchgoers. Down a meandering blacktop road where dusty soybeans were being cut one October near Walls, Mississippi, Lizzie "Kid" Douglas Lawlers—Memphis Minnie—was celebrated in New Hope Baptist Church by pastor Roger Brown, family members, her biographer Paul Garon, and RCA officials from New York City, who documented her talents in remastered Bluebird recordings. Jim O'Neal, cofounding editor of *Living Blues* magazine, and Skip Henderson officially unveiled the marker.

There are many Delta landscapes I love to share, from the sublime to the ridiculous: a pristine plantation church on Stovall Road surrounded by cotton; Daniel's fishing truck parked in Clarksdale's New World District, offering fresh turnip greens for sale; and a gentleman in Sunday attire advertising parched peanuts. The symmetry of three silent guitar cases lined up beneath my dining room windows during the filming of a John Hiatt video for MTV has a rhythm all its own, mimicked again by artistic graphics painted on the side of a tiny grocery store in Tchula, while a highway billboard proclaims the extension of a fundamentalist revival, and an old Dairy Queen site offers a still-life collection with John boat, its catch of the day, and Bible books. The sun setting on Moon Lake amid cypress trees is sheer poetry.

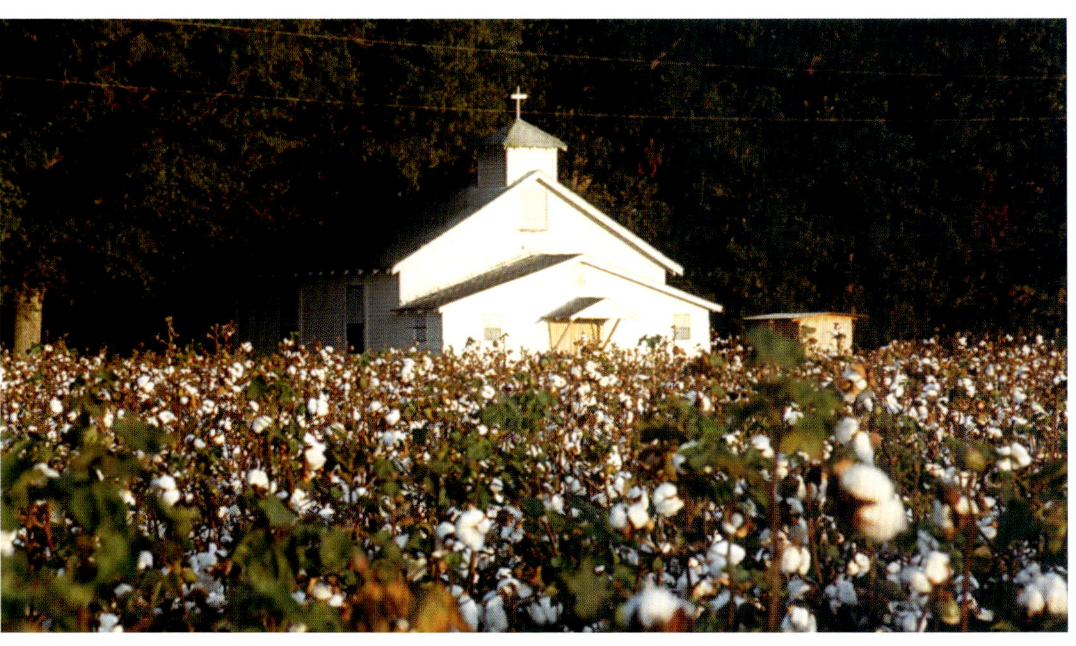

A pristine plantation church on Stovall Road in Coahoma County is surrounded by cotton.

There are many Delta landscapes I love to share, from the sublime to the ridiculous: Daniel's fishing truck parked in Clarksdale's New World District offering turnip greens; a gentleman in Sunday church attire offering peanuts for sale; an Issaquena street scene; fresh fish and Bible books in an old Dairy Queen; and a tiny grocery's road art in Durant.

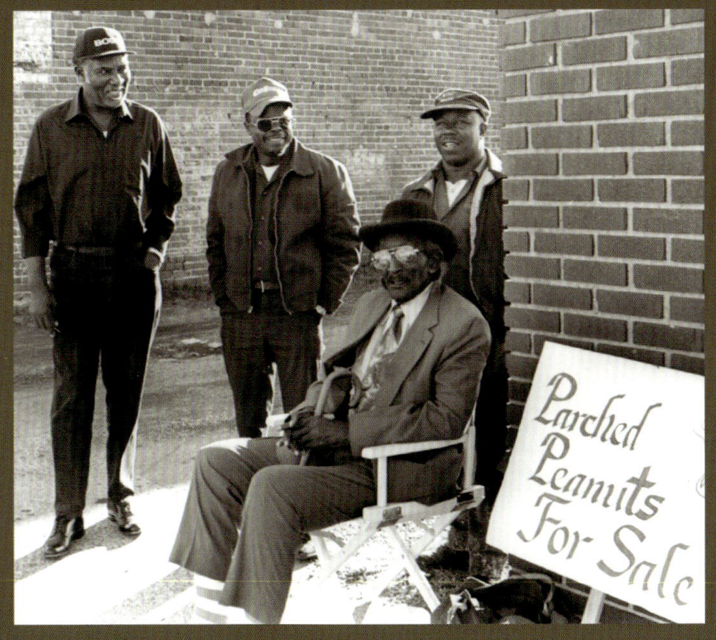

Parched
Peanuts
For Sale

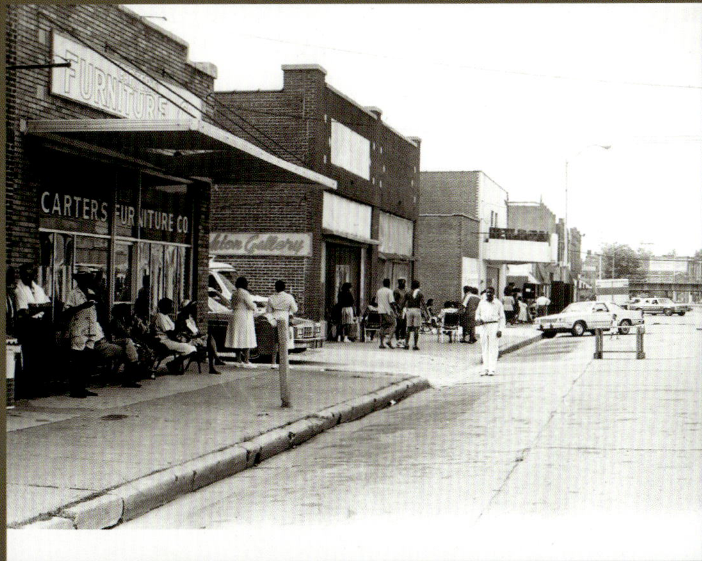

FURNITURE
CARTERS FURNITURE CO

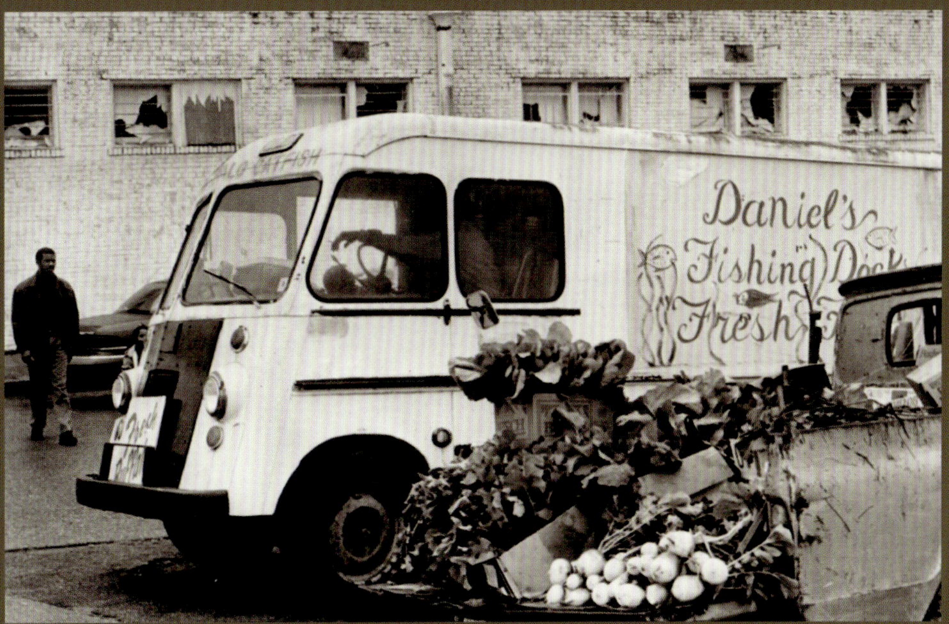

Daniel's
Fishing Dock
Fresh

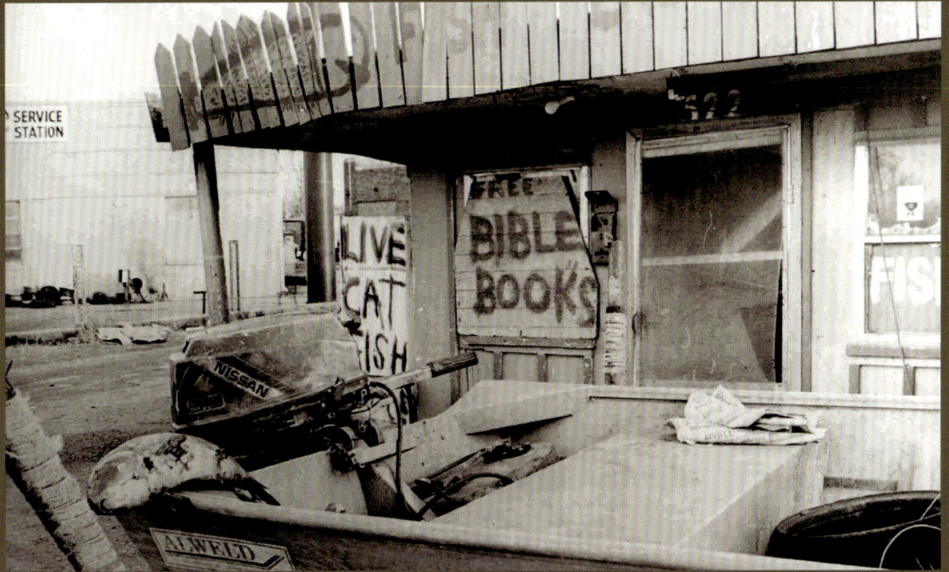

SERVICE
STATION
FREE
BIBLE
BOOKS
LIVE
CAT
FISH
NISSAN
FISH

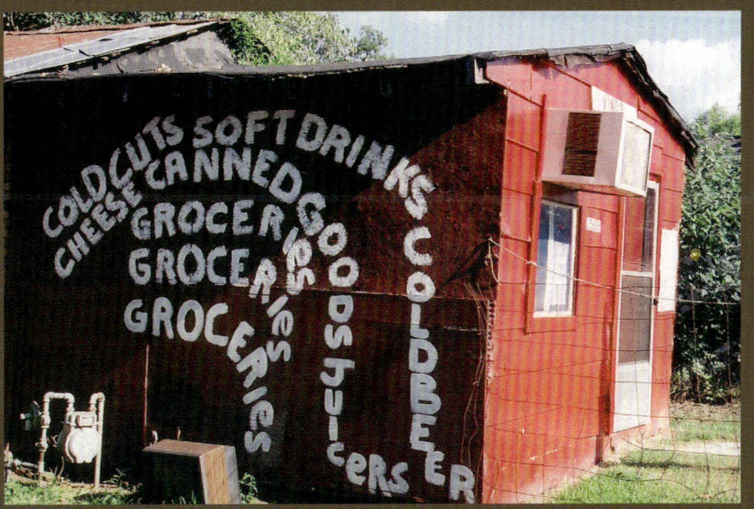

COLD CUTS SOFT DRINKS
CHEESE CANNED GOODS COLD BEER
GROCERIES
GROCERIES
GROCERIES JUICES

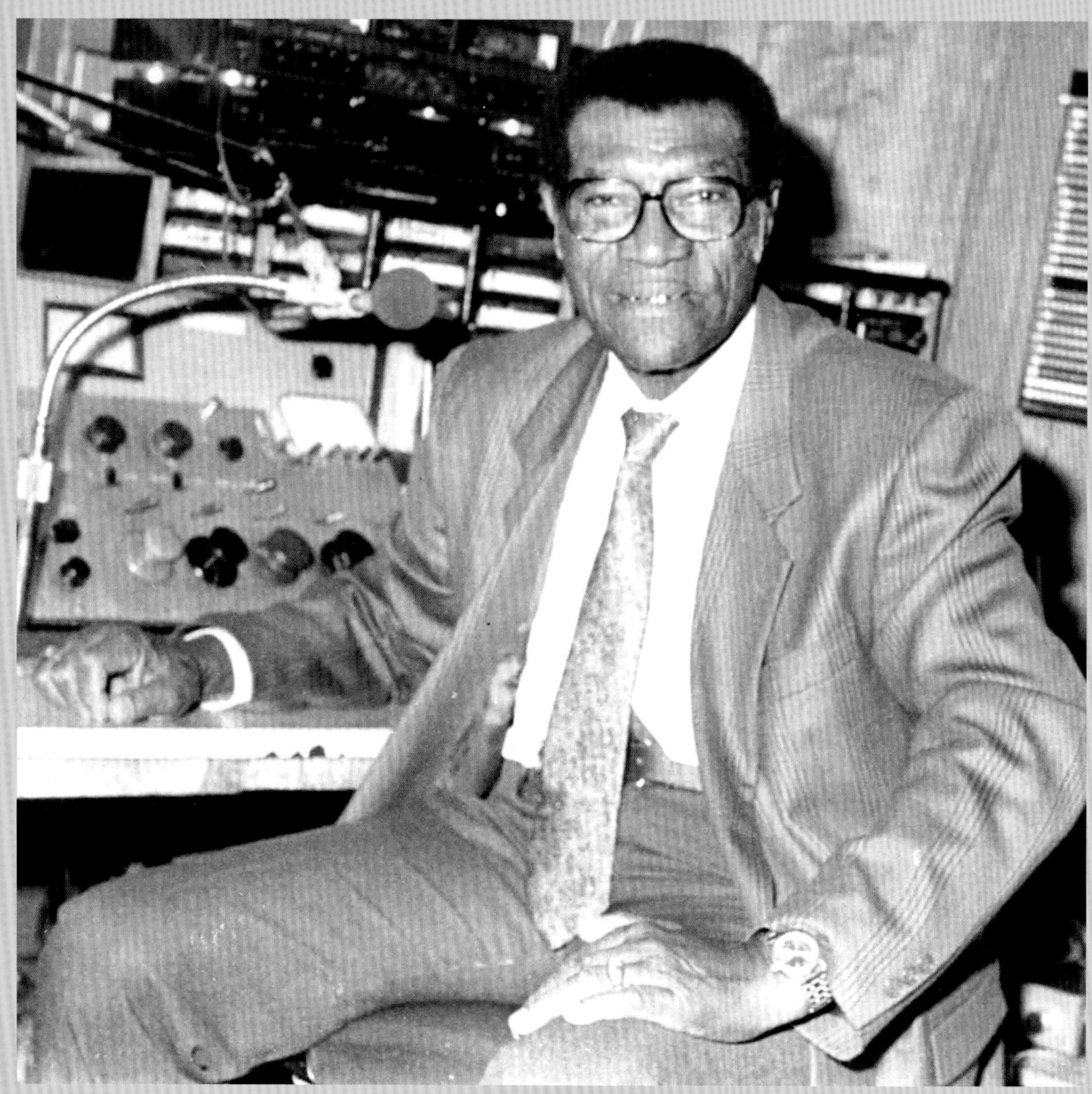

▲ Early Wright, Mississippi's first black disc jockey, who broadcast nightly blues and gospel shows on WROX radio for more than fifty years, was as artistic and colorful as the celebrity musicians he interviewed.

3

HOMEGROWN ICONS

At times when I consider this narrative frivolous, I think of the remarkable individuals—Mrs. McCoy, Mrs. Annie Myles, Sam and Doris Carr, and many others—who would never be known if their stories were not told. So I leave Delta landscapes and talk about homegrown icons and musicians who did not take Highways 49 and 61, the blues routes, to chase fame and fortune in Memphis, West Memphis, East St. Louis, Chicago, and Detroit. They stayed at home in the Mississippi Delta.

▼ In elegant formal attire at the scholarship banquet, Early and Ella Wright accept congratulations from Bill Ferris, director of the Center for the Study of Southern Culture at the University of Mississippi. (second photo) Other dignitaries on stage beneath a banner honoring Early Wright in Clarksdale's Civic Auditorium are Jim O'Neal, founding editor of *Living Blues* magazine, celebrity entertainer Bobby Rush, drummer Sam Carr, and barber/bluesman Wade Walton.

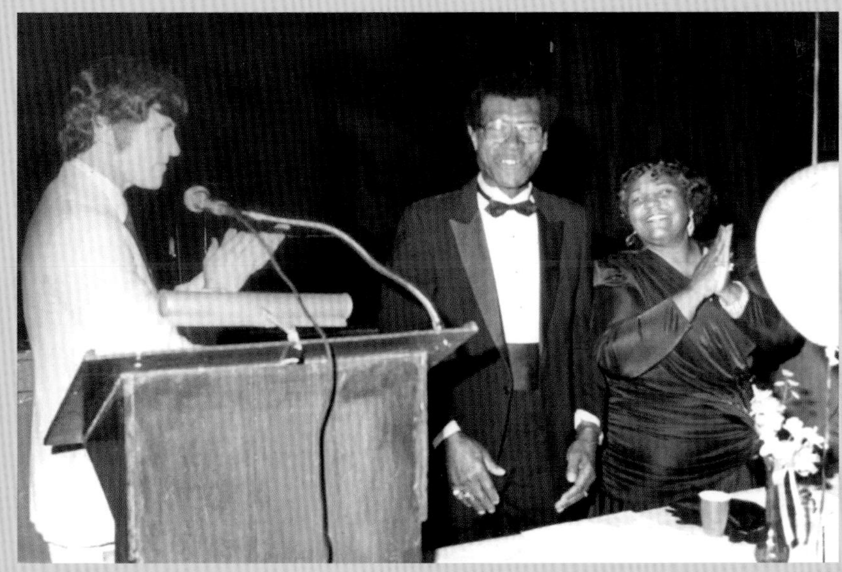

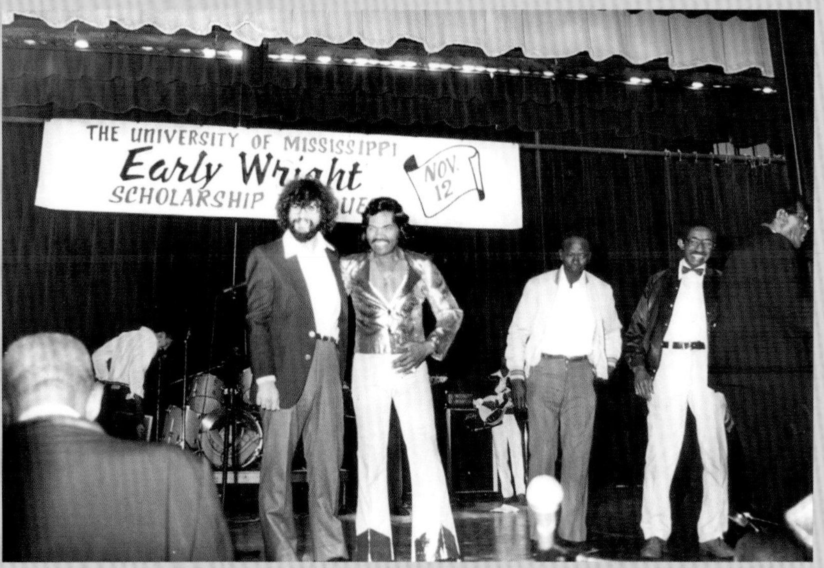

Long before the Delta Blues Museum opened in 1979, and before tourism commissions were anyone's brainchild, two figures in Clarksdale had established tourism bases of their own: disc jockey Early Wright and barber/storyteller/bluesman Wade Walton.

EARLY WRIGHT

Early Wright, Mississippi's first black disc jockey, who broadcast nightly blues and gospel shows on WROX radio for more than fifty years, later became a media favorite. He was featured by CNN, CBS television, the *Washington Post*, the *Los Angeles Times*, and other giants of the print world. On his show, he interviewed many celebrities, including Muddy Waters, Ike and Tina Turner, Little Milton, Bobby Rush, Rufus Thomas, Charley Pride, and even Elvis Presley. He also welcomed visitors after hours when the station was closed. Placing a record on the turntable, Early raced downstairs, unlocked the door, and catapulted back to the second floor ready to interview guests.

On the air his most impressive messages were his own words: greetings to listeners, dedications, church announcements, obituaries, one-of-a-kind advertisements, warnings for children to watch out for snakes and to stay in school, and pleas for volunteers to deliver lunches for the Jones Activity Center. None were prerecorded. Jim O'Neal said Early was as colorful and as much an artist as the performers he featured on the radio. "People tuned in to hear what he said." From his Alcazar Hotel studio, Early connected with his listeners and loved "dropping" requests on them, riding around in "Rena Lara, Crenshaw, Lambert and Tutwylie."

"Don't stay at home saying 'my vote don't count' during election time. Those are yesterday words. I'm not telling you who to vote for; just vote. If you are a registered voter, you're not a first-class citizen if you don't vote," he continued.

Guy Malvezzi, manager of Conerly's Shoe Store at the time, said, "You got your money's worth with Early's advertisements; they were part of the entertainment package."

"A lot of folks thought they had arthritis or rheumatism because they kept their mattresses too long . . . the shape of them got into the mattress. After they bought a new one from Coahoma Furniture on Delta Ave., they're restin' good," Early said.

In 1988 a fundraising banquet to establish an Early Wright Scholarship at the University of Mississippi took place in Clarksdale's Civic Auditorium. Showman Bobby Rush, Early's longtime friend from the

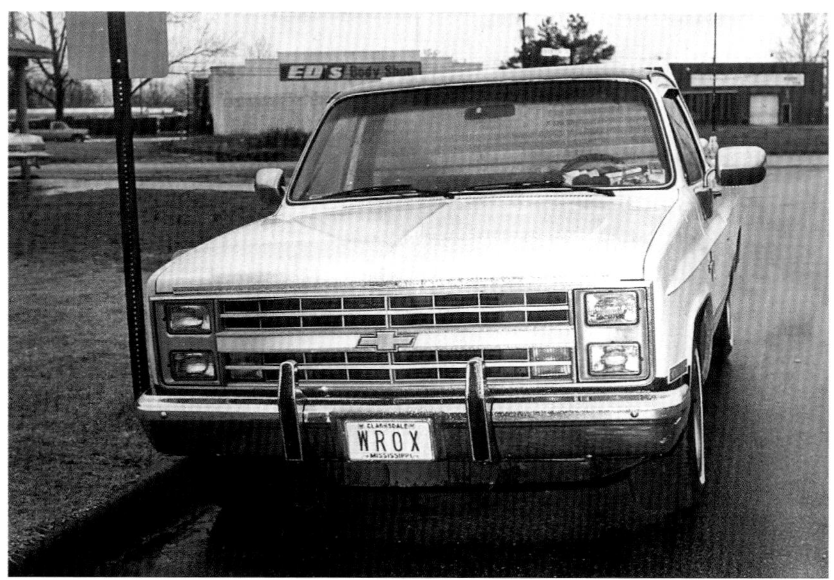

▲ For half a century Early Wright and his WROX pickup truck are part of the landscape as he collects news, announcements, and advertisements for his *Soul Man* show on 1450 AM.

fifties, told me most DJs warned him his records sounded "too black."
"But Early never turned his back on blues like a lot, or on what he was,"
he said. Several hours later I witnessed what he meant.

In formal attire, Early and Ella Wright accepted congratulations
from Little Milton Campbell; WDIA radio executives from Memphis; Bill
Ferris, director of the Center for the Study of Southern Culture; and
local officials, friends, and sponsors. Opening the musical program,
church soloists and choirs frequently featured on WROX radio and
gospel shows organized by Early evoked "amens" and "all-rights" from
crowds spilling over into the aisles. But when Bill Ferris announced
it was time for the evening's headliner, Bobby Rush, the entire gospel section stood up and left. Bobby's show, including its racy "Sue"
segment, roared forward, onward, and upward into a sensational success. Months later at Ole Miss, Early and actor James Earl Jones were
inducted together as Outstanding Black Mississippians.

No one ever figured out how Early was accepted by both church
and blues crowds. But he was, "that's for sure"—to borrow an Early
Wright expression I frequently use. Melville Tillis, longtime cochairman of the Sunflower River Blues Association said, "Early played blues
records when no one else would. He did many things for the community that will never be known; he was a mediator between the races."

Standing tall at six feet, he was a snappy dresser, seldom seen out
of coat and tie. "When I was a boy, I wore cotton sack shirts my mother
and I made," he told me. "I grew up on the hard part of the highway,
but I always went to church in what I had; I have always had sympathy
for the poor," he said.

I interviewed him before his 1988 banquet program, and Early
told me: "I was born at 3 A.M. on a Monday morning in 1915 in Jefferson,
Mississippi, Carroll County. I was first a farmer, then a hostler tending
to stock at Council Spur, and I moved to Clarksdale in 1937." After learn-
ing to drive a train, he became a mechanic for Roberson Motor Com-
pany and opened his own business: Simmons and Wright Garage on
Fourth Street. He became manager for the Four Star Quartet gospel
group when he was hired by WROX station manager Buck Hinman.

Although the Sunflower River Blues and Gospel Festival was
founded by Jim O'Neal and Patty Johnson, Early Wright was its sym-
bolic leader, and he never missed a meeting. The blues festival's highest honor is the Early Wright Blues Heritage Award presented annually
for "outstanding work to preserve, promote, perpetuate, and docu-
ment blues in its homeland, the Mississippi Delta."

When Early Wright died in December 1999, his obituary was
printed prominently in the *New York Times*. Hundreds filled the Civic

Auditorium, with Bobby Rush playing farewell on his harmonica. Less than a month later, Clarksdale lost its second major icon when Wade Walton died in January 2000.

Mourners packed Lyon's Liberty Baptist Church and heard Kenneth Lackey playing his father's harmonica and talking about Wade's philosophy of integrity and the importance of a neat appearance and a sharp shoeshine. At Kenny's feet sat "Flukie," a stuffed monkey who rode on the front seat of Wade's brown pickup to entertain children.

WADE WALTON

Wade's barber shop on Fourth Street, with his white cat, Missy, in the front room and a recreation room with pool table in the back, was a top tourism attraction in Clarksdale. Later Wade moved into a converted Spur Service Station on Issaquena across from the Greyhound bus station and adopted a black kitten he named Spur.

Almost every week, music fans arrived to meet the energetic bluesman. His first album, *The Blues of Wade Walton*: *Shake 'em on Down,* recorded in 1955 and distributed widely in Europe, made him an international attraction. The album was recorded on the Bluesville label in New Jersey, where Wade said he was paid $600. "When I got home, they sent $400 more, and that was the end of that," he said. He never received any royalties.

Wade's trip to New Jersey in 1958 with two white Pomona College students in a 1947 Volkswagen Beetle packed with sleeping bags is legendary. He said Don Hill and Dave Mangurian booked a recording session for him in New Jersey. However, the night before they planned to leave, the two students were jailed in Clarksdale as freedom riders. The trio eventually left Clarksdale heading for New York City and New Jersey, spending one night in a cemetery in Queens. "Later we stayed in the YMCA," he says. When the album was finished, Wade came home on a Greyhound bus. Among the songs recorded were "Big Fat Mamma"; "Choo De Shoo Shoo,"—an instant hit; "Rock Me, Mamma"; "Parchman Farm," which Walton wrote about a real incident with Bill Harpole, assistant prison superintendent; "Big Six," his first barber shop; and "Shake 'em on Down."

One of seventeen children, Wade was born at Lombardy on one side of Parchman and was familiar with the Mississippi State Penitentiary. He told me he was raised on the Lee Mays plantation and grew up hearing prisoners singing and playing the blues. However, he learned blues guitar from his brother, Hollis "Honey" Walton, whom

▶   In 1955 barber/bluesman Wade Walton recorded an album in New Jersey that was distributed internationally, and for decades his barber shop on Fourth Street was Clarksdale's top tourism attraction. Renowned also as a storyteller, Walton installed a stuffed monkey named "Flukie" on the front seat of his vintage pickup to entertain children. Spur, successor to his famous cat Missy, was named for his new shop on Issaquena, a renovated Spur Service Station.

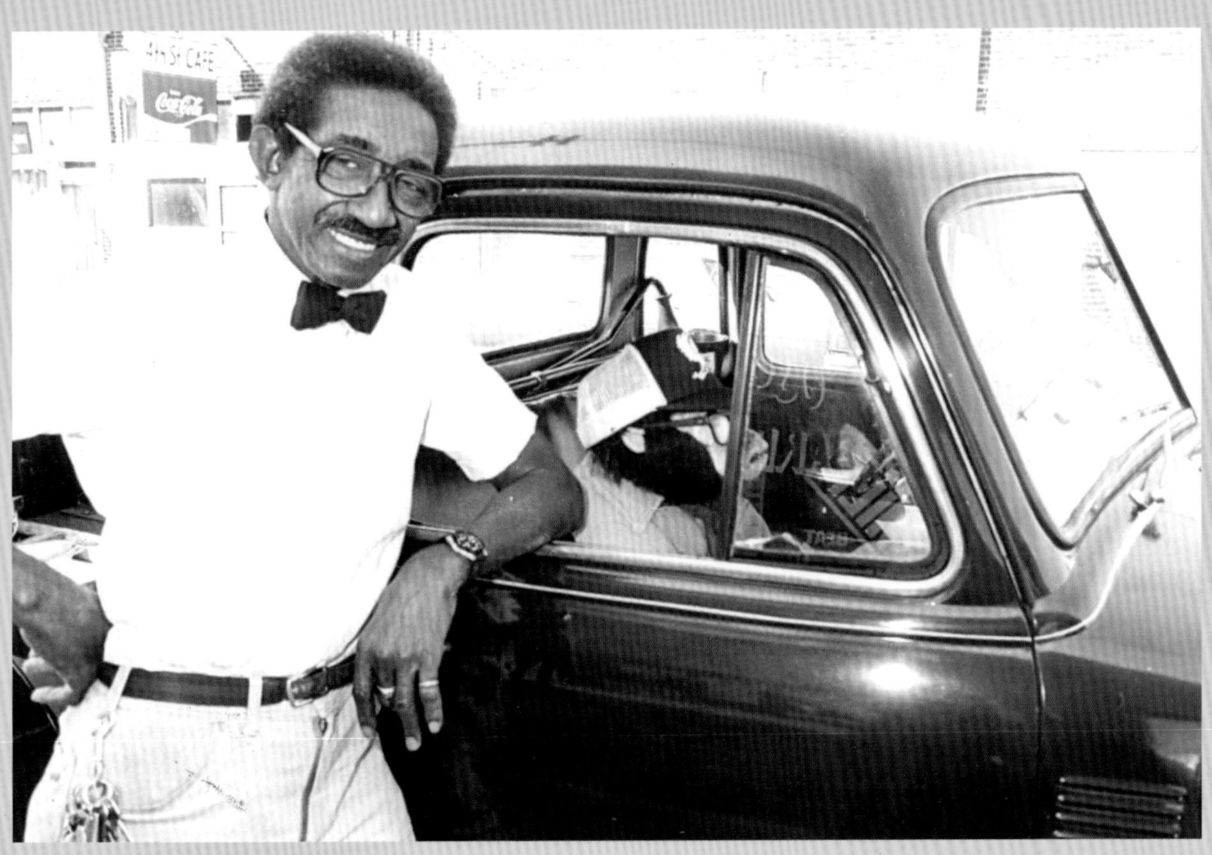
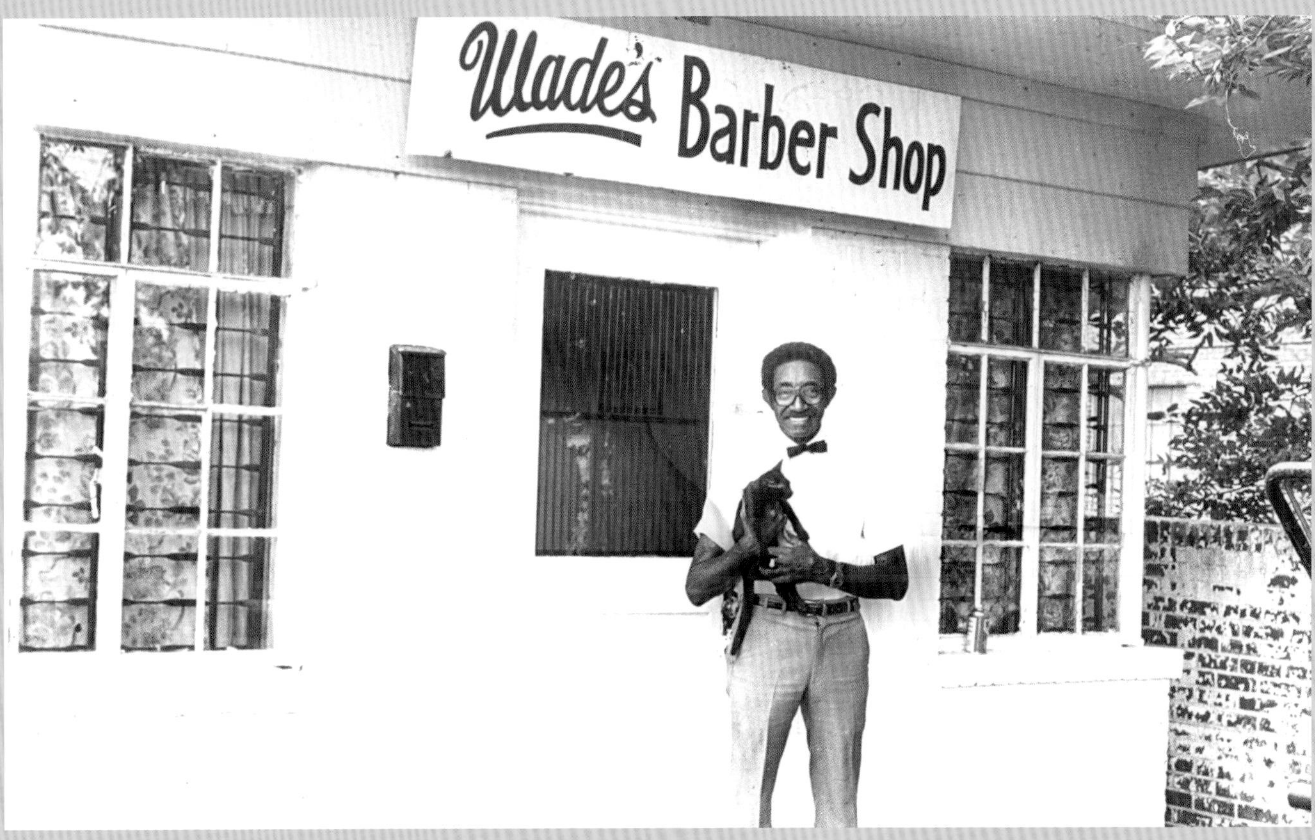
Wade's Barber Shop

he later visited by train every Sunday. Wade was a natural storyteller and recounted a tale about his daddy—a one-armed man who had learned to drive the plantation owner's T-Model Ford and one day steered the vehicle by the Walton house for the first time. Wade recalled, "My brother got the muzzle-loader behind the bed and shot the car, saying, 'I made it leave Papa alone.'"

In the 1940s Wade went to Memphis to Lumpkin Barber College, where he learned his trade. He moved to Clarksdale and started barbering at the Big Six Shop on Fourth Street owned by G. D. Sharp. "He had six chairs and rented chairs to two barbers," said Wade. In 1972 Wade opened his own shop. Years later a fast-talking out-of-towner convinced him to expand it into a club and take him in as a partner. Two weeks later the new partner skipped town, taking most of the equipment and leaving a $400 phone bill.

"He was not the right kind of man; no one heard from him since," says Wade, who estimated his loss at $4,500. Although it put him out of business and propelled him into bad health, Wade rid himself of negative memories by writing a song about his bad times. He called it "Leaving Fourth Street." Revered by both black and white citizens, he was named to Clarksdale's First Hall of Fame and rode in a convertible in the Christmas parade with another Hall of Famer: Mary Jo McIntosh.

Wade enchanted members of the Opera Study Club one night singing "Caldonia (What Makes Your Big Head So Hard?)" at Carnegie Public Library. During the civil rights era, he traveled across Mississippi setting up branches of the NAACP with Dr. Aaron E. Henry. Later, he closed Dr. Henry's extraordinary funeral service, in May 1992, with a harmonica solo in the Pinnacle of Coahoma Community College. Among thousands of mourners were many distinguished politicians, including Dr. Benjamin Hooks, former executive director of the National Association for the Advancement of Colored People; Mike Espy, former U.S. secretary of agriculture; congressman Bennie Thompson; and former Mississippi secretary of state Dick Molpus.

When I stopped to ask Wade about his rumored move to St. Louis, he was wearing his usual bowtie and white coat with "Wade Walton" embroidered over the pocket. He also was busy adjusting a towel around a customer sitting in the barber chair. "This is Samuel Jordan," Wade said. "He used to work for the railroad."

▼ Customers line up for a haircut and a shave, and Clifford Gibson says, "No one but Wade has cut my hair since 1965."

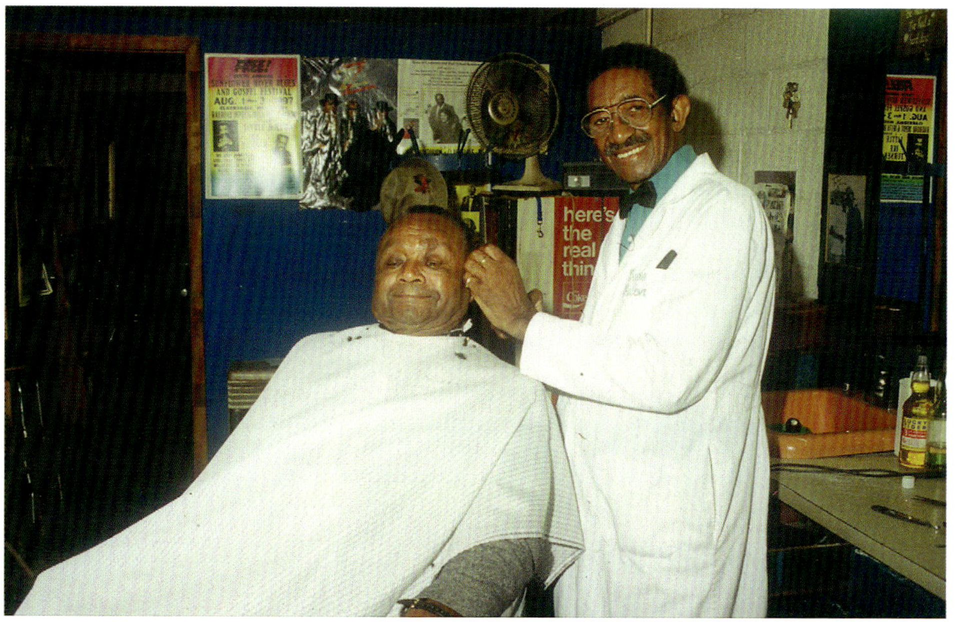

▶ Both born in October, Wade Walton and Leland bluesman Son Thomas celebrate their joint birthdays outside the Delta Blues Museum. Both musicians performed regularly at the Sunflower River Blues Festival, and Walton delighted members of Clarksdale's Opera Study Club in the museum with "Caldonia (What Makes Your Big Head So Hard?)"

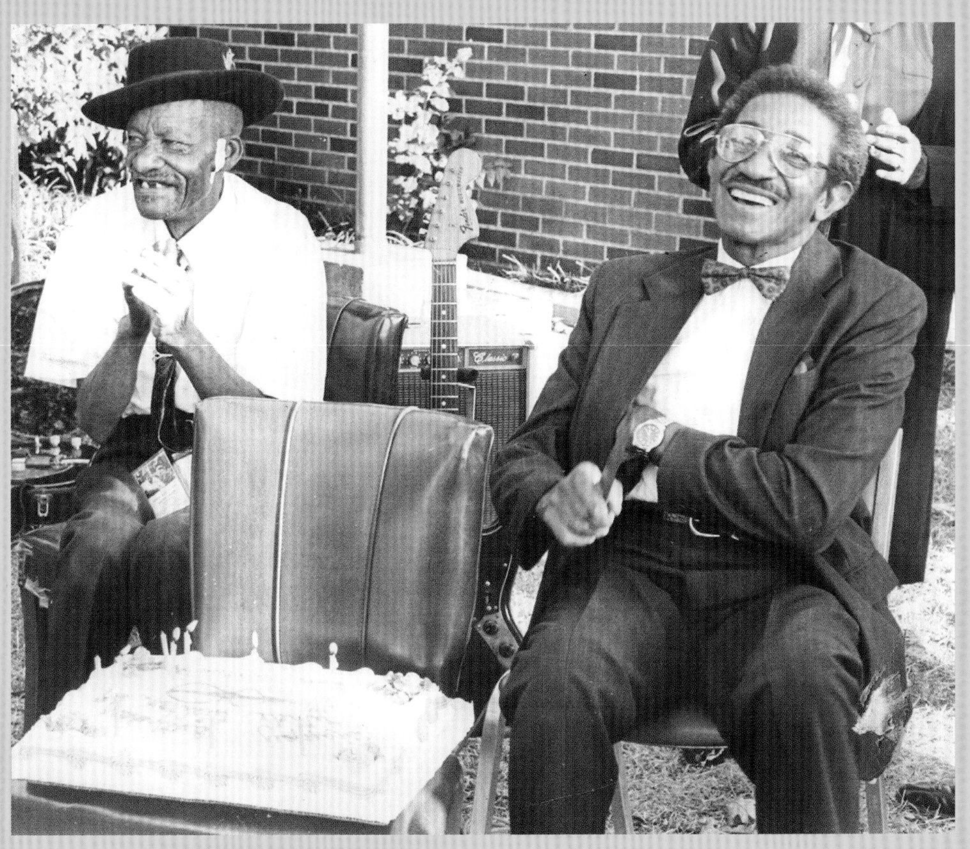

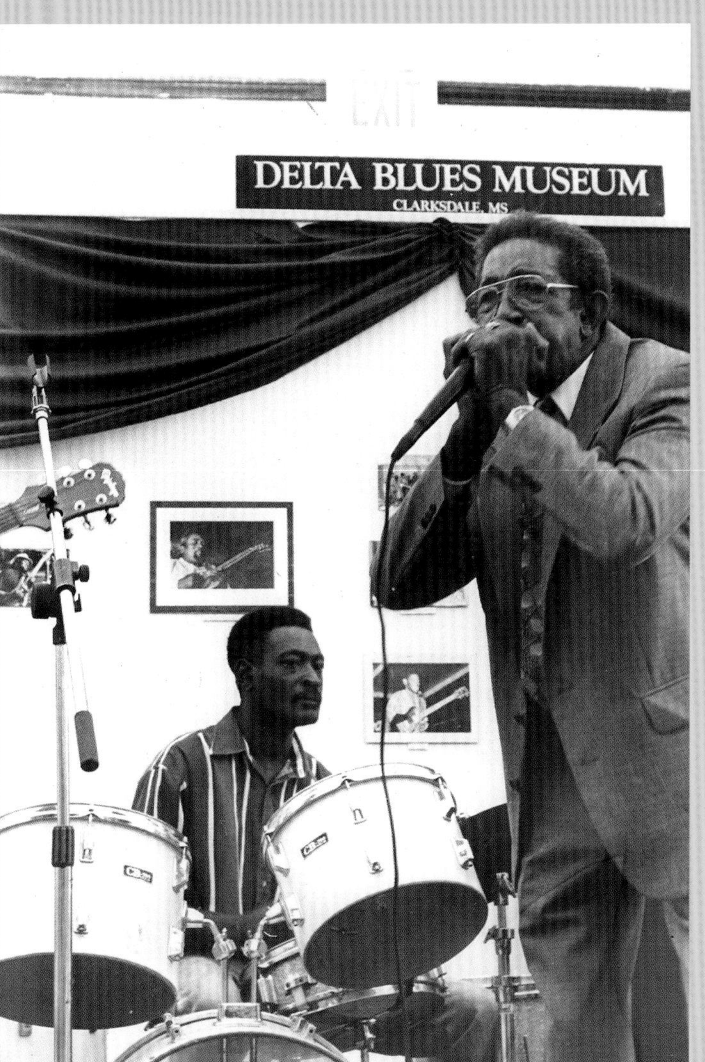
DELTA BLUES MUSEUM
CLARKSDALE, MS

Jordan smiled and replied, "That's right. I maintained the tracks from Lula to Land for forty-four years." With other customers lined up for a haircut and a shave, Clifford Gibson from Jonestown waited his turn, saying, "No one but Wade has cut my hair since 1965." Conversations turned to Wade and his wife, Rose, moving to St. Louis, where Rose's only daughter, Lilly Porter, lived. "Clarksdale is home for me, and I don't want to go," said Wade. "I hate to leave. I've been living here all these years; it's nothing but home." Before moving to St. Louis, he and Rose were honored inside Clarksdale Station with a party and a tribute organized by Marco Stewart and Super Chikan Johnson.

THE JELLY ROLL KINGS

An iconic pair of Delta bluesmen known as the Jelly Roll Kings—drummer Sam Carr and guitarist Big Jack Johnson, minus Frank Frost, their late vocalist/keyboard/harmonica giant—once took me on a fishing trip with them, in the spring of 2003.

"If I could see my past life on television, I wouldn't believe it myself," Sam told me on the way to Phillips Bayou near Moon Lake. Swapping tales about their early Jelly Roll King days, Big Jack said, "Sam was the boss. He'd get in a fight with someone, and if he couldn't whip him, he'd go home, rest up, and come back and fight him again. That's probably because he was raised up by himself." The transformed mild-mannered and courtly drummer playing beneath a feather-trimmed straw hat agrees. "I was raised by myself and had to defend myself. After I whipped the first boy with a jelly bucket at school, that was it; they left me alone," Sam says.

Sam's daddy was Robert Nighthawk, a blues legend, who wasn't around when his son was growing up. "The Carrs raised him," said Doris Carr, his wife of fifty-six years. Sam says, "I grew up between Jeffrey and Dundee, and learned what I did on my own. Doris says Sam was fifteen when he went to Helena, Arkansas, later to stay with his daddy. She said, "Robert Nighthawk came back again to Helena in 1941, and he didn't drink. He played slide and he kept his guitar strings loose, never tight. His voice was sweet. He never sang louder than my speaking voice."

Describing the spell of Robert's performances, Sam said, "Men fell out when he sang 'Annie Lee, This Is My Last Goodbye,' and 'Sweet Black Angel.' People around here were used to picking and chopping cotton and didn't go anywhere to festivals like they do now. People didn't have money, but they paid a dollar to hear him."

▶   An iconic pair of Delta bluesmen known as the Jelly Roll Kings—drummer Sam Carr and guitarist Big Jack Johnson (minus Frank Frost, their late vocalist/keyboard/harmonica giant)—once took me on a fishing trip with them.

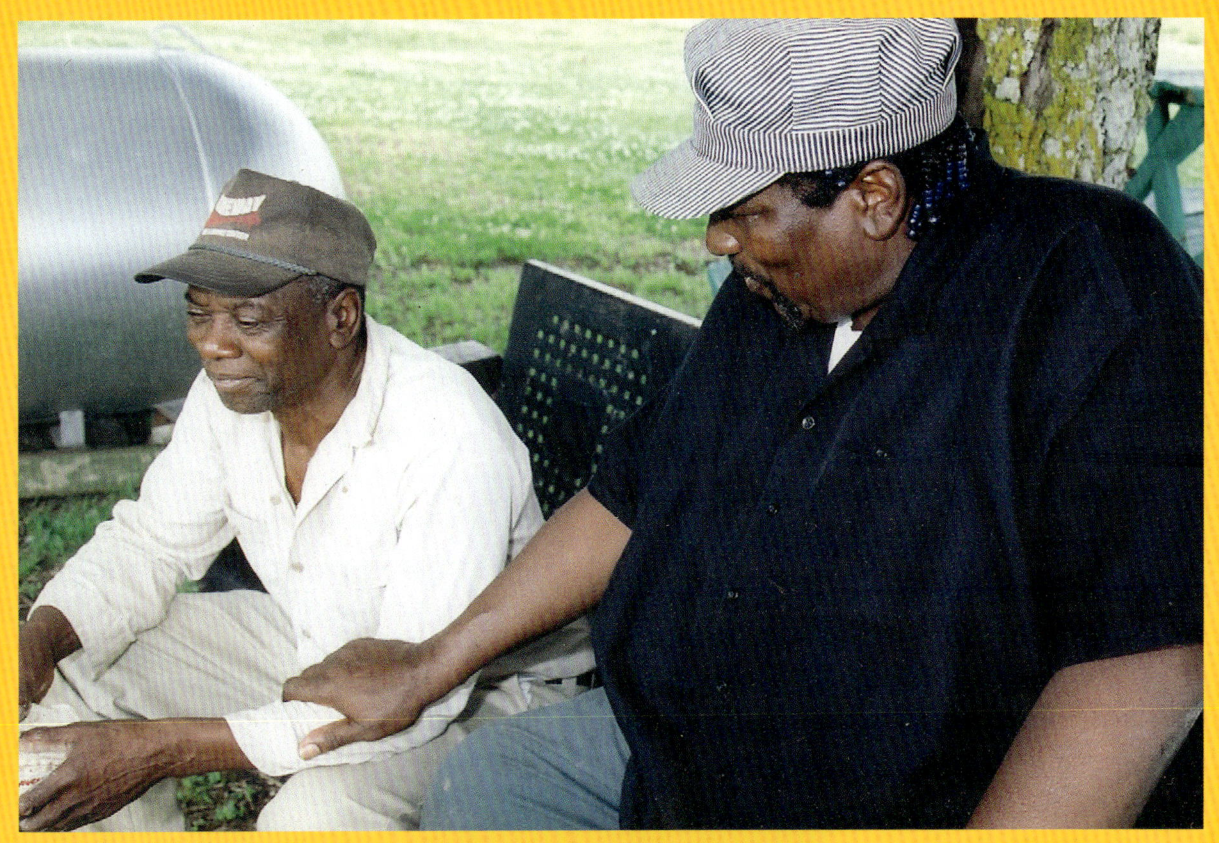

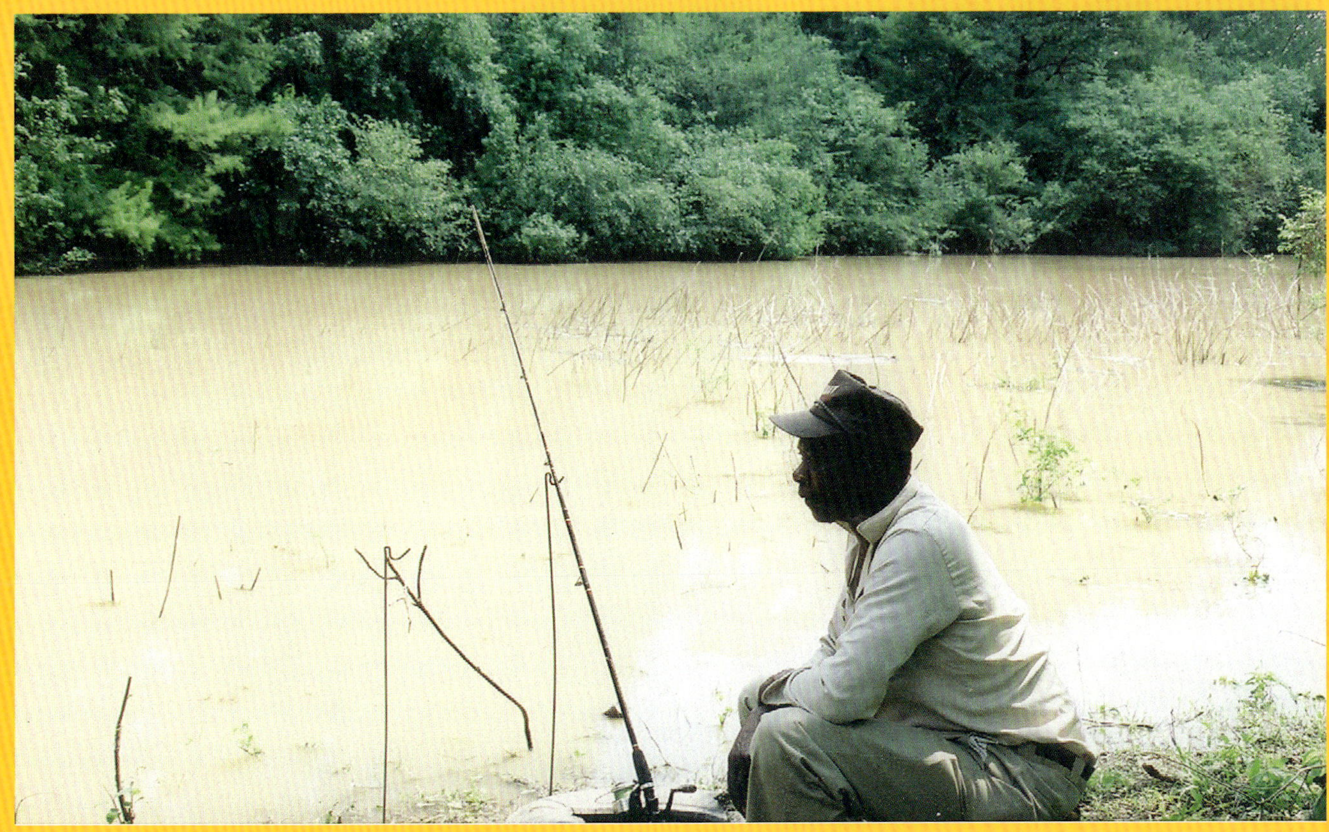

In 1935 Sam moved to St. Louis and put together Little Sam Carr's Blues Band. Ellis Johnson, Big Jack's brother, played with him four or five years, and also Big George Brock. "I played guitar, but I couldn't keep a drummer," said Sam. "I bought one drum a week until I had a set and learned how to play. I never wanted to sing; I couldn't remember the words."

Sam said blues bands in the country didn't have drums like city bands but kept time with a one-string bass wire and foot on a tub. In St. Louis Doris sang with the band, and Frank Frost, who was living in East St. Louis at the time, learned to play guitar listening to Nashville radio shows. "You and Frank had a special routine playing the same guitar together," prompted Doris. Sam said he followed his daddy's backbeat style of playing—changing right on the top of a song.

On October 6, 1960, Sam says, he and Frank left St. Louis for Coahoma County to help pick cotton on his family's farm. "Frank could pick five hundred pounds a day," said Sam. "It rained and rained, and it took three days getting to the house." During their stay, they heard Jack Johnson playing "Big Boss Man" at the Savoy Theatre by the railroad tracks in Clarksdale. "Frank didn't want to hire Jack, because he was blowing harp, playing guitar, and singing," said Sam. He said, "We don't need nobody; we've been playing together two years." Sam said, "I hired him anyway. We found out he was pretty good." They became the Jelly Roll Kings around 1962. "In those days we played 'back in the woods' music," says Big Jack. "We're uptown now."

Asked what the early days were like, both described playing after midnight at Smitty's in Clarksdale and taking off for the country through muddy fields to Fred's near Dundee, where buffalo (fish) was cooking and corn whiskey was for sale. Sam said he'd announce: "I'm not going to play a goddamn thing till I get a drink." Asked what he drank, Sam replied, "Anything. I'd start with a full fruit jar." Big Jack said, "We drank all that whiskey, we didn't care. We played all day Sunday with no sleep; got home sick Monday morning and had to face the boss man."

Wearing white coats, the Jelly Roll Kings were the house band at Conway Twitty's Club on Moon Lake. "One night there was a shooting. Sheriff Jessie Bonner came in there, pulled off his belt and pistol, and stopped the fight," Big Jack said. Recalling another gig in a country juke, Sam says, "I've seen a man killed over a pack of Camel cigarettes, and I stopped a man once from whipping a horse. I told him, 'You hit him again, and I'll cut your head off,' and put a knife on his neck. I was really pushing my luck, but the man stopped.

"The Lord stopped my ways when I was fifty years old, and I changed overnight," Sam said. "Nobody liked me; no one would give me a drink of whiskey. I wanted people to like me like they did Jack and Frank."

Praising Frank Frost, Big Jack said, "I tried my best to keep him alive. He was a monster—he played guitar, harp, keyboard, and sang at the same time. He was a monster. Frank had all kinds of women. There were so many Doris (Carr) had to keep a book for him," said Jack. "We didn't have money, but we lived like real folks and enjoyed ourselves to the highest," said Sam.

Frank Frost died October 12, 1999, in Helena. Jack says, "I wrote the song 'So Long, Frank Frost' the day I got the call." It is part of his *Roots Stew* album, and Jack played it during Frank's funeral in Helena's Malco Theatre on Cherry Street.

Since then, both Sam and Jack experienced serious health problems. "You ain't nothing but a machine—like a car with parts that wear out," said Sam. "When I got sick, I could hear these pumps working and not just my heart. When you do something bad, it comes back to hound you. I did many bad things, and I know that's why I've suffered," Sam continued. "When Jack was sick, he was shaking; his whole body was shaking," said Sam.

In May Jack was performing in London when his wife, Angenette, picked up his 2003 W. C. Handy Award in Memphis. Sam packed festivals in Australia and Scandinavia and earned more Handy nominations than he could count. "The Lord put you all together," said Angenette Johnson. "No one could play like Sam and Frank and Jack."

MRS. HILL AND THE RIVERSIDE HOTEL

In 1944 when Mrs. Z L Hill opened her boardinghouse at 615 Sunflower Avenue, she didn't count on the Riverside Hotel becoming a historic landmark. She was a businesswoman with a young son to raise. She also became "Mama" to a roll call of musicians whose names are important in blues, gospel, and rock 'n' roll music. Today the site is an

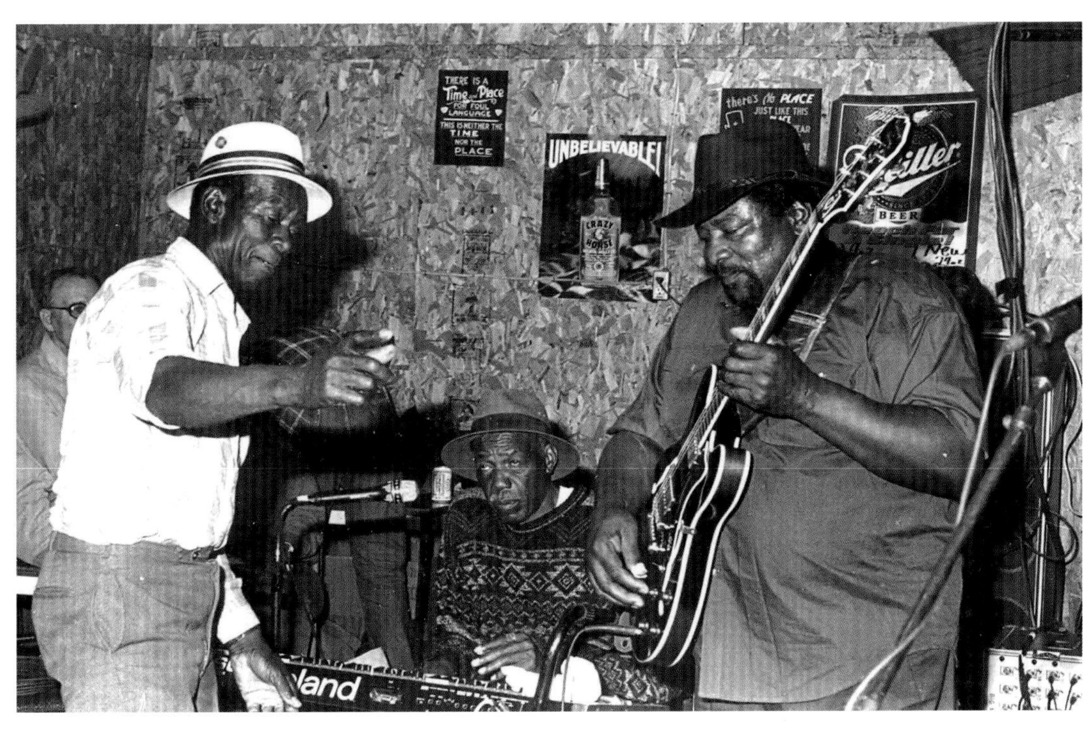

▲

The Jelly Roll Kings: Sam Carr (dancing), Frank Frost (seated at keyboard), and Big Jack Johnson are filmed performing at the Bobo Grocery in one segment of the Smithsonian Institution documentary *River of Song* series featured in 1999 on public television.

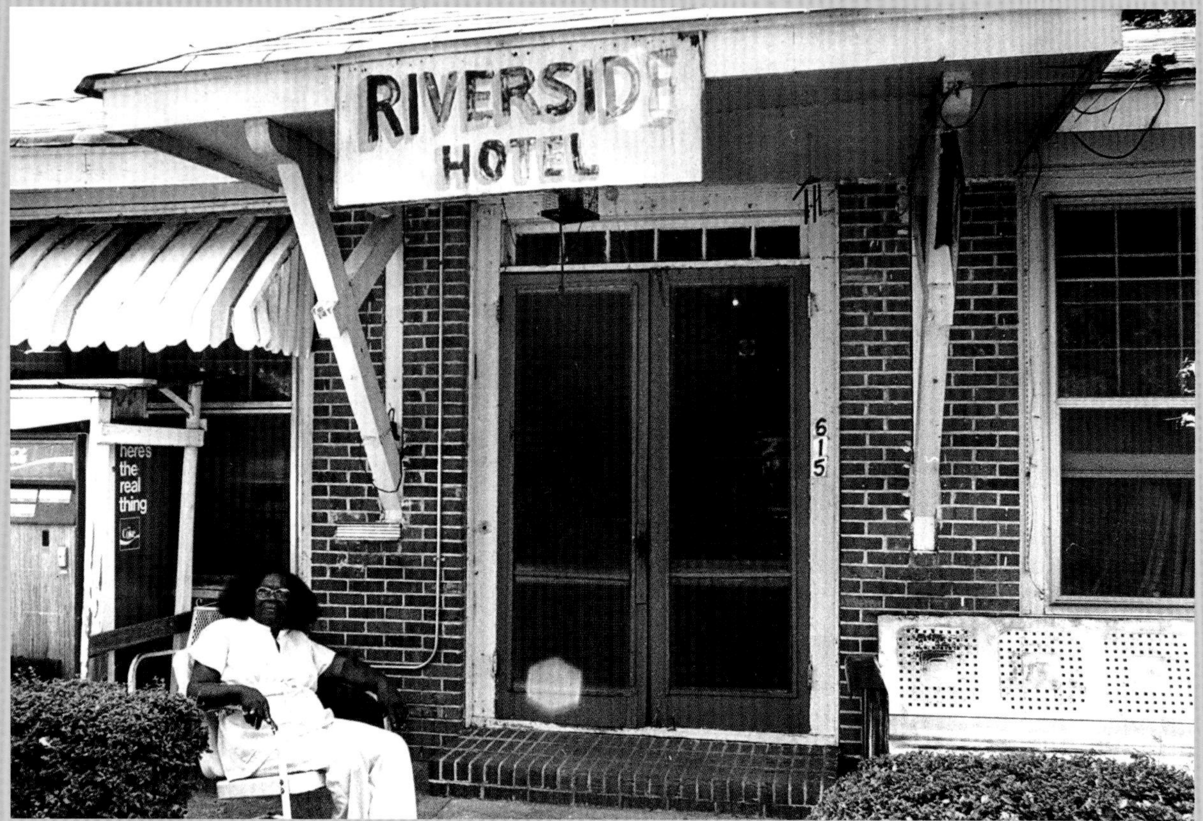

Z L Hill and her Riverside Hotel at 615 Sunflower Avenue dominate every tourism map as a boardinghouse for many early blues musicians. In earlier years, when it was the G. T. Thomas African American Hospital, it became tragically linked to Bessie Smith, the Empress of Blues, who died there in 1937 following an automobile accident on Highway 61 north of Clarksdale.

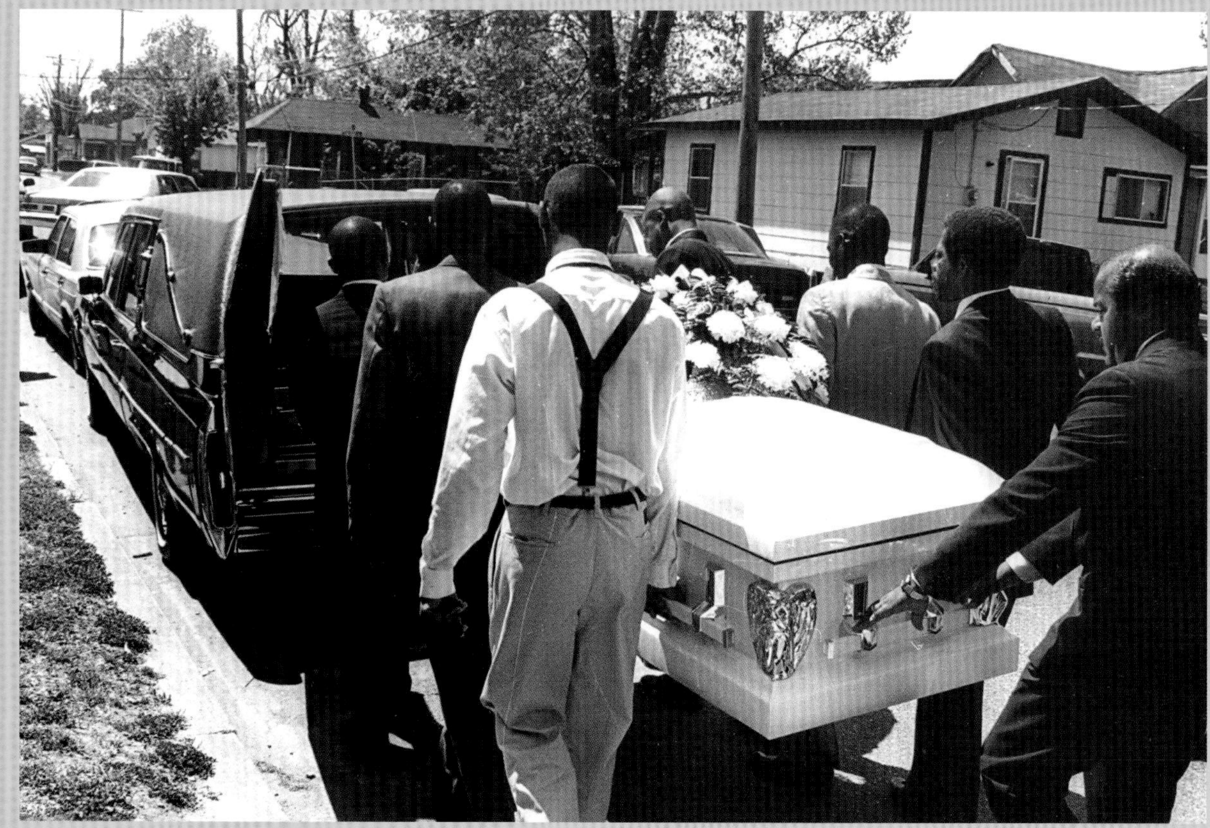

When Mrs. Hill died in 1997, a large crowd attended her funeral, where she was praised for her energy, her success as a businesswoman, and her commitment to community.

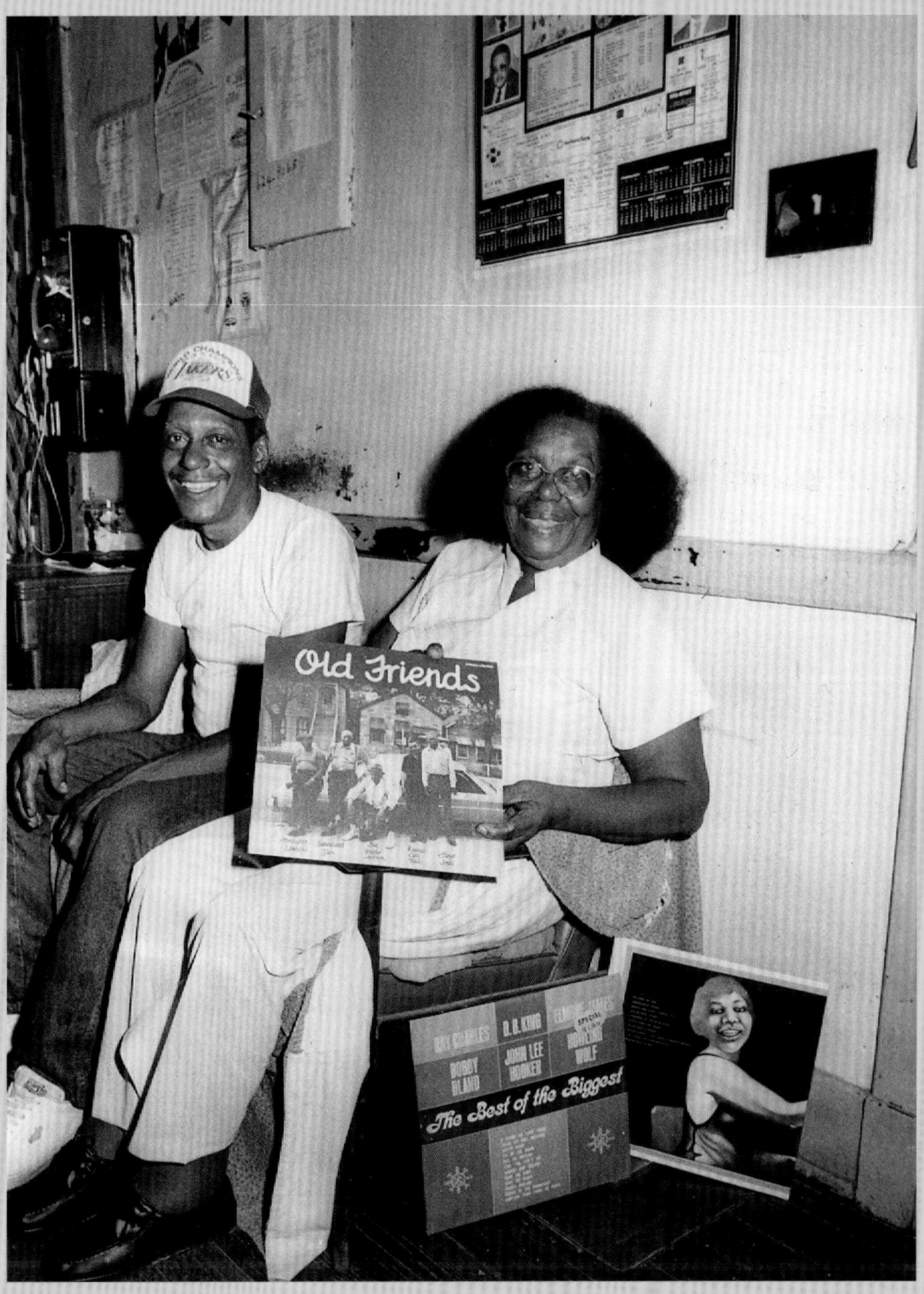

Sitting with her son Frank "Rat" Ratliff in the Riverside entry, Mrs. Hill enjoys relating stories about her boarders, including Sonny Boy Williamson, Jackie Brenston, and the "Rocket 88" gang with Ike Turner, the Reverend C. L. Franklin, and others. Later, John F. Kennedy Jr. enjoyed a Riverside weekend. Mrs. Hill and Frank enjoyed taking international guests to neighborhood ball games and barbecues.

international treasure and features one of Mississippi's early Blues Trail markers. Her "boys" included Robert Nighthawk, Sonny Boy Williamson, Ike Turner, Raymond Hill, Jackie Brenston, C. V. Veal, and Joe Willie Peck, among others. John Lee Hooker boarded with her at an earlier residence on Fourth Street, she told me.

"I embroidered 'Rocket 88' on ties for the band," Mrs. Hill told me while reminiscing about Jackie Brenston's song recorded in Memphis, now regarded as the first rock 'n' roll record. She said her "boys" lived from day to day playing Moorhead one night, Hezekiah Patton's place in Winstonville the next, and Charleston another.

She told me she never had to pay to get in clubs where they played. "We were a family, and at Christmas we exchanged gifts." In those days Mrs. Hill cooked meals for her boarders and for many children attending school across the street. She also ran a florist business and took in sewing. When her boys tried their luck in St. Louis, Chicago, and Detroit, she says, they stayed in touch. She recalled Ike Turner returning to Clarksdale with his wife Tina for a big show at the auditorium. "Tina introduced me as Ike's Mama, and we stayed up visiting till 4 A.M., when their chauffeur took them back to Memphis," she said.

Aretha Franklin's father, preacher C. L. Franklin, brought his gospel show to town, and all the performers, including conjoined twins Yvonne and Yvette McCarter, and a woman midget, stayed at the Riverside Hotel, she said. "We ran out of rooms, so the preacher and I sat up all night talking," she continued. Mrs. Hill remembered the day her former boarder Sonny Boy Williamson came home from Europe wearing a checkered suit. "He put on a show in front of the hotel with crowds so big they blocked the street; he was really stepping out."

Reminiscing about the Riverside's colorful past, Mrs. Hill enjoys listening to records and tapes sent to her from many parts of the world. One features the classic voice of Bessie Smith singing "High Water Blues" about the levee break and the Mississippi flooding the Delta. "She was a big star, and when she came to town, crowds were so big, you couldn't get near her," she said. "She sang in a side tent with people throwing money at her feet."

Those were the early days, before Bessie Smith's tragic link with 615 Sunflower Ave. when it was the G. T. Thomas African-American Hospital. She died there in 1937 following an automobile accident on Highway 61 north of Clarksdale. Newspaper accounts report the Empress of Blues sustained serious injuries, including an arm that was practically severed; she died about an hour after it was amputated. Many blamed other hospitals for turning her away because she was

African American. Playwright Edward Albee wrote a drama based on this belief: *The Death of Bessie Smith.*

In 1944 the hospital was sold to Mrs. Hill, and its twenty-five rooms became the Riverside Hotel, where many famous guests have stayed, including the late John F. Kennedy Jr. All enjoyed extraordinary hospitality—being taken to barbecues, to ball games, and back to the bus station when it was time to leave. Inability to speak English was never a problem; in fact, a visitor from Japan became a regular member of the family through the years.

Mrs. Hill told me her grandfather was a blacksmith in St. Elmo. "I moved to Clarksdale with my parents, Ed and Florence Barnes, when I was five years old," she said. She explained her name is not an abbreviation for anything. "I was born in 1907, and my aunt named me Z L, she said, to give me a name 'nobody had but you.'" When she walked to an early Sunflower Festival, a short distance from her home, she had a special sponsor seat waiting for her. Emcee C. V. Veal called for a round of applause to recognize "his mama."

Mrs. Hill died in 1997, and at her funeral service a friend praised her commitment to community, her energy, her success in business: "Early in the morning when farm trucks stopped on Fourth Street to pick up cotton choppers and pickers, Z L was never in the crowd. But she'd be there when they returned in late afternoon to sell them peanuts and snacks."

Until his death in 2013, her son, Frank "Rat" Ratliff carried on in his mother's traditions and initiated others bearing his own signature style. Today, they have been adopted by other family members. "Rat's" many contributions were recognized and praised by the Sunflower Festival with its highest honor: the Early Wright Blues Heritage Award.

MR. JOHNNIE BILLINGTON

Many of the professional bluesmen performing in the Clarksdale area credit "Mr. Johnnie" Billington with launching their careers. They also agree he taught them much more than music. Along with instrumental lessons, his students were taught to perform and dress with pride and confidence in front of audiences. They played with ZZ Top and Buddy Guy; they exchanged licks with National Symphony Orchestra professionals; they guzzled soft drinks and appetizers in the East Room of the White House; and they exchanged conversation with President Bill Clinton. Mr. Johnnie often organized after-school activities:

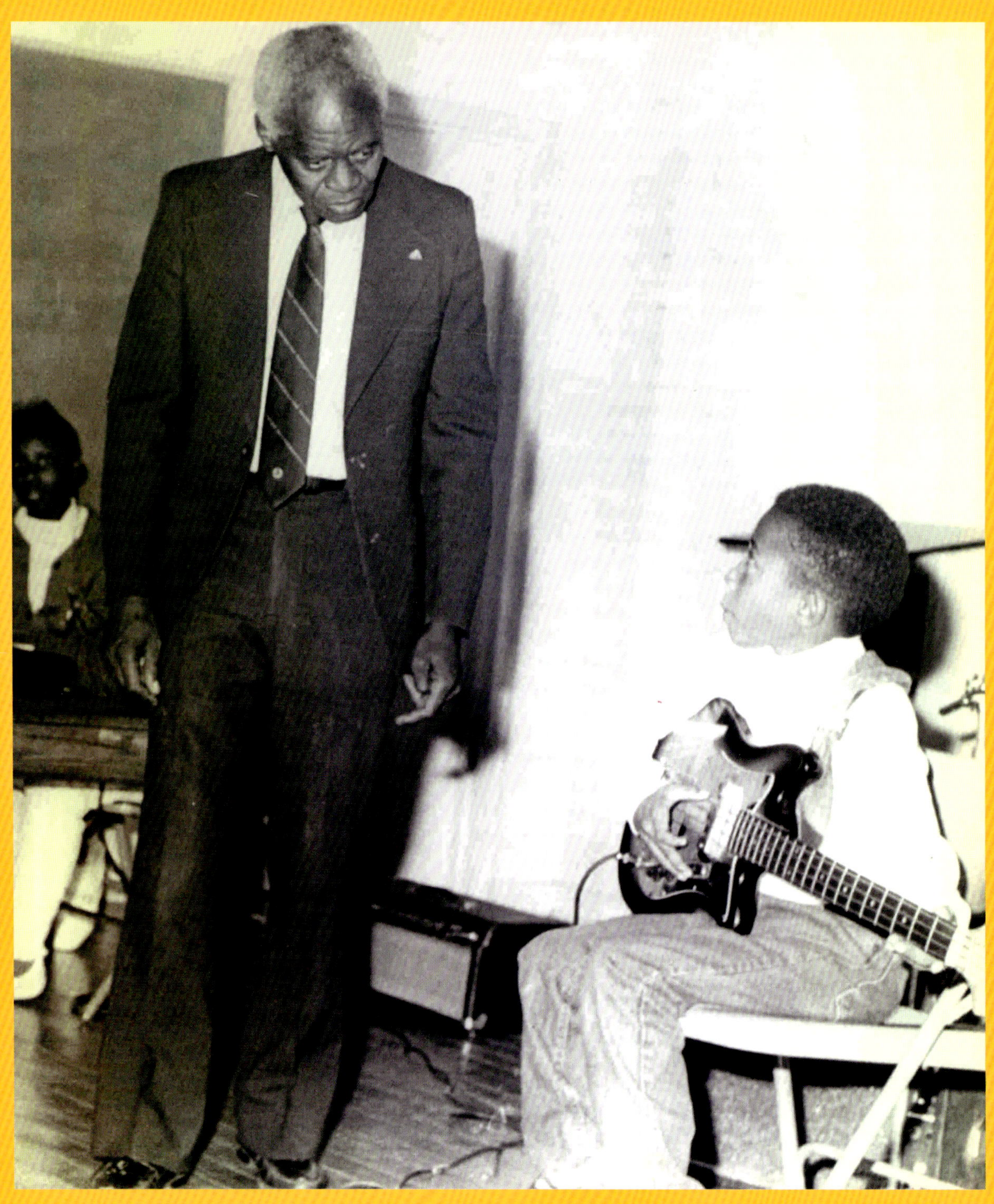

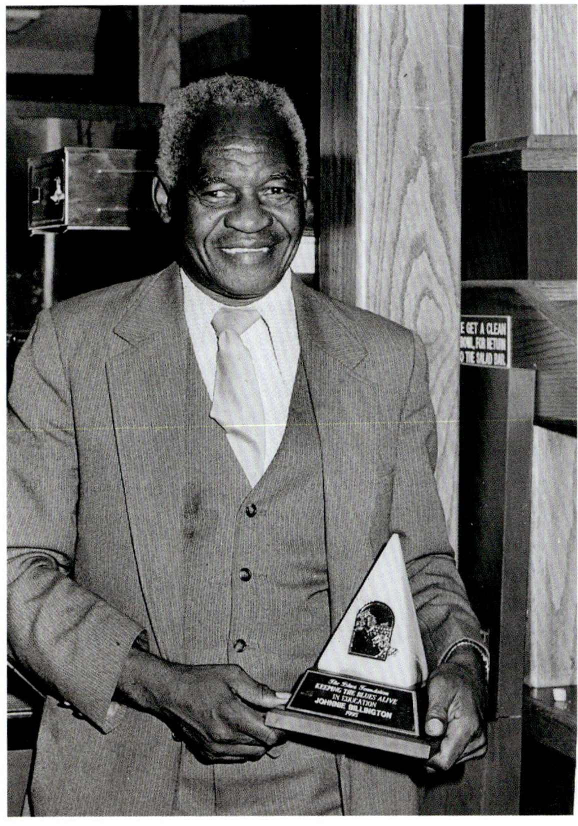

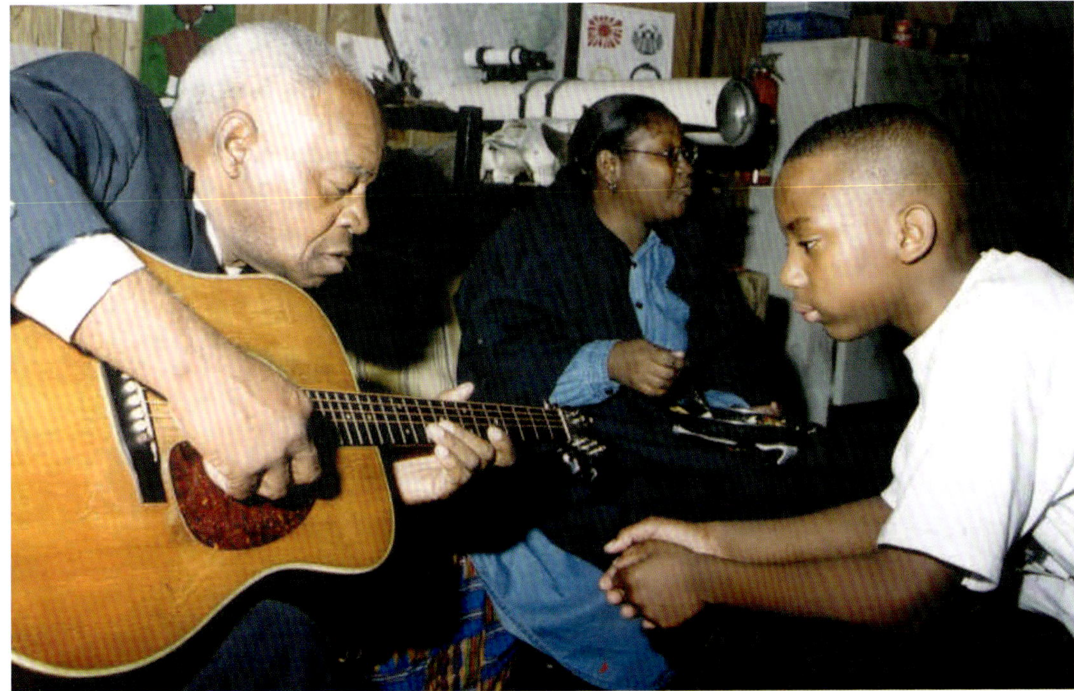

▲

Although blues lessons can take place informally, Mr. Johnnie's attire is always stage-ready. He teaches his students to perform and dress with pride and confidence.

◀

Most of the professional bluesmen performing in the Clarksdale area credit "Mr. Johnnie" Billington with launching their careers. They also agree he taught them much more than music.

lawn-mowing services generating spending money and keeping kids off the streets. He also taught them about sharing and teamwork.

Following one rainy King Biscuit Blues Festival in Helena when the band had to perform without a keyboard, some of the kids wanted to exclude the pianist because he didn't play. Mr. Johnnie said, "It's not his fault rain cancelled out his instrument; he made the trip; he's here; he's a member of the band, and he gets an equal share." This philosophy marked his lessons in the early Delta Blues Museum and still evoke misty-eyed memories for Anthony Sherrod playing the Sunflower Festival's acoustic stage decades later.

In 1999 Clarksdale was one of a handful of cities hosting Bill Clinton's presidential initiative on poverty. Arriving by helicopter at Fletcher Field, where cadets earned their wings in World War II, the president was spirited down U.S. Highway 61 in a procession flanked by Mississippi highway patrolmen. He was taken immediately to Issaquena Avenue in Clarksdale's New World District, where Muddy

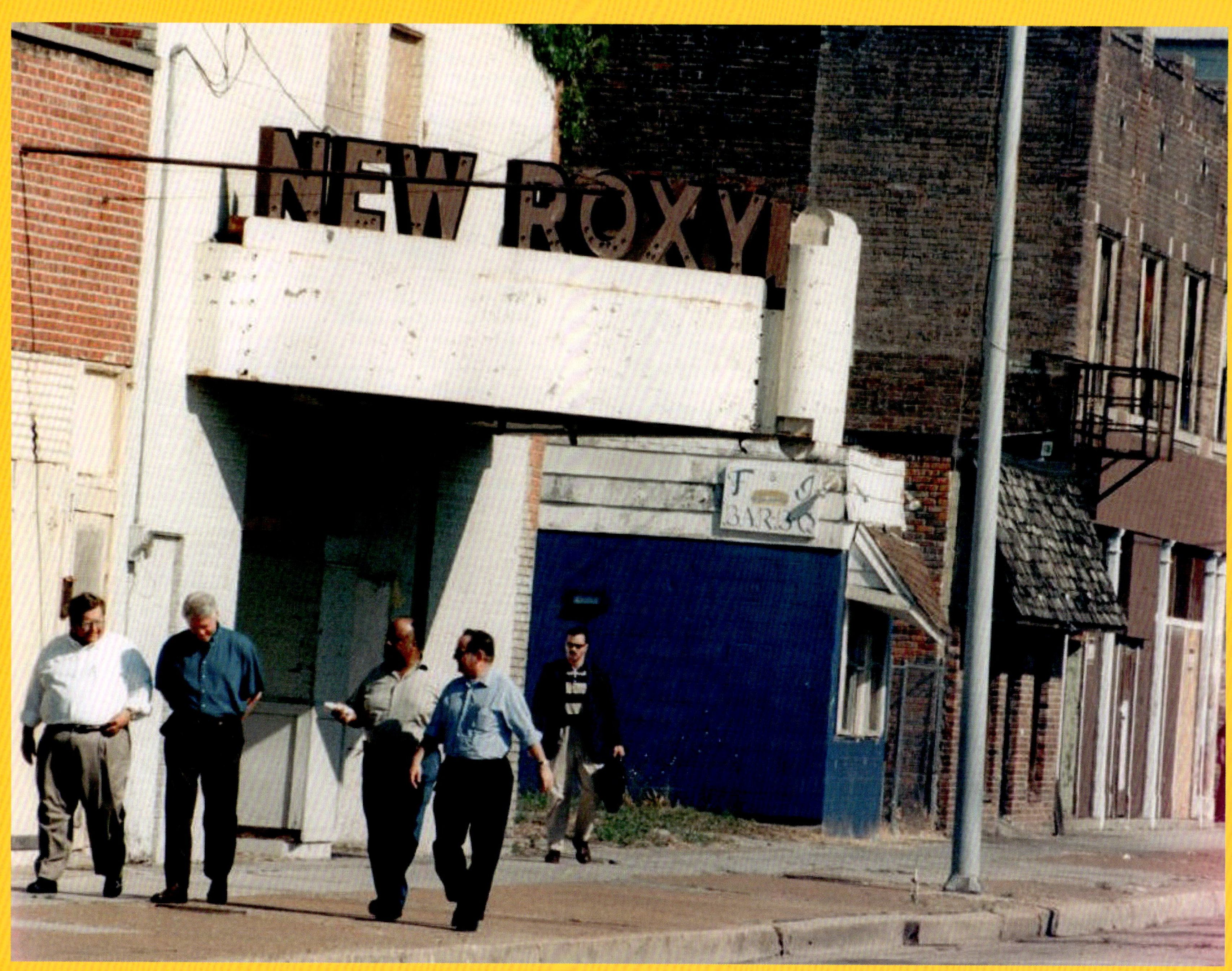

NEW ROXY
BAR-B-Q

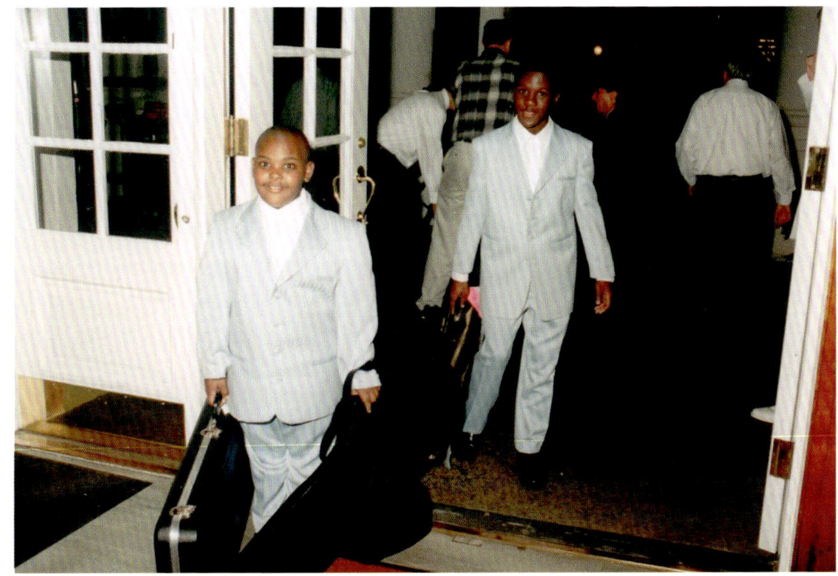

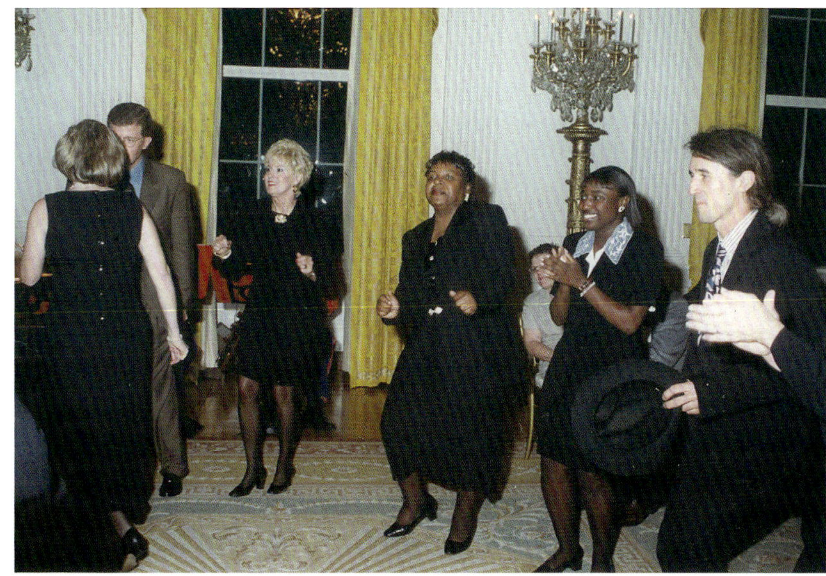

Waters and Honeyboy Edwards once played on street corners in this flourishing area with busy weekend crowds.

In 1999 there were no performing bluesmen but several former governors, state officials, Jesse Jackson, and hundreds of fans cheering behind barricades. The president and congressman Bennie Thompson walked slowly beneath the New Roxy marquee, where Sam Cooke once sang, and into Shirley Fair's florist shop to hear tough economic stories of the Delta. They also heard about the city's great music legacy and the Delta Blues Museum's thriving education program keeping it alive.

A year later, the president reciprocated the hospitality by inviting Delta residents to a White House reception, with a special invitation to the blues education students to perform there. Two sets of kids performed. Twelve-year-old drummer Quotasse Williams and seven-year-old Jarvis Cole, six inches shorter than the bass guitar strapped across his chest, followed the lead of Mr. Johnnie playing "Big Boss Man." For Quotasse, Jarvis, and the other students, accompanied by their teacher, Michael James, it was the gig of a lifetime.

Being off-beat or off-key, whether at 1600 Pennsylvania Avenue or in their storefront studio in Lambert, Mississippi, was sufficient grounds to be called down in public by their teacher. But that didn't happen, and the very best surprise was waiting in the wings. The entourage was whisked away to the circular diplomatic reception room for a private audience with the president. President Clinton shook hands and spoke at length with each member of our group; he

Following his visit to Clarksdale, the president invited the Delta Blues Education students to perform in the White House in 2000, and two sets of kids played, including twelve-year-old drummer Quotasse Williams and seven-year old Jarvis Cole, six inches shorter than his bass guitar (pictured leaving the White House with their instruments). Despite the historic surroundings, members of the Mississippi entourage, including John Ruskey, who organized the student trip, all danced like crazy to music by the U.S. Marine Jazz Band.

In 1999 Clarksdale was one of a handful of U.S. cities hosting Bill Clinton's presidential initiative on poverty. The president and congressman Bennie Thompson (D-Mississippi) walk slowly beneath the marquee of the New Roxy, where Sam Cooke once sang, and into Shirley Fair's florist shop to hear tough economic stories from the Delta. They also heard about Clarksdale's music legacy and the Delta Blues Museum's thriving education program keeping it alive.

talked to me about his good friend and my Clarksdale neighbor Walter Thompson—one of his first major fundraisers. He also expressed great admiration for Mississippi civil rights pioneer Dr. Aaron Henry. Afterward beneath gilt-framed portraits of George Washington, we danced like crazy to the U.S. Marine Jazz Band. The kids swilled vast quantities of soft drinks and enjoyed an East Room buffet lavishly decorated with golden candelabra. Leaving afterward in the van, I asked what they would remember most about this trip. All agreed that meeting the president was the best.

BIG JACK JOHNSON

Glory came at last for Big Jack Johnson—but not in his lifetime. On August 8, 2014, during the twenty-seventh annual Sunflower River Blues and Gospel Festival, Big Jack officially took his seat among other blues giants when he was honored with a Mississippi Blues Trail marker. Cited as a dynamic performer/songwriter with an important legacy to the world, Big Jack was Clarksdale's most famous bluesman since the days of Muddy Waters, John Lee Hooker, and Ike Turner. Once heralded by music critic Robert Palmer as "possibly the most original bluesman alive," Big Jack wrote songs attacking issues such as war, domestic violence, abortion, Hurricane Katrina, AIDS, and the 1994 ice storm that paralyzed Clarksdale.

For almost three decades, Jack toured the world—Europe, Canada, Australia, and Japan—connecting global blues fans with Mississippi, collecting a Handy Award and several Living Blues Awards, appearing in films and recording for the Earwig, M. C., Rooster Blues, and Fat Possum labels. Big Jack's birthday on July 30 was often celebrated with a mini-blues festival in his own neighborhood with musicians playing on a flatbed truck. In his final years he performed regularly with the Cornlickers, Pennsylvania-based musicians who revered his dedication to family, friends, and his role as a goodwill ambassador.

"On stage, he worked to bring Mississippi to the world. Off stage he worked to bring the world to Mississippi," said Dale Wise, Jack's longtime drummer. When he was home, he played regularly at Red's Club for his longtime friend Red Paden, who sometimes could be talked into relating a few memorable Big Jack Johnson stories. One involved Jack winning a $100 bet after wrestling a bear and flipping him to the ground. "Actually, Jack flipped the bear not once but two or three times," said Red.

Jack died March 14, 2011, and thousands attended his funeral in Coahoma Community College's Pinnacle.

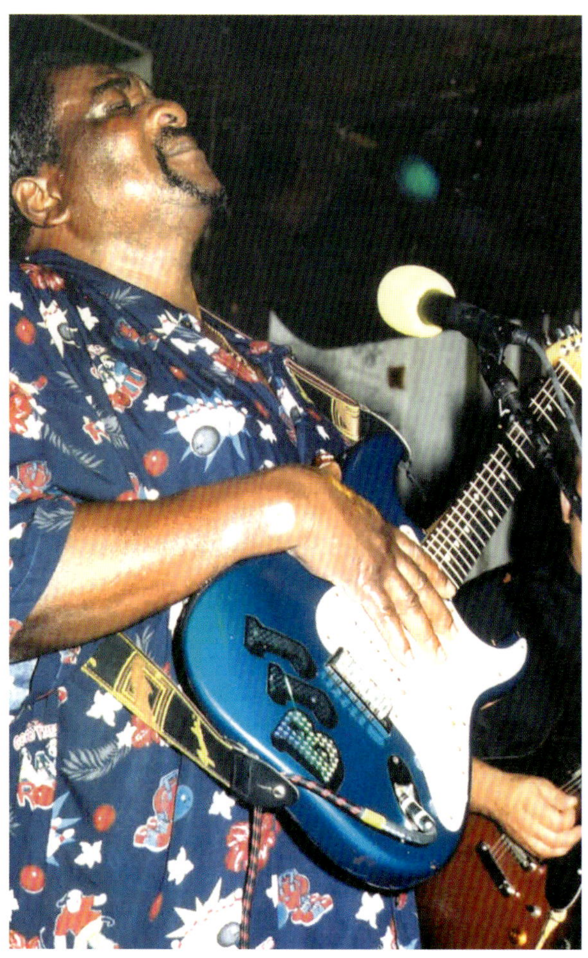

▲   For almost three decades Jack toured the world, including Europe, Canada, Australia, and Japan, connecting global blues fans with Mississippi. With his distinctive BJ guitar, he packed Ground Zero Blues Club at home. He frequently played mandolin and often interjected country favorites, such as "You Are My Sunshine," in his shows.

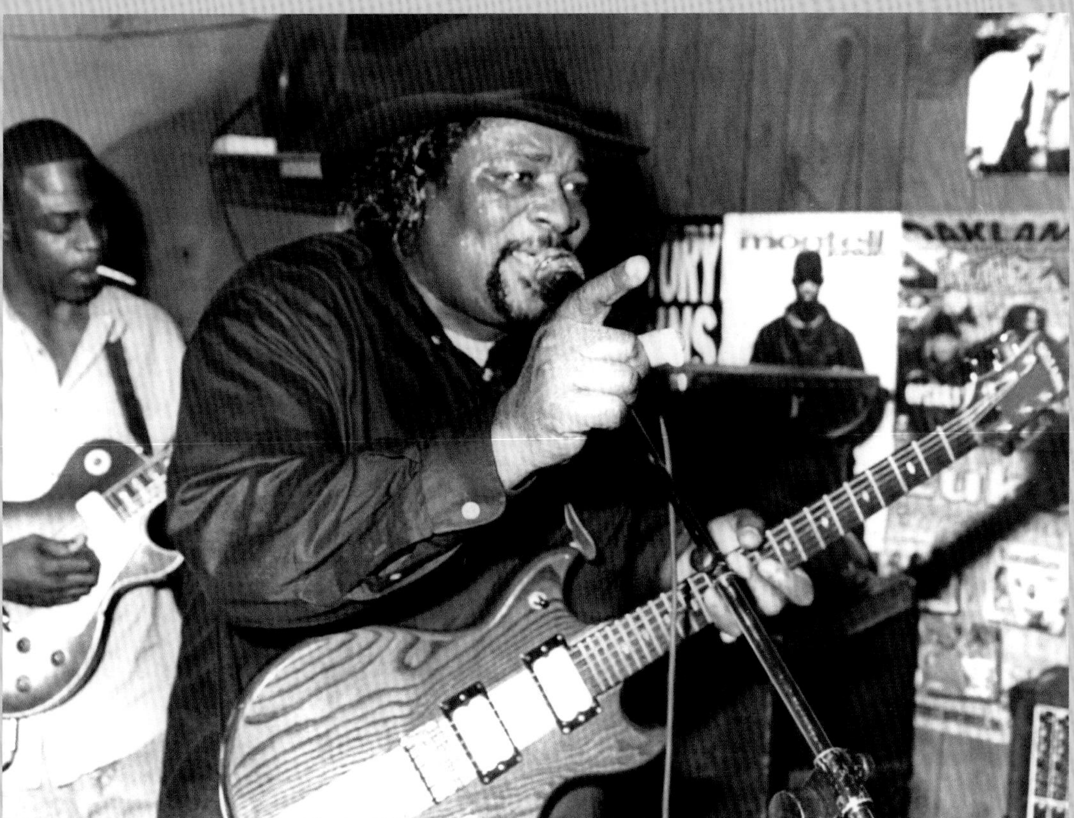

When he was at home, Big Jack Johnson played at Red's Club for his longtime friend Red Paden, who sometimes could be talked into relating memorable Big Jack stories.

Cited as a dynamic performer/songwriter leaving an important legacy through his music attacking such issues as war, domestic violence, abortion, Hurricane Katrina, AIDS, and the 1994 ice storm that paralyzed Clarksdale, Big Jack was the area's most famous bluesman since the days of Muddy Waters, John Lee Hooker, and Ike Turner. He was a regular performer at the annual Sunflower River Blues and Gospel Festival.

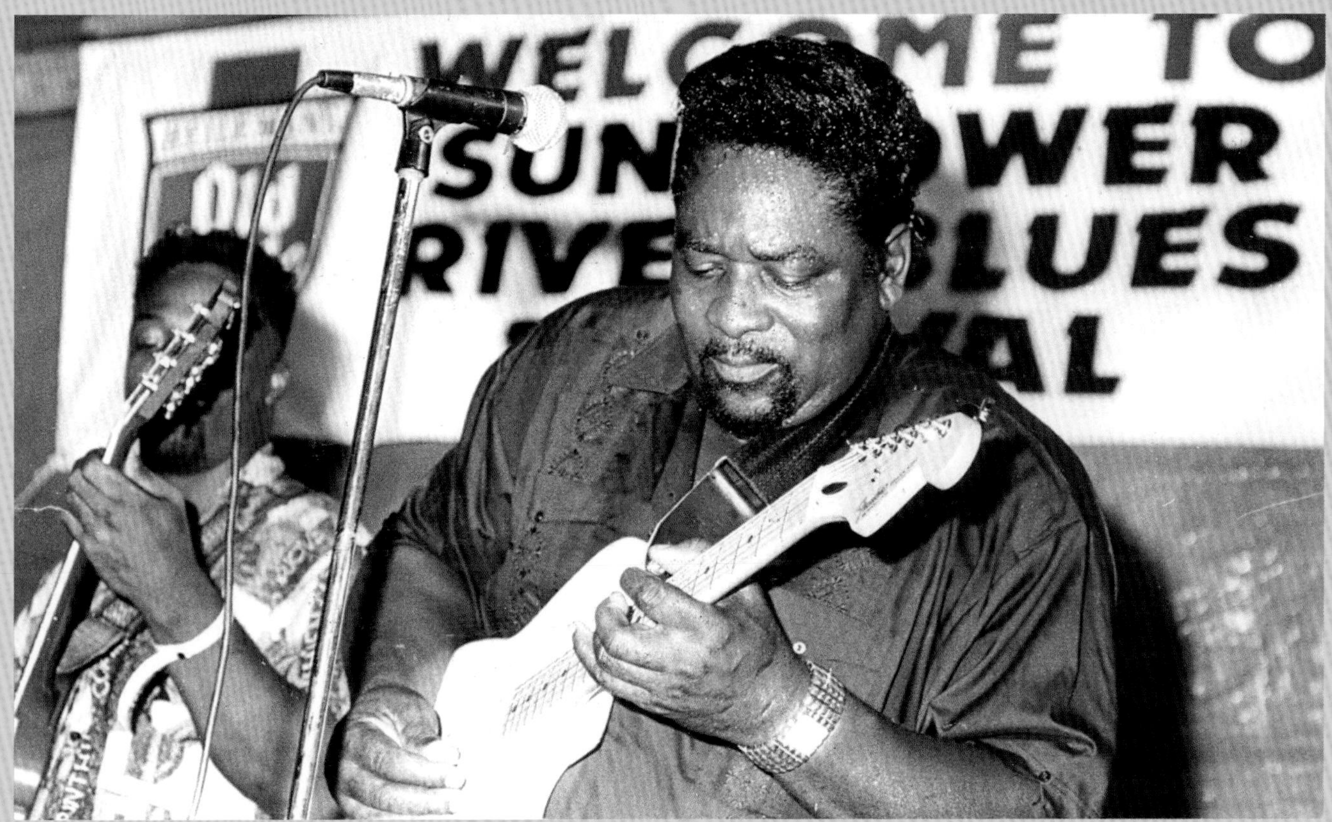

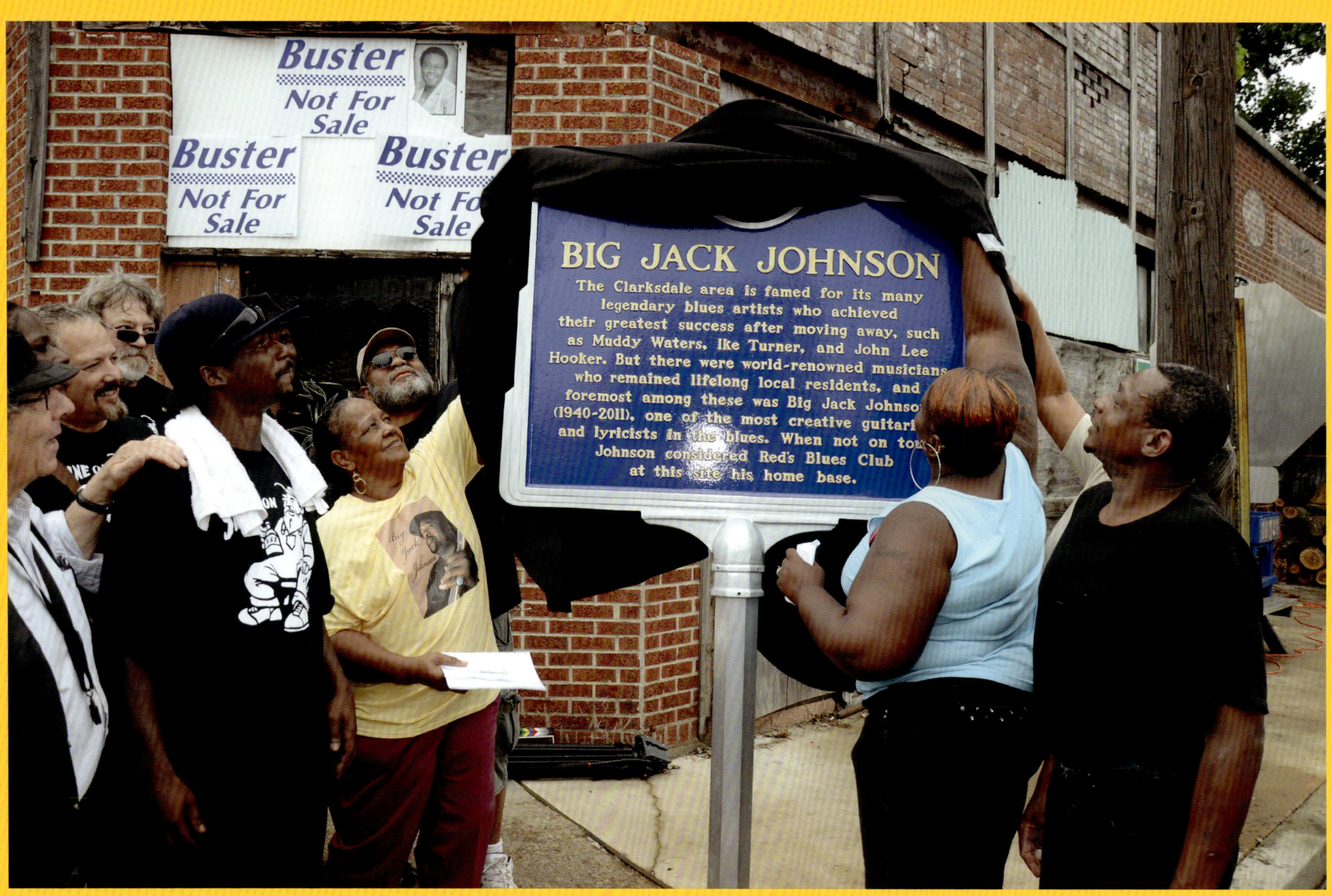
Buster
Not For Sale
Buster
Not For Sale
Buster
Not For Sale
BIG JACK JOHNSON
The Clarksdale area is famed for its many
legendary blues artists who achieved
their greatest success after moving away, such
as Muddy Waters, Ike Turner, and John Lee
Hooker. But there were world-renowned musicians
who remained lifelong local residents, and
foremost among these was Big Jack Johnson
(1940-2011), one of the most creative guitarists
and lyricists in the blues. When not on tour,
Johnson considered Red's Blues Club
at this site his home base.

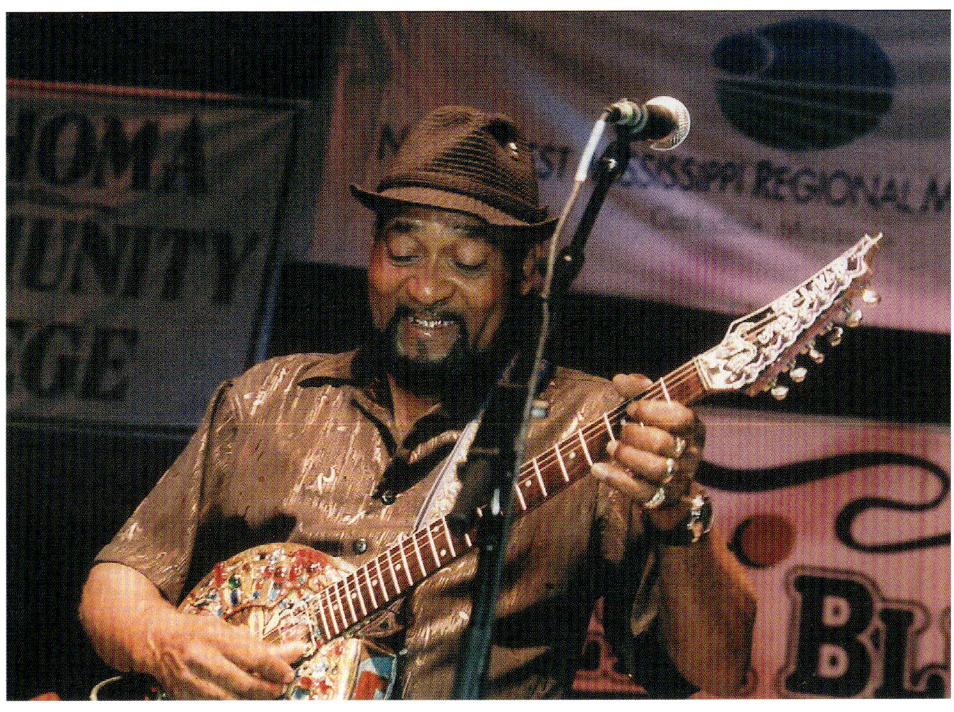

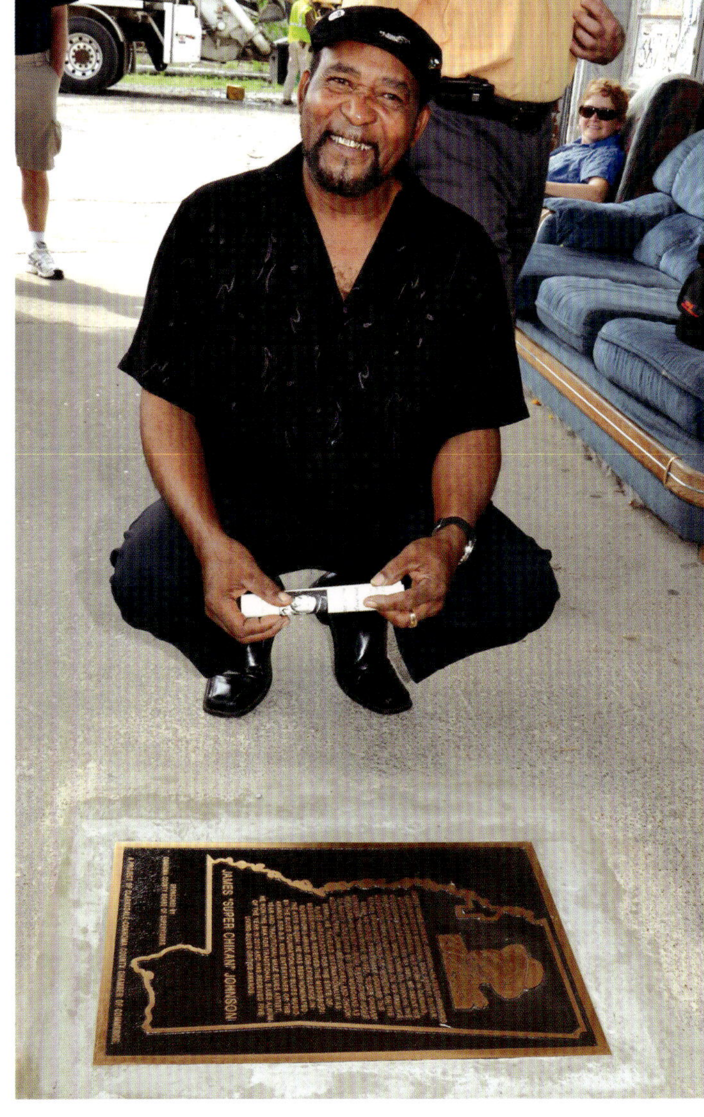

James "Super Chikan" Johnson shares the Johnson family flair for creativity, showmanship, and globe-trotting diplomacy. Additionally, his bold, bejeweled handmade guitars and didley-bows are one-of-a-kind works of art that function professionally as instruments.

Blues Super Chikan Johnson is all smiles over his Clarksdale Walk of Fame bronze plaque outside Ground Zero Blues Club, where he is a favorite performer. Additionally, Johnson is a Governor's Award recipient and once accompanied Gov. Haley Barbour to Japan to open the Mississippi Pavilion at the World's Fair.

Glory came at last for Big Jack Johnson, but not in his lifetime. On August 8, 2014, during the 27th Sunflower River Blues Festival, Big Jack took his seat among other blues giants via a Mississippi Blues Trail marker. Unveiling it are his wife, Angenette, and family, Red Paden, and members of his band, the Cornlickers.

SUPER CHIKAN JOHNSON

Big Jack's nephew, James "Super Chikan" Johnson, shares the Johnson family's flair for creativity, showmanship, and globe-trotting diplomacy. Outstripping any parameters of "folk art," his bold, bejeweled handmade guitars and diddley-bows are one-of-a-kind works of art that function professionally as instruments. He plays them onstage during his high-octane performances that showcase his talents as a guitarist/songwriter. Frequently his shows incorporate storytelling in dialects mimicking barnyard creatures and eccentric family characters. He's never met a stranger. Chikan is a Governor's Award recipient and once accompanied Gov. Haley Barbour to Japan to open the Mississippi Pavilion in the World's Fair.

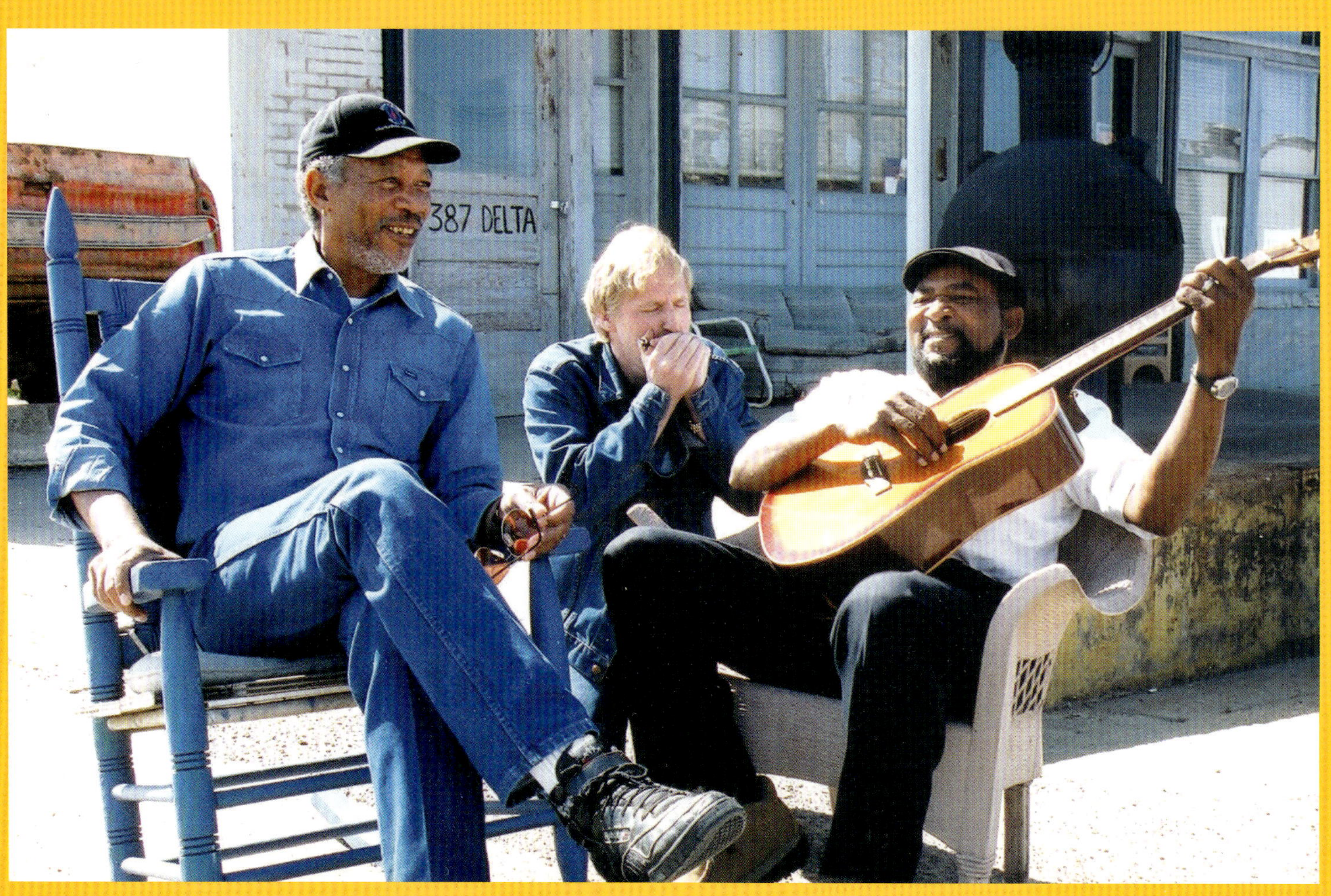

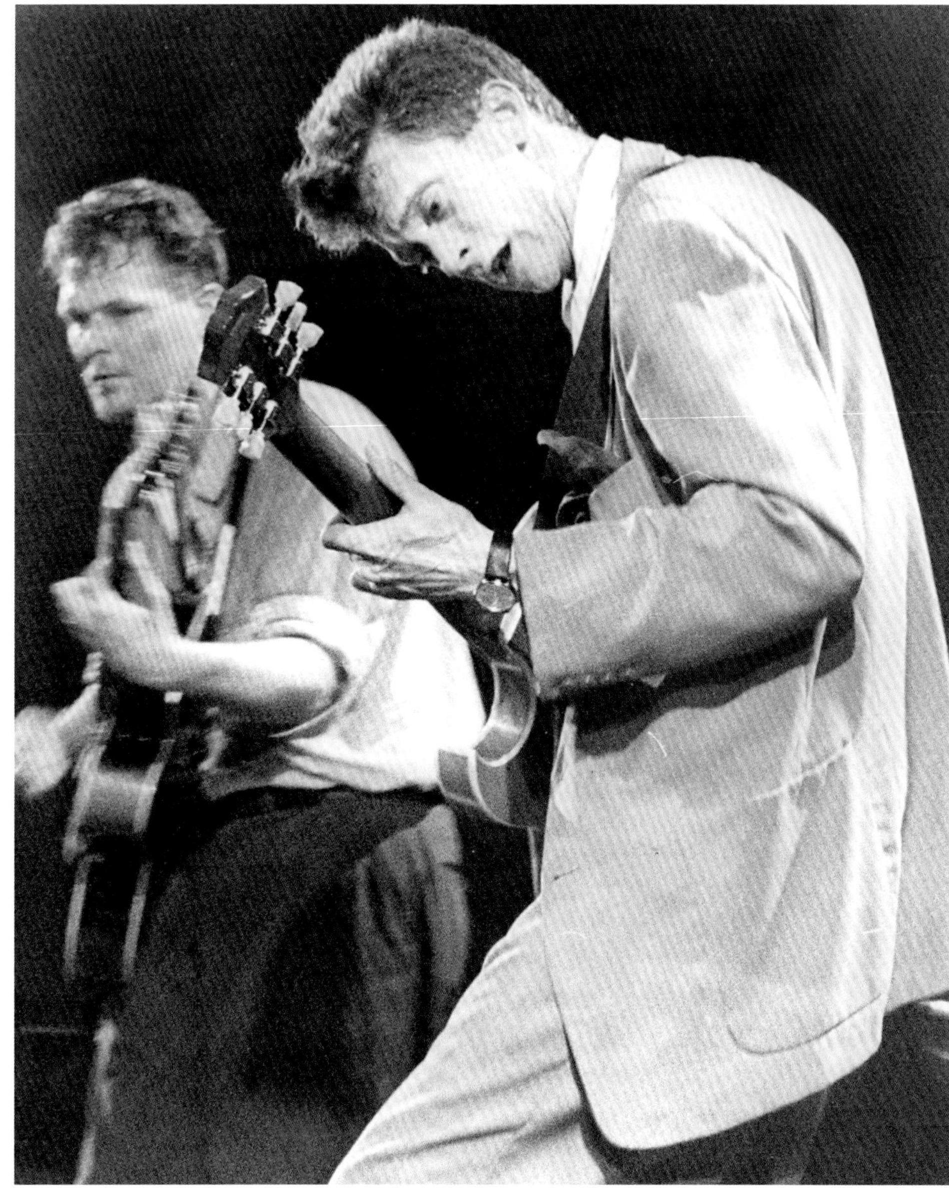

ROLL CALL

The roll call of iconic figures who stayed at home enriching local clubs and juke joints includes Wesley Jefferson and his great vocalist/bass player Rip Butler; philosopher/songwriter/harp master and leader of the Stone Gas Band, Arthneice Jones, with Harvel and Deon Thomas; Othar Turner, his daughter Bernice, and granddaughter Sharde, leading the Rising Star Fife & Drum Band from Gravel Springs; and the North Mississippi Allstars: Luther and Cody Dickinson plus Jimbo Mathus—all exploring their multifaceted creativities.

▶

The career of one of Mississippi's most talented and versatile musicians, Jimbo Mathus, nourished by his childhood babysitter Rosetta Patton Brown, morphs continually in musical exploration. He is pictured playing guitar during his Squirrel Nut Zipper days, when his wildly popular swing band toured nationwide, followed by hordes of fans wearing similar attire.

◀

Outside Ground Zero Blues Club in Clarksdale, Super Chikan Johnson on guitar teams up with Jostein Forsberg, leader of Norway's Notodden Blues Festival, on harmonica, for a rocking-chair serenade to actor Morgan Freeman. The Academy Award winner is co-owner of the popular blues club, with attorney Bill Luckett.

Educator/athlete/musician Melville Tillis ran the great River-mount Lounge, a hangout for Little Milton, Ike Turner, Bobby Rush, and many others, including R. L. Burnside and Billy Gipson. When we often introduced Melville as a musician who played trumpet for Ike Turner, he quickly made this correction: "Ike Turner played with us." A historian who remembered Rabbit Foot Minstrels, Melville was a tireless ambassador for Clarksdale and the Sunflower River Blues and Gospel Festival. He served as chairman of the city's public utilities commission for many years and so praised his hometown to America's energy czars from coast to coast that they often traveled to Clarksdale to experience its aura. He was honored as Clarksdale's Citizen of the Year at the annual Chamber of Commerce banquet.

► In the roll call of iconic figures who stayed at home enriching Mississippi are Othar Turner, his daughter Bernice, and their Rising Star Drum and Fife Band from Gravel Springs, pictured leading a procession in the Old Capitol with First Lady Pat Fordice, following a Governor's Award Ceremony in Jackson.

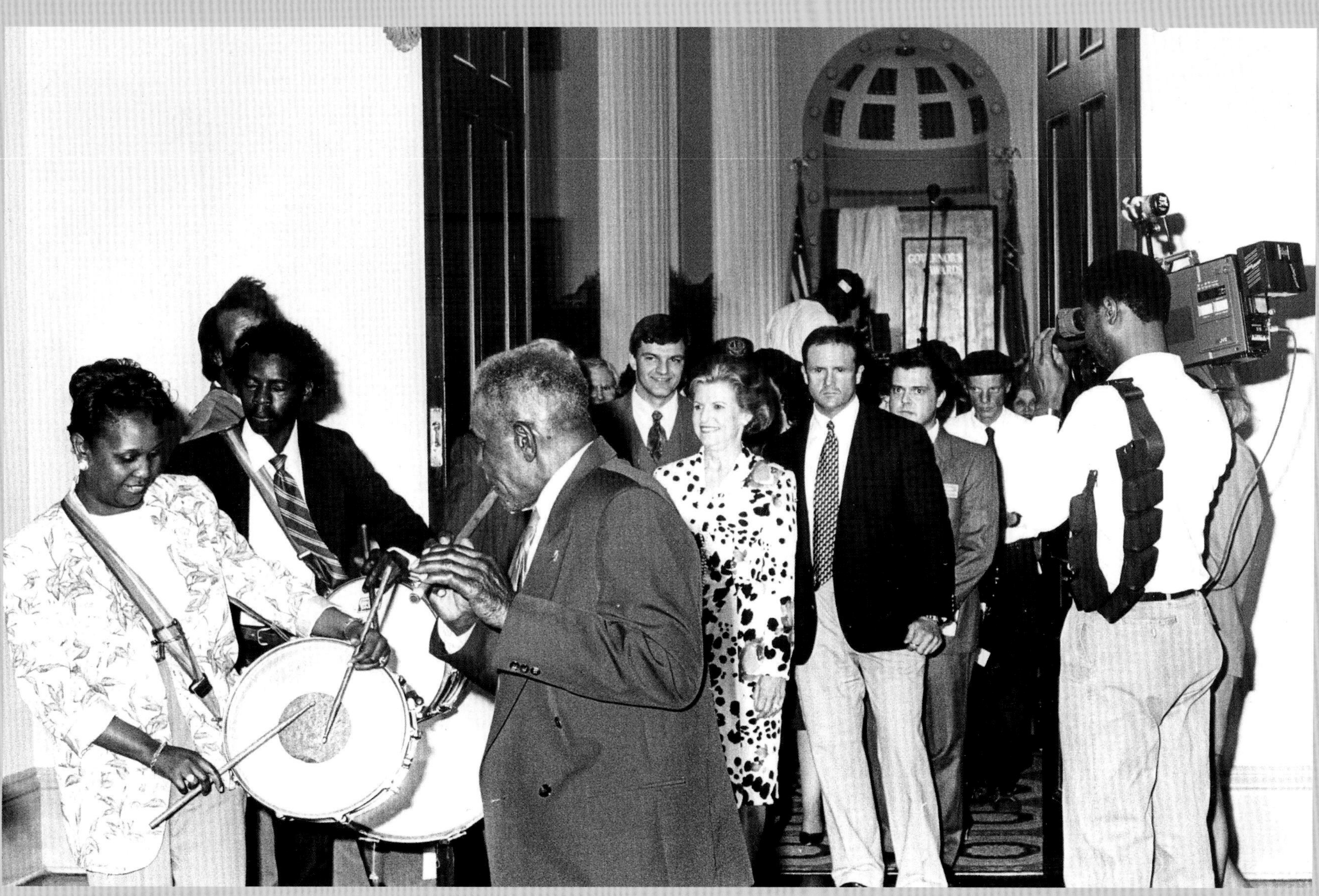

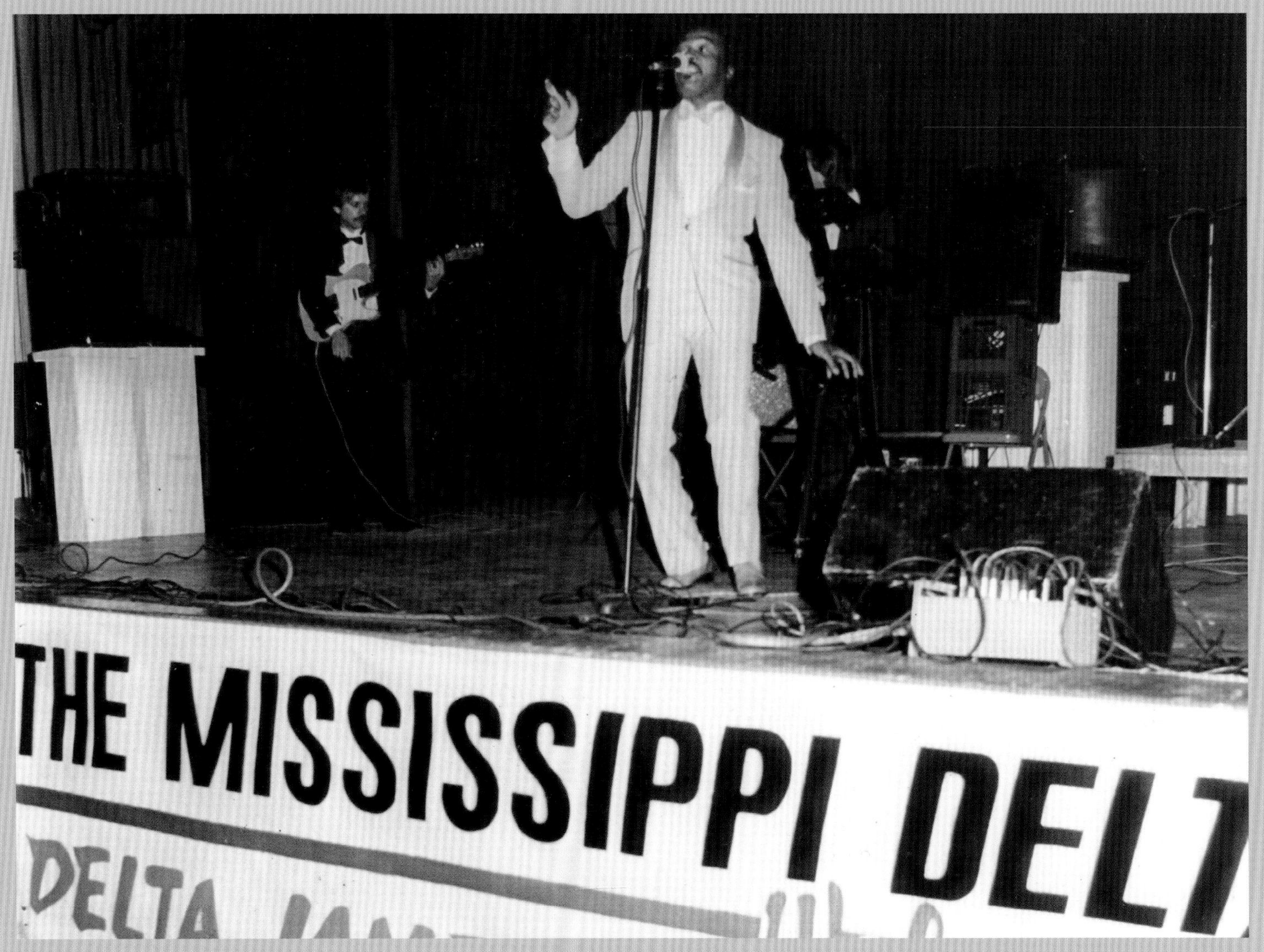
THE MISSISSIPPI DELTA
DELTA
DELT

4
FESTIVALS AND CELEBRATIONS

A successful series of concerts in the Civic Auditorium featuring local and regional musicians, patterned on the *Saturday Night Live* television show, was organized by Jim O'Neal and Dr. Patty Johnson. One of the shows featured Tommy Smiley, lead singer for the Platters. In formal attire he staged a sophisticated review and later showed up at our house to sing with a zydeco band from Eunice, Louisiana.

Wade Walton, Early Wright, Mrs. Z L Hill, the Jelly Roll Kings, Mr. Johnnie Billington, and Melville Tillis were missed everywhere but in no venue more profoundly than Clarksdale's Sunflower River Blues and Gospel Festival. All were active participants and were revered as living legends.

The Sunflower was inspired by a successful series of concerts featuring local and regional musicians. It was patterned on the *Saturday Night Live* television show in the Civic Auditorium organized by Jim O'Neal and his partner, Dr. Patty Johnson. One of these shows sponsored by the Mississippi Delta Arts Council featured Clarksdale native Tommy Smiley, lead singer for the Platters. In formal attire, he staged a sophisticated review and showed up later at our house to sing with Rockin' Dopsie, a zydeco band from Eunice, Louisiana, we had met earlier in a visit through the Southern Arts Alliance.

Jim O'Neal said agreements with the University of Mississippi to move *Living Blues* magazine from Chicago to Oxford began in 1983 and led to

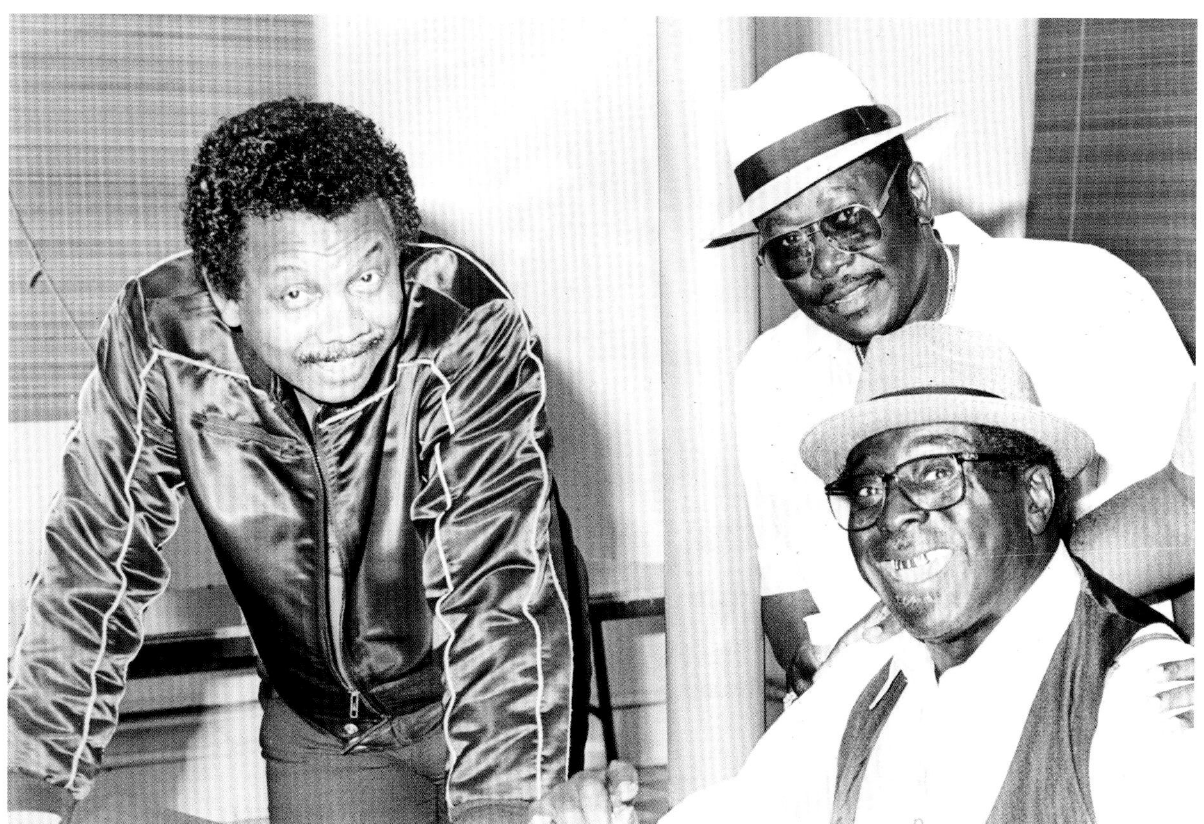

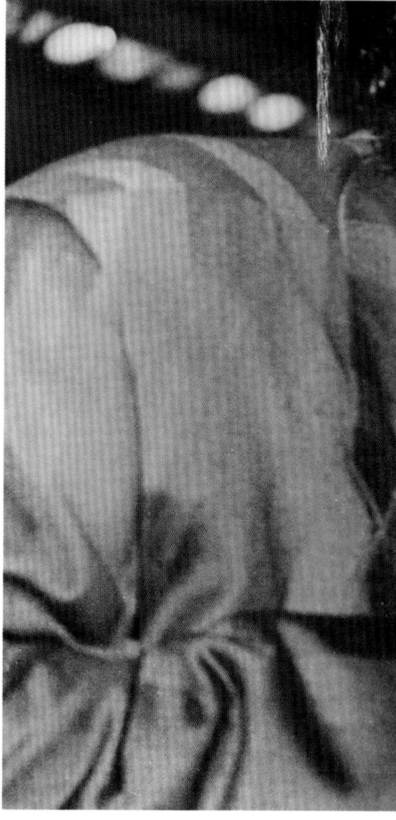

his moving to Oxford in 1986 to edit the publication. "I was always drawn to the Delta and kept going there to find blues, and so I decided to resign from LB . . . and I moved to the Delta in the summer of 1987 with the intention of starting a recording studio and retail store," he said. In 1988 he and Dr. Patty Johnson opened the Stackhouse on Sunflower Avenue in a mini-steamboat-shaped building in downtown Clarksdale and bought a house on Clark Street. "The store opened on Muddy Waters' birthday, April 4," Jim continued. Their recording studio, Rooster Blues, and the Stackhouse became a magnet and center of blues activities drawing musicians, visitors, and organizers planning celebrations and festivals. When Jim and his wife Selina moved to Kansas City, Missouri, ten years later, everyone (especially myself) felt the void and a great loss without his presence and encyclopedic knowledge of all things blues.

Simultaneously, auditorium manager Eddie Rolling, a veteran music promoter and the author of a popular casino blues song apparently "borrowed" and recorded by musician friends, organized shows with topnotch celebrities that I loved to cover. Eddie knew how to put together a classic evening and pack it with a partying crowd.

Wedging myself and my camera between diagonally placed tables near the stage, I was welcomed by fans attired in sequins and

▲ With abundant hair and a velvet delivery punctuated by his signature snort, Bobby "Blue" Bland performs "Stormy Monday" in high style.

◄ Simultaneously, auditorium manager Eddie Rolling, a veteran music promoter, organized shows with topnotch celebrities that I loved to cover. Superstar Albert King came to visit with Tyrone Davis in the break room before Tyrone's performance in a green crushed-velvet jumpsuit open to the waist.

► I loved photographing Denise LaSalle singing "Drop That Zero, Find Yourself a Hero" in her tiger-striped mermaid gown.

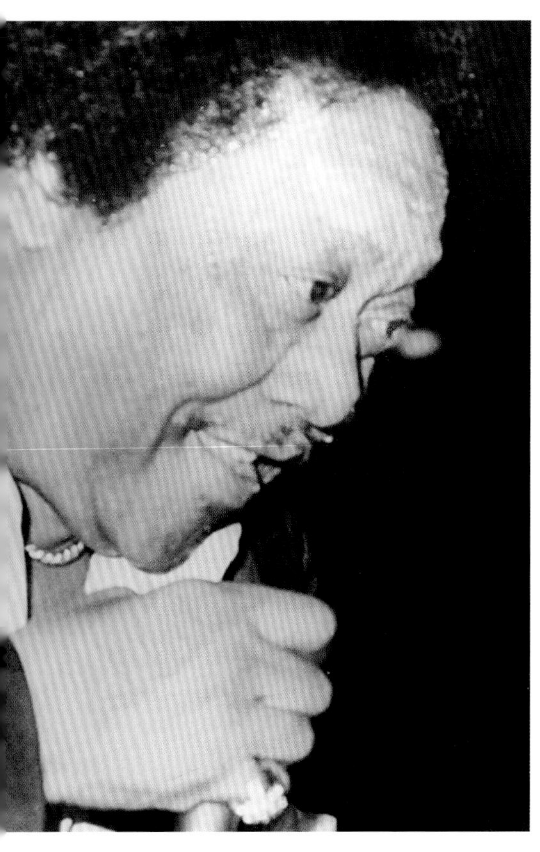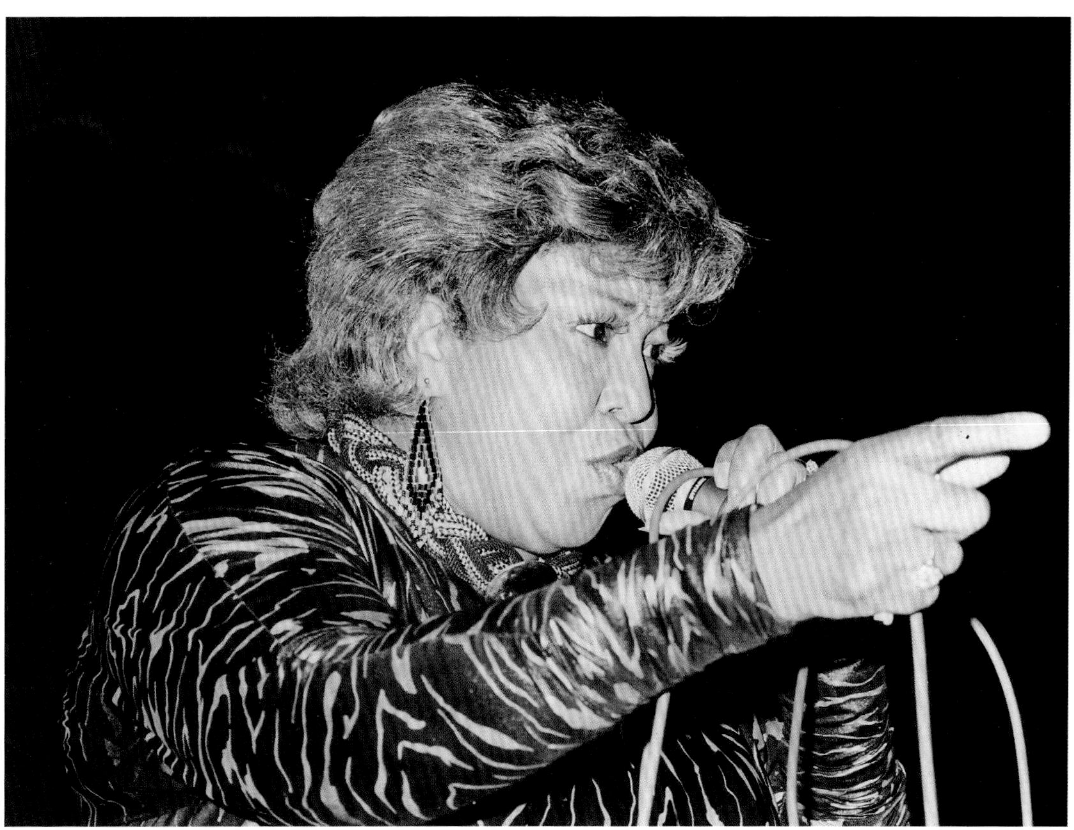

gold lamé. I loved photographing Denise LaSalle singing "Drop That Zero, Find Yourself a Hero" in her tiger-striped mermaid gown. The elegant chaise longue/lavish backdrop settings for souvenir glamour photos were as glorious as the music and the long-stemmed silk roses sprinkled with twinkling lights. Tyrone Davis performed in a crushed green velvet jumpsuit open to the waist. Curly-haired Bobby "Blue" Bland's classic lyrics punctuated by his signature snorts and Marvin Sease's pelvic thrusts kept crowds wide-eyed at 2 A.M., including the dignified mayor of Notodden, Norway, on his first trip to Clarksdale.

The consummate "Boss," James Brown gave me advance permission to attend his three-hour sound check and show at the Isle of Capri Casino in Lula. Berating his magnificent band and its three drum sets with scathing commands, forcing vocalists to repeat lyrics over and over and over till he got the perfection he demanded, this small figure in high-heeled western boots departed the hall, parting the crowded lobby like Moses crossing the Red Sea. Later, when he returned wearing his show smile, crimson cape, and costume, with vocalists in glittering grey gowns he personally designed, the standing-ovation crowd never sat down but kept dancing in the aisles. Only Little Richard's "Tutti-Frutti" came close to the James Brown Isle spectacular.

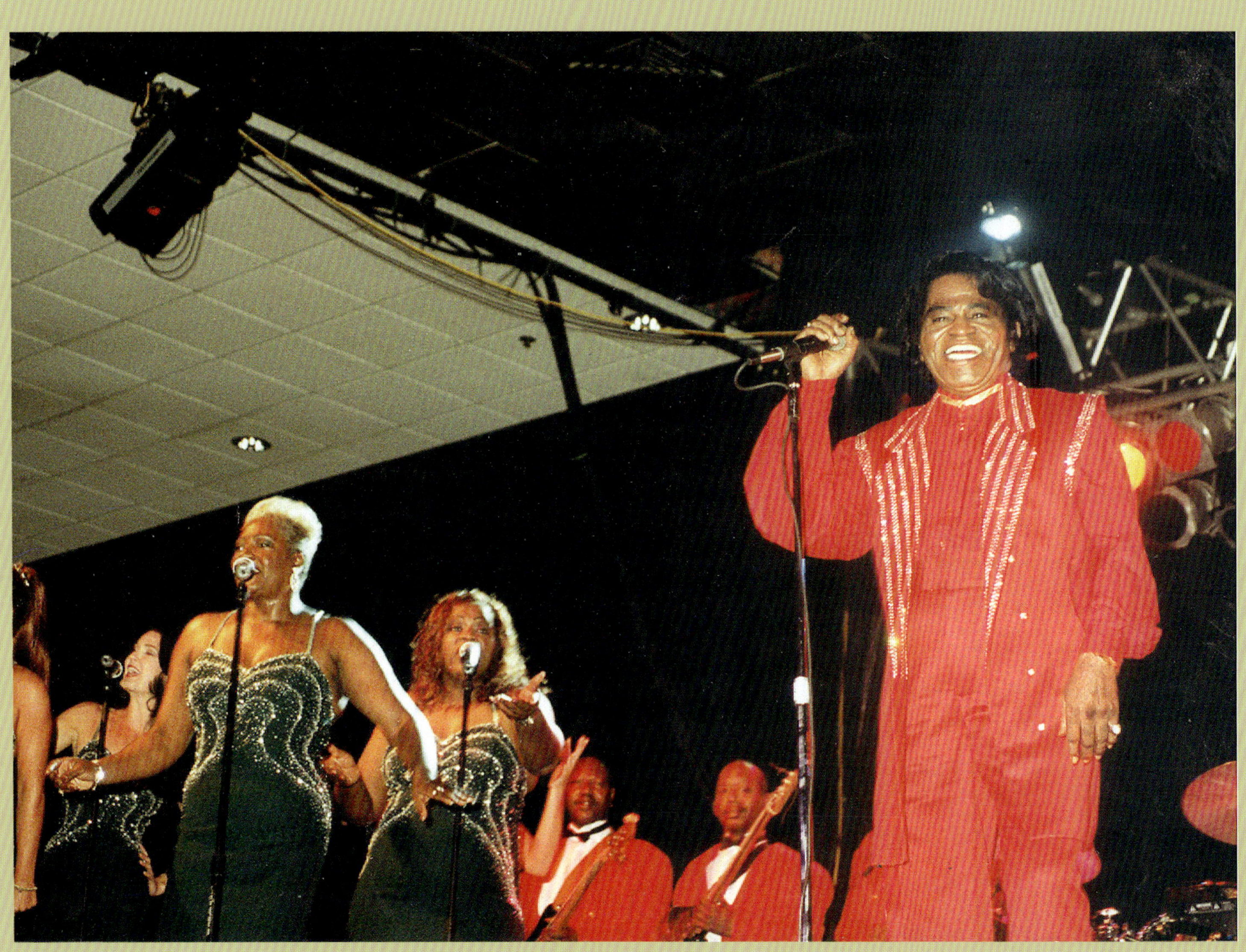

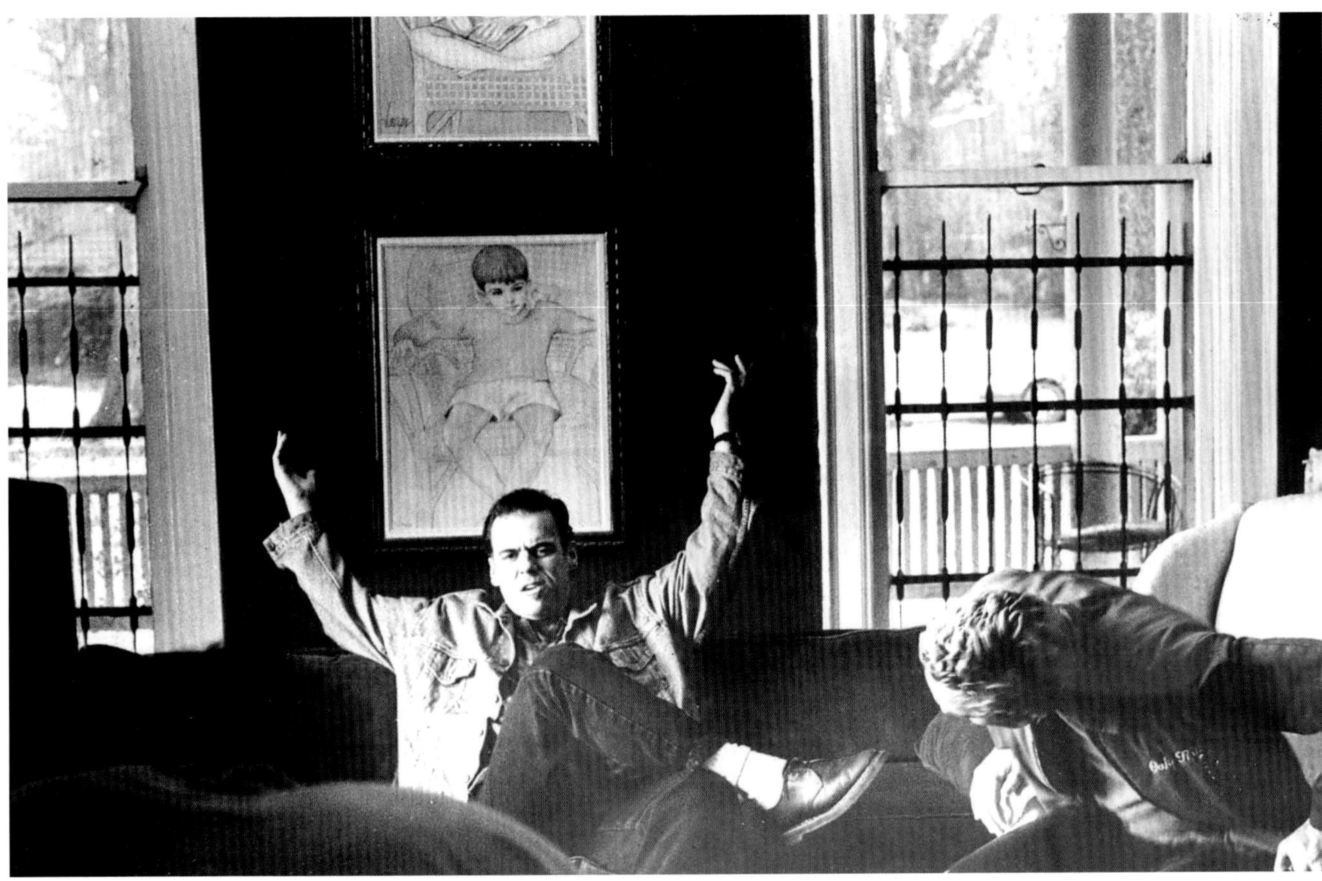

▲

In 1994 John Hiatt and his band filmed a video, *Buffalo River Home*, in several locations, including our living room and front porch, which prompted telephone calls asking, "Did we just see you and Laura on MTV?"

◄

The consummate "Boss," James Brown gave me advance permission to attend his three-hour sound check and show in 1999 at the Isle of Capri in Lula. Berating his magnificent band with scathing commands, forcing vocalists to repeat lyrics over and over and over until he got the perfection he demanded, this small figure in high-heeled western boots departed the hall, parting the crowded lobby like Moses crossing the Red Sea.

However, other celebrities have been drawn to the Delta to perform as well.

Celebrity John Hiatt and his band filmed a video, *Buffalo River Home*, in several locations, including our living room and front porch, which prompted telephone calls asking, "Did we just see you and Laura on MTV?" It was great fun with makeup artists standing by and caterers on the second-floor landing preparing meals for the large film crews. Other segments were filmed at the homes of Jennie Neblett, Shirley Fair, and Howard Stovall, and also at the D'Oyley House.

Garth Brooks once visited R. H. Bearden Elementary School near Webb following screenings of *LaLee's Kin*, an award-winning Sundance Film Festival documentary by the legendary Al Maysles that earned an Oscar nomination. I was asked to take still shots for the project and experienced this fast-moving cinema verité style in action. The storyline focused on education, and the high cost of growing cotton

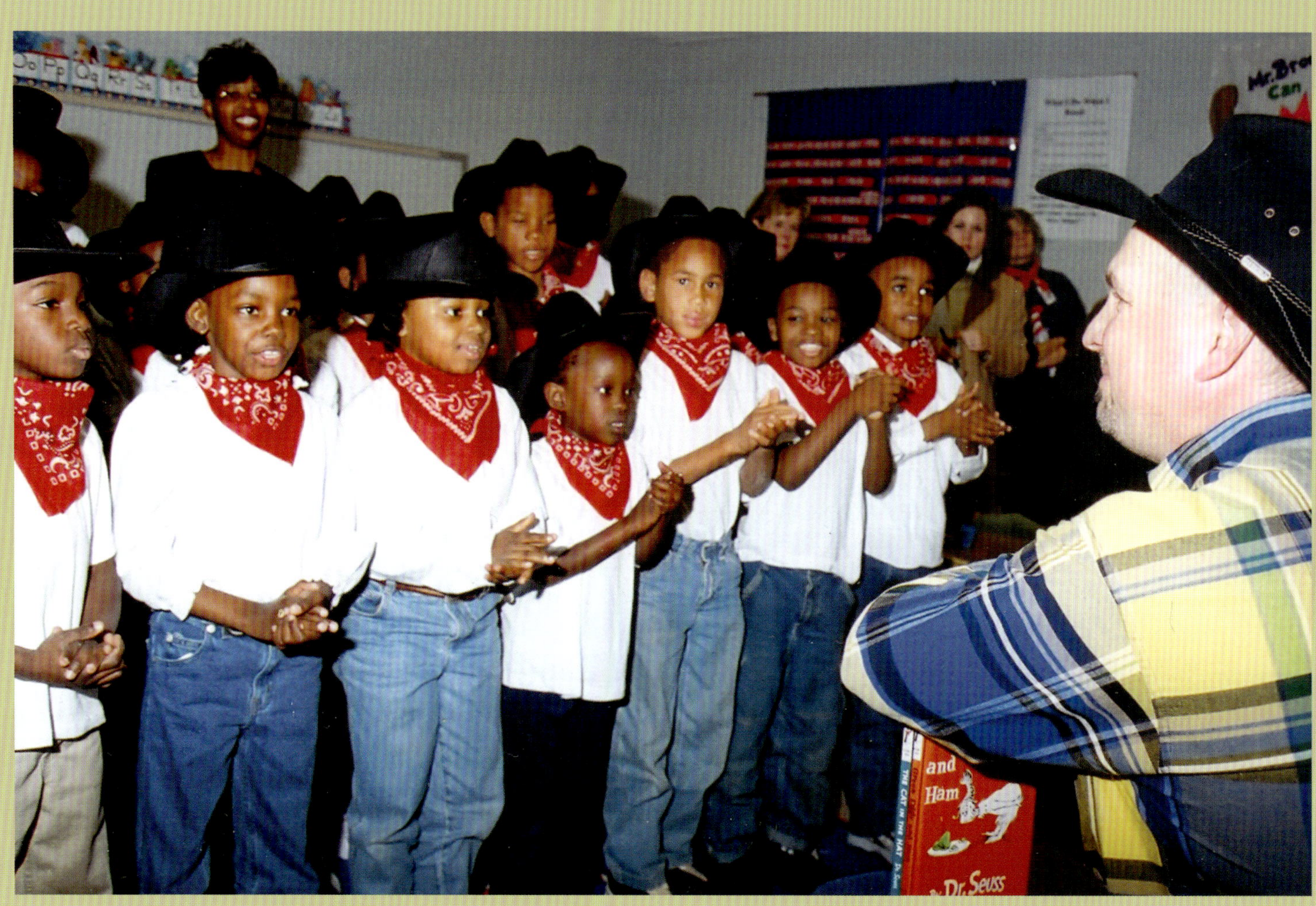

on multiple generations of Delta families. It tracked a powerful matriarch, her family, and a grandson, Redman, named after the chewing tobacco. Redman and his grammar school classmates wore Garth Brooks attire: red bandanas and broad-brimmed hats for the country music star's appearance at their school to read Dr. Seuss.

The combined successes of regional concerts and the abundance of local talent spawned an interest in staging a full-fledged festival, and in 1988 the Sunflower hit the ground running as a unique quasi-volatile celebration of Mississippi Delta blues. Early Sunflower meetings took place in the Bobo Building, the Rivermount Lounge, the Crossroads Blues Club, Sarah's Kitchen, Hicks, local restaurants, and the Delta Blues Museum. They also were held outside Delta Wholesale (now Ground Zero Blues Club), where members picked up beer cans and trash on the railroad tracks before the festival kicked off. Three decades have refined its edges and brought accolades, including its own Mississippi Blues Trail marker, but the Sunflower continues an unbridled spirit, its mission to remain free, to preserve its laid-back style and its refusal to be categorized.

The Sunflower's twenty-fifth anniversary celebration in 2012, headlined by Led Zeppelin's Robert Plant, rocketed into history as Clarksdale's largest outdoor music celebration, with an estimated 40,000 fans standing shoulder to shoulder cheering in John Lee Hooker Lane and Yazoo Avenue to watch the show live and on giant video screens. The reality that the Sunflower's modest membership, composed of 50 percent African American and 50 percent Caucasian members ranging from professionals and secretaries, to cooks, road crews, and even a prison guard from Parchman, was able to pull off this extravaganza and offer it free is testimony to the "can-do outlaw spirit" with which it was founded, and the generosity of Robert Plant, his band, and their reverence for the roots of Mississippi Delta blues. In November 2011 when Robert Plant graciously and officially accepted our invitation to perform in 2012 (after enduring years of good-natured hounding), funding became a priority. The Sunflower board met for weeks with officials of a large out-of-state entity interested in sponsoring the event. This was great news, with plenty of money on the table. However, it came with baggage: the Sunflower was expected to charge admission.

Keeping the festival free and accessible to everyone who wanted to come has always been a mainstay of the Sunflower's mission statement. Blues members met on my front porch, talked it over, and took a vote; it was unanimous: we would *not* charge admission, and we

◄

Garth Brooks visited R. H. Bearden Elementary School near Webb in 2001 following screenings of *LaLee's Kin*, an Oscar-nominated documentary about education, filmed in Tallahatchie County by renowned filmmaker Al Maysles. LaLee's grandson, Redman, and his third-grade classmates wore Garth Brooks attire to welcome the country music star, who read Dr. Seuss to the class.

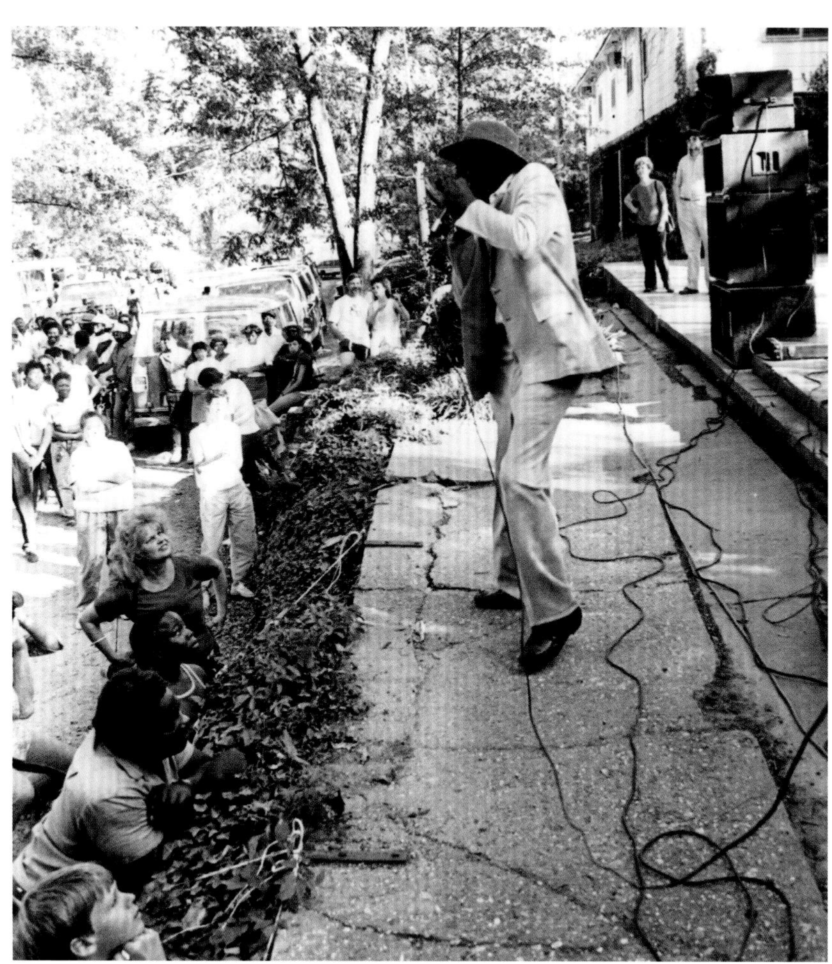

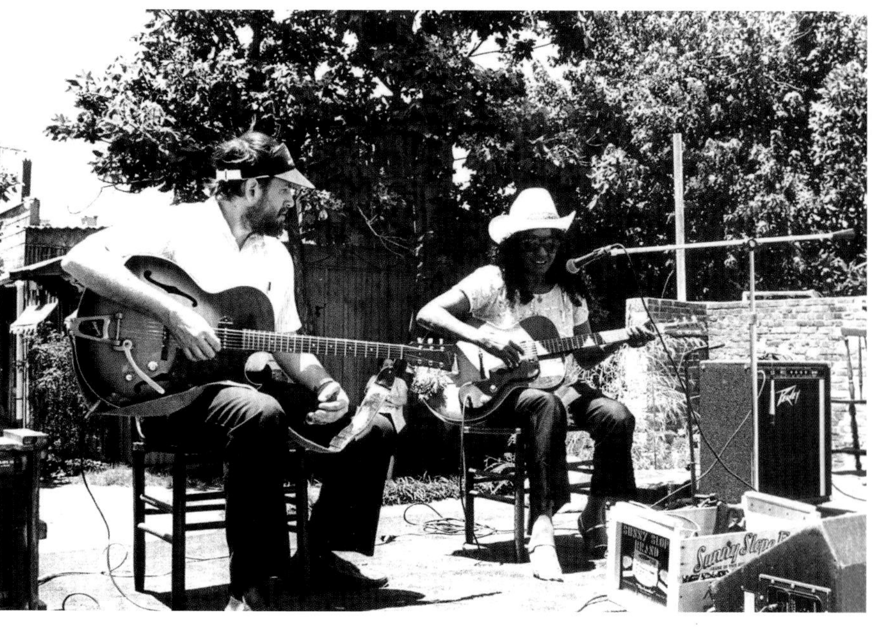

turned down the big money. Later I told Robert Plant about the vote, as we left Sunday services at Liberty Baptist Church.

We were warned by many, "You won't be able to put on this show; you can't do it." John Sherman and Melville Tillis, festival cochairs, replied, "Yes, we can," and practically moved into John's law office for the next ten months to figure it out. In the spring we sent a delegation to check out the Audubon Park Concert series in Memphis. Their organizers featured special seating for VIP patrons and charged general admission cover. We adopted some of their VIP seating suggestions, but no general admission. Even though some out-of-towners complained because they could not get close to the stage, if admission were charged, the festival would have been completely off-limits to many low-income residents.

The first Sunflower featured two outdoor stages: one behind the Riverside Recreation Center facing the Sunflower River, and the other in the open space between Delta and Sunflower Avenue. Headliner Otis Rush closed the festival that evening inside the Thompson Center,

▲ The second outdoor stage was a flatbed truck parked in the open space between Delta and Sunflower Avenues, where singer/songwriter Jessie Mae Hemphill was accompanied by musicologist David Evans.

◄ In 1988 the first Sunflower River Blues Festival featured two outdoor stages, one behind the Riverside Recreation Center (Cat Cave), where renowned musician Frank Frost played harmonica. The stage was across the Sunflower River from downtown Clarksdale.

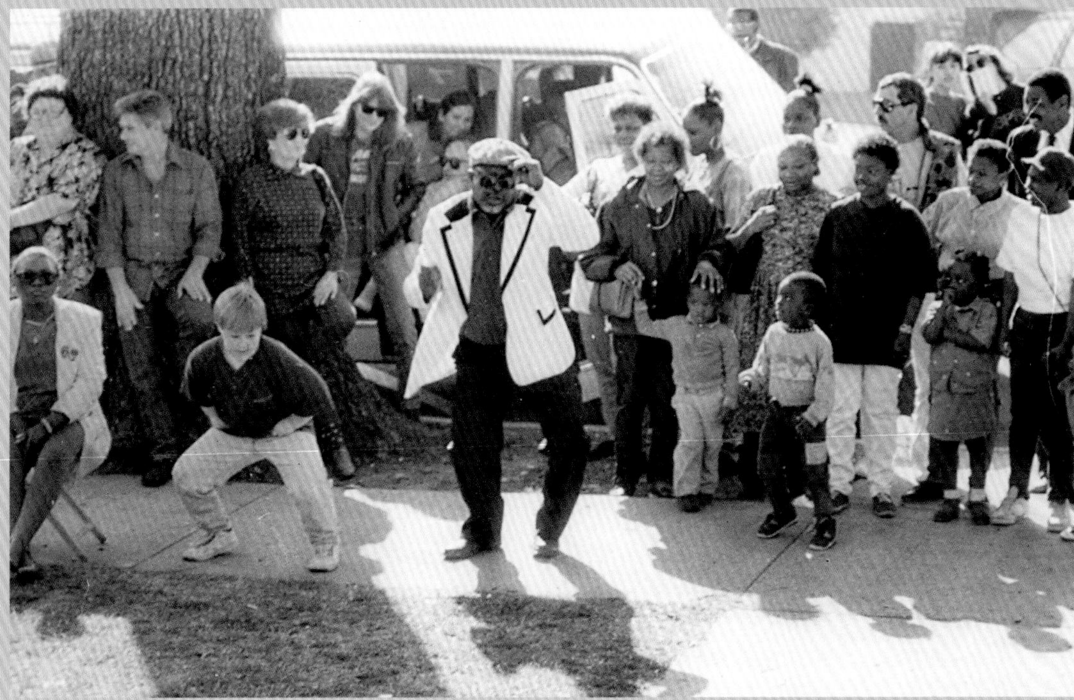

Impromptu dancing is the sign of good music at the Sunflower's early acoustic stage outside the Delta Blues Museum.

Early Sunflower blues fans take advantage of elevated seating on tank cars when the loading docks outside the Delta Blues Museum were converted into the festival main stage at the foot of Delta Avenue.

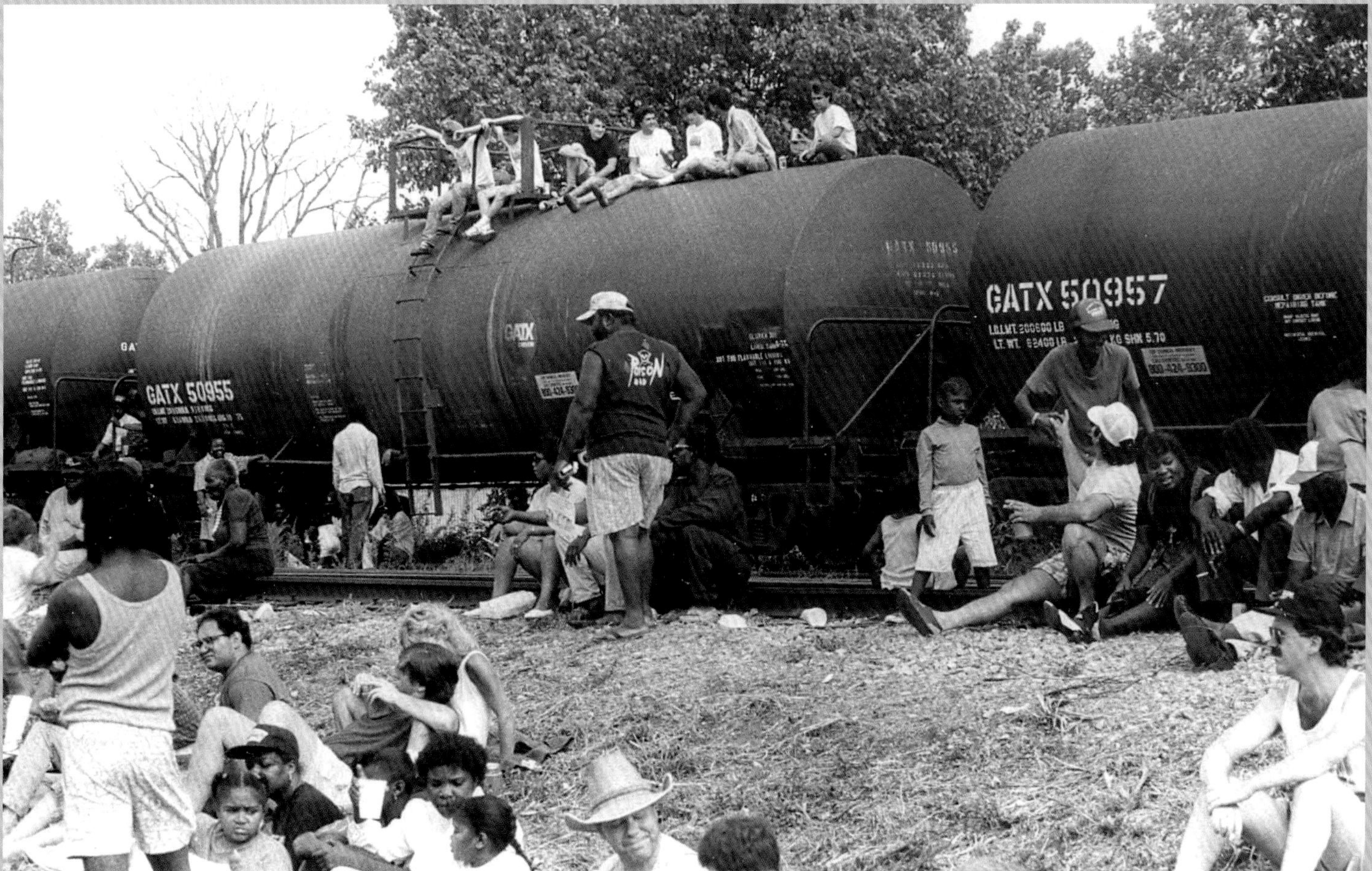

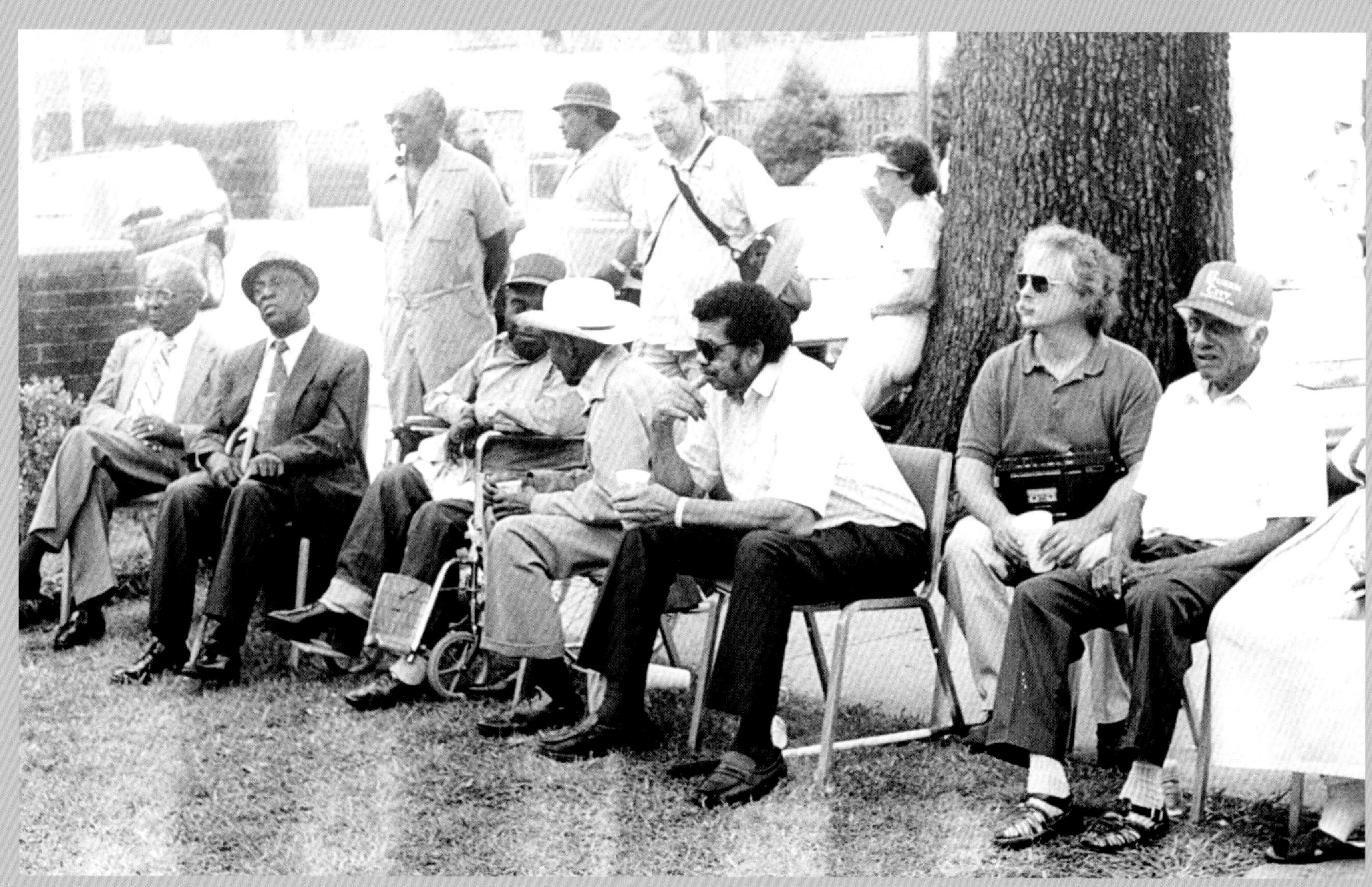

A rare gathering of legendary musicians visiting and enjoying acoustic blues together takes place at an early Sunflower Festival outside the Delta Blues Museum. Included are (from left) Elder Roma Wilson, the Reverend Leon Pinson, CeDell Davis, Jack Owens, Bud Spires, author Barry Lee Pearson, and Eugene Powell.

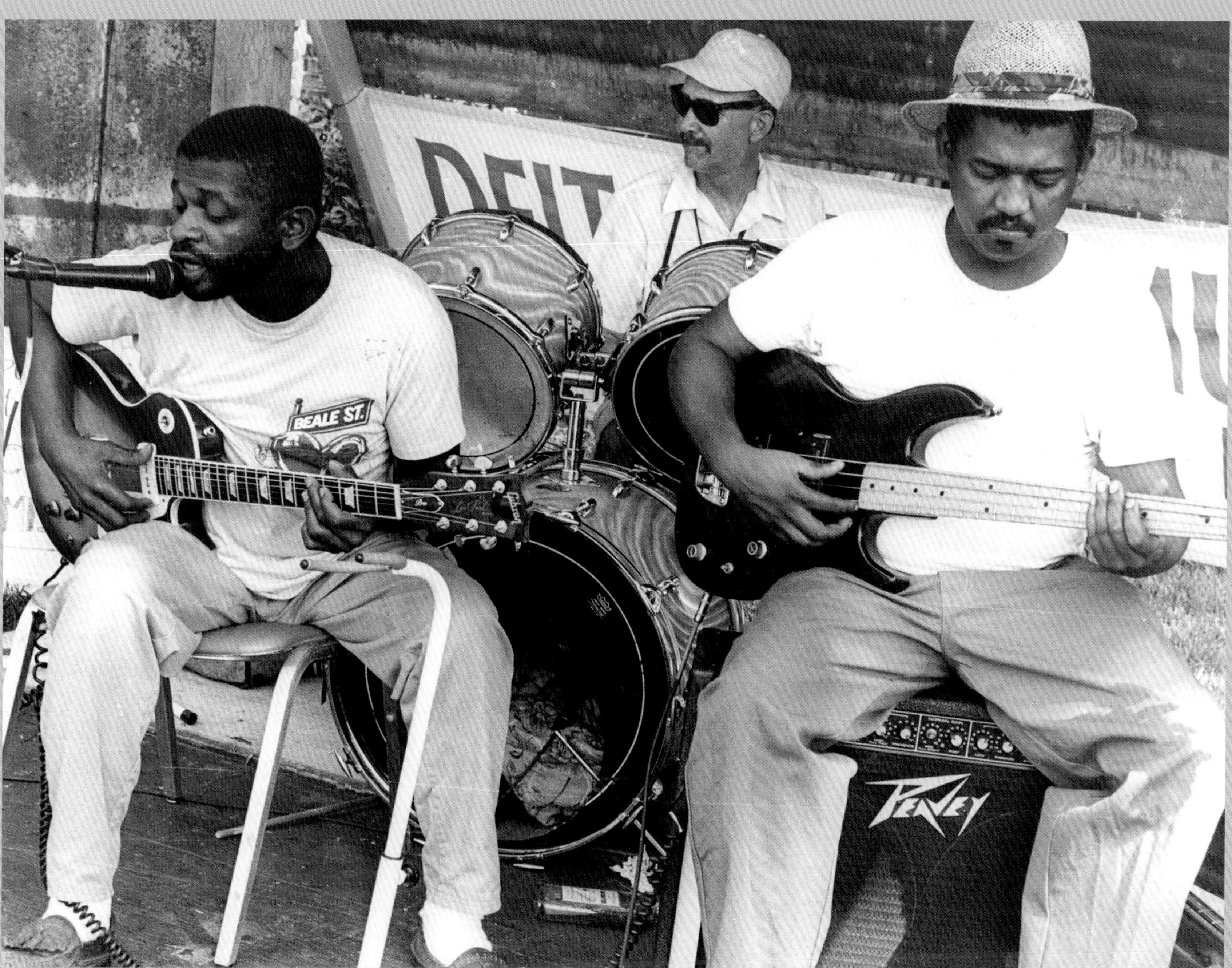

The informality of a visiting drummer sitting in with super-talented Lonnie Pitchford (left), renowned for his Robert Johnson–style guitar performances, including a Smithsonian Institution showcase in Washington D.C., and guitarist Michael James, is the Sunflower Festival's laid-back signature.

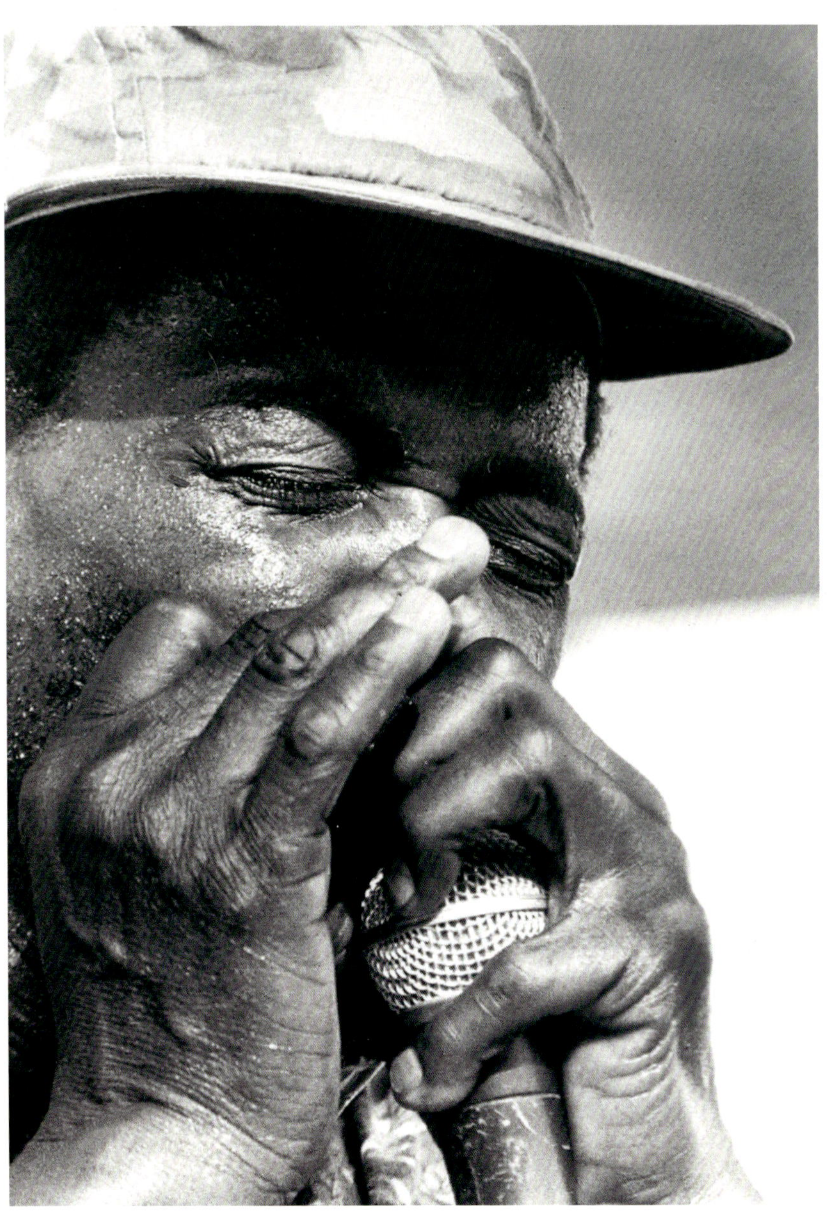

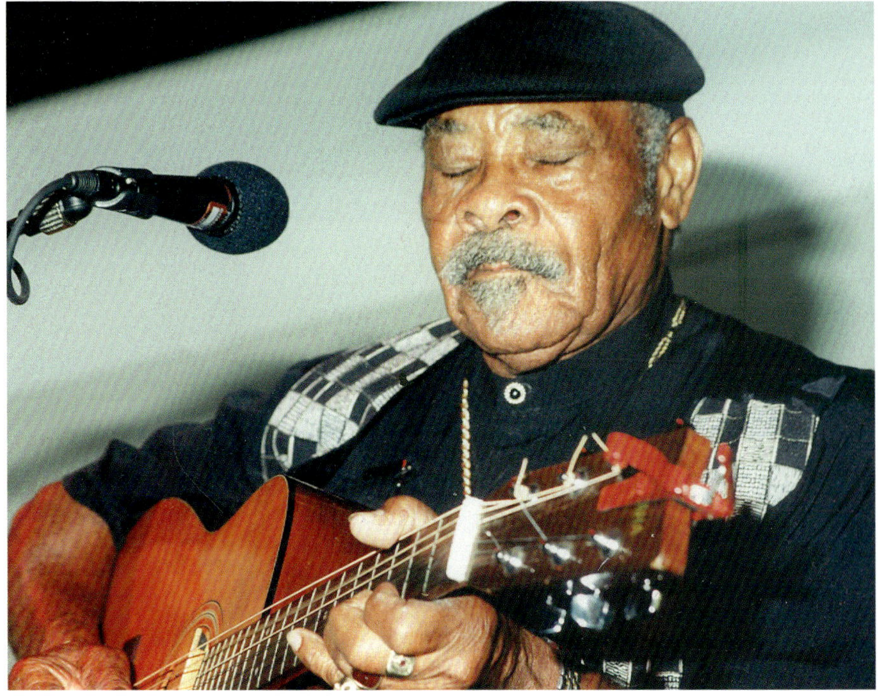

and it was a near-disaster. After a full day of sun and blues, the audience was blistered and bleary. The Indianola band booked to back Otis Rush apparently never rehearsed his songs. Fortunately, Mississippi ETV crews who documented the day left early and missed the finale.

On its acoustic stages, Arthneice Jones, Eddie Cusic, T-Model Ford, Robert Belfour, Pat Thomas, and other revered artists have mixed sidewalk philosophy with music. They connect intimately with the audience, including a contingent of Oklahoma lawyers who came ten consecutive years just to hear Arthneice.

A harp virtuoso, Arthneice worked in bricks and concrete, spoke in abstraction with the wisdom of a street scholar, and played with

On its acoustic stages Arthneice Jones (left), Eddie Cusic (right), T-Model Ford, Robert Belfour, Pat Thomas, and other revered artists have mixed sidewalk philosophy with music and connect intimately with the audience, including a contingent of Oklahoma lawyers who came for ten consecutive years just to hear Arthneice.

Blues ladies reigning over Sunflower Festivals through the years include the incomparable Koko Taylor singing "Wang Dang Doodle," and duets with Bobby Rush; daring Shirley Brown warning the audience her 2005 performance would be a "grown folks show"; super-talented young Shemekia Copeland as a fledgling headliner in 2008; and Dorothy Moore evoking remarks from Manchester fans: "Hearing her sing 'Misty Blue' alone in 2011 was worth the whole trip over from the UK."

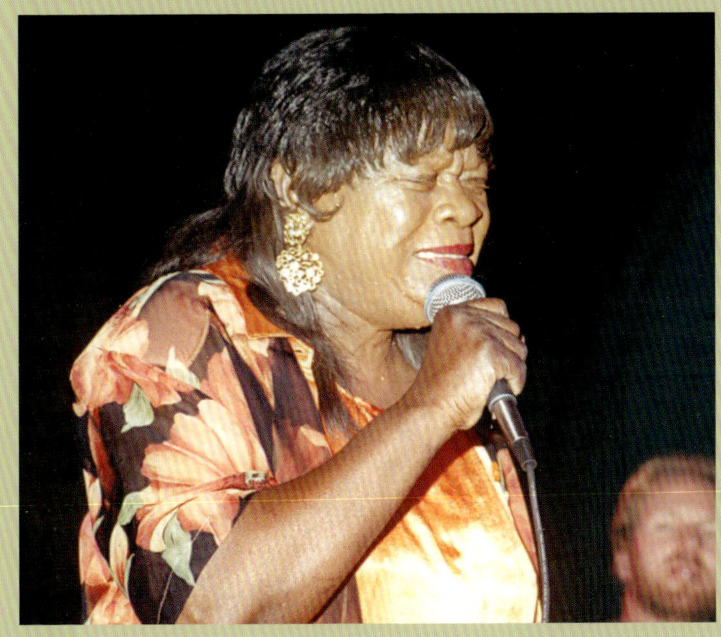
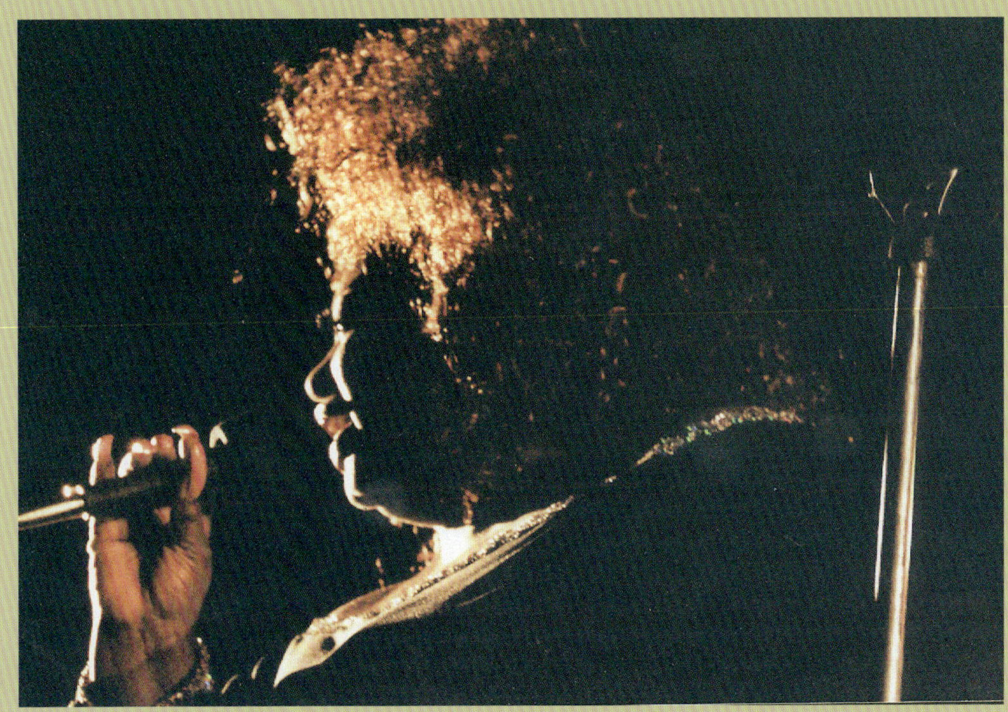
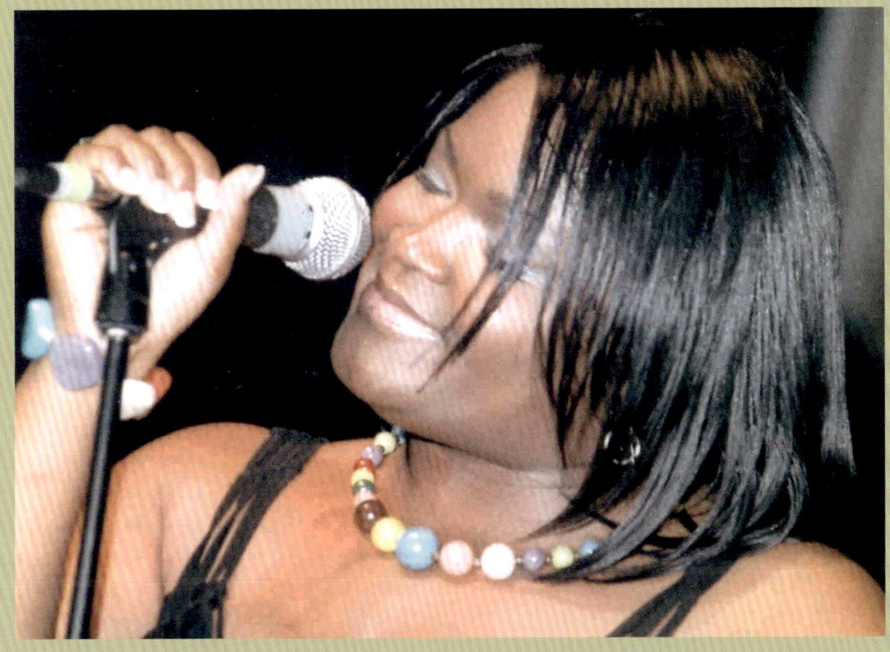
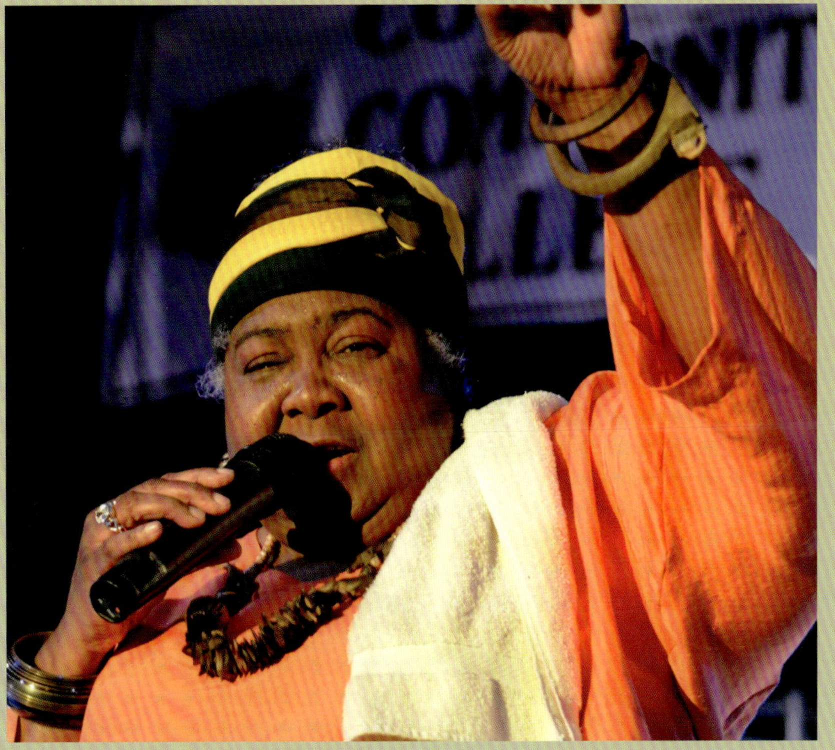

the best in the business. Admired by many, including Grammy Award winner Charlie Musselwhite, Arthneice was leader of the Stone Gas Band that once performed extensively in north Mississippi and Memphis. In recent years he was semiretired as a musician and focused on his business as a contractor. However, each summer his performances with Terry Williams drew large crowds eager for his music and commentary on life, its troubles, traditions, joys, and sorrows, often laced with humor. The connection between musician and audience was rare and intense. It closed with entreaties for more and more and more.

Plagued by respiratory problems, Arthneice died May 22, 2013, outside his home in Clarksdale's Riverton subdivision. Services were held May 30 inside the packed Real Faith Church, with Delta Burial in charge of arrangements.

Stuff happens during the Sunflower Festival's hot August days; music and relationships merge or explode; class reunions produce unlikely pairings; and an aura of excitement permeates the very breath of bodies pressed together against the downtown stage. Its headliners, from Koko Taylor, Bobby "Blue" Bland, and Shemekia Copeland to the North Mississippi Allstars, Dorothy Moore, and Charlie Musselwhite are selected by the Sunflower's biracial membership, equally divided between African American and Caucasian music fans.

On the Sunflower's twenty-fifth anniversary, Robert Plant and his Sensational Space Shifters skyrocketed Clarksdale into another orbit. Drawing the largest crowd in downtown history, the festival also required the combined security forces of Homeland Security, the Clarksdale City Police, Coahoma County sheriff's deputies, and Wood Security, a private firm contracted by the festival. One black-suited ninja refused to let Clarksdale mayor Henry Espy cross a barrier into the VIP tent because he was not wearing his All-Access ID. Stalkers were identified, monitored, and distanced from celebrities, outlawed video cameras hidden atop the VIP tent were ferreted out and removed, media were screened, coverage was restricted, and private interviews were granted by the headliner only to Mississippi ETV, CNN, and Paul Sexton, a writer from the *Daily Telegraph* who flew from London for the one-night assignment. After the concert, with no place to lay his weary head, Paul Sexton went home with us, slept in an attic room with no lights, and interviewed Robert the next morning on our front porch.

In addition to Robert Plant, the lineup included two other superstars: Charlie Musselwhite and Bobby Rush. Actor Morgan Freeman and attorney Bill Luckett were honored onstage to accept the Early

▲ Hill Country blues direct from the Zebra Ranch in Coldwater paired with the Burnside legacy from Holly Springs, Gravel Springs, Como, and Senatobia takes over the Sunflower River Blues Festival in a finale duet with Luther Dickinson (left) and Duwayne Burnside in 2006 and again in 2013.

▶ The Sunflower's salute to Muddy Waters is transformed into a magical Year of the Blues celebration in 2003 with members of Muddy's band, including guitarist Bob Margolin (left) and keyboard giant Pinetop Perkins coming together with Hubert Sumlin and Carey Bell in a dynamic main stage finale.

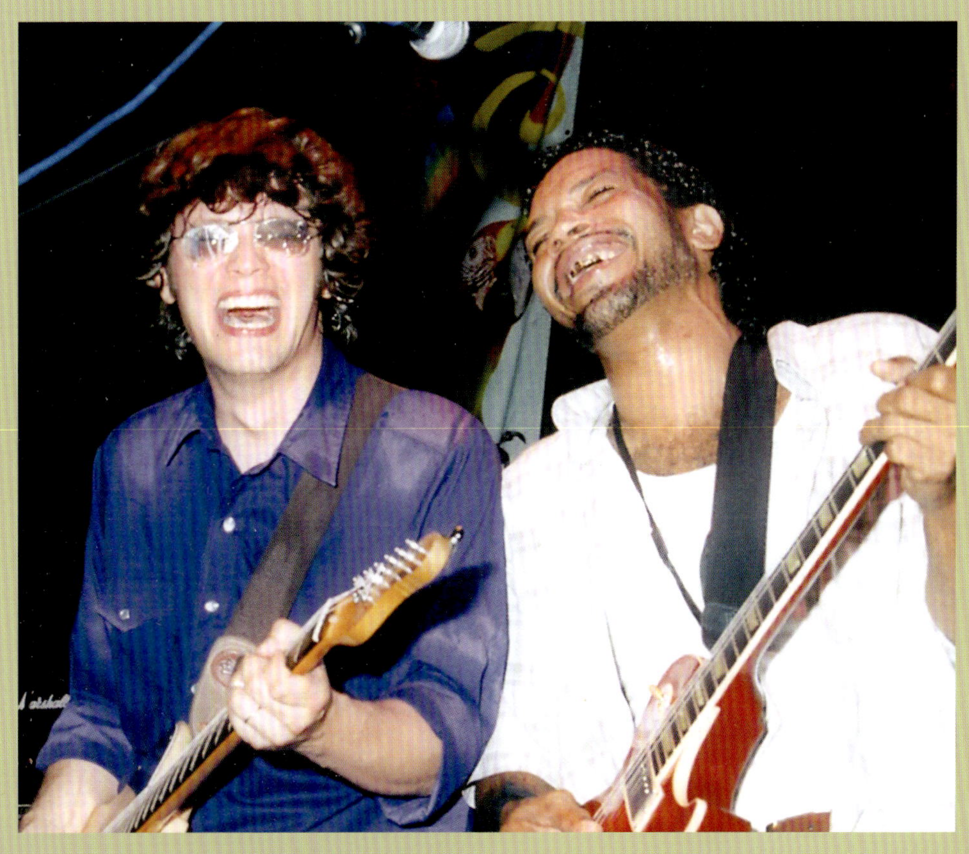

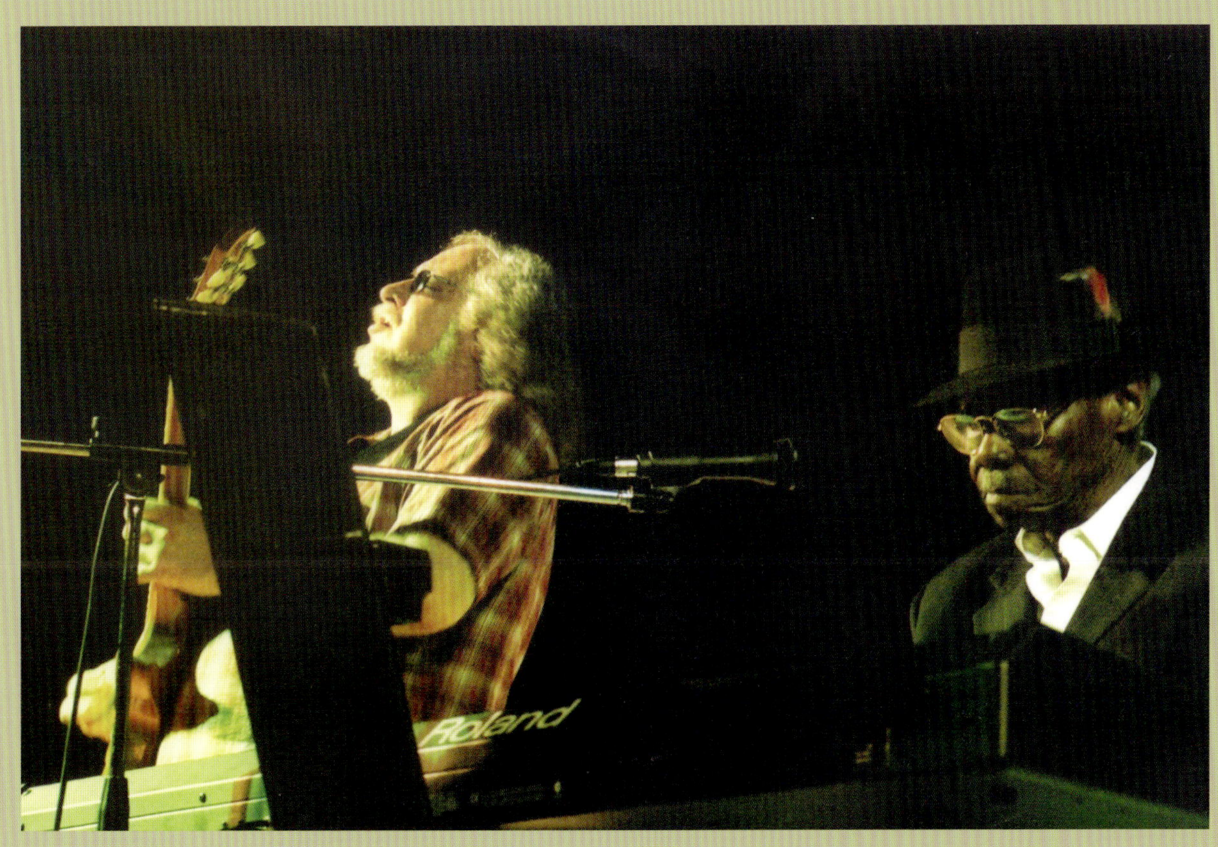

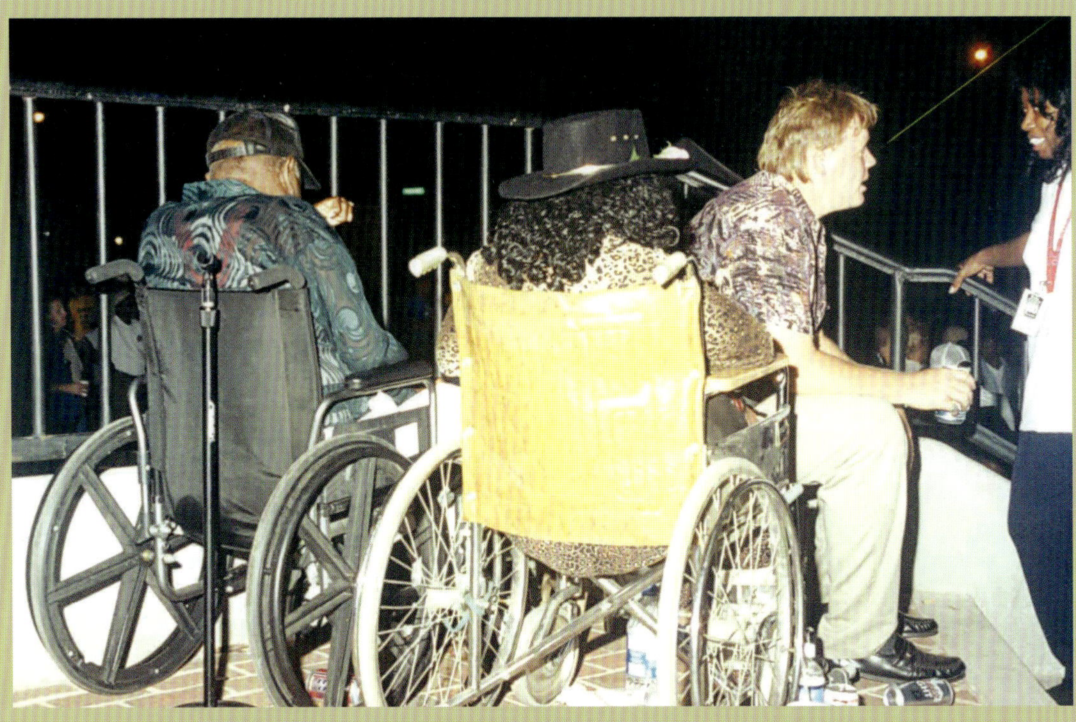

Sitting side-by-side in their wheelchairs near the Sunflower's main stage, CeDell Davis and Jessie Mae Hemphill enjoy watching the crowd in action on Blues Alley, while "Lightnin'" Malcolm and Maie Smith visit.

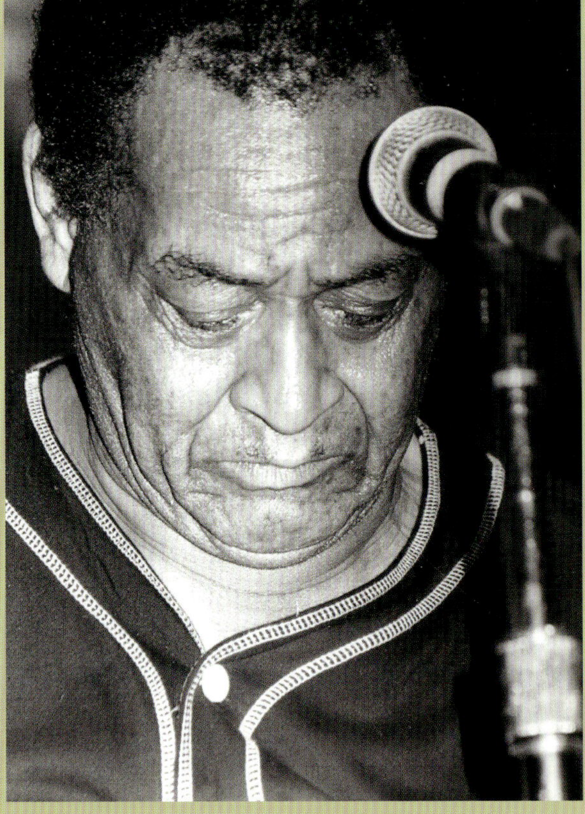

Although Junior Kimbrough and R. L. Burnside, both Hill Country, played the Sunflower Festivals, I took this photograph of Junior in total concentration at the Music Heritage Festival in downtown Memphis.

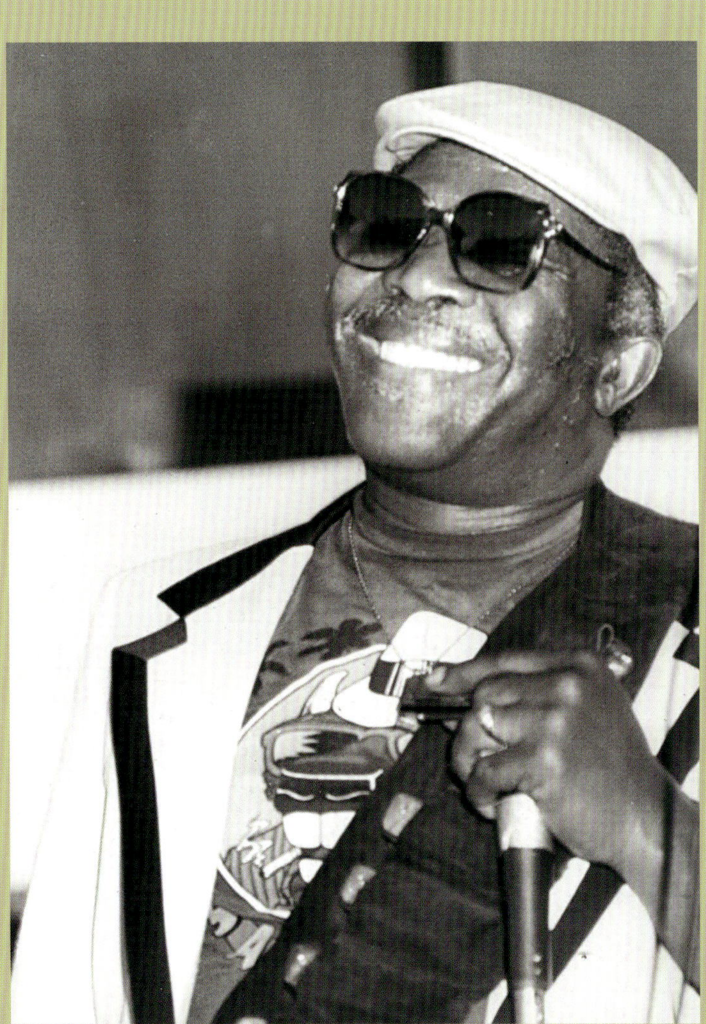

The sheer joy of Mojo Buford, wearing his leather brace of harmonicas and about to perform on the Sunflower stage, is contagious. Mojo was a member of Muddy's band in Chicago.

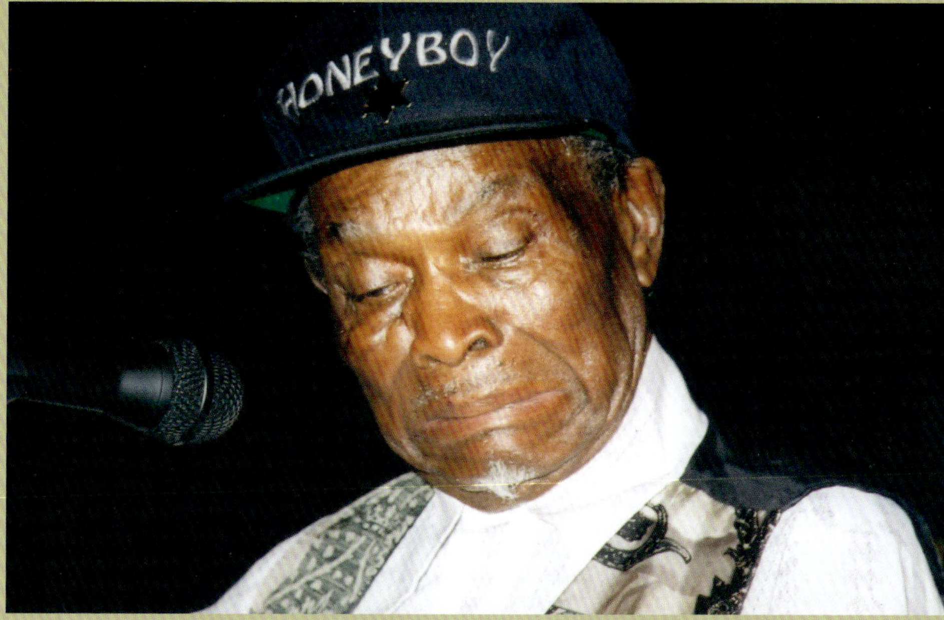

Honeyboy Edwards, who grew up on a farm out from Shaw and hopped trains all over the Delta, was a Sunflower favorite. He told me stories about getting caught as a youngster, pulled off a train, and confined for a while in Vance, where the plantation commissary manager supplemented his prison diet with fresh fruit. Honeyboy talked about being recorded for the Library of Congress by Alan Lomax in a plantation church on the King and Anderson farm outside Clarksdale. I drove to a vacant building in downtown Shaw one night when Michael Frank was recording segments of Honeyboy's documentary, and Sam Carr was there playing drums.

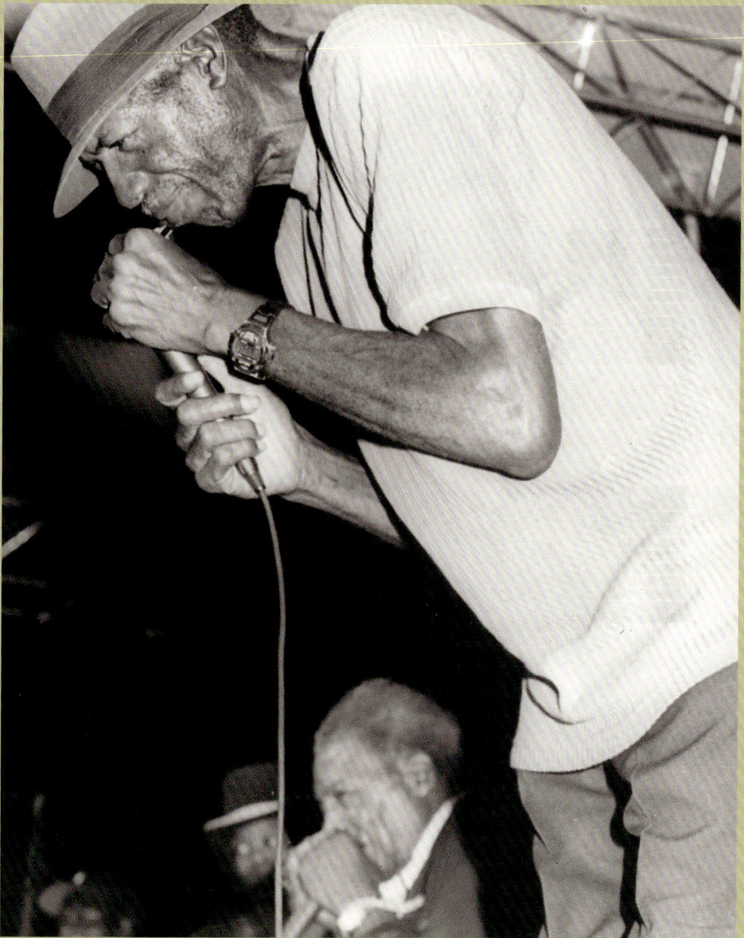

Two harmonica virtuosos, Frank Frost (in foreground) and Willie Foster, perform in tandem for a rare Sunflower River Festival.

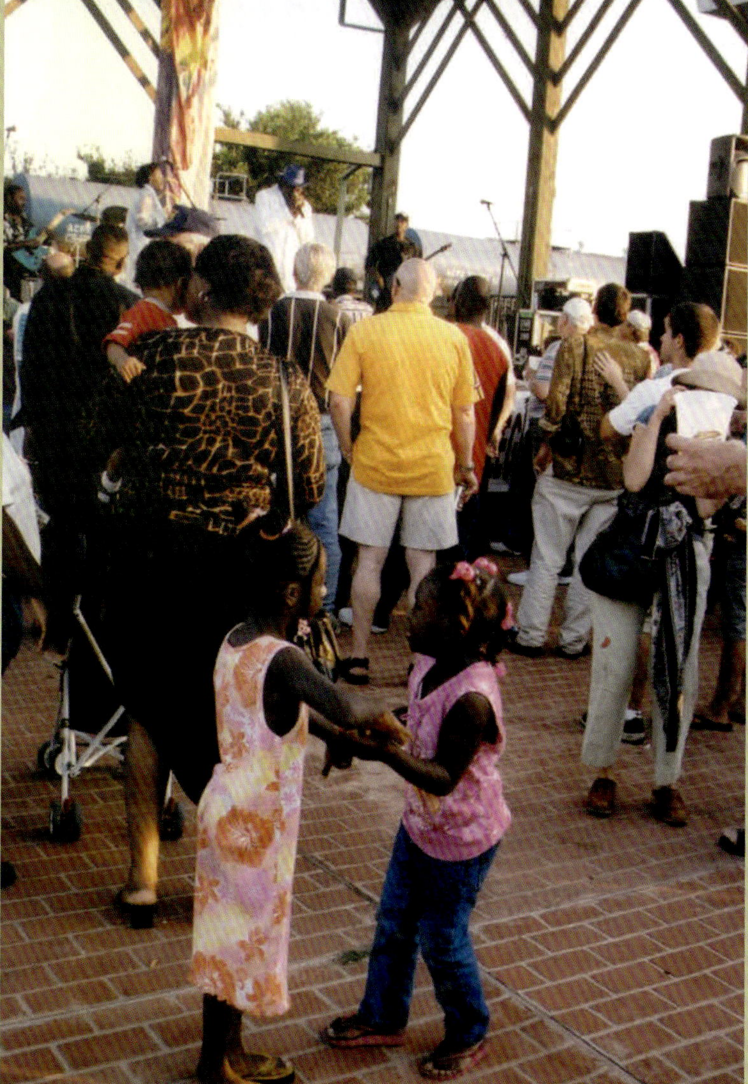

This photograph of two children dancing within the crowd captures the Sunflower River Blues and Gospel Festival's joyous spirit.

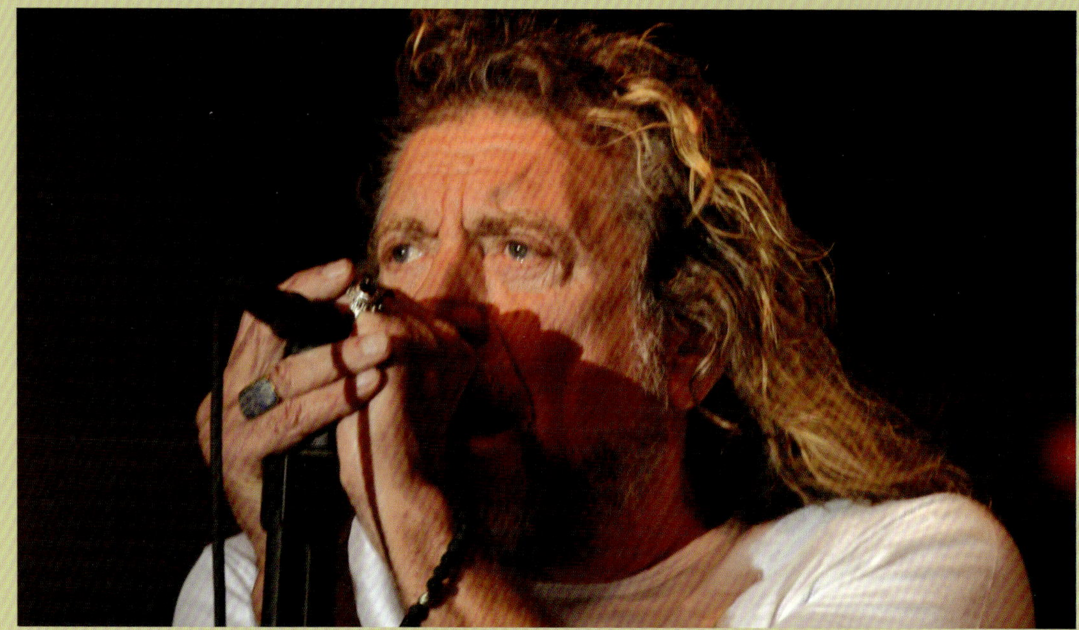

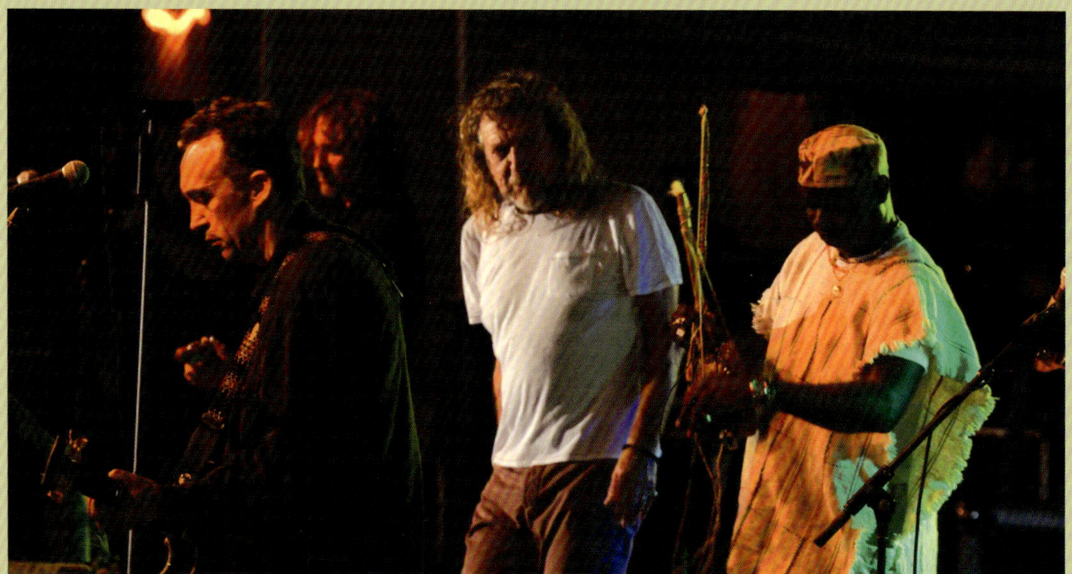

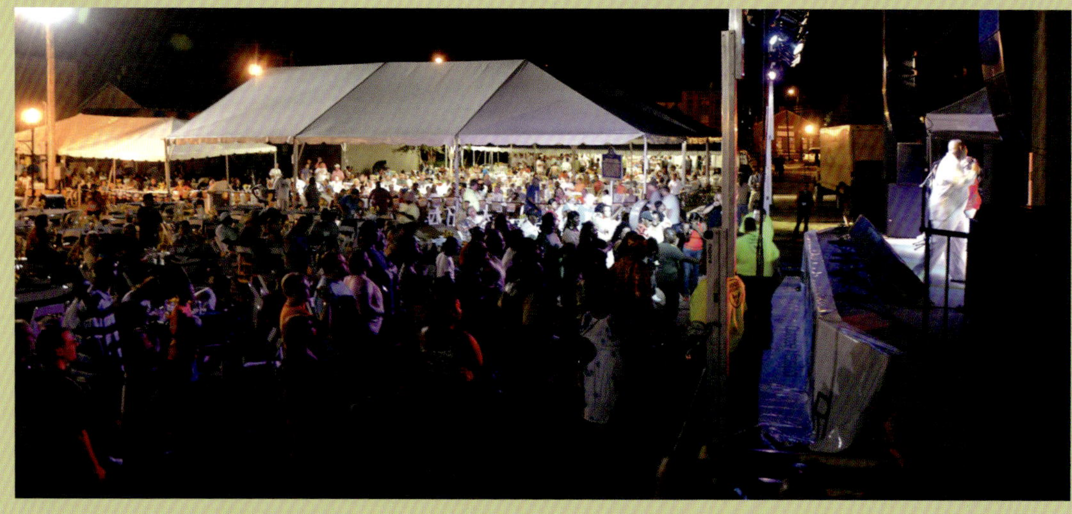

In 2012, on the Sunflower's twenty-fifth anniversary, Robert Plant and his Sensational Space Shifters (pictured: Justin Adams, Liam Sean "Skin" Tyson, Robert Plant, and West African musician Juldeh Camara) rocketed Clarksdale into another dimension. The outdoor crowd remains the largest in Clarksdale history, with music fans standing shoulder-to-shoulder across Blues Alley and down Yazoo Avenue to Second Street, where images were projected on a super-sized television screen.

Wright Award. A fantastic time most definitely was had by all, and nothing's been quite the same since.

NOTODDEN

In 1996, following an initial trip by Scandinavian journalist Tore Hvaal, a second visit by Jostein Forsberg, Espen Fjelle, and Wendy Fjelle, and finally a large delegation of city officials, the Sunflower Festival and Norway's Notodden Blues Festival became sister cities/festivals. The Norwegian mayor and council members were wined and dined on catfish and treated to live blues at the Rivermount Lounge and Smitty's, a concert by Marvin Sease at the City Auditorium, and Sunday services at Friendship M. B. Church in Friars Point, where the entire congregation lined up to shake their hands.

Through the years, cultural exchanges between the two cities have forged unique bonds and lifetime friendships. However, attending both festivals back to back requires physical stamina, because the Norwegian celebration takes place in August one week before the Sunflower opens.

My "Live from the Mississippi Delta" collection of fifty or so blues photographs was exhibited on my second trip to Notodden in 1998. It was opened formally by the Norwegian minister of culture. With the Myles Family singing "Amazing Grace," it became such an emotional experience for me that I blubbered and became a complete mess while being escorted through the exhibit by the culture minister.

Speaking at a blues educational program in Norway in 2002, headliner Tony Joe White talked about his growing-up days in Louisiana. Not only was this "Polk Salad Annie" musician/songwriter interesting and humorous, he segued into light-hearted commentary on Scandinavian trolls and his recording "Even Trolls Love Rock & Roll." Which brings up the seemingly unlikely affinity of Norwegians for blues and especially Mississippi Delta Blues. Jens Haugen, bassist for the Norwegian band Spoonful of Blues, likens the solitude of Delta

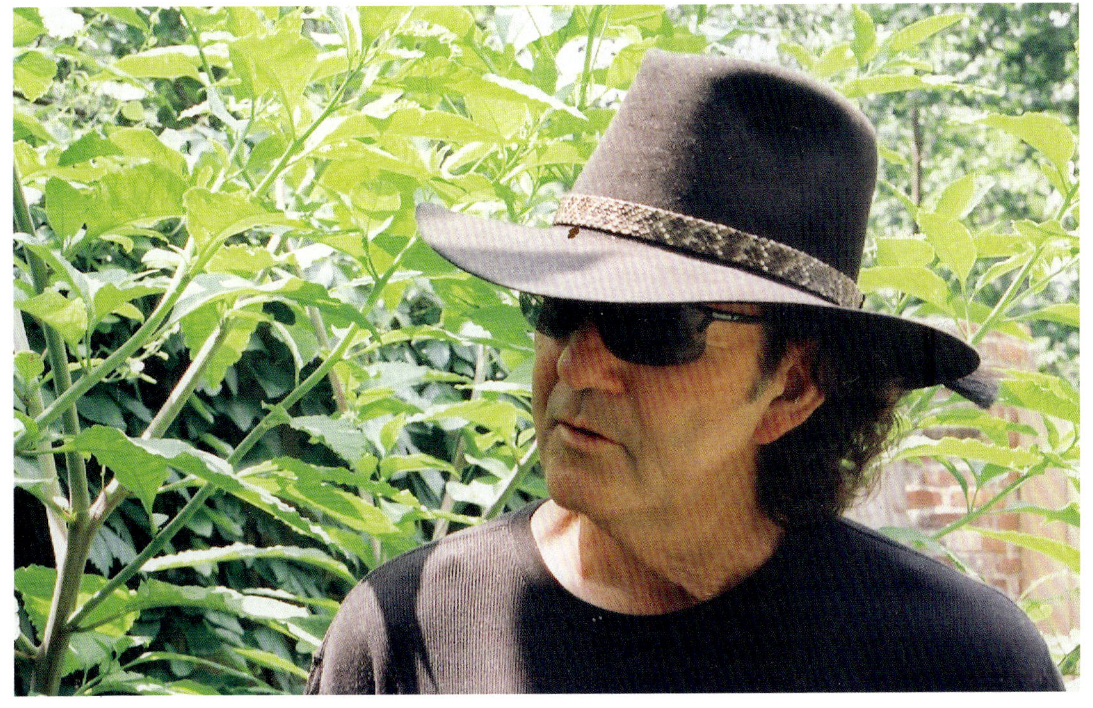

Speaking at a blues educational program in Norway in 2002, headliner Tony Joe White talks about growing up in Louisiana and recording "Polk Salad Annie" and "Even Trolls Love Rock & Roll."

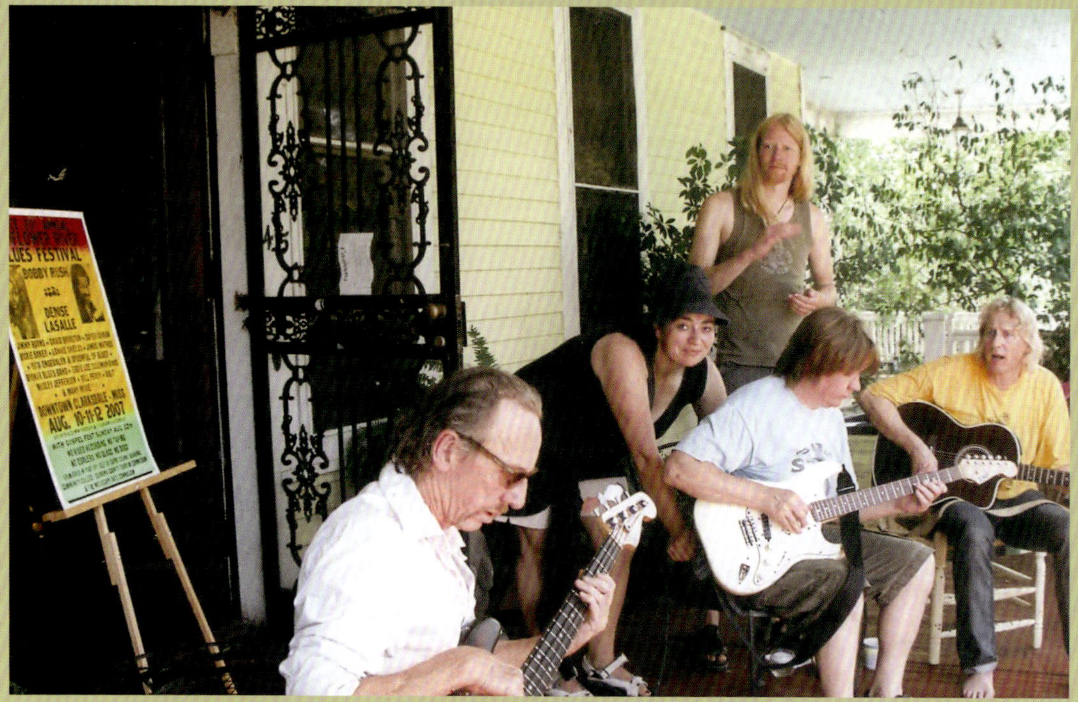

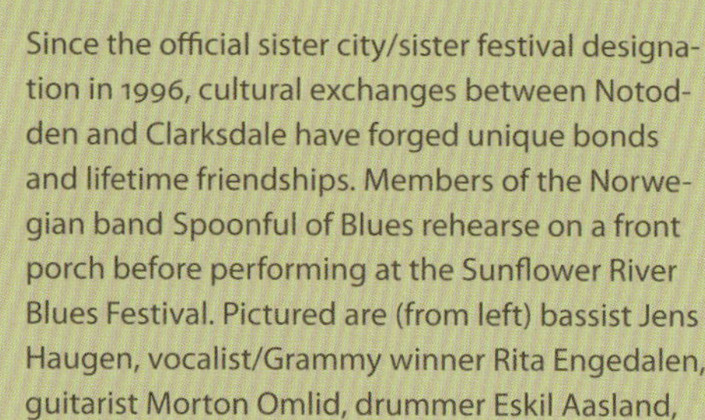

Since the official sister city/sister festival designation in 1996, cultural exchanges between Notodden and Clarksdale have forged unique bonds and lifetime friendships. Members of the Norwegian band Spoonful of Blues rehearse on a front porch before performing at the Sunflower River Blues Festival. Pictured are (from left) bassist Jens Haugen, vocalist/Grammy winner Rita Engedalen, guitarist Morton Omlid, drummer Eskil Aasland, and Jostein Forsberg, festival leader/harmonica.

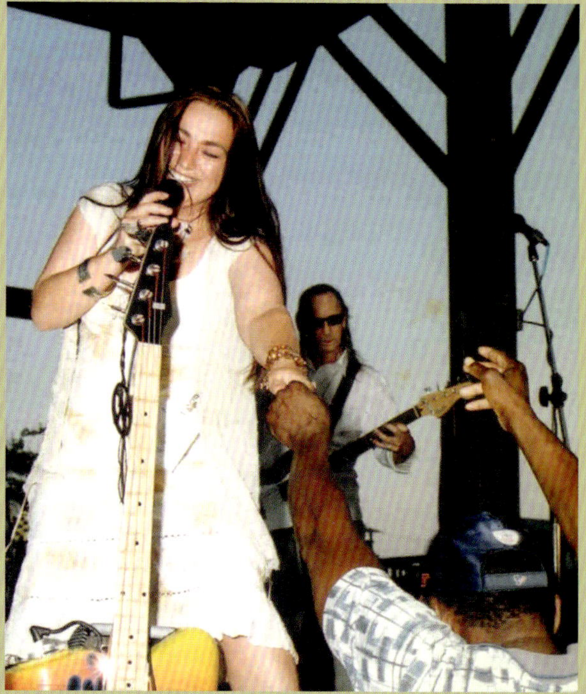

Singer/songwriter Rita Engedalen is well known in Mississippi and has performed several times at the Sunflower River Blues Festival and headlined the main stage in 2015. She has recorded several of her songs in Clarksdale with gospel soloist Myra Turner, first cousin of Ike Turner, and with members of the Coahoma Community College Concert Choir.

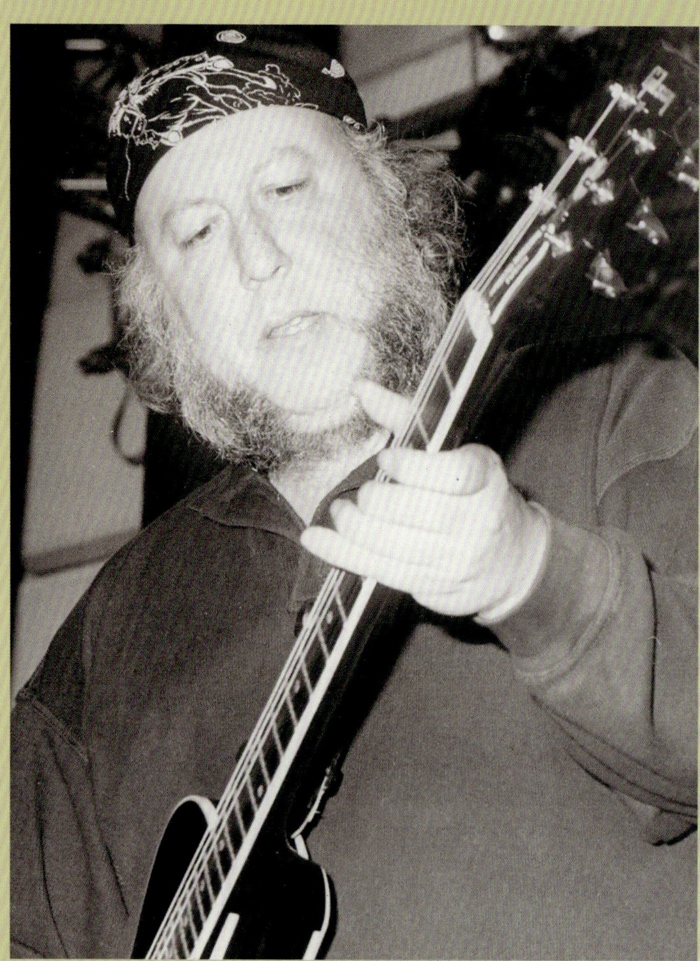

On my first trip to Norway's Notodden Blues Festival in 1996, I was privileged to be one of ten photojournalists to photograph the reclusive British rock guitarist Peter Green, founder of Fleetwood Mac, in his first public performance in decades.

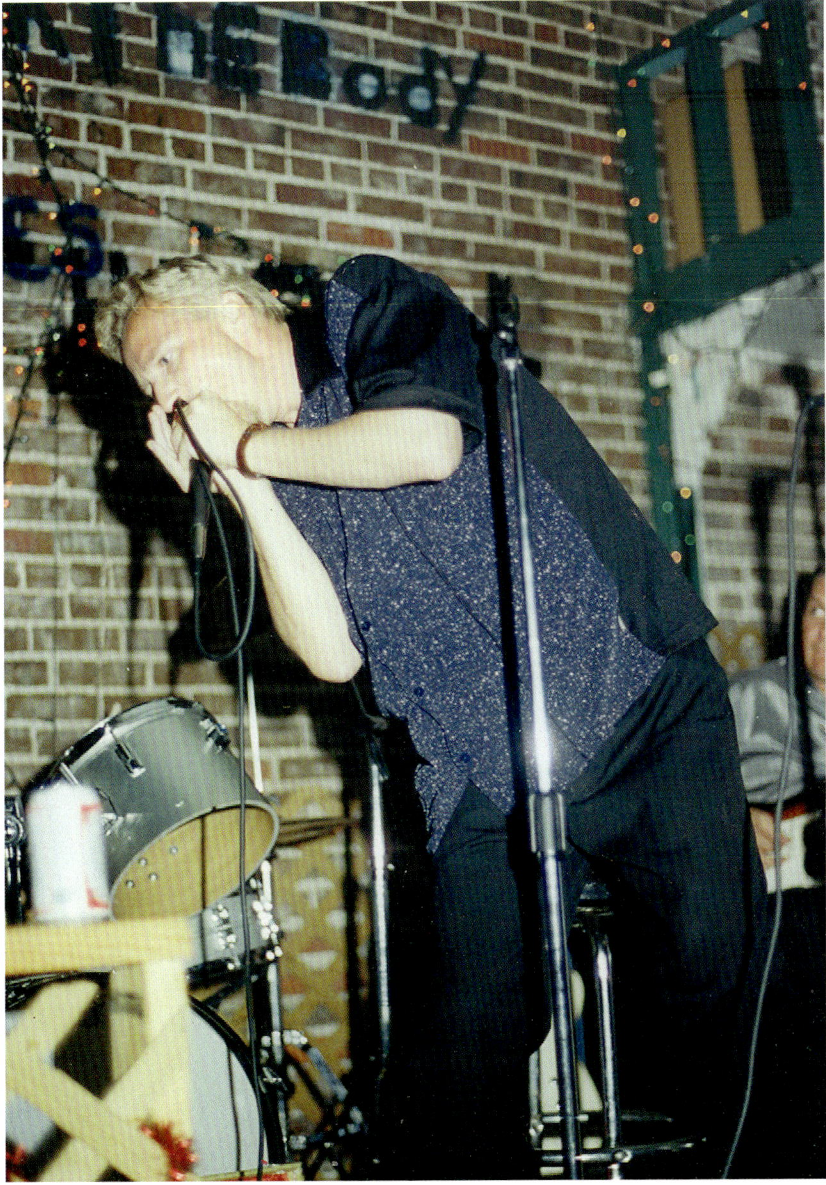

plantations to the remote high mountains of Scandinavia as similar breeding grounds for musical creativity. For many centuries his country has produced traditions of great fiddlers.

Norwegians have traveled often to Mississippi's blues sites and juke joints, and the Sunflower created its popular "Grits, Greens, and Barbecue" supper to introduce them to soul food. The late Grady Palmer, a Clarksdale city commissioner, attended several Notodden festivals, where he relished being introduced as the "Prime Minister of Mississippi." Kids from the Delta Blues Museum's Educational Program have spent a seminar week with youngsters from all sections of Scandinavia. They also have performed with the Blues Brothers and Wilson Pickett, and wound up helping teach some of the blues seminar classes. "How is it that Delta kids sound like B. B. King?" we were asked. The only reply—must be simply that it's something they hear and absorb from birth. Big Jack Johnson, Sam Carr, Super Chikan Johnson, Jimbo Mathus, the Myles Family, and many other Mississippi musicians have performed on their stages and enjoyed Scandinavian hospitality. Notodden residents I had never met frequently offered me rides to events all over the city.

Knut Slettemo, my journalist friend, drove me through the mountains surrounding Notodden, where his heroic countrymen led by Lt. Col Knut Haukelid sabotaged Nazi attempts to secure "heavy water" produced in occupied Norway during World War II. "Heavy water," he explained, was vital in Hitler's race with the United States to develop the atomic bomb. Viewing the sheer cliffs where Norwegian paratroopers from the United Kingdom landed and attacked the heavy-water plant at Vemork in 1943 was mind-boggling. The deep-water Lake Tinnsjo, where many countrymen were sacrificed to sink the ferry steamer *Hydro*, laden with barrels of heavy water bound for Germany, was equally impressive. On the night before I left Notodden, I was honored to speak by telephone to one of the saboteurs who participated in these actions that eventually freed Norway from German control. Unfortunately, I had to leave the next day without meeting him.

However, when Knut and I were in the high mountains, I listened to the haunting voice of a woman calling her cows, and Jens's comments about solitary Norwegians relating to lonely blues musicians came home to me. While abroad, the Myles Family stayed in the home of a city official. Aboard ship, during a blues cruise offering mountains of shrimp, they became homesick for southern cooking. Their hosts took them grocery shopping afterward and then turned their kitchen over to Olivia Myles, and she produced a southern downhome fried chicken supper.

▲

Notodden Blues Festival leader Jostein Forsberg, who has visited the Mississippi Delta so many times he could probably vote here, plays harp inside Sarah's Kitchen in Clarksdale.

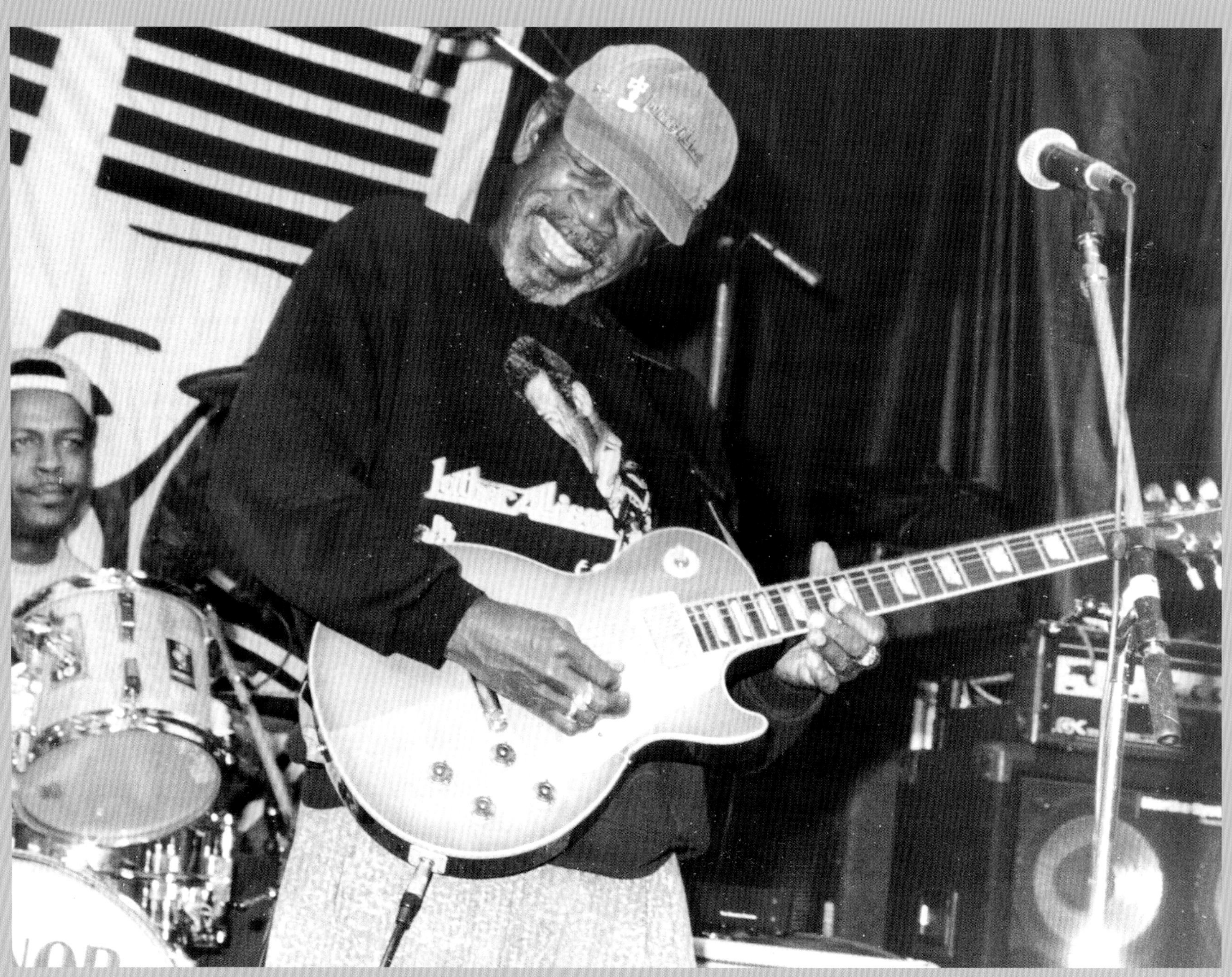

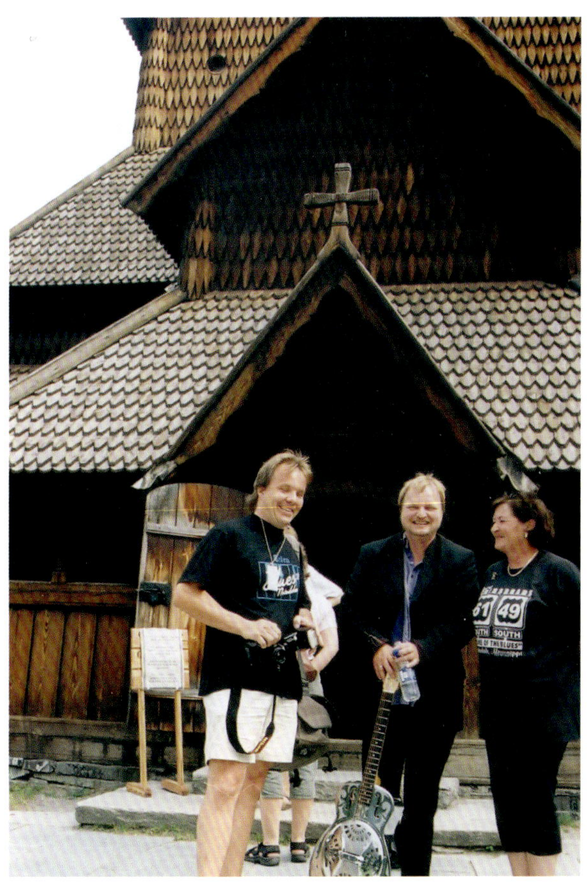

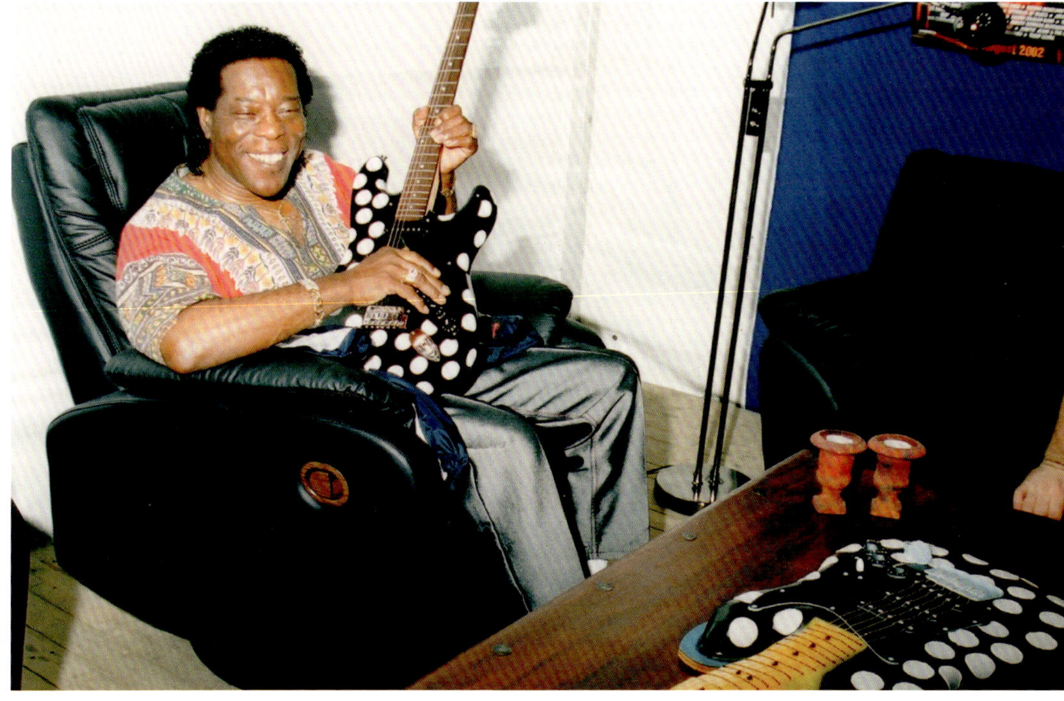

▲

The Myles Family singers from Clarksdale and Kosciusko received a rare invitation to perform in Notodden's ancient twelfth-century stave church, a veritable fairytale structure. The concert was broadcast on Norway's equivalent of National Public Radio. Pictured outside the church are (from left) journalist Knut Slettemo and virtuoso guitarist Knut Reiersrud.

▶

Notodden Festival headliner Buddy Guy celebrates his birthday with a unique polka-dotted cake mimicking his trademark guitar.

◀

Among my experiences and the celebrated artists I met from several trips to Notodden are Robert Cray, the Blues Brothers, Dr. John, Bo Diddley, and an interview with the extraordinary Luther Allison, who performed even his sound check with drop-dead intensity.

The Myles Family received a rare invitation to perform in Notodden's ancient twelfth-century stave church, a veritable fairytale structure. The concert was broadcast on Norway's equivalent of National Public Radio. Among the extraordinary artists I met on several trips to Notodden were Buddy Guy, celebrating his birthday with a black-and-white spotted guitar-shaped cake, Peter Green from Fleetwood Mac, the Blues Brothers, Robert Cray, Dr. John, Bo Diddley, and the fabulous Luther Allison, in a sound check interview.

Norwegian diva and Grammy Award winner Rita Engedalen has recorded gospel songs in Clarksdale with the Coahoma Community College Choir and Ike Turner's first cousin, Myra Turner, soloist with Chapel Hill Baptist Church. Jostein Forsberg, Morten Omlid, Jens Haugen, and Eskil Aasland from the Spoonful of Blues Band have been favorites on the Sunflower Blues Festival main stages. In 2015 Rita and Margit Bakken presented their Women in Blues program on both acoustic and main stages. It's been a rich exchange, with Notodden opening its fabulous, long-awaited European Blues Center and Robert Plant headlining their 2015 Notodden Blues Festival, Clarksdale expanding its historic Delta Blues Museum, and its Blues Education Program students performing at the White House for the second time.

KING BISCUIT BLUES FESTIVAL

If August and the Sunflower resurrect memories of hot music and explosive relationships, October and Helena's King Biscuit time dance to another rhythm. Blue skies of such intensity occur only in October—a signal, perhaps to live hard and fast before winter, often the cold/ brown season.

One fall there were three vintage Cadillacs parked frequently outside our house at 415 Court Street. One had tiger-striped seat covers and belonged to my good friend John Ruskey, who was curator of the Delta Blues Museum at that time and was living temporarily upstairs in our house. We roared to Indianola in it for B. B. King Homecoming concerts. We also coasted to an early conference in Greenville when Shelby Foote, its principal speaker, declared straight on how much he hated tourists.

Another Caddy belonged to Tad Pierson, who moved to Memphis, where he offers custom blues tours. This, however, was his debut venture into blues country. One of the wheels on his Cadillac collapsed, and he parked his client—a sophisticated New York psychologist, on my front porch swing for the day. Afterward, she mailed me her vintage ballet first-nighter gowns to wear at our Tennessee Williams Festival parties in October, and I also took them to Paris.

While I was away, a legendary blues wedding took place in my house. The ceremony I had envisioned was a small affair on the front porch. However, it ballooned into a global event, with invitations sent bulk mail, an African-robed minister, and celebrated bluesmen wearing golden usher badges while seating guests in my living room/ chapel. Around 3 A.M., several wedding guest/friends called me in Paris with an update, and again from the Rivermount Lounge, where a reception with red beans and rice was in progress. Months later I was still discovering strange souvenirs in my house.

The third Caddy belonged to Skip Henderson—a New Jersey promoter, whose Mt. Zion Fund kicked off the first blues trail marker program in Mississippi or anywhere else. He initiated the campaign to save Clarksdale's passenger depot and convinced community leaders that Memphis was stealing Clarksdale's blues heritage. An application for Mississippi's Transportation Department's (MDOT) first Iced Tea grant cleared its first hurdle. Hugh Jack Stubbs, county administrator, a veteran official with connections across Mississippi, and I attended a two-day MDOT conference in Jackson. He lobbied engineers more accustomed to building bridges than to preserving train stations, while I visited with archives and history folks. Thanks primarily to

▶ Skip Henderson, a New Jersey music promoter, whose Mt. Zion Fund kicked off the first blues marker program in Mississippi, convinced community leaders that Memphis was stealing Clarksdale's blues heritage and initiated a campaign to save Clarksdale's passenger depot as a tourism attraction. An application for one of the first ICED TEA grants from Mississippi's Transportation Department (MDOT) was successful and provided funding. Architects Richard Dickson and Jack Tyson (pictured inside) took on the daunting job of saving the historic but neglected building overgrown outside with brush and containing animal pelts from a taxidermy business and trash from vagrants sleeping and cooking inside.

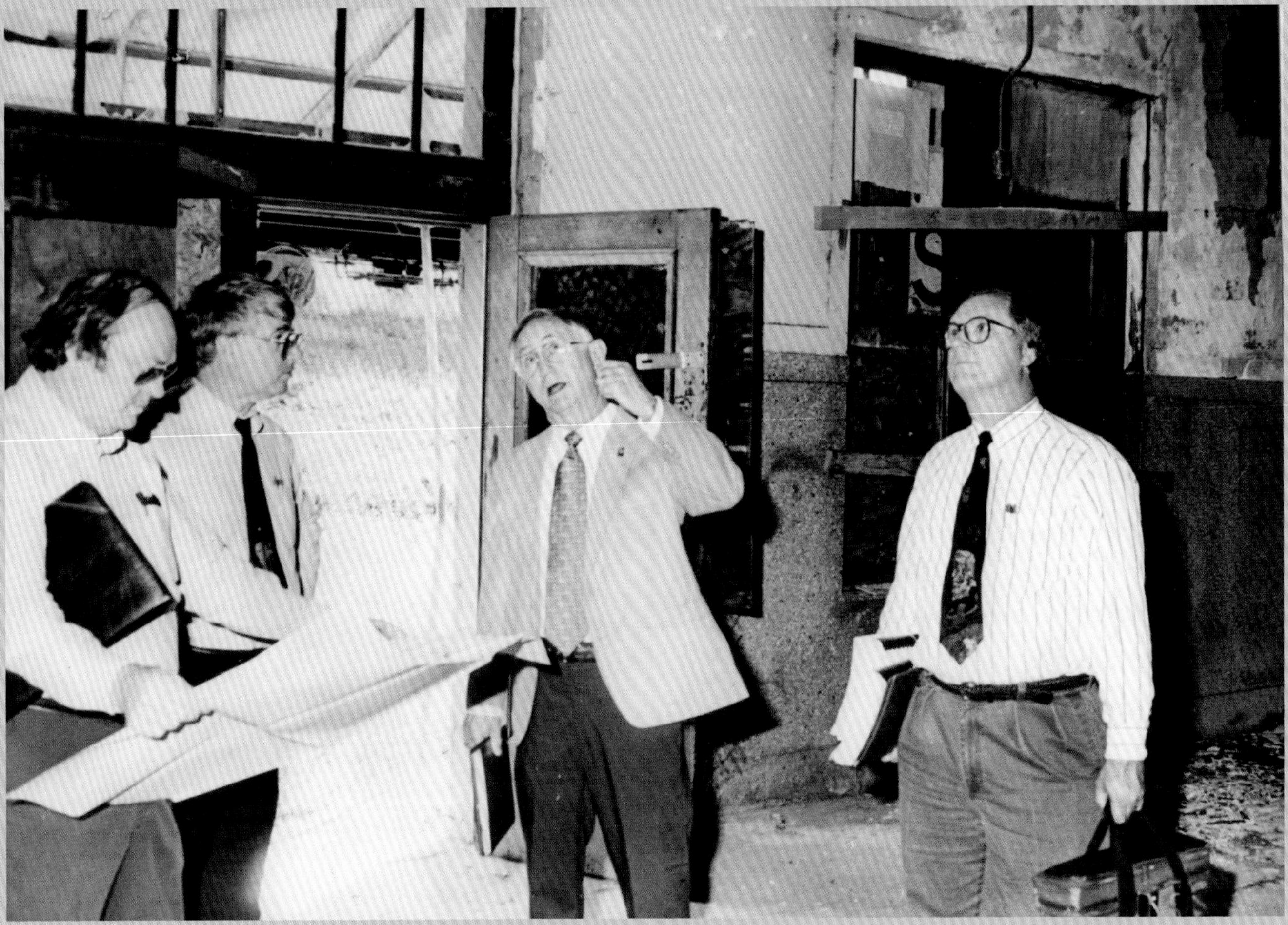

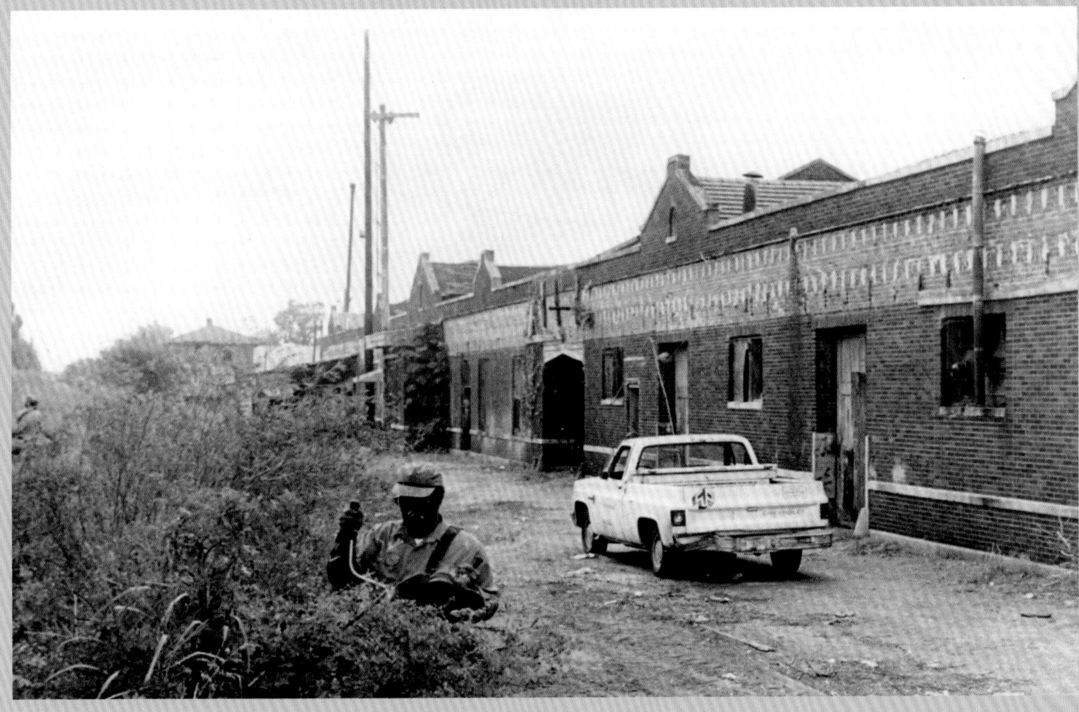

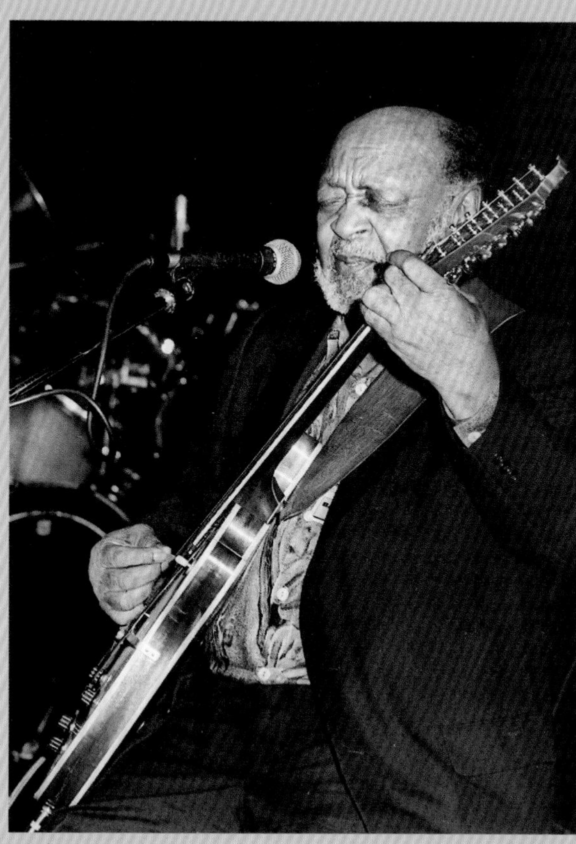

Robert Junior Lockwood learned to play guitar from Robert Johnson, and until his death in 2006, he was a sensational anchor each year for the King Biscuit Blues Festival in Helena.

This photograph of phenomenal guitarist Albert King performing in Helena in front of the famous King Biscuit logo with Sonny Boy Williamson, taken either at the first King Biscuit in 1986 or the third in 1988, is a special favorite of mine.

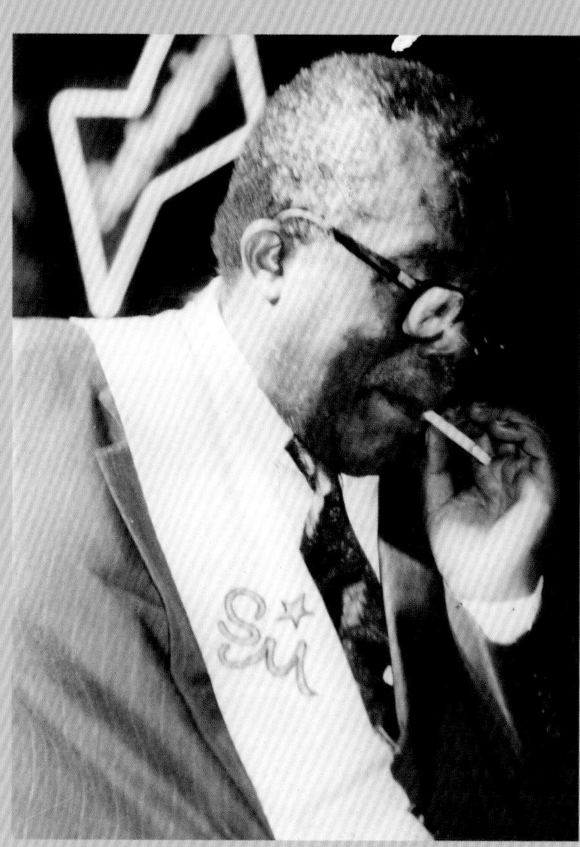

Other great musicians playing King Biscuit through the years include Anson Funderburgh and harmonica great Sam Myers, smoking a pack of cigarettes onstage during his performance.

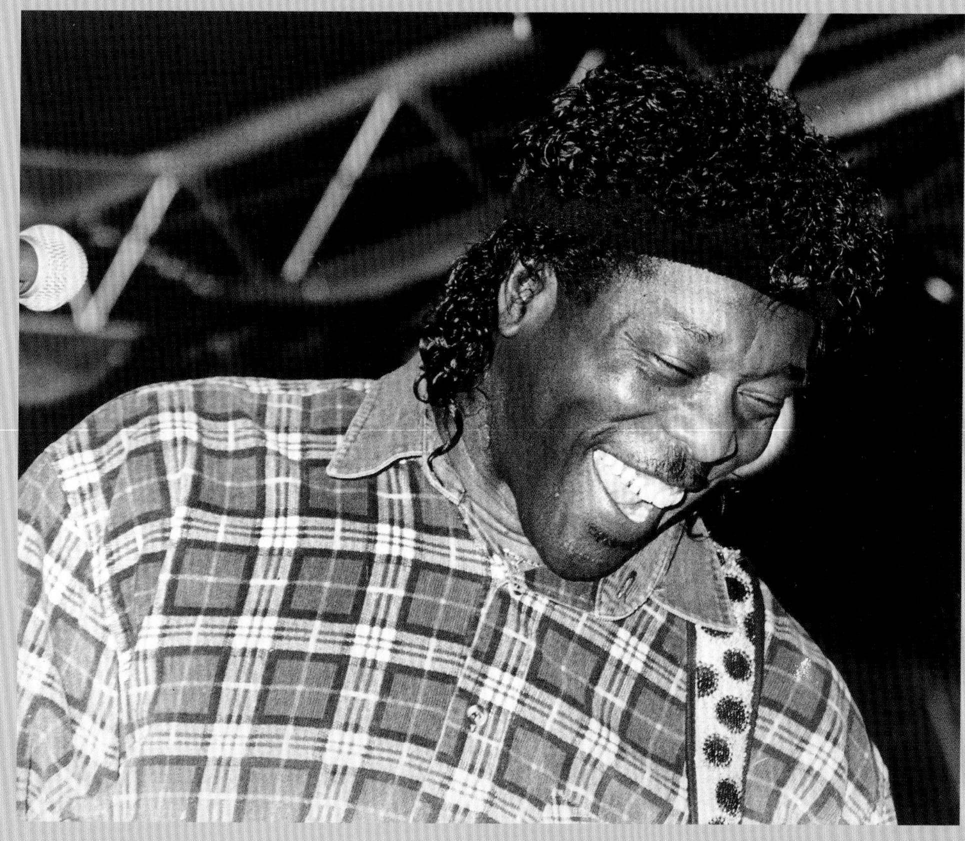

Having a great time playing and flipping his famous polka-dotted guitar, Buddy Guy headlines Helena's 1989 King Biscuit Festival.

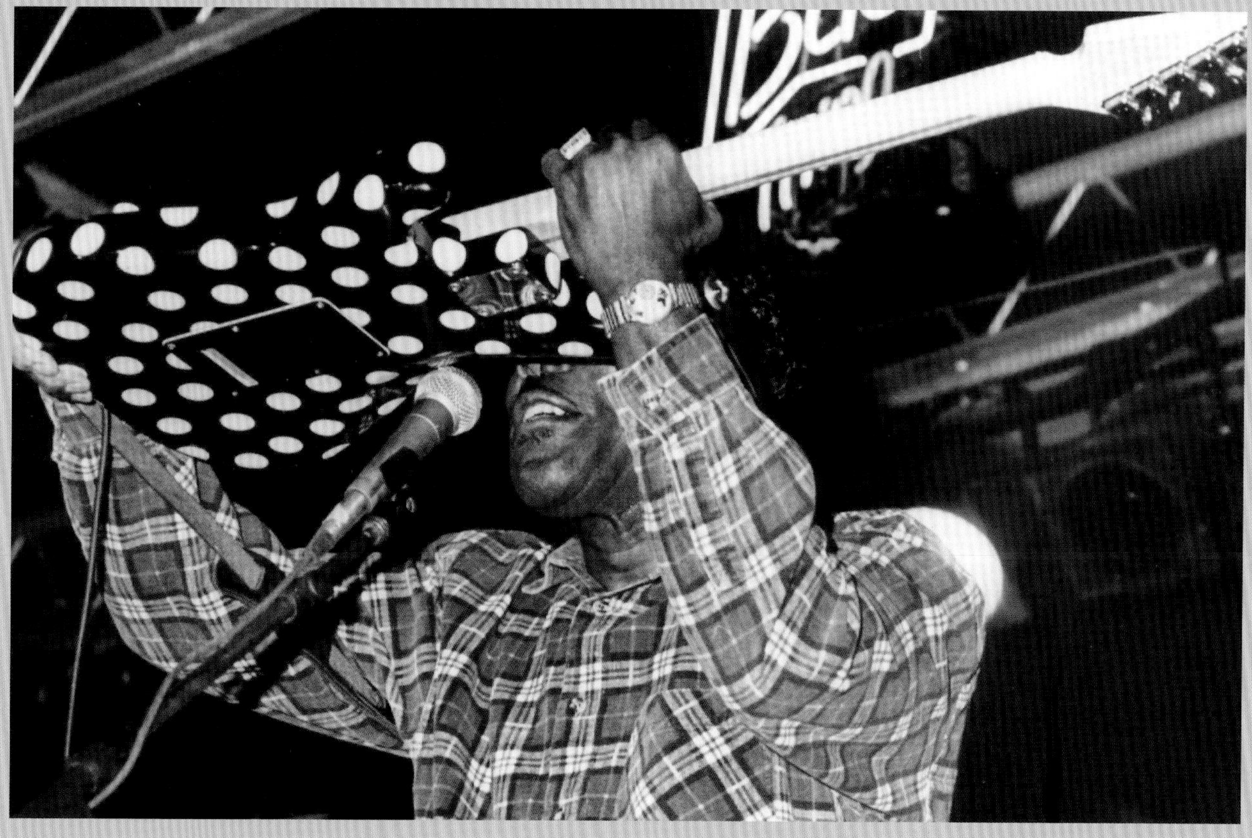

Hugh Jack's persistence, the station, which contained animal pelt remnants from a taxidermy business and trash from vagrants sleeping and cooking inside, was saved.

Renovation had setbacks, including a collapsed ceiling, but a poignant ceremony documenting the structure's historical importance in the community was unforgettable. Aaron Kline described how the Torah was shipped from the East Coast to the depot for Clarksdale's Beth Israel congregation in the 1920s, and its members took turns walking it in procession to the temple on Delta Avenue. Veterans recalled World War II cadets arriving by train for flight instruction at Fletcher Field, and caskets returning brave soldiers home for interment. Athletes talked about football teams leaving the station for Big 8 Conference games across Mississippi, and musicians described Muddy Waters leaving Stovall Plantation and buying a ticket for Chicago, where he became king of the electric guitar.

In Helena, Bubba Sullivan, Jerry Pillow, KFFA's Sonny Payne, and others kicked off King Biscuit in 1986 two years before the Sunflower. It has become one of the country's largest blues festivals and a major tourism event in Arkansas. For years it remained admission-free and open to the public. Although Robert Junior Lockwood, who learned guitar from Robert Johnson, was a classic regular at King Biscuit, his wife/manager halted photography after the first few numbers of his set. She'd announce, "That's enough now," and everyone obeyed.

Other great musicians playing there through the years have included Anson Funderburgh and Sam Myers (smoking a pack of cigarettes onstage during his performance), Marsha Ball, Irma Thomas, Bobby Rush, Albert King, Buddy Guy, Charlie Musselwhite, and the quintessential bluesman: Luther Allison.

The most memorable King Biscuit performance I experienced in Helena was Luther Allison's. Beneath a full moon, the musician became a wild man, jumping off the stage without interruption to his guitar playing, and roaming through crowds high atop the Mississippi River levee. He probably would have played another hour, but a tech pulled the electric cord and silenced the magic.

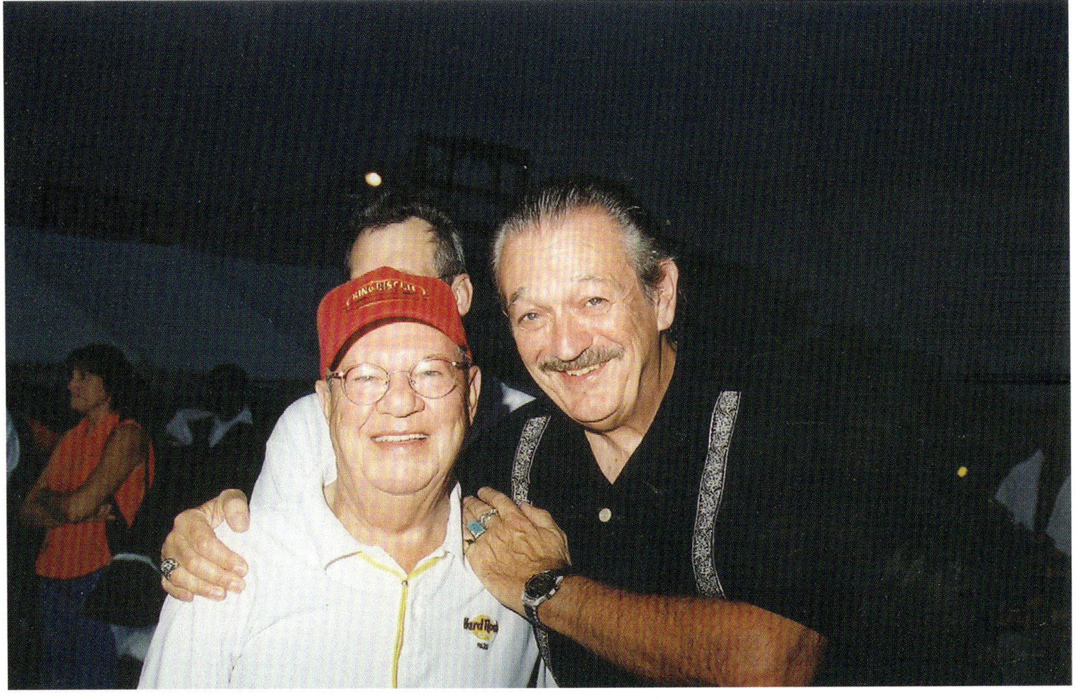

▲ The main man and voice of Helena blues, KFFA radio's famous Sonny Payne, and Charlie Musselwhite are longtime friends.

▶ Luther Allison's kamikaze performance roaming through crowds on the levee beneath a full moon at King Biscuit is still recalled with awe by blues fans.

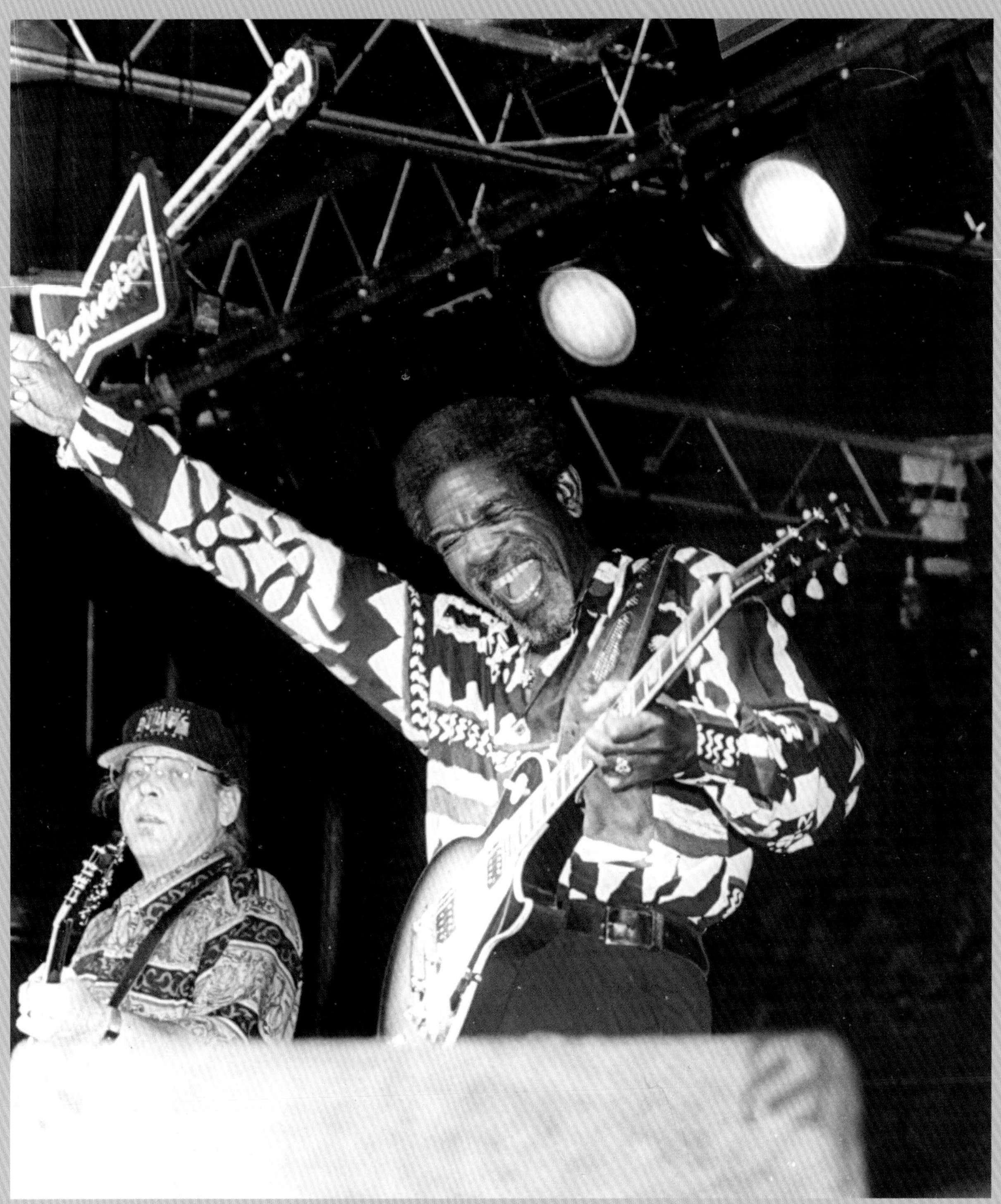

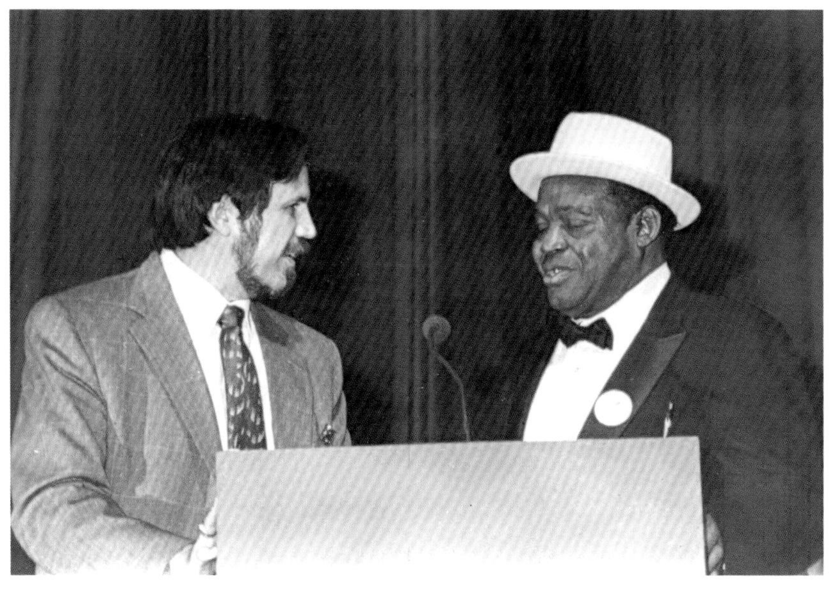

BLUES MUSIC AWARDS

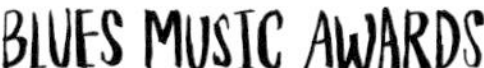

I'm not sure why the Blues Foundation changed the name of its awards from W. C. Handy to the Blues Music Awards (BMAs); the movie industry still retains its "Oscars," television its "Emmys," and theater the "Tonys."

The ceremony sites also moved around for a while. On its tenth anniversary, November 5, 1989, I sat on the floor for a very laid-back ceremony in the Memphis Convention Center with Willie Dixon onstage, *Roots* author Alex Haley a couple of rows behind me, and Ruth Brown, MC for the program. Jessie Mae Hemphill, honored for excellence in traditional blues, was there in cowboy hat and boots. Others wore glamour and glitter. I attended extraordinary Handy ceremonies in the beautiful, friendly, but cramped Orpheum Theatre, where Little Milton and Bobby Rush clowned together perhaps remembering their early days in the Chitlin' Circuit.

Harmonica virtuoso James Cotton earned standing ovations, and I came very close to disaster. Photographers that year were assigned to the orchestra pit in front of the stage, with instructions not to use a flash. With two cameras I staked out a center position in front of the skirted circular stage and began shooting film. When one roll (this was before digital) was full, I'd switch to another camera, reload, and continue through the ceremony. Near the finale, I reached for my second camera, and it wasn't there. When I parted the stage curtains in front of me, I was aghast to find a twenty-five-foot drop down to the concrete basement floor where my camera was a shattered black spot. An Orpheum roadie retrieved it for me.

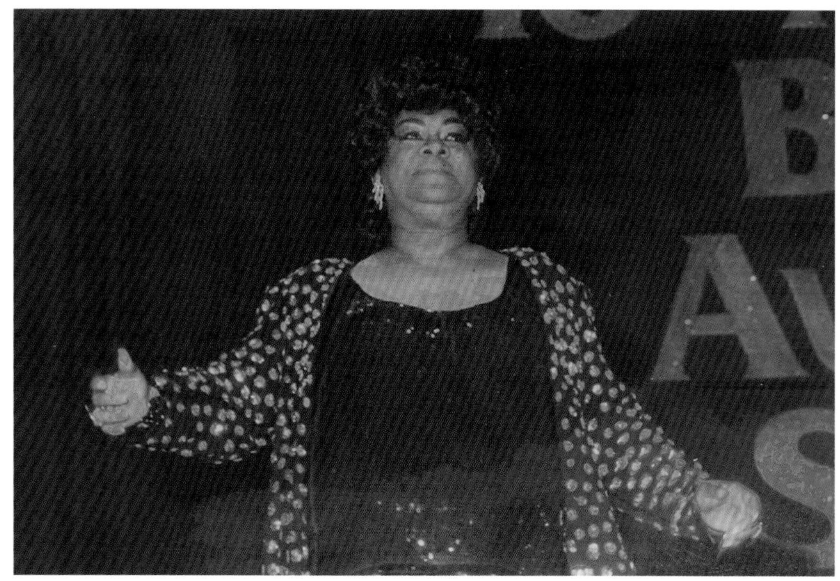

▲ On the tenth anniversary of the Handy/Blues Music Awards in 1989, I sat on the floor of the Memphis Convention Center for a very laid-back ceremony with Willie Dixon on stage as guest host, *Roots* "author Alex Haley a couple of rows behind me, and Ruth Brown, emcee for the program.

▶ I attended extraordinary Handy Award ceremonies in the beautiful but cramped Orpheum Theatre, where Little Milton and Bobby Rush clowned together, probably remembering their early days in the Chitlin' Circuit.

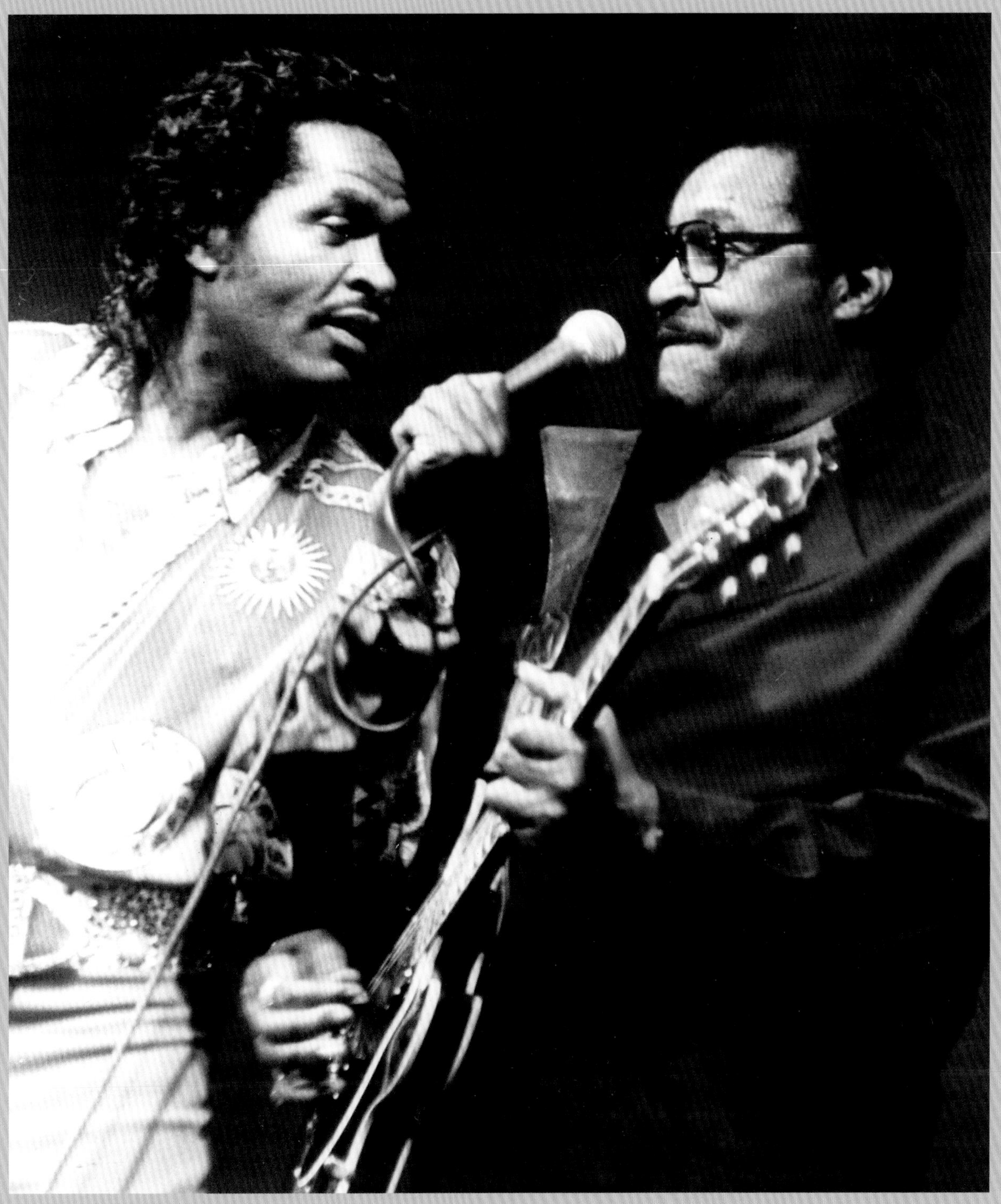

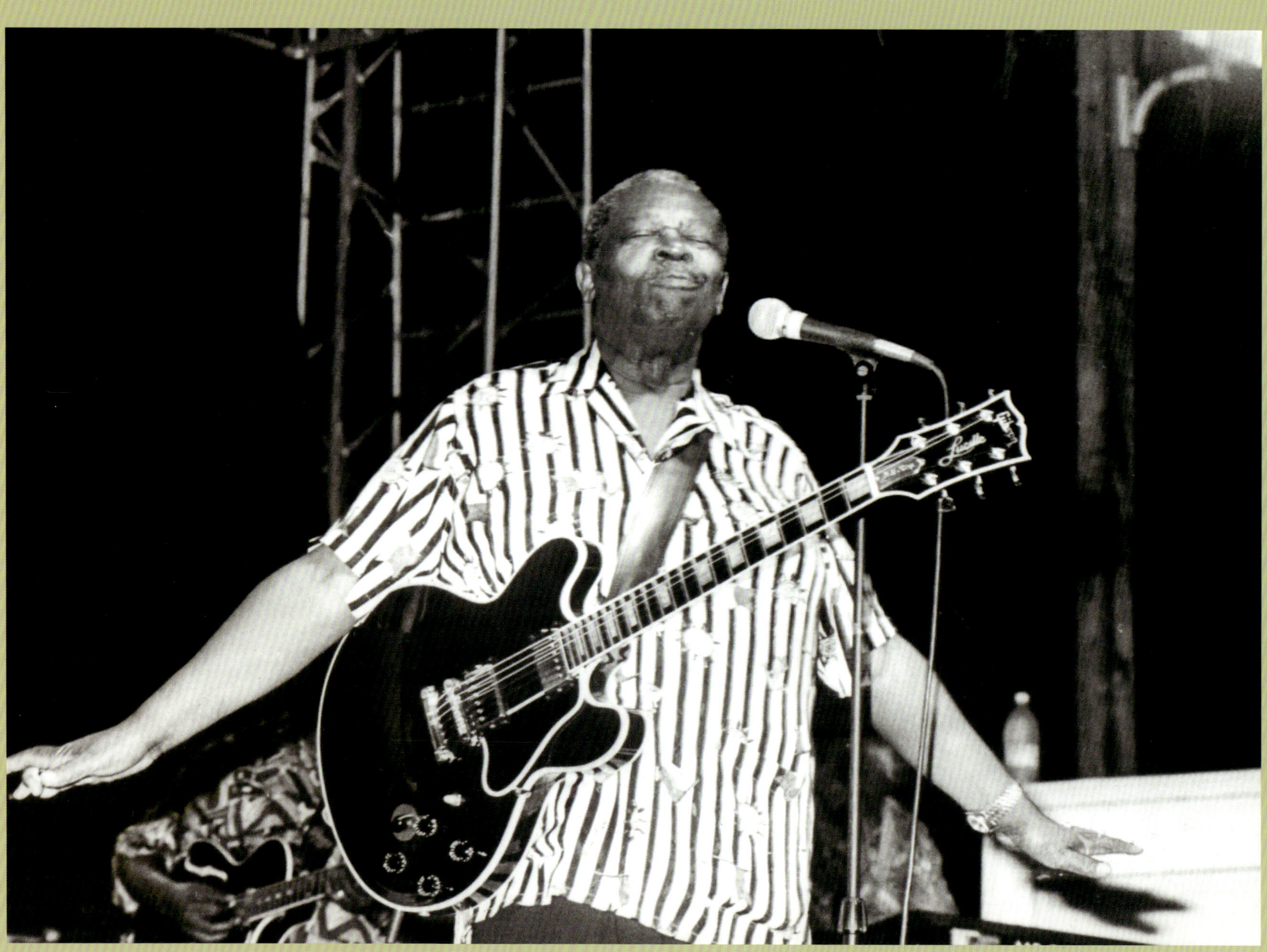

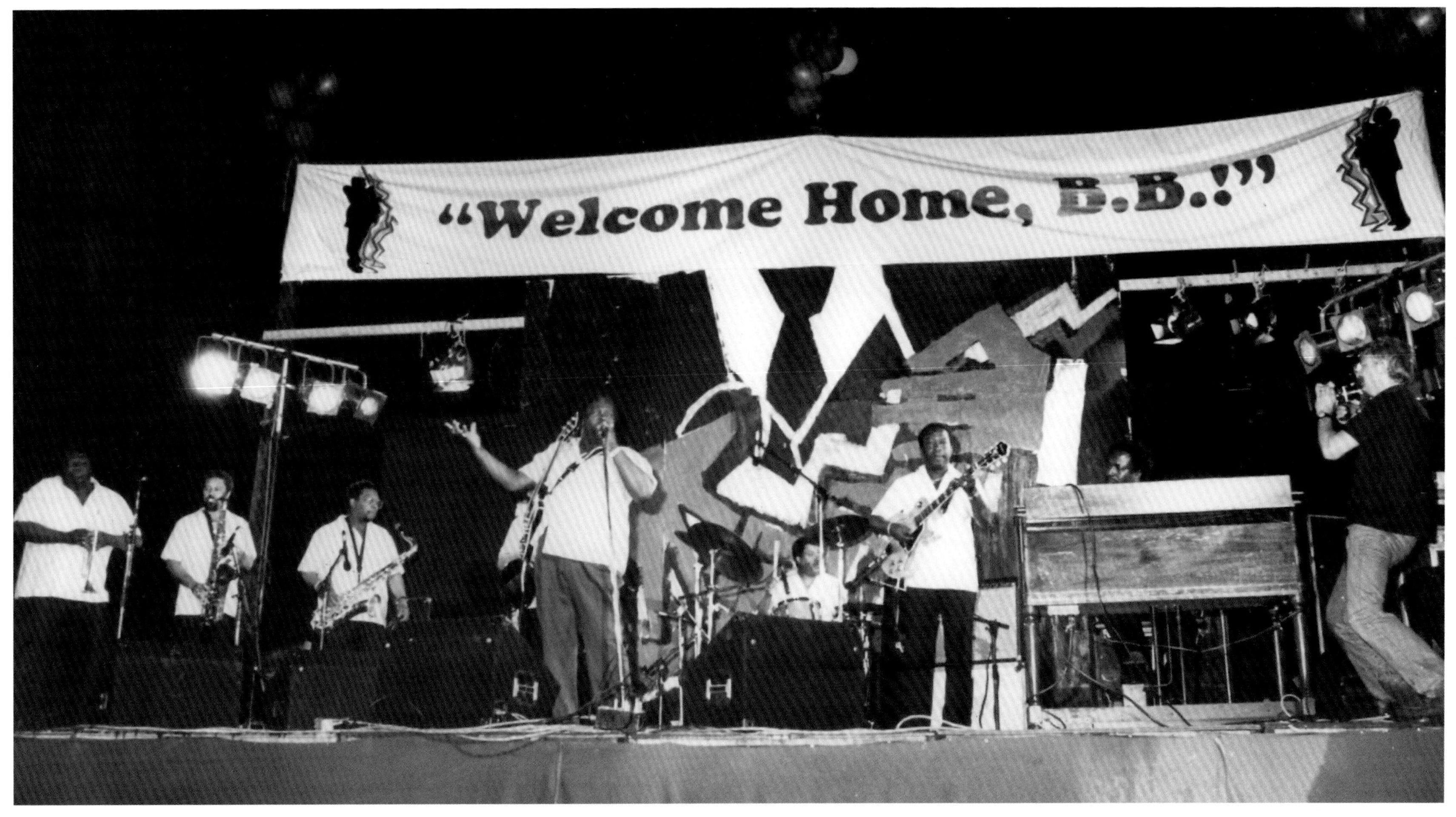

BB KING HOMECOMING CONCERTS

Recalling many events/ceremonies I've photographed as a journalist, I must rate B. B. King's Homecoming Concerts among my favorites. A primary problem was getting there. The date—usually the last Friday in May or the first Friday in June—frequently conflicted with a championship barbecue competition in Clarksdale, Delta Jubilee. Another problem was weather. For years, it rained—farmers almost counted on it—and the Memphis Cotton Carnival, practically a rain magnet, took place about the same time. But when the weather cleared and B. B.'s bus pulled into Indianola's community park, "The Thrill Is Gone" and "When Love Comes to Town" made everything perfect.

In 1989, probably my first year to attend, the BBC filmed a documentary of his concert beneath an enormous "Welcome Home, B. B." banner. Despite occasional drizzles, the show went on, and volunteers took turns holding a large umbrella over B. B. Inviting kids onstage with him for a dancing competition was always a big part of his show;

▲

In 1989, probably my first year to attend, the BBC filmed a documentary of his concert beneath an enormous "Welcome Home B. B." banner.

◄

Recalling many events/ceremonies I have photographed as a journalist, I must rate B. B. King's Homecoming Concerts in Indianola among my favorites.

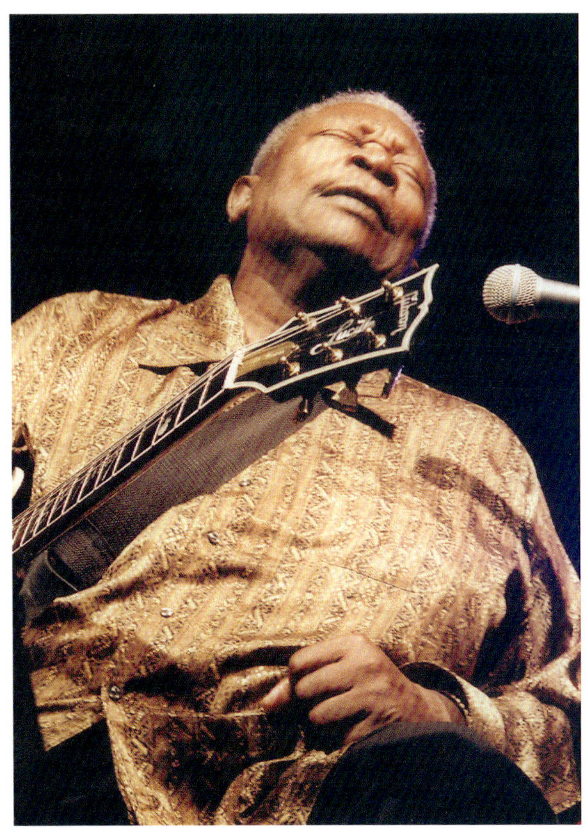

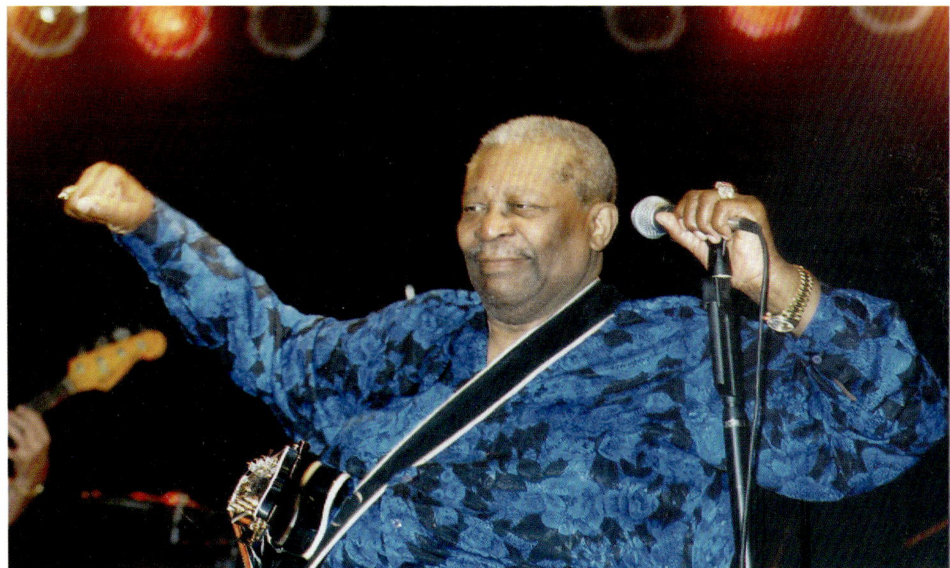

later he even donned a cape and let ladies massage his neck and arms with lotion. Always a gentleman, always connecting with his audience, surely B. B. was the quintessential ambassador for Mississippi and America. At a Mississippi Valley State University press conference, he generously autographed my photos of him reproduced in Sebastian Danchin's biography published by University Press of Mississippi. Asked if he would change anything in his life, he named two things: "I would get an education," he said, and, "I would not marry till I was 40."

GOVERNOR'S AWARD FOR EXCELLENCE IN THE ARTS

During Black History Month in 2004, Sam Carr was presented an extraordinary award for a blues musician: an engraved plaque from Thompson Chapel praising his accomplishments, and an invitation to perform music not normally welcomed by preachers. The plaque honored him for the excellence of his representation of Lula, Moon Lake,

▲ Inviting kids on stage with him for a dancing competition was always a big part of his show. Always a gentleman, always connecting with his audience, surely B. B. was the quintessential ambassador for Mississippi and America.

During Black History Month 2004, Sam Carr was presented an extraordinary award for a blues musician: an invitation to perform music not normally welcomed by preachers. While drumming inside the small white frame church beneath the Mississippi River levee near Lula, Sam cried but he never missed a beat.

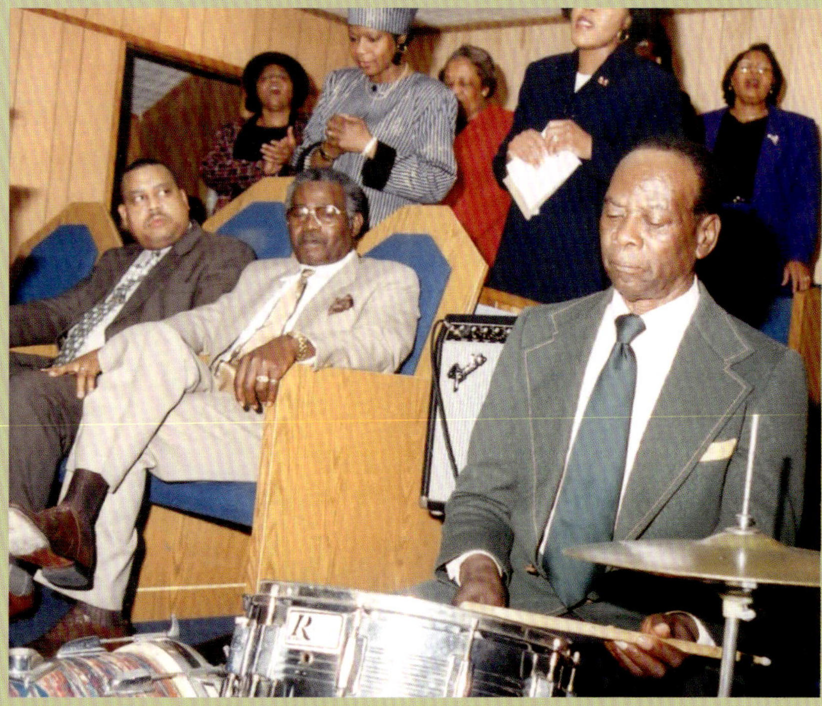

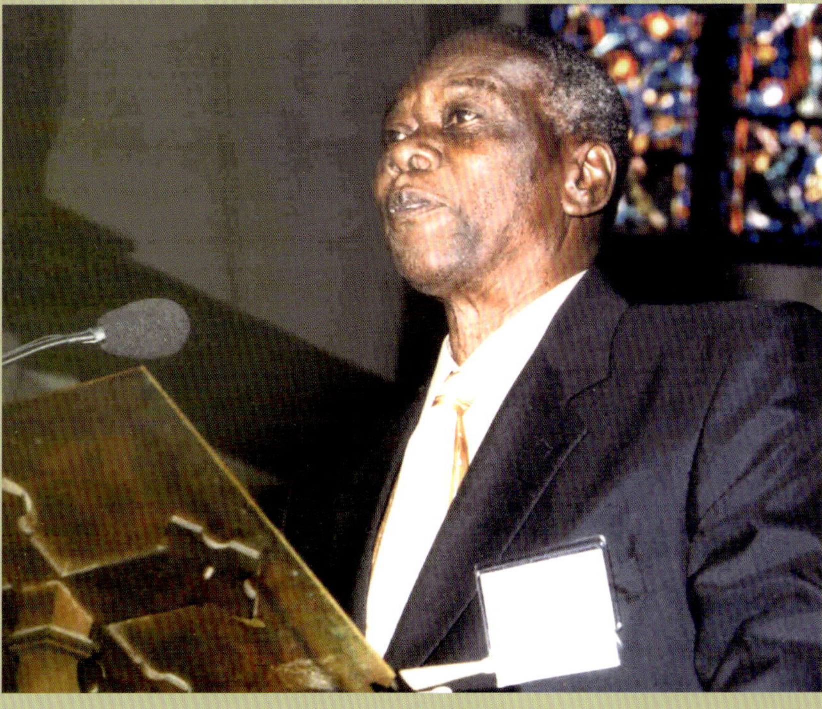

Three years later, inside St. Andrew's Episcopal Cathedral of Jackson before a larger audience, Sam was cited for his contributions to Mississippi's heritage as a Governor's Award recipient.

At an elite gathering in the Governor's Mansion, Sam and the governor reminisce about Conway Twitty's Club on Moon Lake when Barbour was a college student and Sam and the Jelly Roll Kings were the house band.

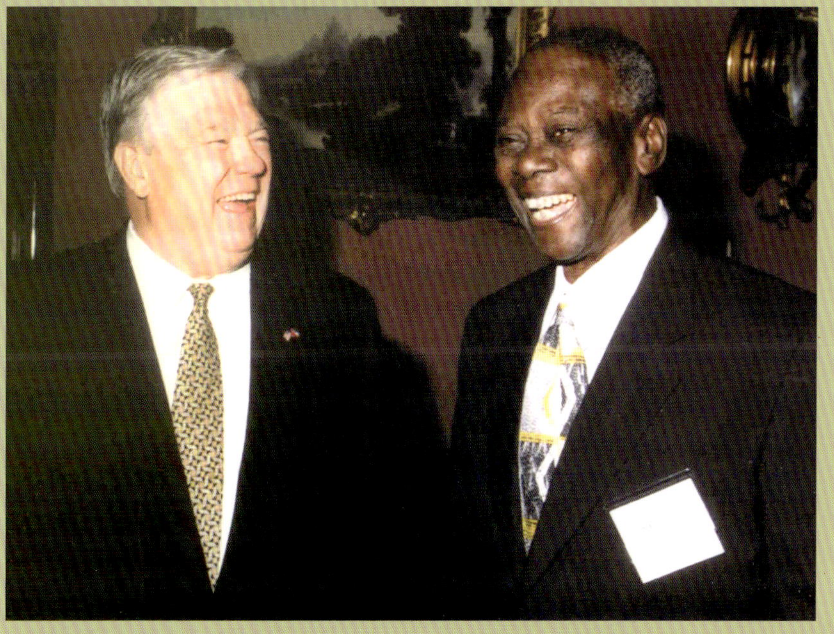

and the Mississippi Delta in capitals around the world. While drumming inside the small white frame church beneath the Mississippi River levee near Lula, Sam cried, but he never missed a beat.

Three years later, inside St. Andrew's Episcopal Cathedral of Jackson, he was cited before a larger audience for his contributions to Mississippi's heritage as a Governor's Award for Excellence in the Arts recipient. "Sam's gonna cry," predicted Doris Carr, his wife of sixty years. Wrong. Beneath the hundred-year-old cathedral's soaring gothic arches and brilliant stained glass windows, Sam Carr stood tall and dignified as he spoke from a bronze lectern. "I thank everybody for coming," he said simply after shaking hands with Gov. Haley Barbour and First Lady Marsha Barbour.

While playing with Bo Diddley the night before at the Mississippi Arts Commission reception, his drumsticks spoke eloquently for him before cheering fans and flashing cameras. At an elite gathering at the Governor's Mansion, Sam and the governor reminisced about Conway Twitty's Club on Moon Lake when Barbour was an Ole Miss college student recruiting bands, and Sam and the Jelly Roll Kings were the house band. Later surrounded by guests and fans requesting autographs and private conversations, Sam held his own in the impressive dining room glittering with silver and gold. I asked him what he thought of the governor. "Which one was he?" Sam replied.

▶ While playing with Bo Diddley at the Mississippi Arts Commission reception, Sam's drumsticks speak eloquently for him before cheering fans and flashing cameras.

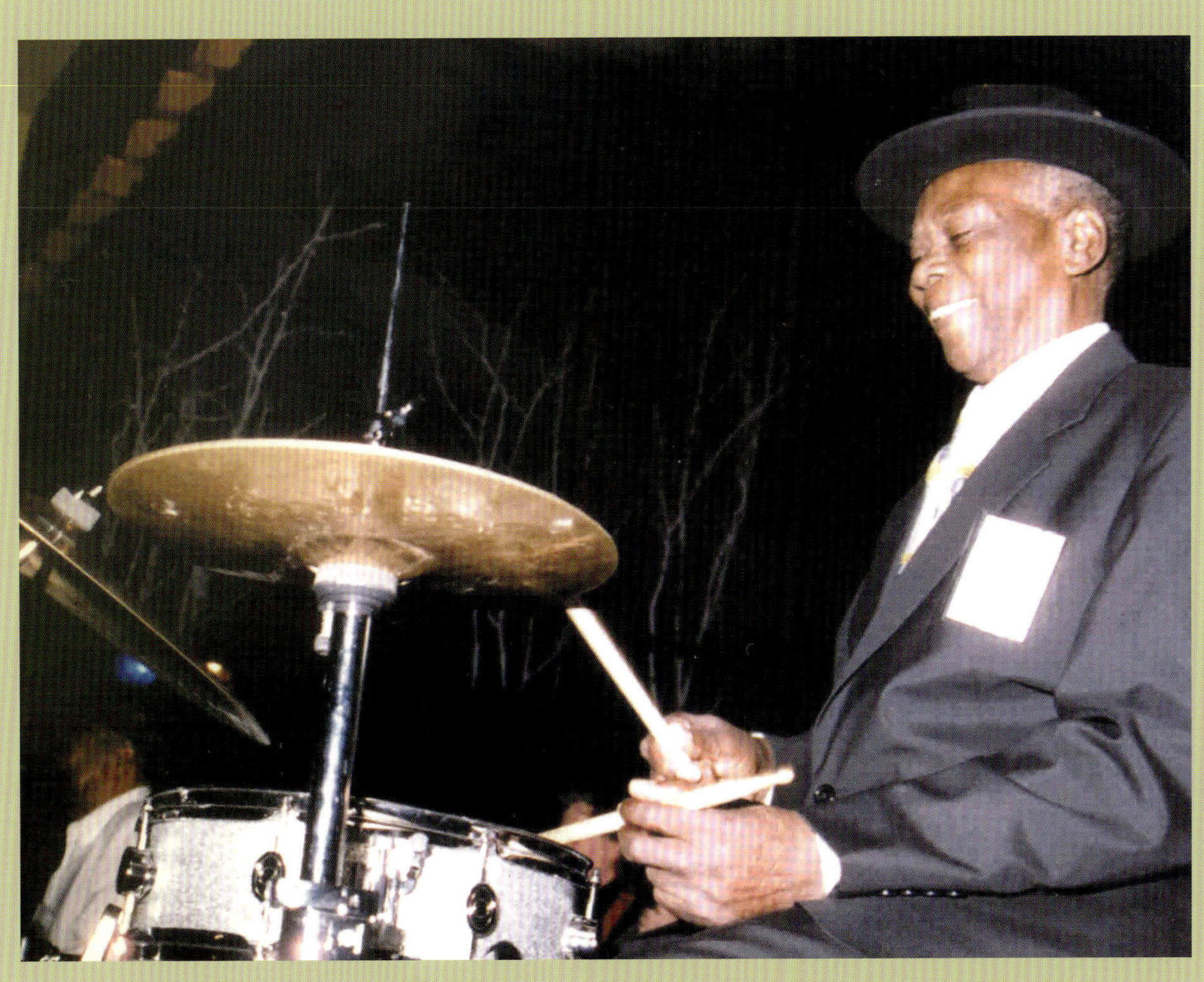

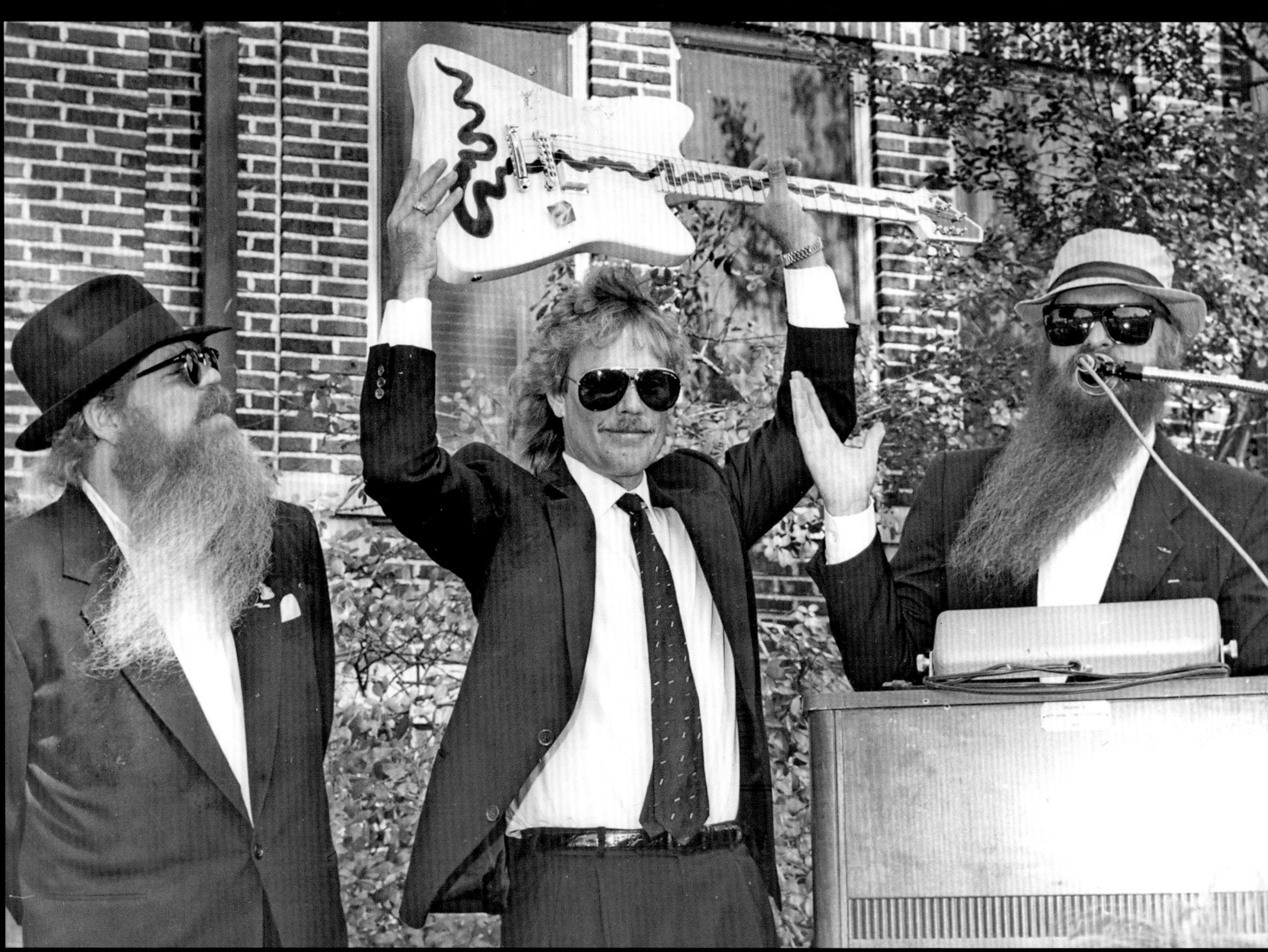

5

INTERNATIONAL ICONS

As a journalist for a relatively small daily newspaper, I supplemented my income photographing events, and writing features for larger publications and magazines. This was great fun, and it also introduced me to some amazing individuals and international icons. Billy Gibbons and ZZ Top were the first major rock band to attract global audiences here. In the 1980s between recording sessions at Ardent Studios in Memphis, Billy Gibbons, Dusty Hill, and Frank Beard drove down Highway 61 to visit Stovall Plantation, home of Muddy Waters, their spiritual and musical godfather influencing their bluesy roots.

Muddy's performances on ZZ's spectacular 1976 Worldwide Texas Tour, with live animals and plants onstage, are documented in the September 1989 *Musician* magazine article titled "How Tres Hombres Discovered the Electric Guitar" by Timothy Wade. The stage is described online as having a 180-foot hand-painted backdrop where

In the 1980s Billy Gibbons and ZZ Top were the first major rock band to attract global audiences to Mississippi Delta Blues via a tribute to their mentor and Coahoma County native Muddy Waters. In a media extravaganza ZZ unveiled a guitar christened the Muddywood, fashioned from cypress taken from Muddy's cabin on Stovall Plantation, and launched a $1 million world tour

a longhorn steer, a black buffalo, two vultures, two rattlesnakes, yucca, and cacti cohabited with the musicians.

To answer Timothy Wade's questions about ZZ's initial contact with Muddy Waters, Billy Gibbons talked about their meeting backstage in 1973 in Burlington, Iowa, on a blues tour described as a poker game that traveled. Gibbons said, "We were so excited because it was our first face-to-face meeting with Muddy, and we asked Freddie King if he could introduce us 'cause we had a coupla records out that were doing okay and we were feeling pretty good about it. So Freddie ushered us in and said, 'Excuse me, Muddy, but these are several fellas on the show tonight. I'd like you to meet them: ZZ Top.'" He said Muddy smiled for about half a second, turned and said, "Pleased to meet-cha," and went right back to the poker game. Following shop talk about Muddy Waters and Willie Dixon blues hits they admired and their own phenomenal success, Wade asked how Muddy "came to open for their 1976 Worldwide Texas Tour."

Gibbons replied: "We had kept up a loose friendship through the years, and when Muddy would play at a place down on Rush Street in Chicago called Mr. Kelly's, we'd always go and see him. It was a real uptown scene, a concert setting that was far removed from the Southside clubs. But we caught him a number of times because we'd walk up the street. So when we came down to Texas to do some home dates that year, we were just wondering what flavorful addition could we include to really embrace the feeling we were trying to give back to our home state. And the blues being such a big part of not only our music but everybody's music in Texas, Muddy Waters seemed the logical choice."

Asked if there was an opportunity at any point to sit down with Muddy informally and have him show a few things about his guitar style, Gibbons said he'd sneak a peek when he could. "One of my favorite licks of Muddy was on 'Rollin' Stone.' That was our best stolen riff, directly out of the Muddy catalogue. See, not only was his singing the most powerful thing you could ask for, but he had a top-flight band at all times, and really employed the inventors of this stuff. Some of the inversions of his, like that famous reversed seventh chord was so definitive in his work." Gibbons added that another tremendous contribution Muddy made to blues and rock 'n' roll was his brilliant Delta slide guitar.

Visiting Clarksdale between recording breaks in Memphis, Billy Gibbons began dropping in on bluesman/barber Wade Walton, with Wade enjoying eyeing and kidding him about his long red beard. The rock star also discovered the Delta Blues Museum inside Carnegie

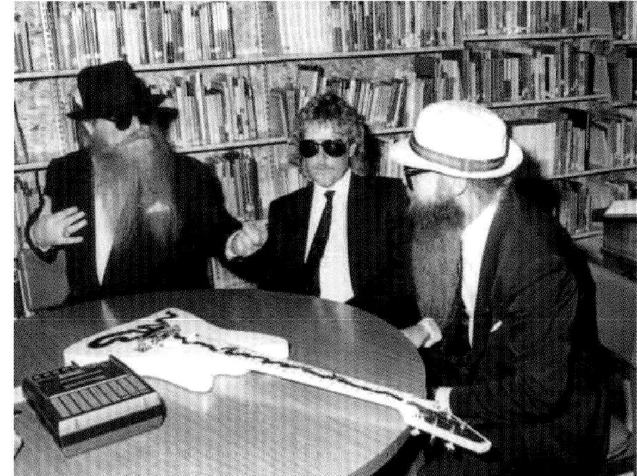

Public Library and visited with Sid Graves, who founded the museum in 1979 with support from the library board headed by David Califf. Impressed with the town's blues heritage, Billy returned from time to time and eventually formed a grand plan to launch a $1 million campaign to honor Muddy and to expand the museum into a tribute to all Delta blues musicians. In 1988 Dassinger Creative Services (DSC), ZZ's public relations firm in New York City, issued dozens of news releases to media emphasizing how the Muddywood guitar unveiling was payback time to their mentor. Their media extravaganza unveiling the Muddywood guitar in April 1988 was successful in attracting dozens of journalists, including Robert Palmer, music editor of the *New York Times*, writers from the *Village Voice*, *People*, *Rolling Stone*, and *Guitar*, plus MTV news anchor Kurt Loder, who conducted live interviews with Early Wright, bluesmen Sam Carr and Frank Frost, city officials, and Warner Brothers executives. The all-day event spotlighted the city of Clarksdale, its diverse musical and multicultural heritage, and culminated in a downhome catfish and hush-puppy supper for hundreds in the City Auditorium, followed by a packed-house late-night gig for original Muddy Waters band members playing in the Crossroads Blues Club.

ZZ's mission and links with Clarksdale continued through the years via the Muddywood guitar tour of international Hard Rock Cafes launched September 4, 1988, on NBC's *Today* show with Dan Aykroyd and Paul Shaffer. The guitar tour traveled to Dallas, Chicago, Houston, New Orleans, Los Angeles, Tokyo, Stockholm, London, Boston, and New York City. ZZ's hospitality extended to museum staffers and myself, given VIP credentials to attend Grammy Night atop the Peabody Hotel's Skyway with Jerry Lee Lewis and Rufus Thomas, attend their 1991 Recycler show in the Memphis Coliseum, and the Beale Street Music Fest they headlined during "Memphis in May." Although thrilled with the posh buffet before the Recycler concert with its junkyard towers on stage, we fell in love later with the Beale Street Fest backstage extravagance for its headliners on the Mississippi riverbanks. I asked which bus in the parking lot belonged to ZZ and was told all three musicians had a bus of his own. A fourth was filled with food and beverages, which Johnnie Billington and his blues students especially enjoyed.

ZZ didn't hit and run but continued the connection, flying a Lear jet full of blondes and well-heeled Texas visitors into Fletcher Field. So did a coordinated extravaganza at Madison Square Garden starring another Clarksdale native, John Lee Hooker. Many staff members went to NYC and hobnobbed with Johnny Winter, Gregg Allman, and John

Camera crews from MTV and other networks, Warner Brothers executives, and print media from *Rolling Stone* to the *Village Voice* interviewed ZZ inside Carnegie Public Library.

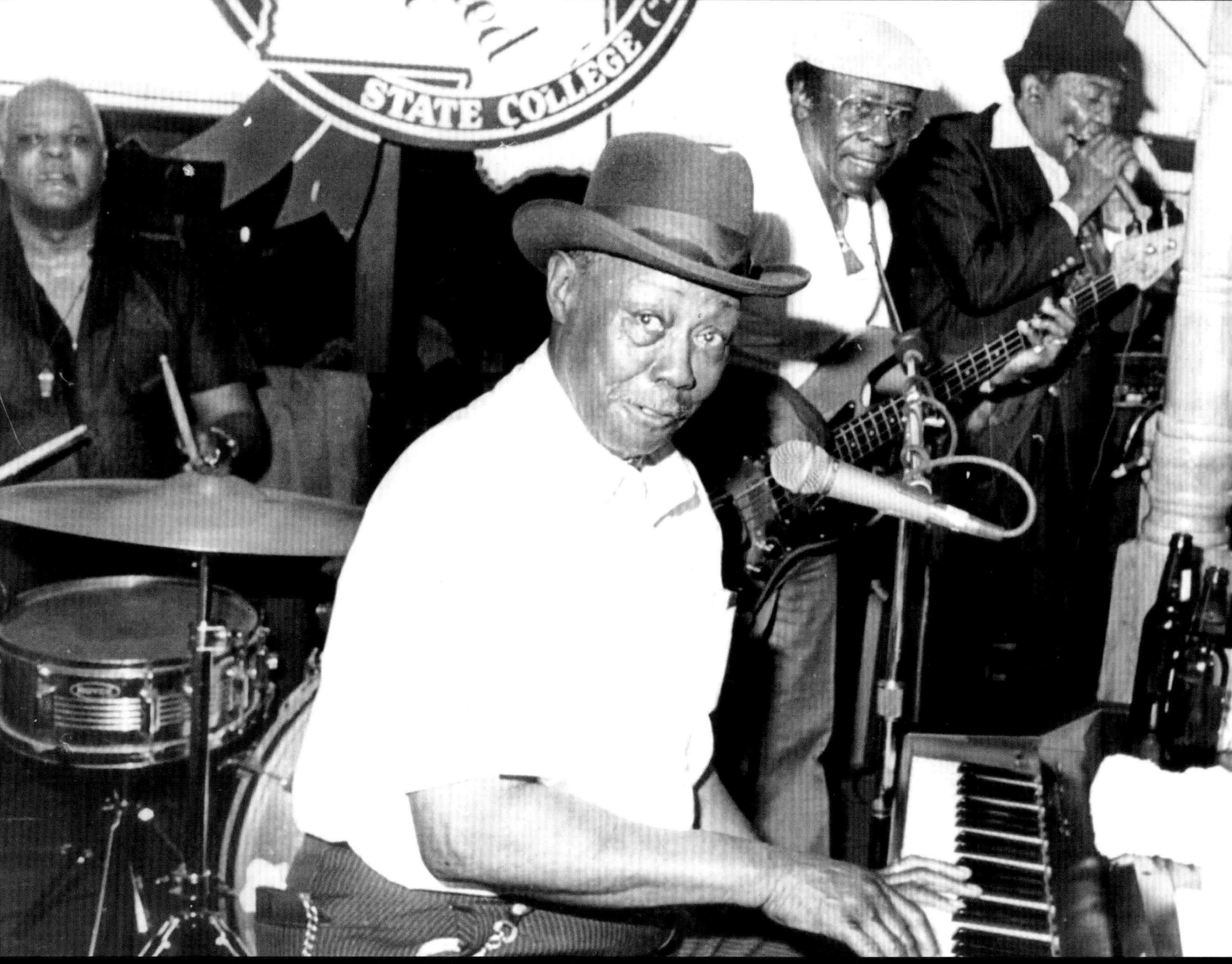

Still hyped and performing in the early morning hours at the Cotton Exchange on Delta Avenue following a catfish supper and ZZ's second presentation in the Civic Auditorium are former members of Muddy Waters Band, anchored by Pinetop Perkins on keyboard.

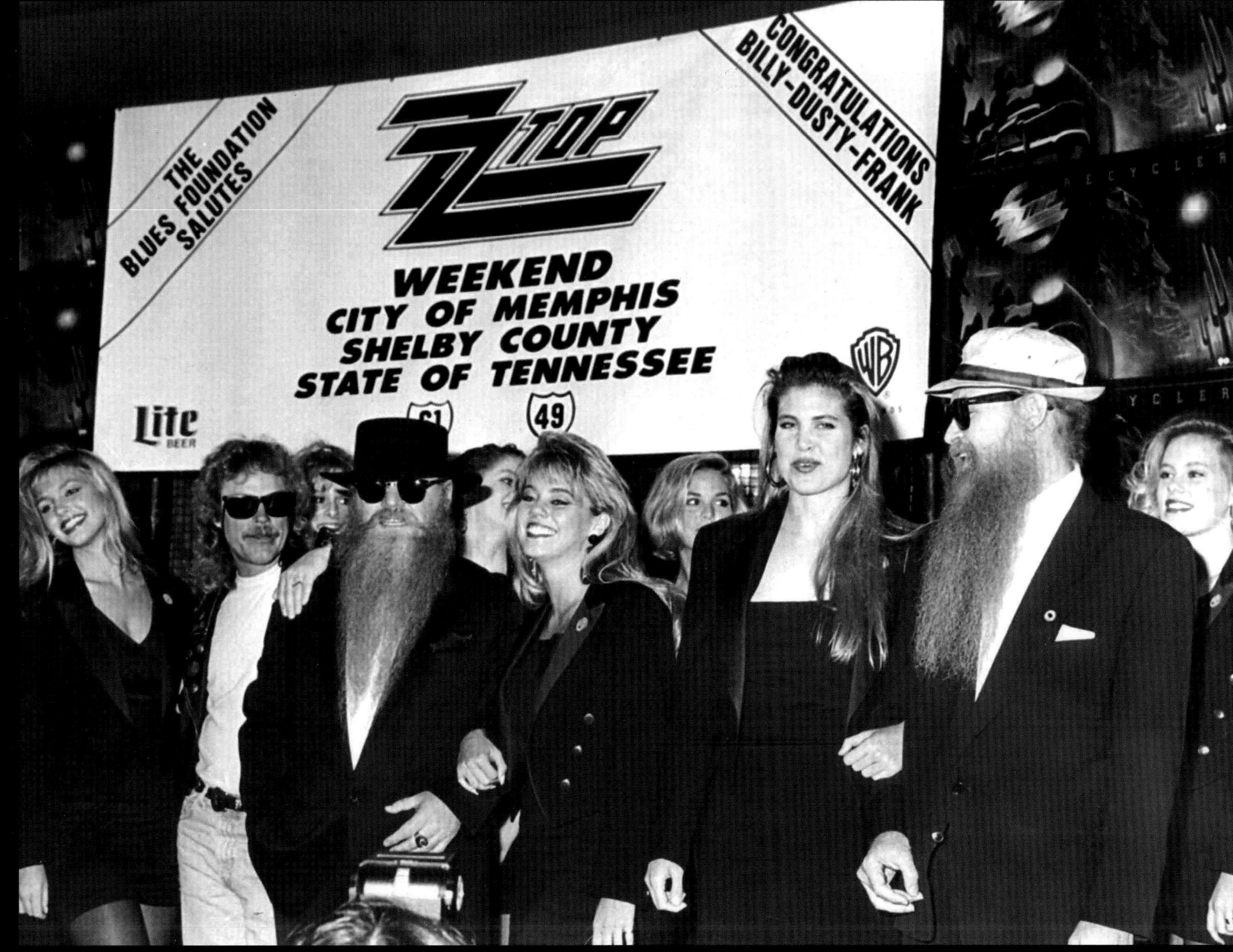

ZZ didn't hit and run; they continued the connection, distributing backstage passes for their rock concerts, flying a Lear jet full of blondes and well-heeled Texans into Fletcher Field, and hosting staffers and blues students on Grammy night at the Peabody.

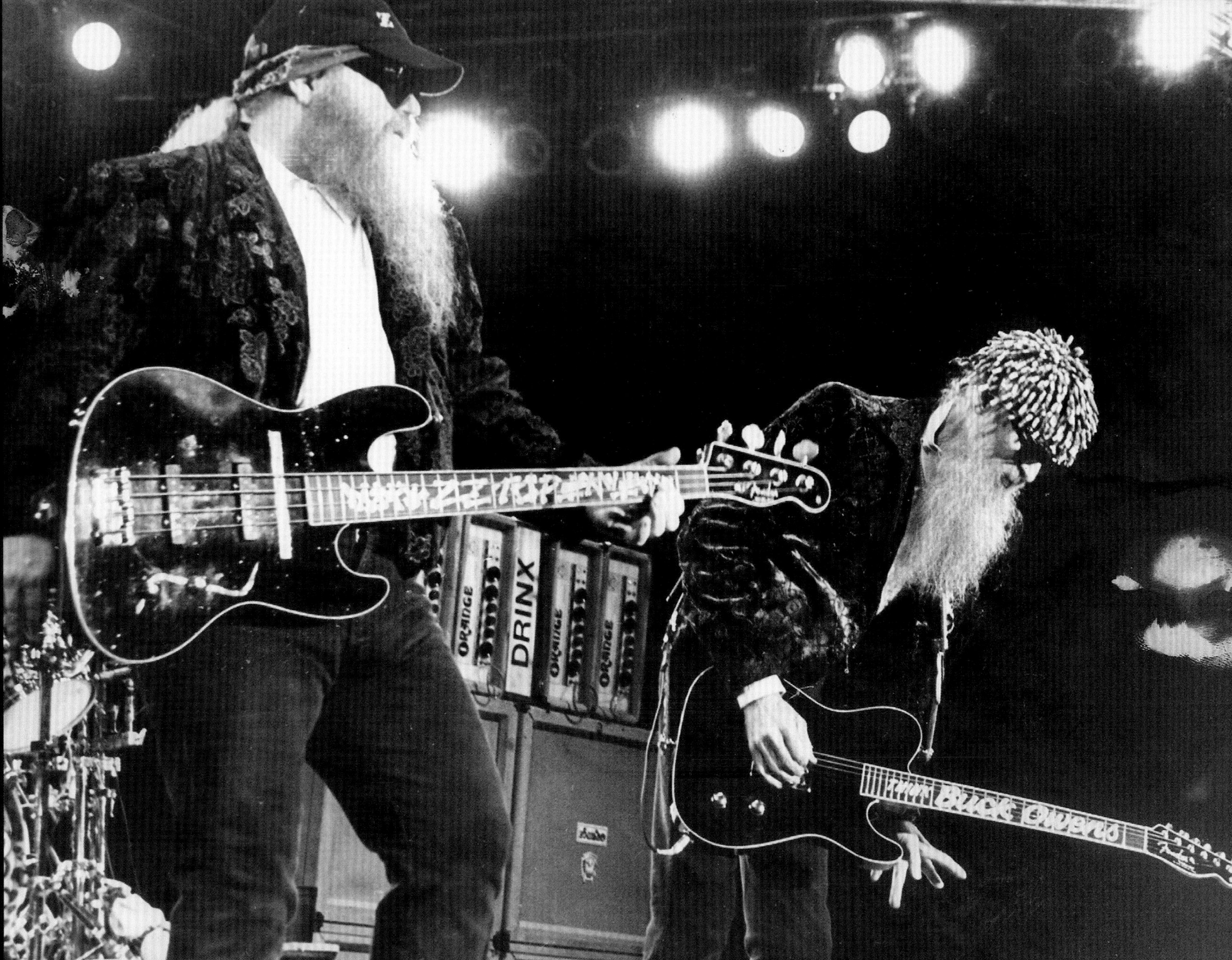

ZZ TOP
DRINX
ORANGE
ORANGE
ORANGE
Buck Owens

On one of his frequent trips to Clarksdale, Billy
Gibbons enjoys an up-close and personal tour of
the Muddy Waters cabin on Stovall Road with Sid
Graves, Carnegie Library and Delta Blues Museum
director, and Jim O'Neal, founding editor of *Living
Blues* magazine.

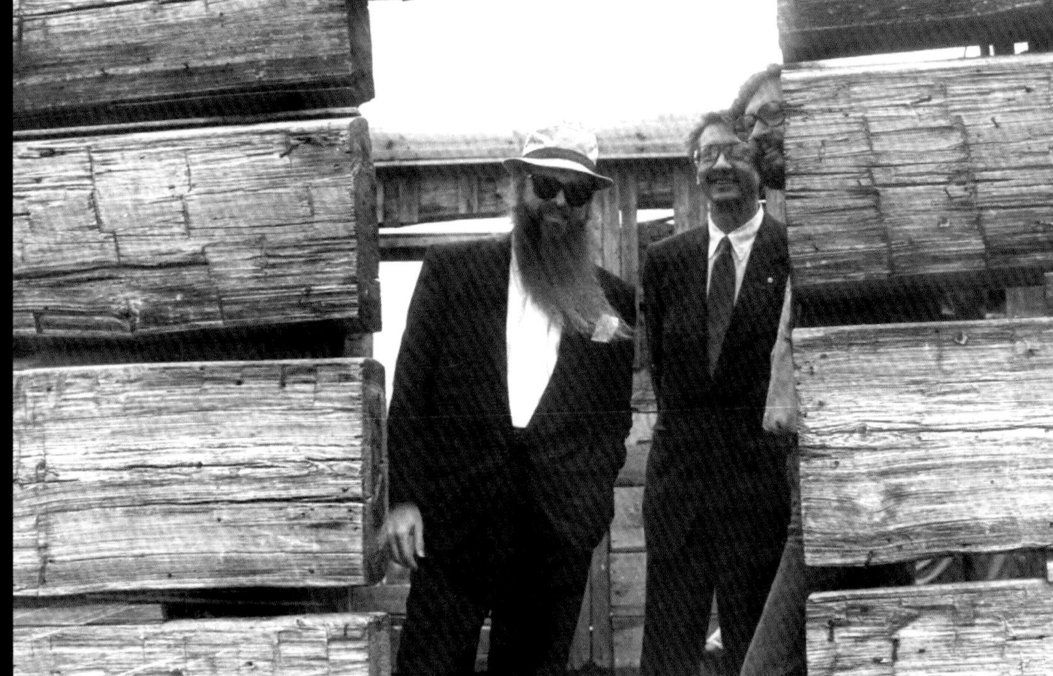

Jerry Lee Lewis joins Sid Graves and ZZ Top at
Grammy Night atop the Peabody Hotel in Memphis.

Lee. Eventually following the museum's relocation from Carnegie Public Library to its present Blues Alley location in a historic former railroad freight depot, it expanded with a Muddy Waters wing. The DBM would later attract other famous patrons—but ZZ's Billy, Dusty, and Frank were the first and are honored in Clarksdale's Walk of Fame.

CHARLIE MUSSELWHITE

It's weird how walls of the Thompson Center, an old vaudeville theater needing renovation, have resounded with incredible talent through the years. Charlie Musselwhite and his band moved their Sunflower concert inside when rain showers started that Friday night in August 1995. Acoustics were bell clear, and Charlie's signature "Cristo Redentor" rocketed through its vaulted ceiling on a direct course to the moon. Charlie told me "Cristo" composer Duke Pearson once said he was coming into the harbor of Rio when he first saw the outstretched arms of Jesus and heard the music. I was so captivated with this composition that the Musselwhites taped ten versions and mailed them back to me.

Charlie and Clarksdale adopted each other that night. On and off the stage, he's a crowd favorite and has returned many times to perform, visit, and enjoy soul food. When friends sympathized over his bad luck and near-fatal collision with an eighteen-wheel rig in Mexico, and Henri's (Henrietta) shark attack in Hawaii, Charlie quickly replied, "Actually we feel pretty lucky."

A tireless ambassador for Mississippi, he was awarded the Governor's Award for Excellence in the Arts in 2000. As a finale on stages from Croatia to Mexico City, to Norway and Brazil and China, Charlie closes his concerts with this admonition: "If you love blues, you need one time in your life to make the pilgrimage—not a trip—but a pilgrimage to Clarksdale and the Mississippi Delta. This is where all the greats come from—Charley Patton, Son House, and Muddy Waters. Blues comes right out of the ground. You can reach down and put some in your pocket and take it home."

Revered globally by musicians of many genres, Charlie is a virtuoso harmonica master. He has recorded with such diverse artists as Tom Waits, whom he brought to Clarksdale for the Tennessee Williams Festival, to renowned Cuban guitarist Eliades Ochoa of Buena Vista Social Club fame. His artistry is so admired in Cuba that he often received emails from members of the Havana Blues Society. He connected me with this group in the early 2000s, and I traveled there

▶   Charlie Musselwhite and his band moved their Sunflower Fest concert inside the Thompson Center, an old vaudeville theater needing renovation, when rain showers started that Friday night in August 1995. Acoustics were bell clear, and Charlie's signature "Cristo Redentor" rocketed through the vaulted ceiling on a direct course to the moon.

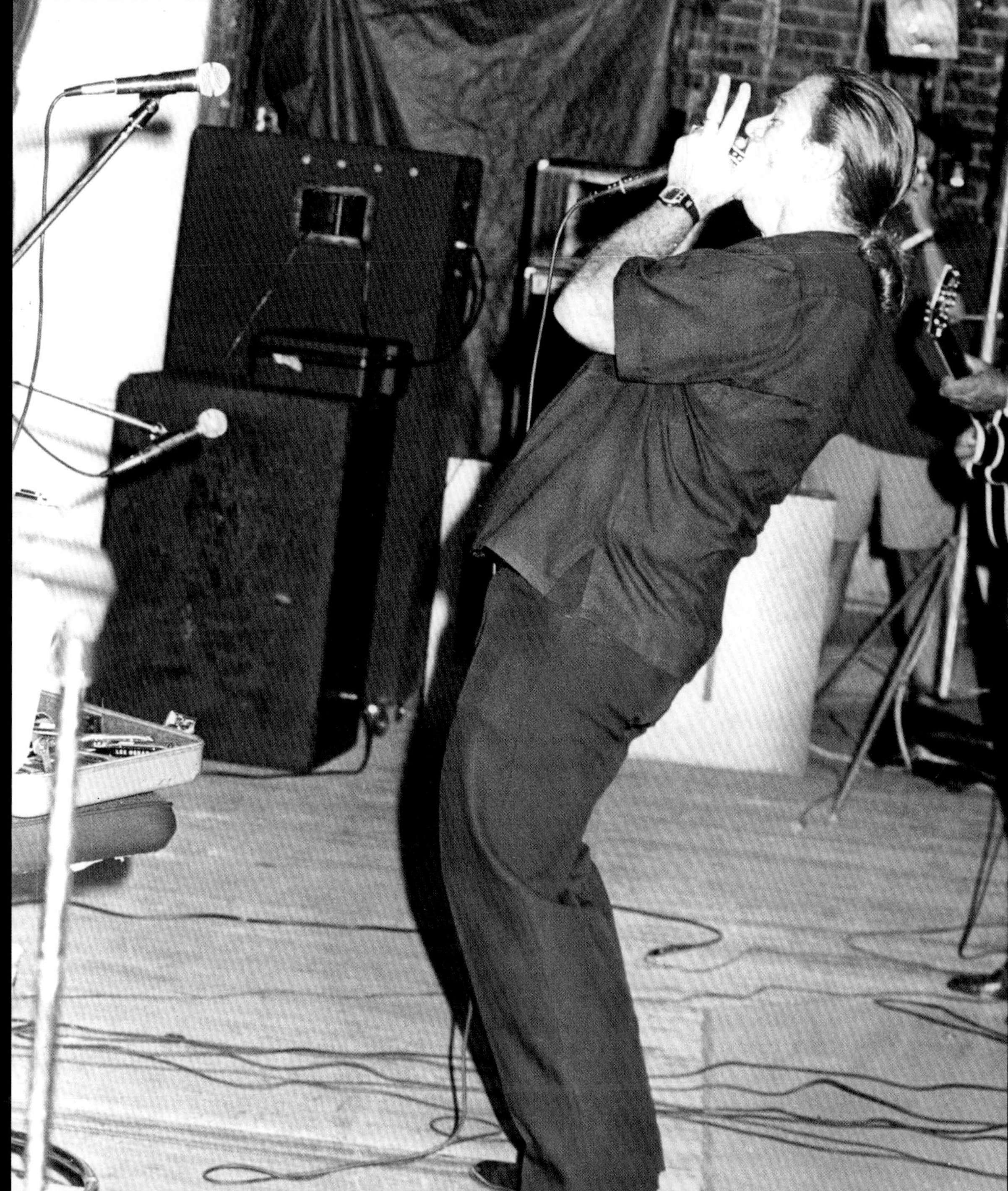

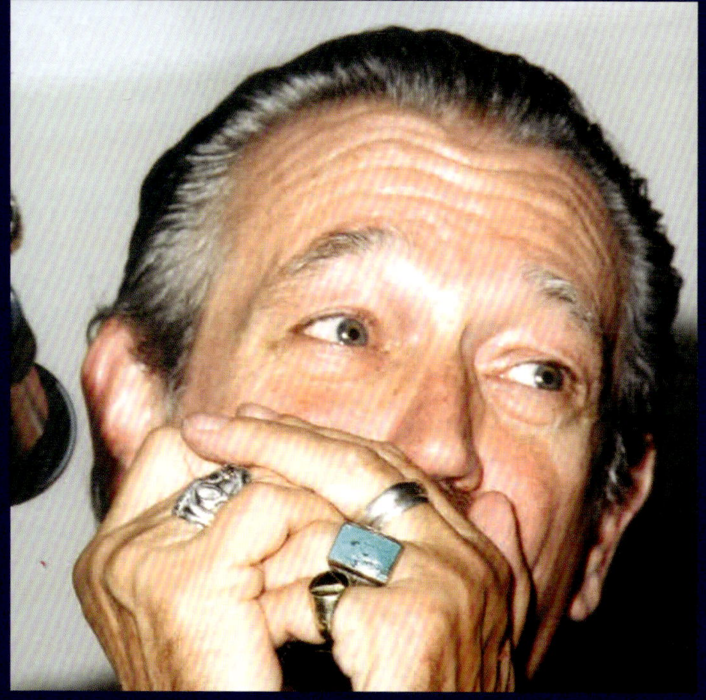

As a finale on stages from Croatia to Mexico City, from Norway to China, Charlie closes his concerts with this admonition: "If you love blues, you need one time in your life to make the pilgrimage—not a trip—but a pilgrimage to Clarksdale and the Mississippi Delta. This is where all the greats come from—Charley Patton, Son House, and Muddy Waters. Blues comes right out of the ground. You can reach down and put some in your pocket and take it home."

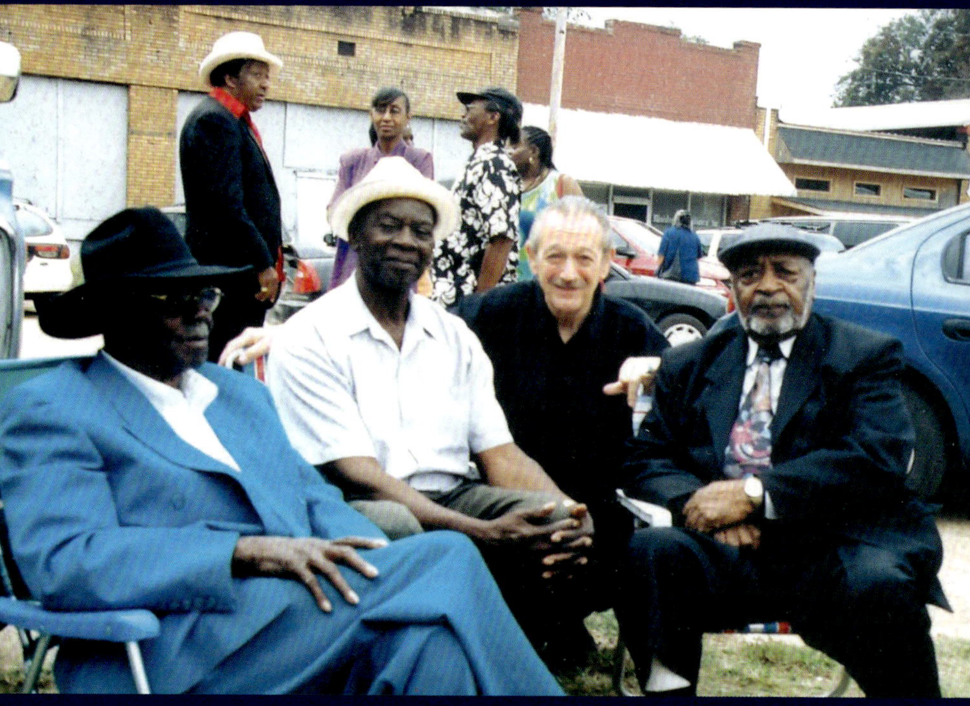

▲

Music legends visiting and celebrating the Year of the Blues Centennial together in Tutwiler in October 2003 include (from left) Pinetop Perkins, Sam Carr, Charlie Musselwhite, and Robert Junior Lockwood.

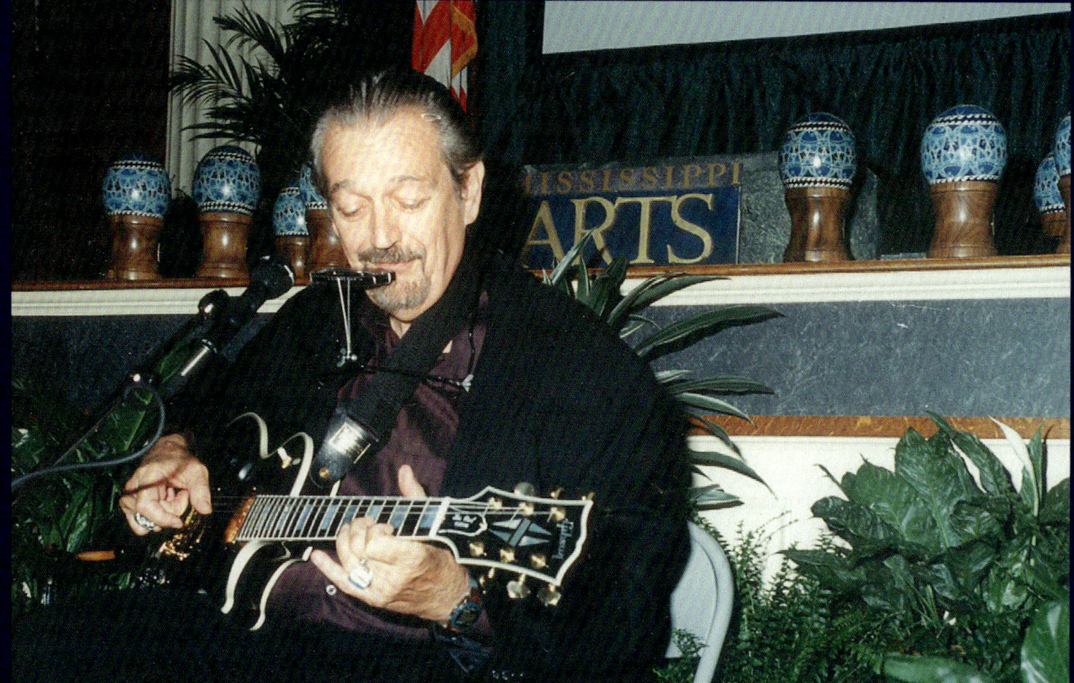

◄

Revered globally by musicians of many genres, Charlie is a virtuoso and a tireless ambassador for Mississippi. He brought down the house in the Old Capitol playing guitar and harmonica accepting the 2000 Governor's Award for Excellence in the Arts.

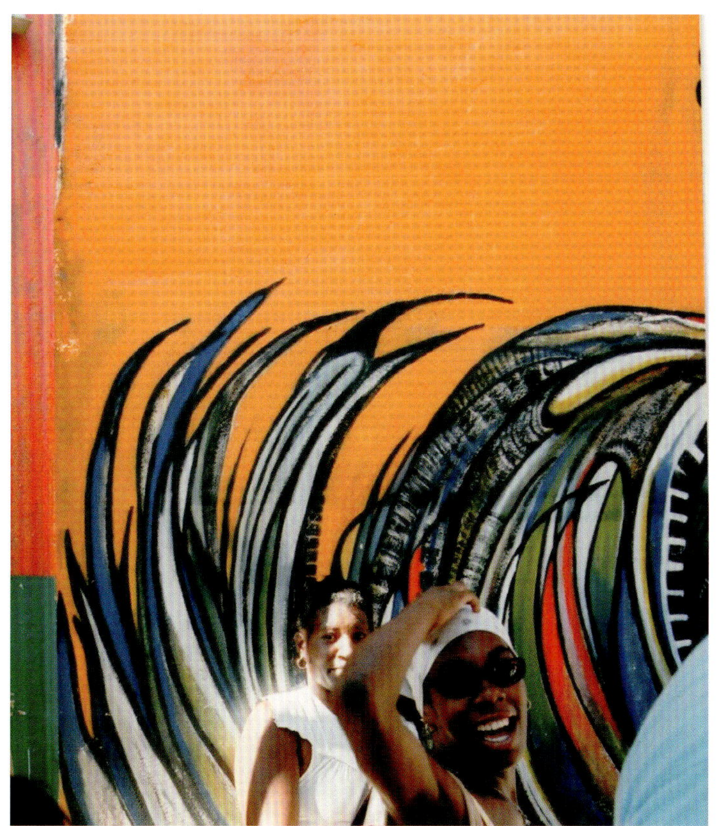

legally on a newspaper assignment to research Mississippi musicians in Cuba during the Spanish American War.

Although I was unable to visit Santiago, Cuba's center of traditional music, I fell in love with Havana and its lovely citizens. Welcoming me to family dinners and dancing to recordings of the Rolling Stones amid colorful caged parrots, I was even talked into puffing on a Cuban cigar and following the exciting rhythms of an Afro-Cuban drumming festival taking place down narrow neighborhood streets. In contrast, an elegant string orchestra played a sunset serenade each afternoon at a promontory overlooking the ocean on the grounds of the Nacional Hotel.

It's no secret Charlie loves soul food. Although the Musselwhites watch what they eat and even outlawed pork, beef, and sugar from their diets at one time, they seek out good country cooking. While headlining the 1995 Sunflower Festival, they feasted several times on black-eyed peas, Louise Campbell's turnip greens, cornbread, fresh tomatoes, cucumber, and cheese grits. But facing a weekend without more, they called one Sunday morning: "What about soul food in Helena?" Charlie asks.

▲

Following exciting rhythms and exotic sounds leads to a colorful Afro-Cuban drumming festival in Old Havana.

▶

An elegant string orchestra plays a sunset serenade each afternoon at a promontory overlooking the ocean on the grounds of the historic Nacional Hotel.

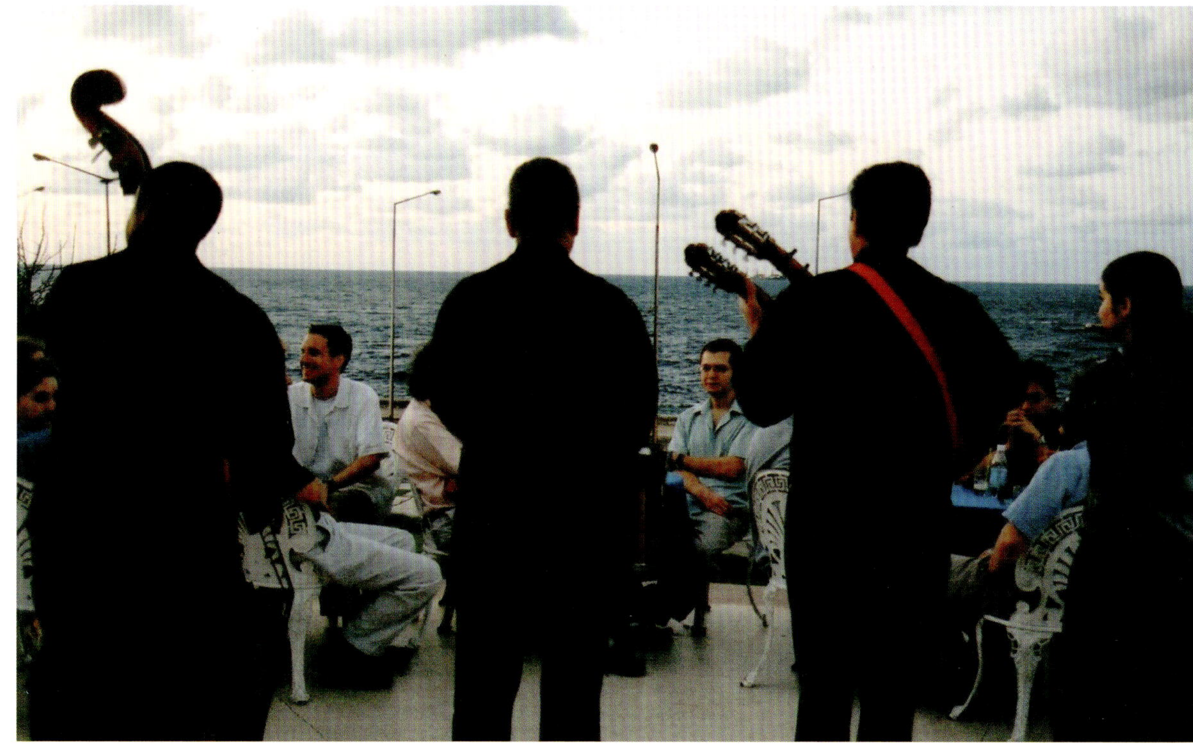

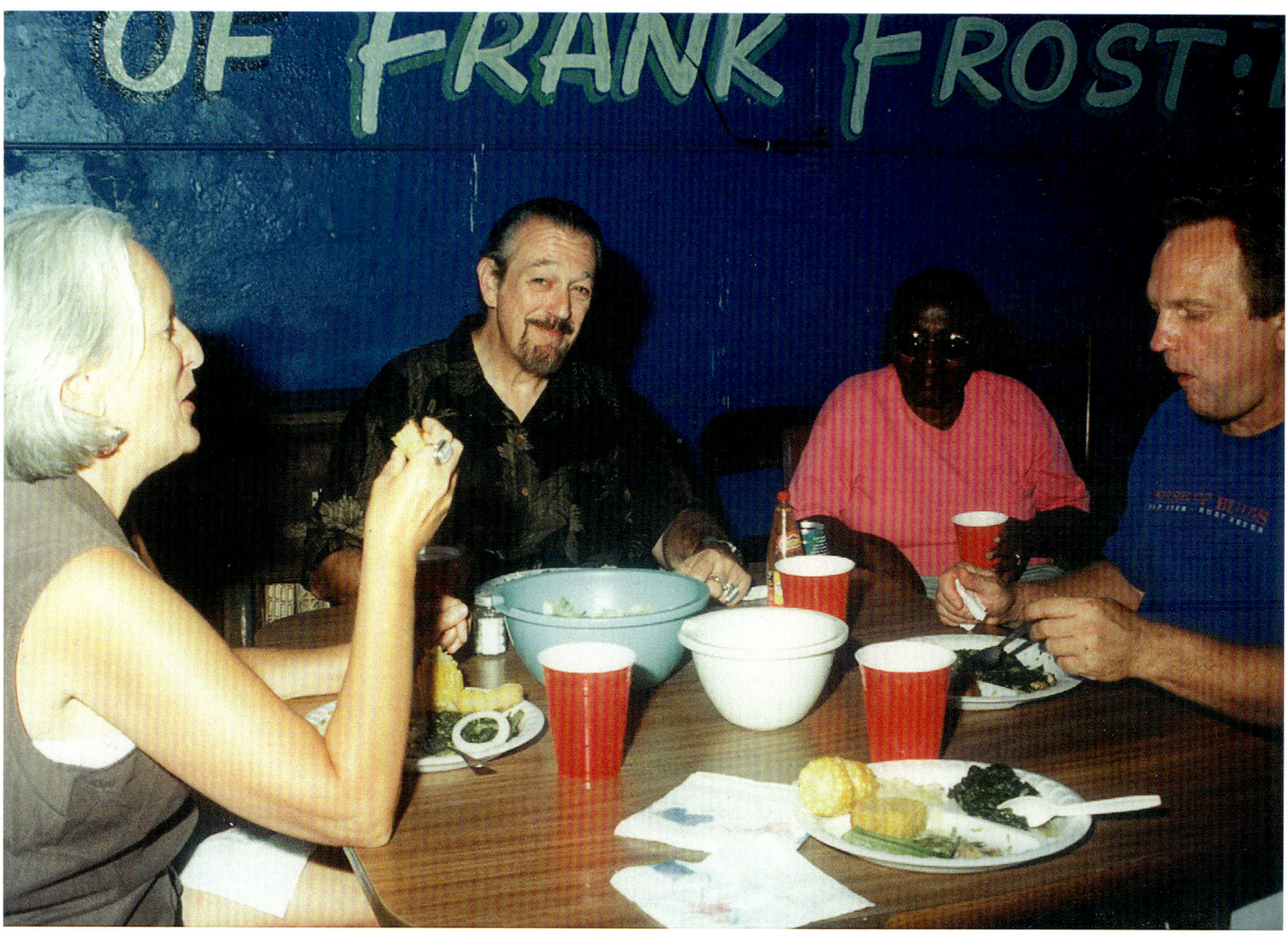

Eddie Mae Walton who runs Eddie Mae's, the hangout of Frank Frost, told me, "If you had called earlier, my friend Nora, who runs a café across the street, would have cooked something for you. But she's not at home now, she's at church." I ask: "What about you, Eddie Mae?" "Well, I'd have to go to the store, but I could get something together in a couple of hours," she replied.

Two hours later, the Musselwhites, Jim Krejici, their sound guy, and I were sitting down at Eddie Mae's chrome dinette table near a freshly painted mural proclaiming, "Home of Frank Frost." She brought out okra, cabbage, corn on the cob, green beans, sliced onions, lettuce and tomato salad, cornbread, and turnip greens. Eddie Mae pulled up a chair and asked, "What did you say your name is?" Charlie replied that he plays a little guitar and harmonica and knows Frank Frost.

A couple of tourists with cameras drifted in from the sidewalk asking, "Is this a café?" Ever a businesswoman, Eddie Mae immediately answered, "Sure is." Disappearing and making rustling noises in the kitchen, she returns to our table. "Are you through with that salad?"

▲ Frank Frost's lady, Eddie Mae Walton, whips up a Sunday soul food brunch in Helena for Henri and Charlie Musselwhite, and Jim Krejici.

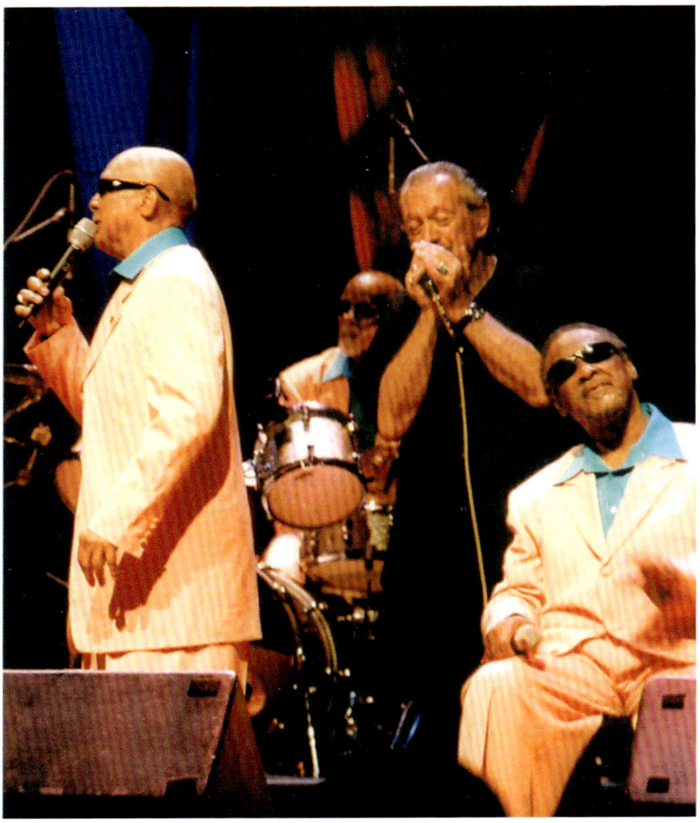

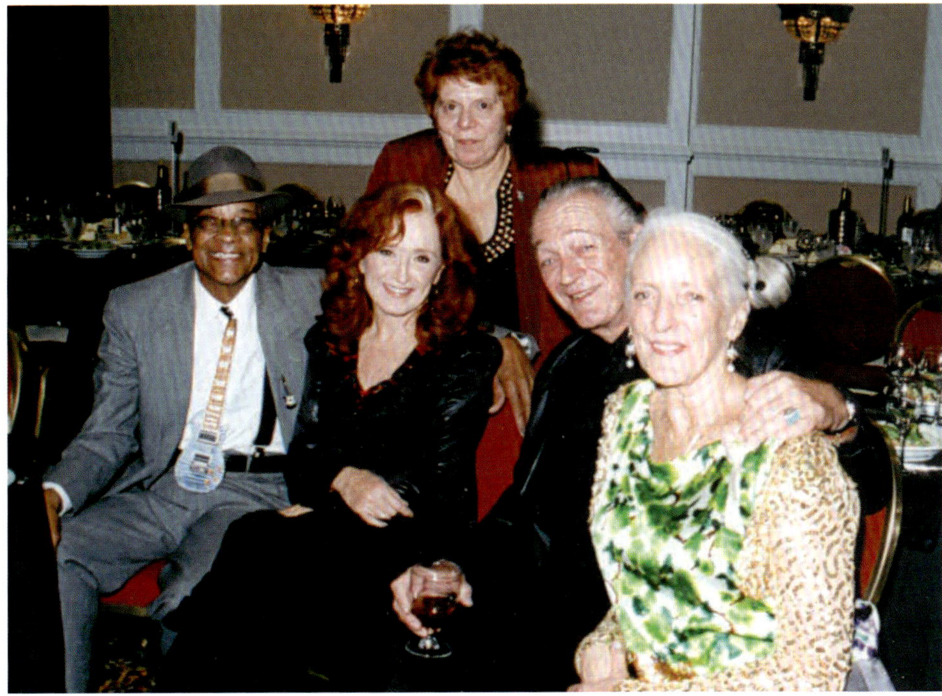

▲

Clarence Fountain (seated) welcomes Charlie Musselwhite into joining their Blind Boys of Alabama if pending eye surgery is not successful.

▶

Celebrating Charlie Musselwhite's induction into the Blues Foundation Hall of Fame in Memphis are (from left) blues musician Hubert Sumlin, Judy Peiser, Center for Southern Folklore director, Bonnie Raitt, and Charlie and Henrietta Musselwhite.

she asked, transferring it to the newcomer's booth. In a minute she returned with another question for Henrietta Musselwhite, "Are you tired of your fork?" Henri smiled and surrendered her fork.

One spring evening after supper, when we were sitting on my front porch, Charlie said something was wrong with one of his eyes—he couldn't see objects on his left. "You're kidding, right?" "Actually, no. I can't see," was his reply. Immediately I phoned our ophthalmologist/friend Tom Cooper, who was not at home. However, we met his partner Victor Pang at their clinic. After his examination, the diagnosis—a detached retina—was not good news. Charlie needed surgery ASAP.

However, he was in the area not only for the Memphis Handy Awards the next night, Thursday but also to play with the Blind Boys of Alabama Friday night at the Gertrude Ford Center in Oxford. With Dr. Pang pulling strings and scheduling specialists for surgery in Memphis Saturday, a plan evolved with Charlie keeping his commitments if he promised to tone down the energy level of both concerts.

I missed hearing him perform at the Handys but drove to Oxford Friday, where Clarence Fountain, leader of the Blind Boys, was making this strange announcement from the stage: "Our good friend Charlie Musselwhite, who is playing with us tonight, is facing a serious eye operation tomorrow in Memphis. I have assured him that if things do not go well, he's welcome to join the Blind Boys of Alabama." The crowd gasped, went silent, then thundered with applause. A rare evening of music followed. Early Saturday morning Charlie's surgery was successful. He was unable to fly home, but he and Henri returned on the train.

IKE TURNER

Behind the white linen shorts, gold chains, designer shoes, and entourage of beautiful women, an utterly charming Ike Turner was a hometown boy revisiting scenes and friends from his childhood on his last trip to Clarksdale. Descending unannounced on Fourth Street and Issaquena in a convoy of Cadillacs, Ike clowned for photographers beneath the city's art deco Greyhound bus station, Haggard's drugstore, and the New Roxy Theatre. Turner, who was living in Los Angeles at the time, was in town for a photo shoot of hometown scenes to publicize his new CD.

"Where's WROX?" he asked, since he once worked as a disc jockey for the historic blues radio station, before his celebrity days on keyboard and his reign as music impresario with his former wife Tina Turner.

"Ike's still the same," says C. V. Veal of Clarksdale, his longtime friend and former drummer, who was still working for Hyde Brothers lumber yard. Things happen when he's around."

Spinning stories from his youth, Ike raced around town leading a procession of visitors, including the acclaimed Memphis photographer Ernest Withers, to Centennial Church, where his father's name is inscribed on the cornerstone as church secretary. "He was the pastor later," added Turner before heading off to view a house where as a child he heard pianist Pinetop Perkins and Sonny Boy Williamson practicing together, and a site on Sixth Street where he cut his first record in 1952 for Joe Bihari of Modern Music. Interested in revisiting the setting also was Bihari, who was living at the time in Beverly Hills and had just finished producing Turner's new CD.

Turner joked, talked about old times, and played keyboard at the home of Marylee Smith on Mississippi Avenue with his current vocalist, a stunningly beautiful woman shot into a gold Spandex pants suit. Next came a pilgrimage to his birthplace at 314 Washington Street. Sharing the living room sofa with Ruth Perkins, his former classmate, who lives there now, he said, "It's funny how things in the past always look smaller later; but you all have really kept the place up. If you

▶   Ike Turner and his Ikettes in gold Spandex stage
an unforgettable 1997 Sunflower River Blues
Festival.

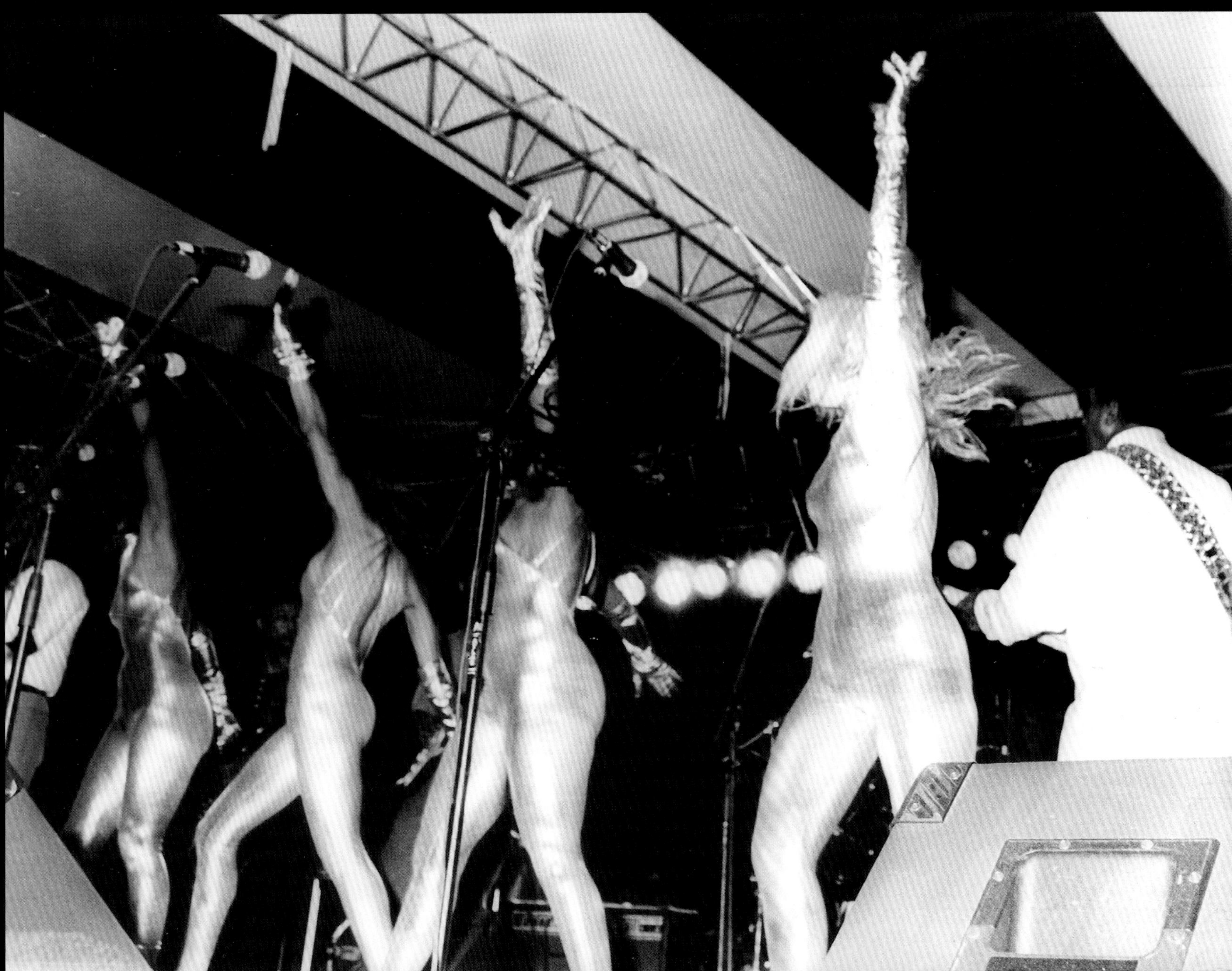

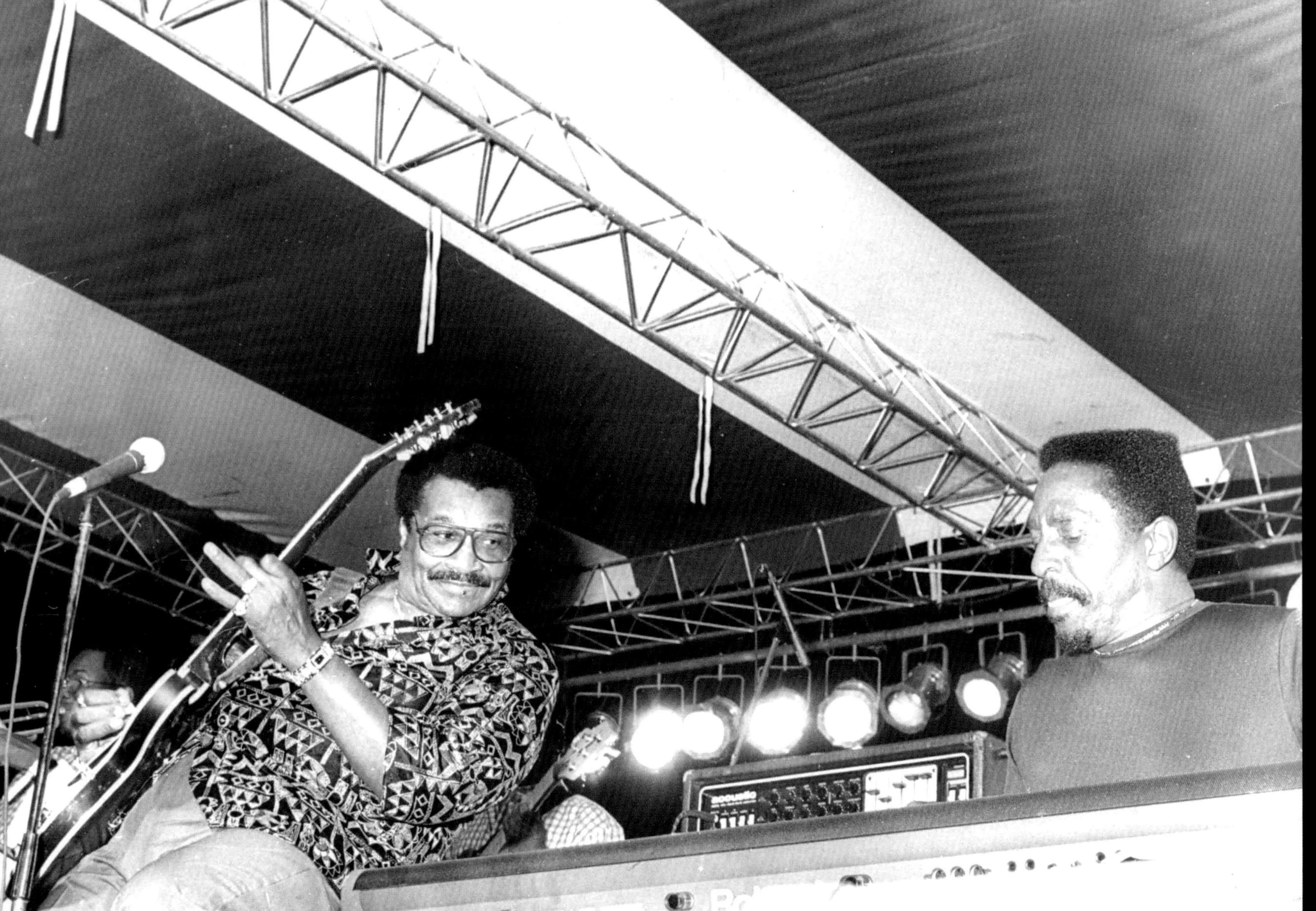

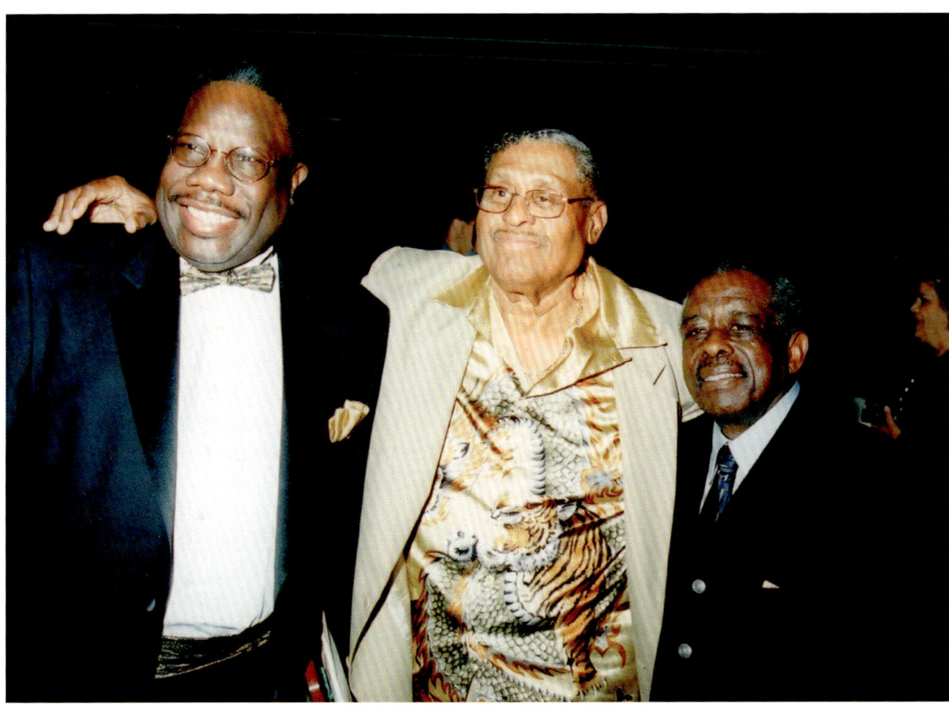

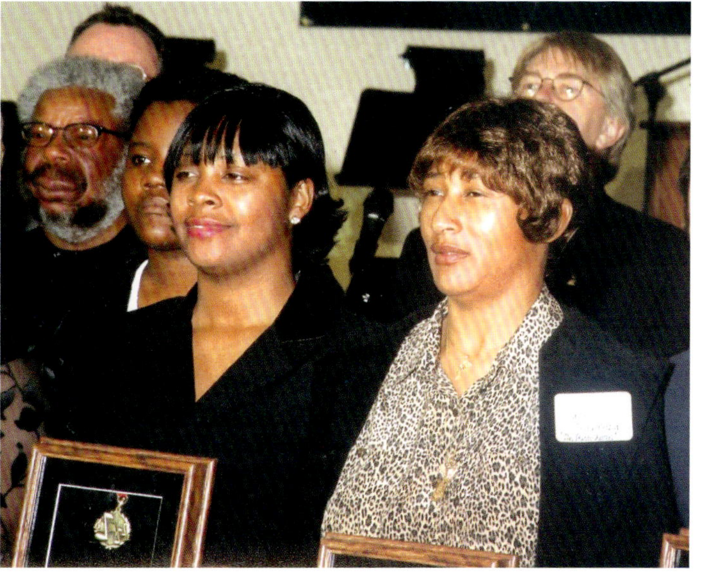

decide to sell it, let me know," he said. Ruth's grandson immediately replied, "How do we get in touch with you?"

Lucille and Larry Turner's Grill on Issaquena specializing in soul food (no relation but close Ike Turner friends) was closed, since it was Saturday. So the entourage adjourned for a catfish dinner at The Ranchero restaurant on Highway 61. Ike picked up the tab and headed back to Memphis.

In 2003 when Ike was inducted into Mississippi's Musicians Hall of Fame at the University of Southern Mississippi, C. V. Veal, his cousin, accepted the award for him. C. V. and I had driven to Hattiesburg for the ceremony and visited with other honorees: Greenville native Horace Turnbull, who founded the Boys Choir of Harlem, and Lillian McMurray's daughter, who talked about her mother padding the studio walls of Trumpet Records with mattresses to enhance its sound. Joining us also was Quincy Ruffin, brother of the late David Ruffin, lead singer of the Temptations, who grew up in Clarksdale's Riverton subdivision. At an earlier Hall of Fame induction in 2001, Charley Patton's granddaughter, Keisha Brown from Duncan, stood in for her grandmother Rosetta Patton Brown. Joining her in the group photo was Marva Morganfield, widow of Muddy Waters, and his longtime agent Scott Cameron.

▲

Blues drummer/vocalist C. V. Veal (center) accepts the Mississippi Musicians Hall of Fame plaque for his cousin Ike Turner in Hattiesburg at the University of Southern Mississippi and visits with other recipients: Horace Turnbull, founder of the Boys Choir of Harlem, and Quincy Ruffin, brother of The Temptations' lead singer David Ruffin.

▶

Keisha Patton Brown, granddaughter of blues pioneer Charley Patton (left), and Marva Morganfield, widow of Muddy Waters, accept Mississippi Musicians Hall of Fame plaques in Jackson for their family celebrities.

Quintessential bluesman Little Milton Campbell and music impresario Ike Turner join forces in August 1997 for a mighty tenth-anniversary Sunflower Festival finale.

BOBBY RUSH

With special ties to Clarksdale and the Mississippi Delta, Bobby Rush has appeared in almost every section of this book. Originally the connections were through longtime friendships with Early Wright and Melville Tillis, but they quickly spread to many more clamoring to book him as a festival headliner. Since then he's returned so many times, no one is sure about the number.

His flamboyant shows on the Chitlin' Circuit paired with burlesque-style dancers have toned down through the years, and he's catapulted into the Blues Foundation's Entertainer of the Year status. How remarkable that his energy level remains intact, and most audiences realize his shows are fun and not to be taken too seriously.

I once covered Bobby's appearances at West Tallahatchie High School in Webb after he had donated a shipment of computers for their classrooms. An early-morning assembly was reserved for

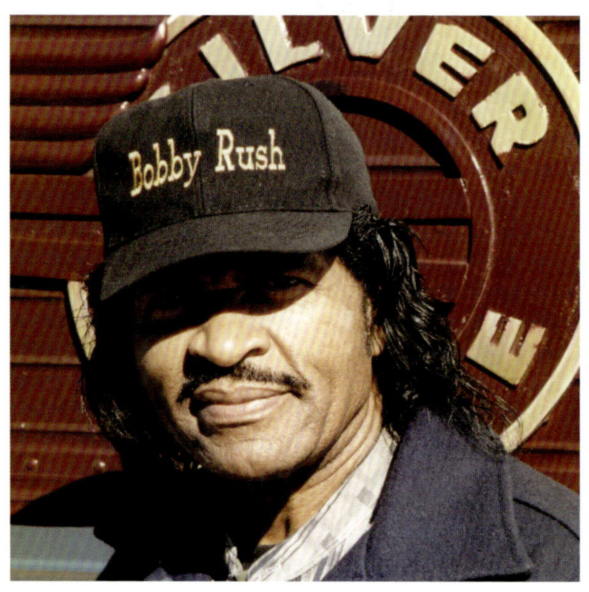

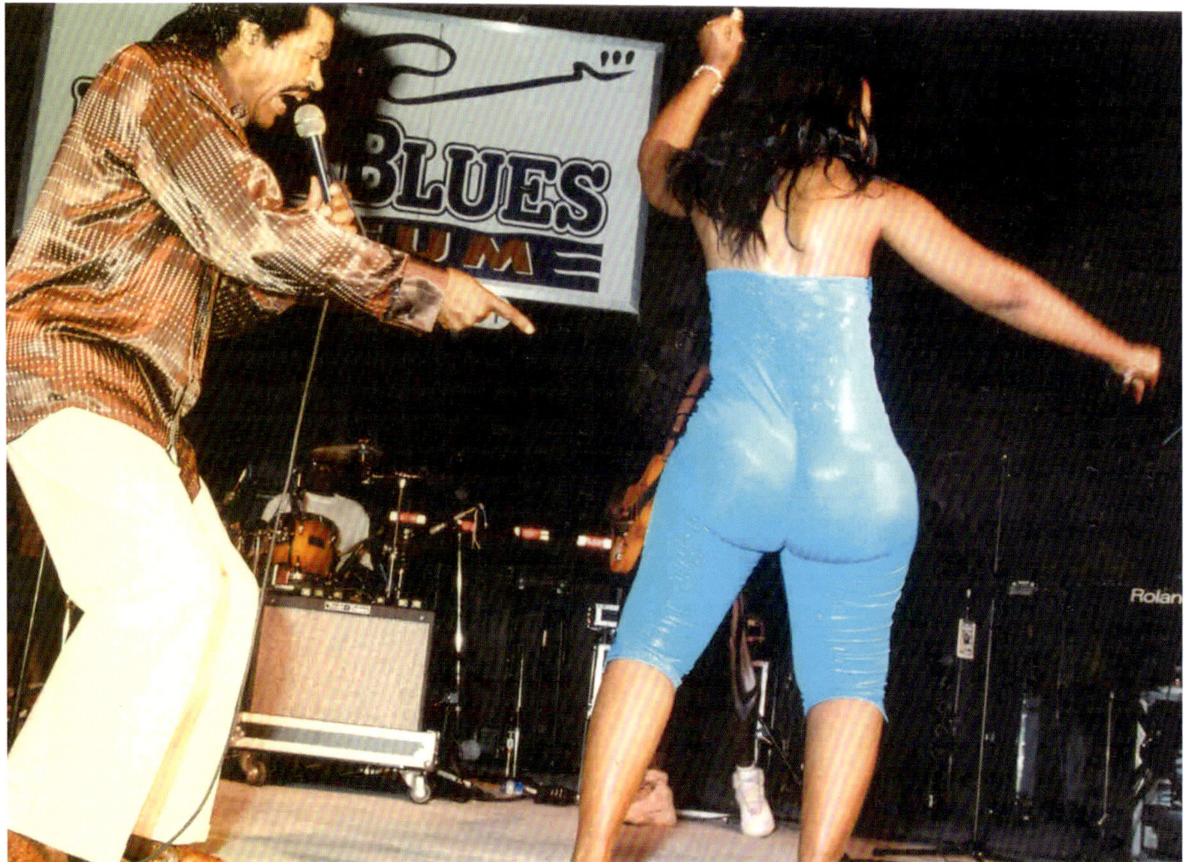

▲

A quiet moment for Bobby Rush outside his bus at the King Biscuit Blues Festival in Helena is rare.

◀

With a master showman's touch, Bobby Rush combines a quasi-bad-boy style with a sense of fun at the 2007 Sunflower River Blues Festival.

▶

Bobby Rush appears in almost every section of this book because he has special ties to Clarksdale and the Mississippi Delta. His flamboyant shows on the Chitlin' Circuit paired with burlesque-style dancers have toned down through the years, and he's catapulted into the Blues Foundation's Entertainer of the Year status. This photograph, however, one of my favorites, is from 1994, and embodies the rhythmic vitality of his performances.

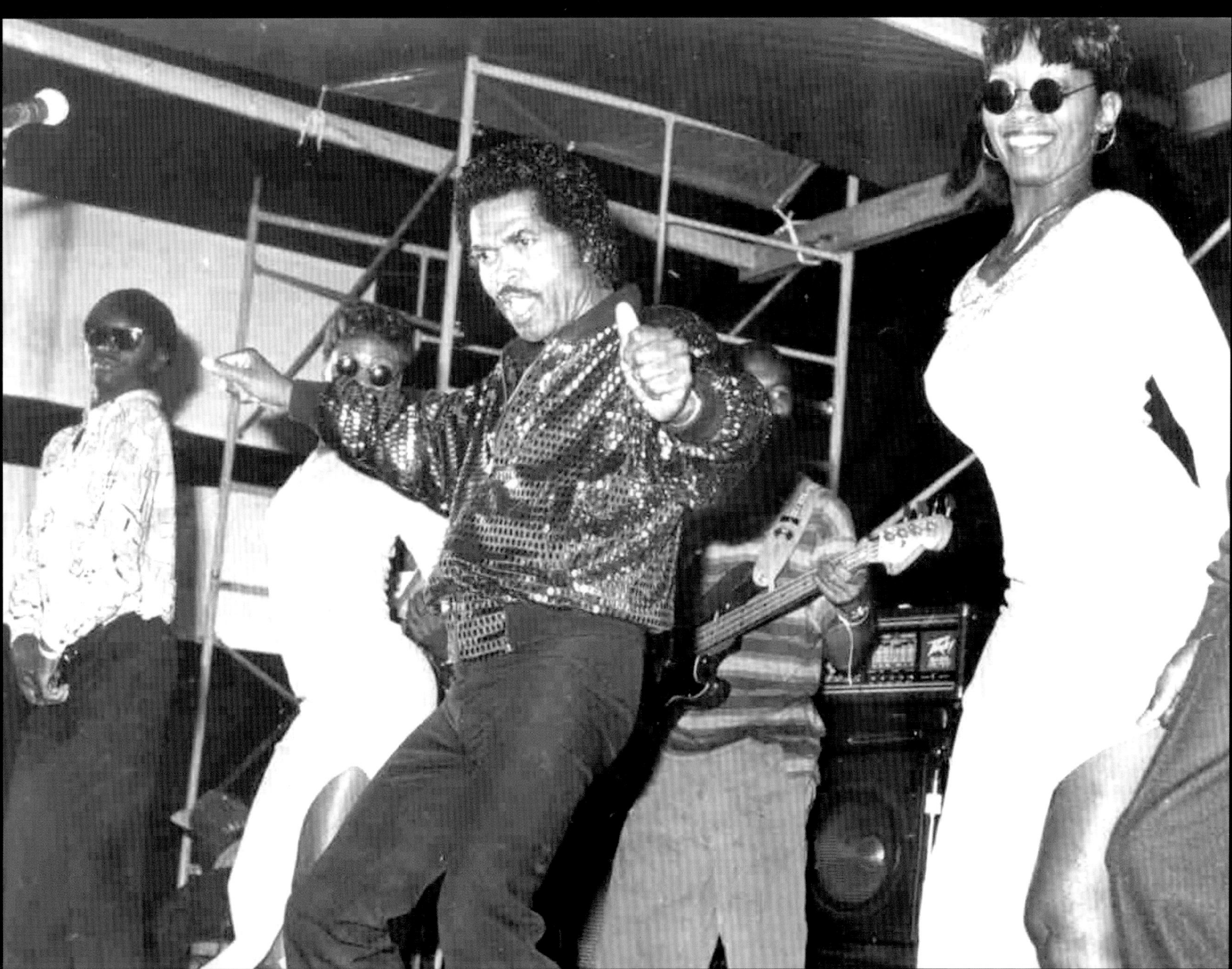

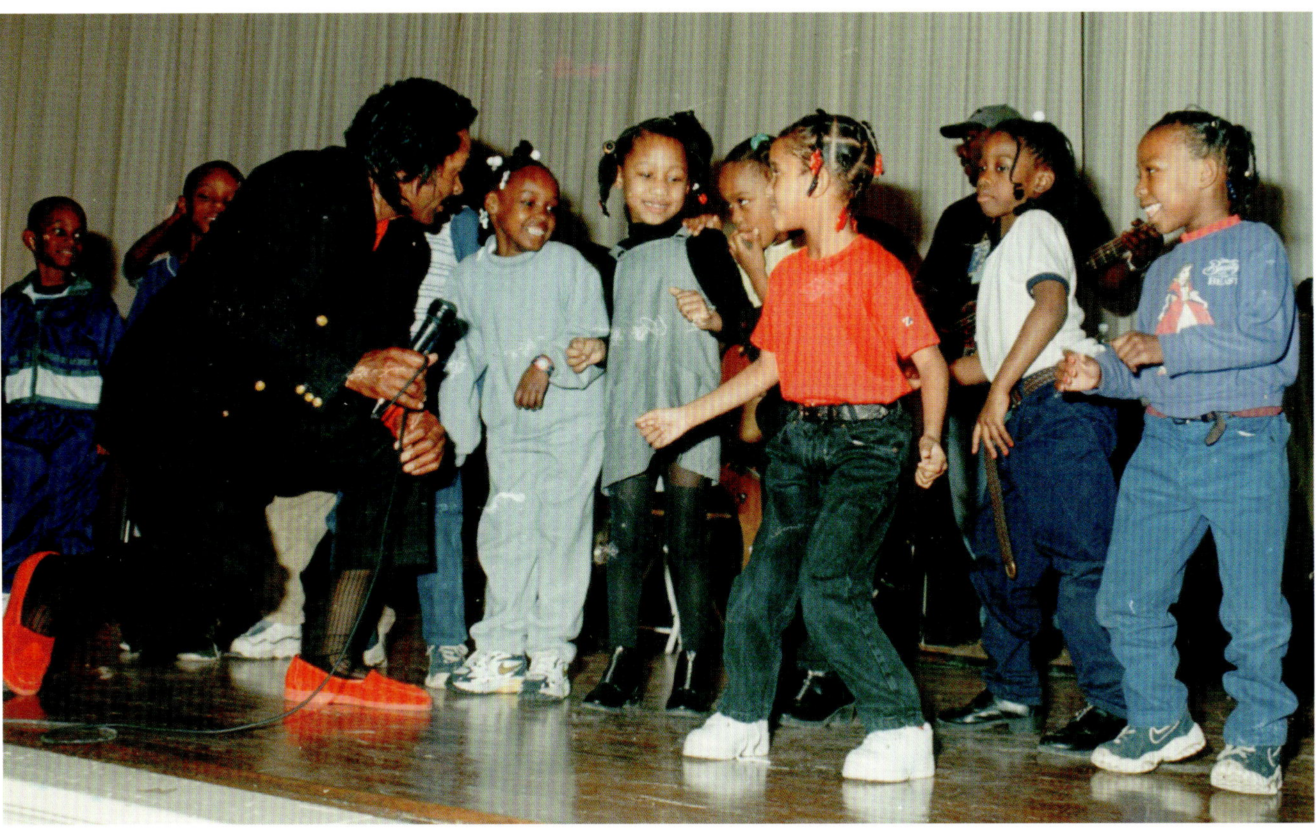

elementary students from schools all over the district, and I pondered how kids would react to this flamboyant entertainer. Absolutely no problem; they loved him. Youngsters were all over him onstage, dancing and singing like crazy. Talking later to high school seniors, Bobby said he was a preacher's boy and stressed the importance of staying in school.

When Early Wright died, Bobby was onstage as part of the funeral service in the Civic Auditorium. Decades later, he returned to speak about Melville Tillis at Haven United Methodist Church, and several days afterward at Clarksdale's City Board of Mayor and Commissioners to request official recognition for his good friend. The meeting adjourned to the downtown Delta Blues Museum stage, which was renamed the Melville C. Tillis Blues Stage before family members and city officials.

TENNESSEE WILLIAMS

Folklorist Alan Lomax includes Tennessee Williams in his *The Land Where Blues Began,* his amazing account of travels in the Delta recording musicians for the Library of Congress.

▲ Attending Bobby Rush's appearance for elementary students at West Tallahatchie High School after he had donated computers for their classrooms, I pondered how these little kids would react to this flamboyant entertainer. Absolutely no problem: they loved him and were all over him onstage, dancing and singing like crazy.

He writes: "It was here that Tennessee Williams did the research for *Cat on a Hot Tin Roof*. Williams was a Southern realist, and I have no doubt that at the time of my visit his fabled 'Big Daddy' was an important figure at the meetings of the local bank, meetings that determined the policy of the cotton lobby in Washington."

Lomax refers several times to Tennessee's "Big Daddy" characters to describe real white plantation owners in Coahoma County. In two other major Tennessee Williams plays, *Orpheus Descending* and *Battle of Angels*, the principal male character is Val Xavier, a macho blues guitarist wearing a snakeskin jacket. In 1991, to prepare for his role as Val in a premiere production of *Orpheus* being staged in Nantes, France, by the Théâtre la Chamaille and the University of Nantes, French actor Gerard Wilkins traveled to Clarksdale to take guitar lessons from blues master Johnnie Billington. Actresses Claudine Hunault, who portrayed Myra/Lady Torrence, and Blondine, who played Carol Cutrer, followed a few days later to learn "how to speak Southern." They stayed at the Riverside Hotel, where they became great friends with Frank "Rat" Ratliff, son of Mrs. Z L Hill, and visited the Grange Cemetery across the street, where Blanche Clark Cutrer and John Wesley Cutrer are buried. Tennessee borrowed the name Blanche, only daughter of Clarksdale founder John Clark, for *A Streetcar Named Desire*, and J. W. Cutrer became the role model for the dashing Dr. John Buchanan in *Summer and Smoke* and *Eccentricities of a Nightingale*.

In March 1992 when the curtain opened on *Orpheus* in France, Mr. Johnnie's guitar pupil was a convincing heartthrob onstage strumming "Heartbreak Hotel." Applauding from the audience were Dr. Kenneth Holditch and myself, invited as a journalist/photographer, to talk and show slides of sites in Clarksdale and the Mississippi Delta tied to Tennessee plays. Still another Mississippian was in the theater lobby, performing during intermission: Handy Award winner/blues guitarist/vocalist Jessie Mae Hemphill of Como. Later, all of us were celebrated at a champagne reception in the Nantes city hall.

The world continued to shrink on this trip when my daughter Laura and I visited the grave of Doors celebrity Jim Morrison in Paris, at Père Lachaise Cemetery. Several devoted fans from Thailand were sitting on Morrison's gravestone passing around a bottle of wine. When they learned we were from Clarksdale, we were welcomed enthusiastically within their circle with toasts to our hometown and the blues. In August 1992 our theater friends from France returned to Clarksdale for the Sunflower River Blues Festival and stayed at our house, along with cousins from San Antonio, Texas. All of us enjoyed an informal concert by Son Thomas of Leland played on the front steps of the Delta Blues Museum.

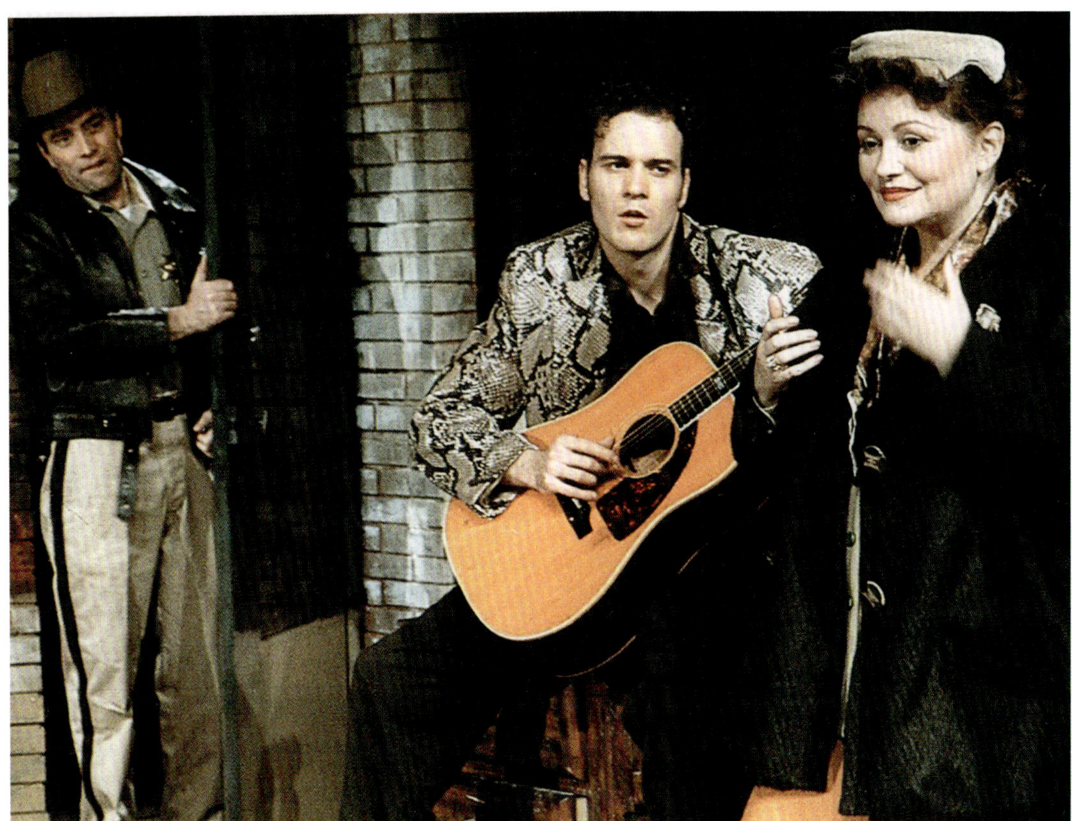

One morning on my front porch, I heard our French visitors discussing a friend who was a theater director at the Comédie-Française in Paris and had an uncle living in "Al-A-Ga-Tour," Mississippi. Guessing at a translation, I telephoned Bruno's, a legendary service station five miles south of Clarksdale on Highway 61, specializing in gas, groceries, and local news. I asked, "Who in Alligator has a niece in Paris who is a theater director?" The rapid reply: "Why, Aaron Kline, of course."

Aaron Kline, a pillar of Clarksdale's Beth Israel congregation and owner of a mercantile establishment in Alligator similar to Tennessee Williams's store in *Orpheus Descending,* was not only thrilled to meet my visitors. He and his wife hosted an elegant Sunday brunch for them in their home on West Second Street. Afterward, we all went down to Issaquena in the New World District for the Sunflower Festival's first gospel concert beneath the New Roxy Theatre marquee.

In its twenty-four-year history, the Mississippi Delta Tennessee Williams Festival has featured blues and gospel music on its program each fall. Starting in 1993 and for several years afterward Clarksdale singer/songwriter Big Jack Johnson opened the festival beneath paper lanterns outside Uncle Henry's Place on Moon Lake. Jim O'Neal lectured on Delta blues music during the literary conference, and Charlie Musselwhite performed in the Gov. Earl Brewer/Dr. William

▲ Wearing a snakeskin jacket as the macho character Val Xavier in *Orpheus Descending* publicity material, French actor Gerard Wilkins strums "Heartbreak Hotel" onstage in the Nantes, France, production of the Tennessee Williams classic drama set in the Mississippi Delta.

▶ In preparation for his major role as the intriguing guitarist opening *Orpheus Descending,* French actor Gerard Wilkins travels to Clarksdale in 1992 for guitar lessons from blues master "Mr. Johnnie" Billington. He and other French actors stayed at the famed Riverside Hotel across from the Grange Cemetery, where Blanche Clark Cutrer and J. W. Cutrer—role models for other Tennessee Williams characters—are buried, and an angel monument is transformed later into the signature set piece for the play *Summer and Smoke.*

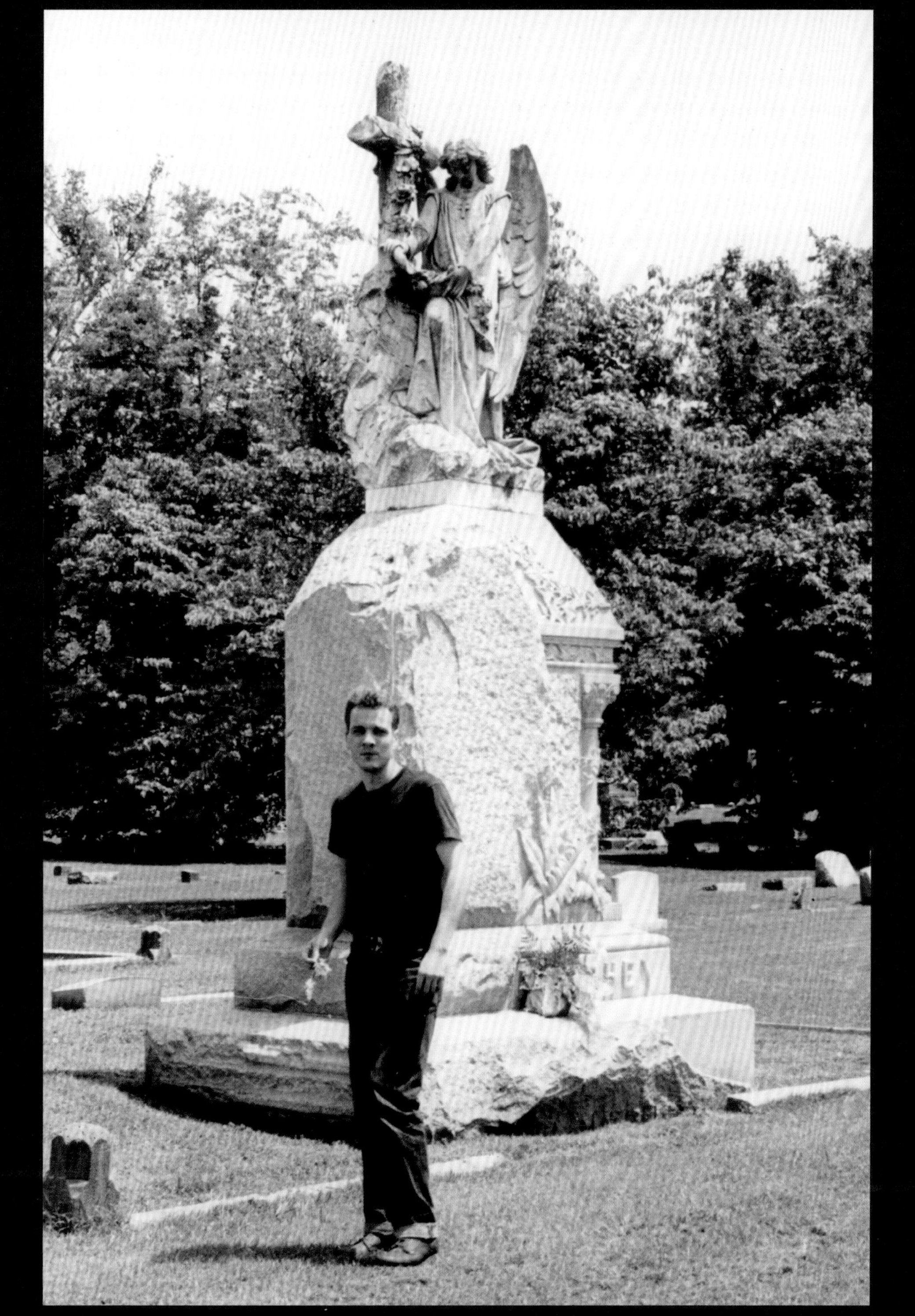

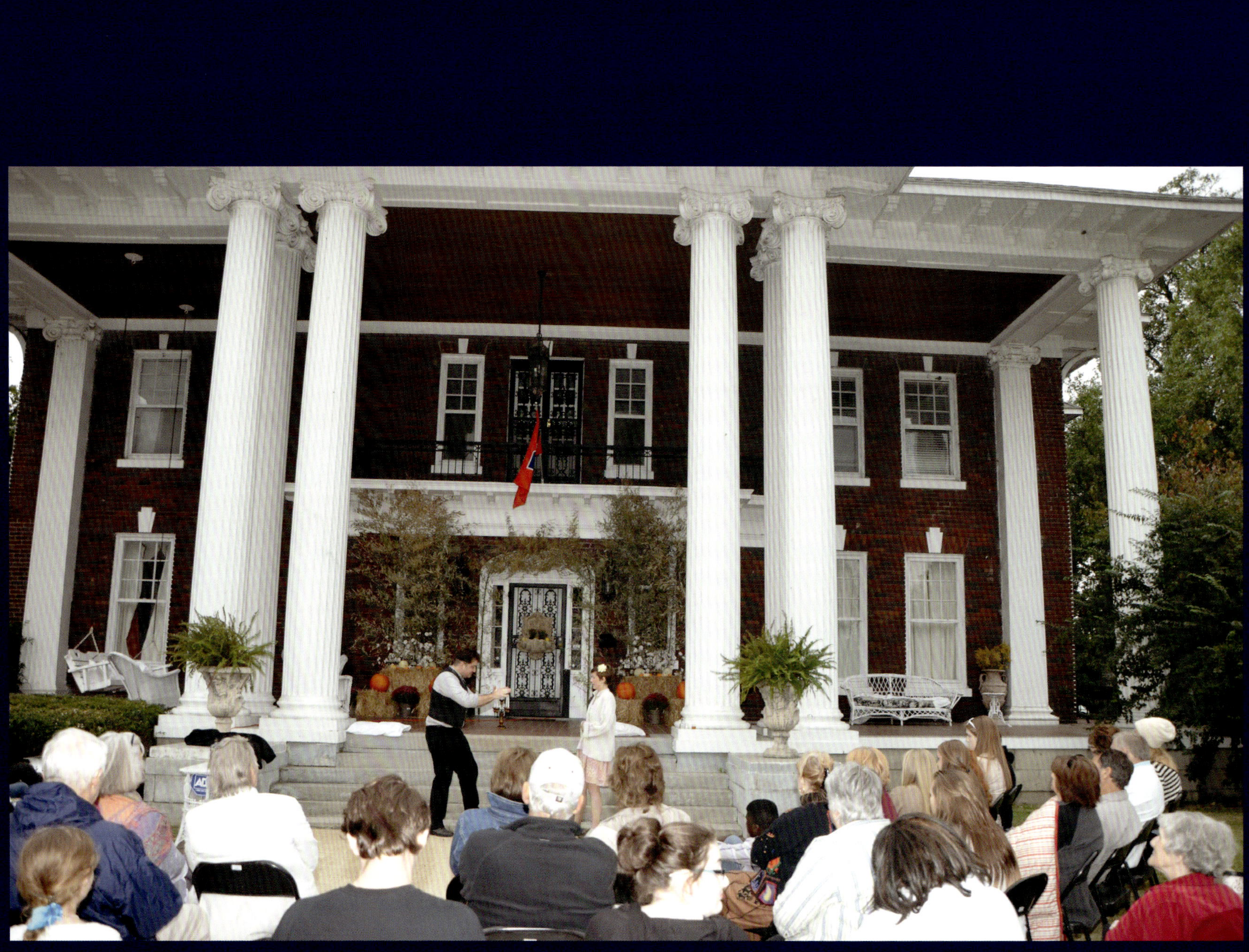

Barr mansion. In 2010 Charlie brought his friend and recording artist Tom Waits to the conference. Musicians John Ruskey and Foster "Tater" Wiley performed Tennessee's blues songs, *Blue Mountain Ballads*, during a Clark House reception.

"Blue Mountain is what he [Tennessee] called Clarksdale in *The Glass Menagerie*," said Dr. Holditch. "He liked the sound of it just as he liked Laurel and used it for Clarksdale in *A Streetcar Named Desire*." The ballads are included in *The Collected Poems of Tennessee Williams*, edited by David Roessel and Nicholas Moschovakis and published by New Directions with a CD of the author reading. David Dunavant, a blues guitarist, has played at the Cutrer Mansion reception from 2012 to 2016, and Richard "Daddy Rich" Crisman entertained earlier between scenes performed by New York actors Tammy Grimes and Joel Vig at Oakhurst Middle School's auditorium.

One year the Tennessee Williams play *Battle of Angels* was performed in Clarksdale's Larry Thompson Center for the Arts as the festival's centerpiece. New York theater director Erma Durico starred in the leading role of Myra. Cast in a signature role as the prophetic conjure man shaking an eerie rattle of dried chicken bones was ebullient Clarksdale blues drummer/vocalist C. V. Veal, organizer of the Top Hatters, an early blues band and also a member of the Kings of Rhythm with his cousin Ike Turner and Jackie Brenston.

The works of Tennessee Williams have been linked with blues in Clarksdale, in Mississippi, and in my own personal life. Scenes from his dramas are performed as popular porch plays in the historic neighborhood where he lived as a child, with audiences sitting informally in lawn chairs. One play takes place at the magnificent mansion of former governor Earl Brewer and Dr. Michael Barr; another, on the double-galleried Patterson/Ross residence, where the Tennessee Williams postage stamp was unveiled in 1995; a third, at the gingerbread-style law office of attorney John Sherman, cochairman of the Sunflower River Blues and Gospel Festival; and last, the rambling raised cottage built in 1894 by Walter Clark, where Tom visited his best friend, Phil Clark, famed director Elia Kazan brought actress Barbara Bel Geddes before her Broadway role as Maggie the Cat, and my own 415 Court Street address, cluttered with photographs of my blues friends.

ROBERT PLANT

When I called Atlantic Records in 1998 to talk about *Walking into Clarksdale*, the Robert Plant and Jimmy Page album paying tribute to

The works of Tennessee Williams have been linked with blues in Clarksdale, in Mississippi, and in my own personal life. Scenes from his dramas are performed as popular porch plays in the historic district where he lived as a child, with audiences seated informally in lawn chairs. The vintage home of former governor Earl Brewer and Dr. Michael Barr is the 2015 setting for *The Glass Menagerie* being performed by the Matt Foss Theatre actors. Afterward they won ovations at the Kennedy Center and the Moscow Art Theatre in Russia.

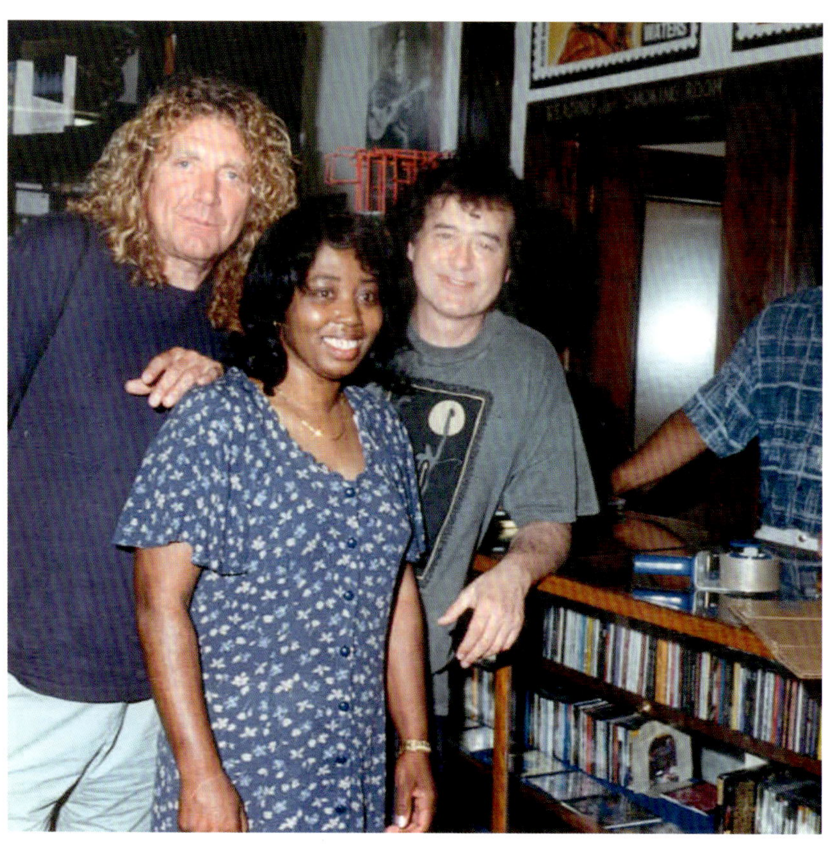

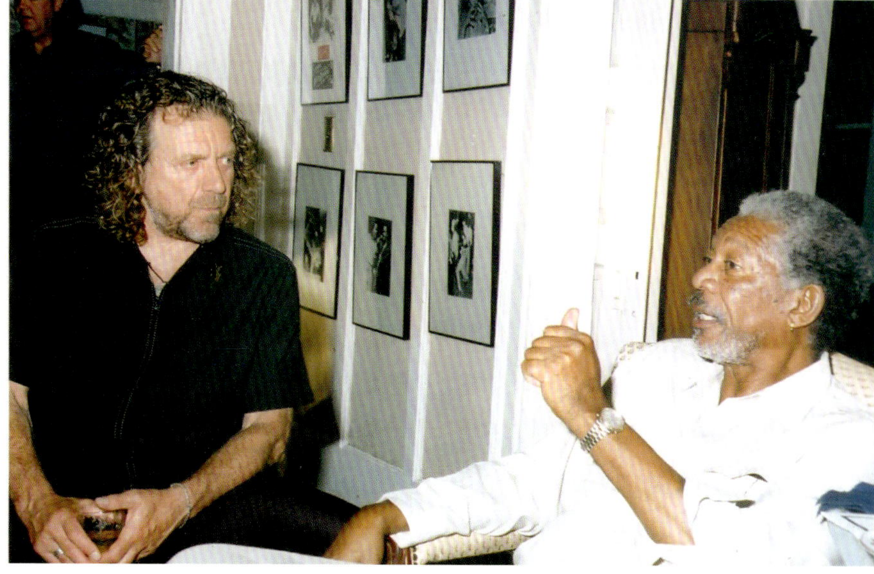

my hometown, I had no clue where this was leading. Within months the two superstars were autographing their album inside my house after our walking together not only in Clarksdale but also in Tutwiler and Friars Point.

On a day off between the Plant/Page concerts, Robert Plant, a serious blues historian, was pointing out blues sites and their significance to Jimmy Page and members of their band. I volunteered to be their tour guide. They declined checking on the renovation in progress at the new Delta Blues Museum in Blues Alley but were interested in seeing Smitty's Red Top Lounge across the railroad tracks. Eyeing Robert's hair and their long Lincoln Town Car parked at the curb, James Alford, club manager, came over with a hello to say he knew who they were. Robert checked out the jukebox and walked around a bit, and we left for Sonny Boy Williamson's grave near Tutwiler and later for Friars Point, where Robert Johnson once played outside Hirsberg's Drugstore.

▲ On a subsequent trip to Clarksdale and the Delta with his guitarist Justin Adams, Robert Plant and actor Morgan Freeman meet for the first time, get acquainted at an informal gathering, and Robert, Jason, and Big Jack Johnson play together.

◄ In 1998 when I called Atlantic Records about *Walking into Clarksdale,* the Robert Plant and Jimmy Page album paying tribute to my hometown, I had no clue where this was leading. Within a year the two superstars were autographing their album inside my house. We began walking into historic blues sites not only in Clarksdale but also in Tutwiler and Friars Point. One of our first stops was the Delta Blues Museum and a warm welcome from Maie Smith.

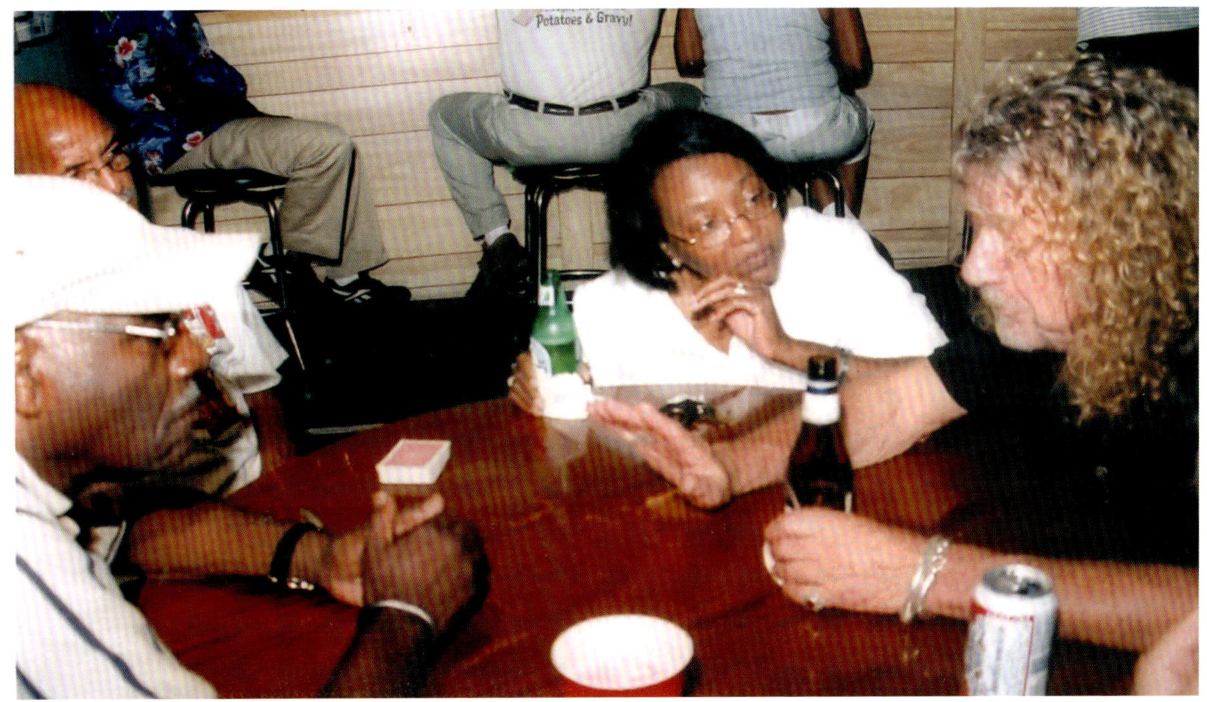

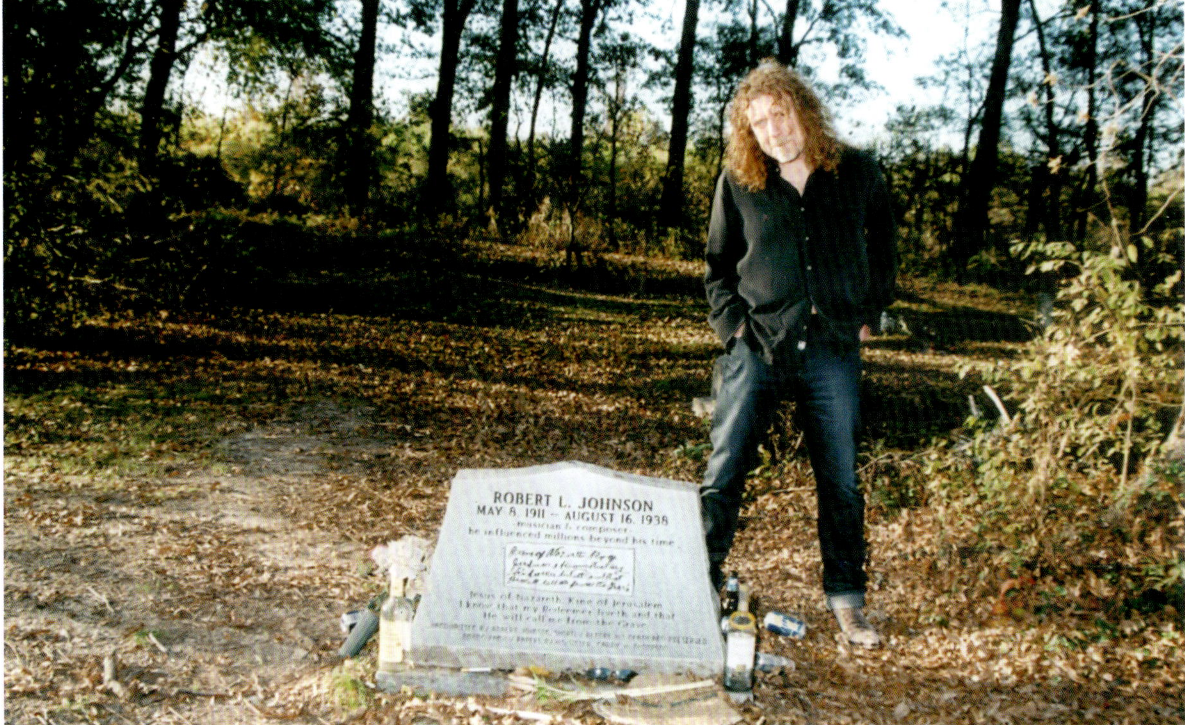

▲

Fleeing a super-sized crowd of fans following his 2008 presentation of a Led Zeppelin plaque to the Delta Blues Museum, Robert escapes to a quiet club on Issaquena Avenue and joins Yvonne Stanford and Melville Tillis (left) at a regular Tuesday-night card game.

▶

Following Robert's unveiling of the W. C. Handy Blues Trail marker in Tutwiler in 2009, he visits the third gravesite of legendary bluesman Robert Johnson outside Little Zion M. B. Church between Money and Greenwood, Mississippi.

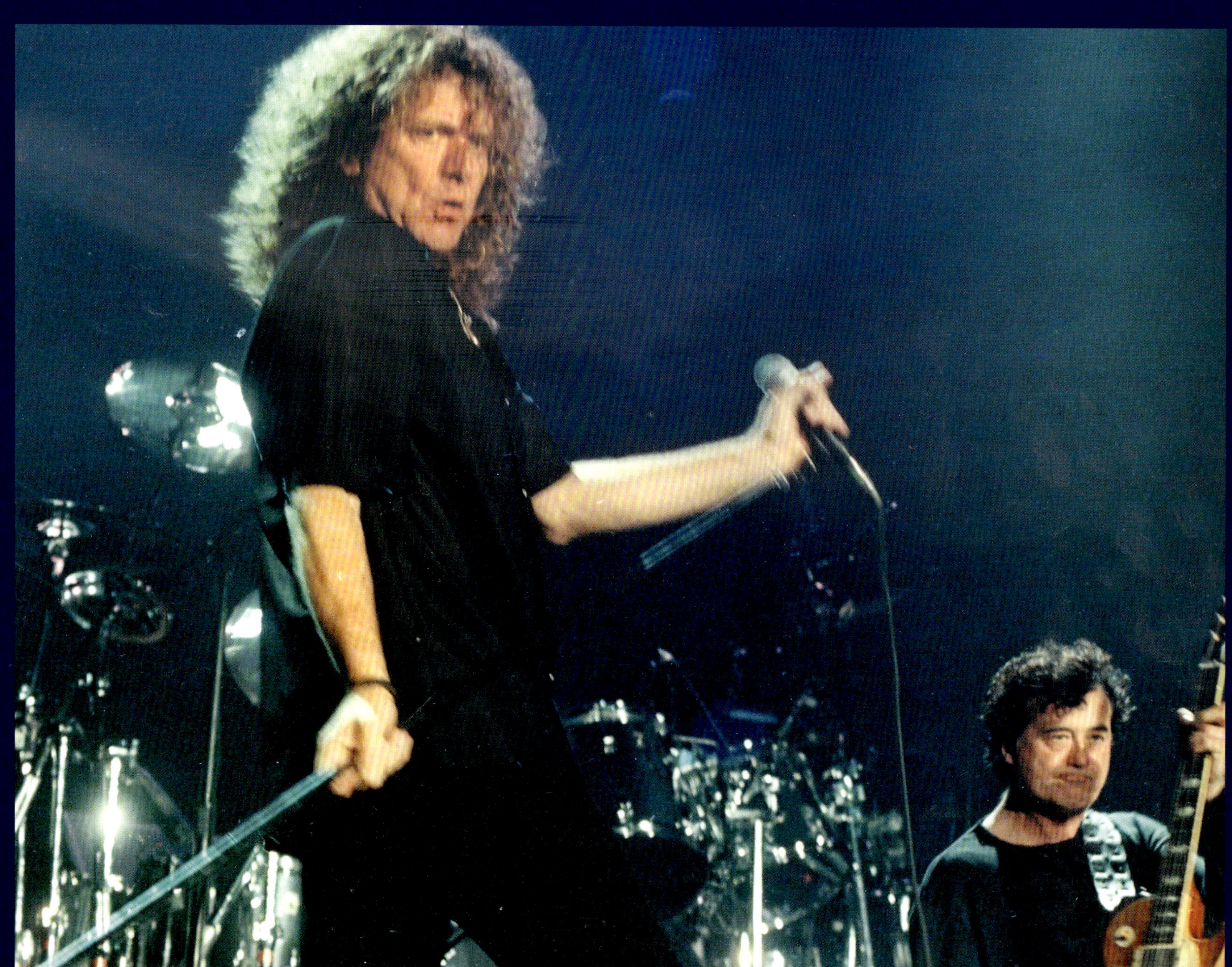

A week or so later, I received a telephone call at the newspaper asking if I'd like tickets to the Plant/Page concert in the Memphis Pyramid. After catching my breath, "Believe I would" was the answer, along with a request to photograph them live in concert. This was the beginning of an eighteen-year friendship with this amazingly talented and charismatic individual—a contemporary Renaissance man of music—open, outgoing, adventurous, inquisitive and interested in new directions and musical combinations that take your breath away yet pay respect to the past. In Strange Sensation and the Robert Plant organization, he has assembled premiere musicians, infused with talent and energy. They love what they are doing. Thanks to Robert's generosity, our family and Delta friends labeling ourselves "the Moon Lake bunch" have enjoyed many of his concerts. Memorable cross-country outings include being smuggled onstage during his Seattle concert, getting stranded on Mud Island after Robert's show with Alison Krauss, and attending the Led Zeppelin reunion concert in London, where we shared an after party table with John Bonham's family. When Led Zep's "Kashmir" finale rocketed into outer space, it took the three of us from Clarksdale along with it.

Unannounced, Robert often spent time in Clarksdale and the Delta before his spectacular 2012 Sunflower Festival performance. He's listened to our blues musicians and a Sunday gospel choir at church; enjoyed local restaurants, homegrown tomatoes, and Mary Patel's spicy vegetarian eggplant casserole; joined Big Jack Johnson and his own lead guitarist, Justin Adams, playing together; met Morgan Freeman; danced anonymously to a jukebox in a local club, sat in on a card game on Issaquena; and presented the Delta Blues Museum with a plaque featuring mini–Led Zeppelin album covers acknowledging their debt to Delta blues musicians. In short, he's at ease here—a home boy.

◄

Following Robert Plant and Jimmy Page's visit to Clarksdale, I receive an inquiry if I would like tickets to the 1998 Plant/Page concert at the Memphis Pyramid. "Believe I would" not only earns guest tickets but also a photography pass producing this live shot from a phenomenal concert, and the beginning of an amazing friendship.

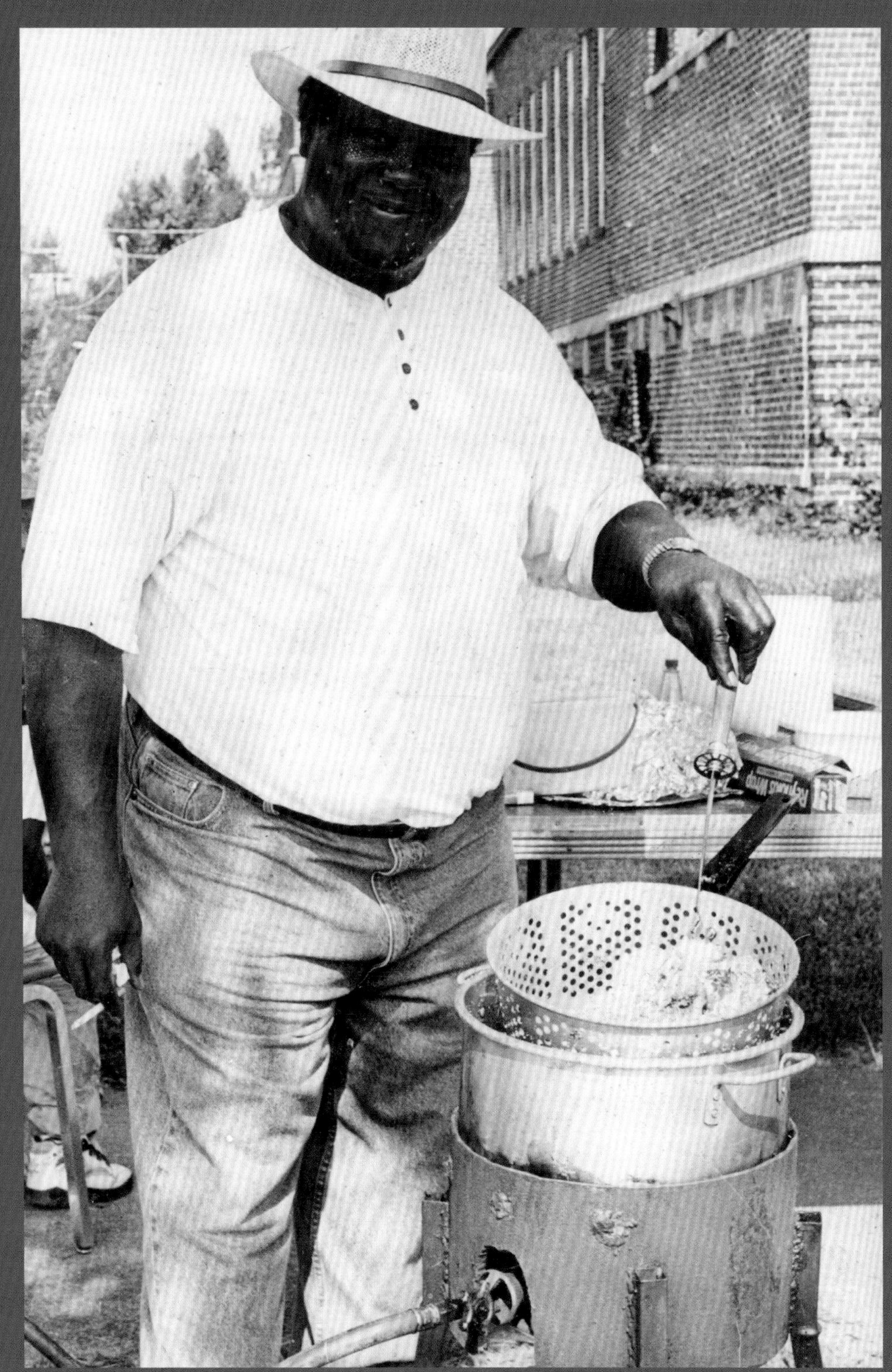

6

DELTA BLUES
MUSEUM

Since its 1979 inauguration as the world's first music museum devoted exclusively to blues, the Delta Blues Museum has been an important center of cultural and community activities. On opening day I met Jessie Mae Hemphill in the museum's original location—a large room inside Myrtle Hall Elementary School on Highway 61. A member of the renowned Sid Hemphill family from the North Mississippi Hill Country, where they made their own leather drums, Jessie Mae was hard to miss. Wearing a white Stetson centered with a semiprecious "diamond," she enjoyed making her presence known.

Early on she christened me "the paper lady," and I photographed her everywhere from Sherman Cooper's mini-festivals in the country between Crenshaw and Como, to a cabaret and university conference in France, where dignitaries toasted her with champagne and roses. The one exception was an evening honoring the late fife master Napoleon Strickland when the house band was tethered so close to the Como

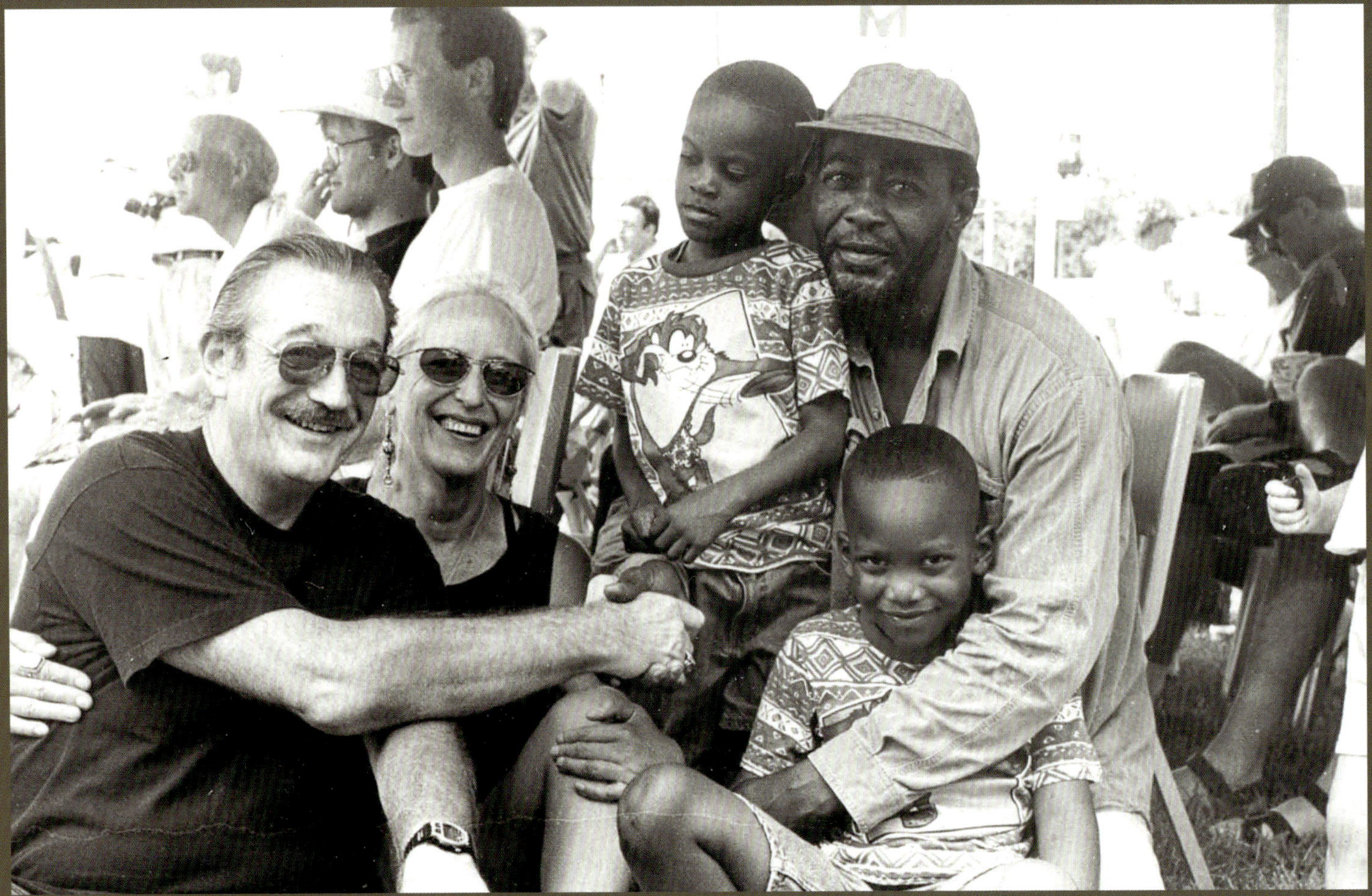

Sitting on the lawn of the Delta Blues Museum when it was located inside Carnegie Public Library, Charlie and Henrietta Musselwhite (left) visit with local songwriter/harmonica master Arthneice Jones and kids during the Sunflower Festival's acoustic program.

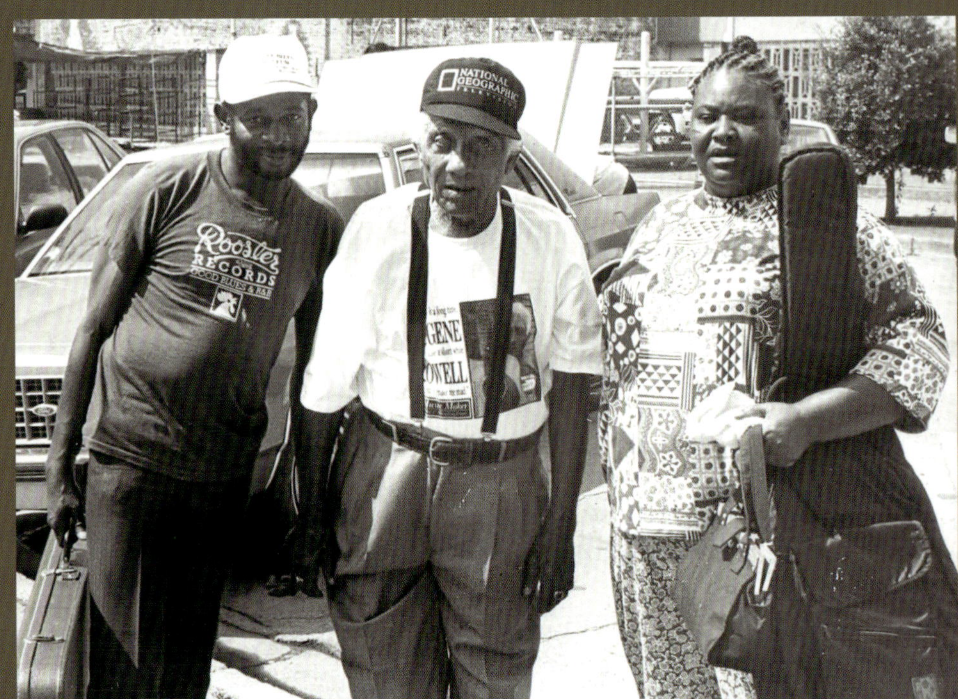

Robert Johnson–style virtuoso guitarist Lonnie Pitchford (left) helps Eugene Powell and his wife prepare for a set inside the Delta Blues Museum.

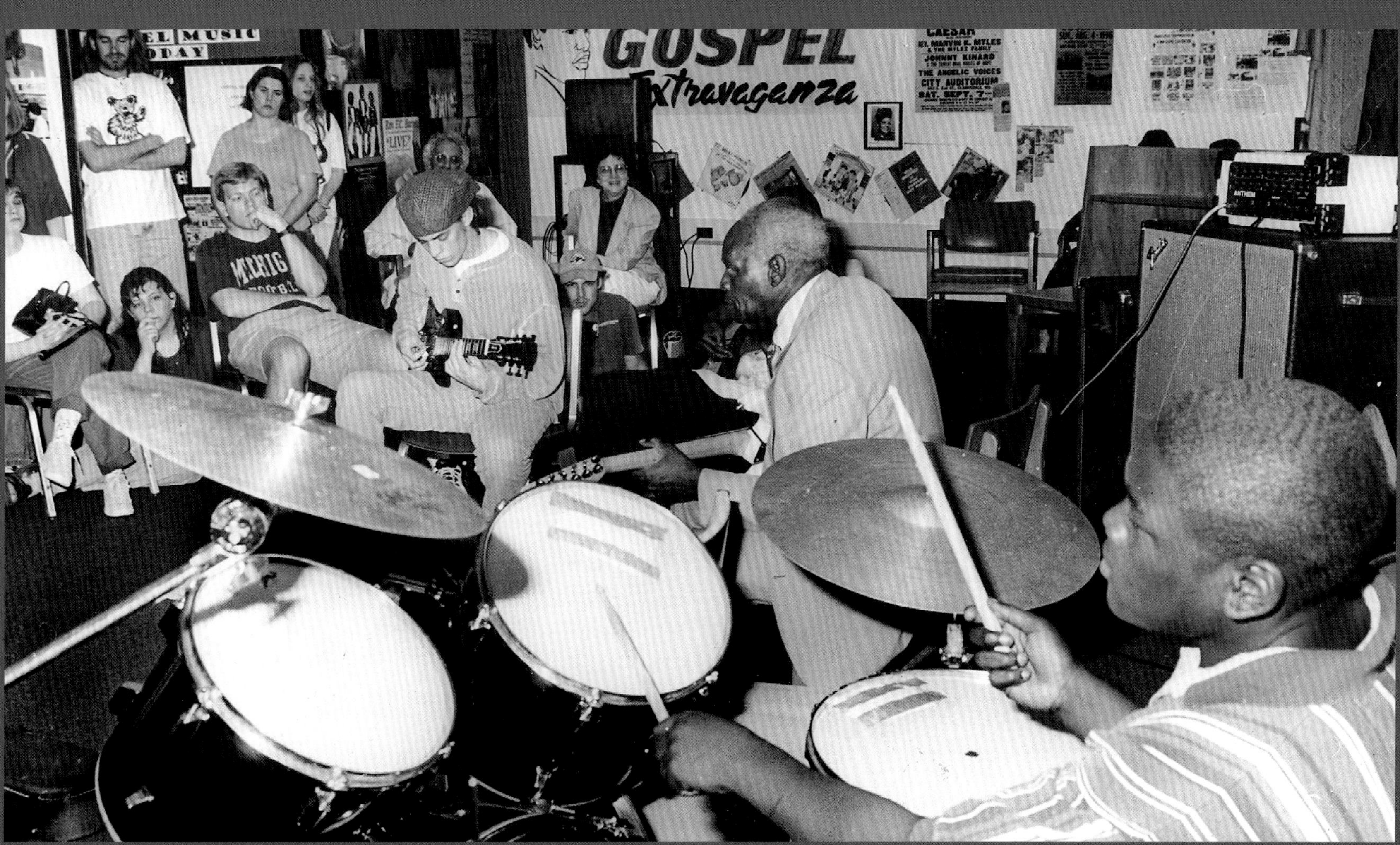

Under the direction of Mr. Johnnie Billington,
a National Endowment for the Arts Master Folk
Artist (center), students in the Delta Blues Education Fund, including Jack Williams on drums,
perform a concert during the 1990s in the Delta
Blues Museum. In 2000 the kids performed in the
White House and enjoyed a private audience with
President Bill Clinton.

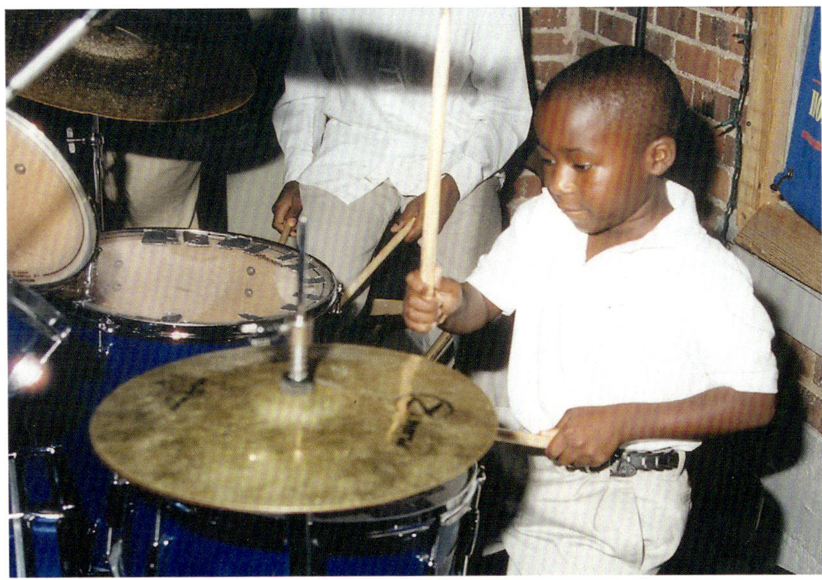

gym walls by too-short extension cords that they could hardly move or play. Jessie Mae was resplendently attired, and when I complimented her and asked permission to take her photo, she tossed her head back and turned away.

After the museum opened, its founder Sid Graves, who was also director of Carnegie Public Library, personally transported the exhibits downtown to the library each night for safekeeping. As interest in the museum grew in size and reputation, it was moved to Carnegie's second floor, where one of Nancy Kossman's kids became trapped inside the elevator during opening week. But the museum became a popular gathering place for the community, and crowds informally celebrated anniversaries and events there organized by curator John Ruskey. There were parties on Muddy Waters Day and Son House Day; someone showed up with a cake; musicians brought instruments and played, and dancing generally followed.

For years the museum hosted the Sunflower Festival's acoustic stages, educational programs, and a showcase of southern soul food. Outside on the lawn, Big John Broom fried catfish; Boss Hogg and his family furnished barbecue; and Shirley Fair offered dishes from Fair's Restaurant on Fourth Street. With Mr. Johnnie Billington in charge of instruction for the Delta Blues Education Program, youngsters learned to play blues after school and later performed in the Kennedy Center and the White House.

Tourists began to arrive. Billy Gibbons entered the picture, and eventually the library's second-floor space was not nearly large enough. Time to move again, this time under the umbrella of the city of Clarksdale. But in 1990 before they moved, artists Ray and Mary Daub of Wilmington, Delaware, donated a five-foot, eleven-inch

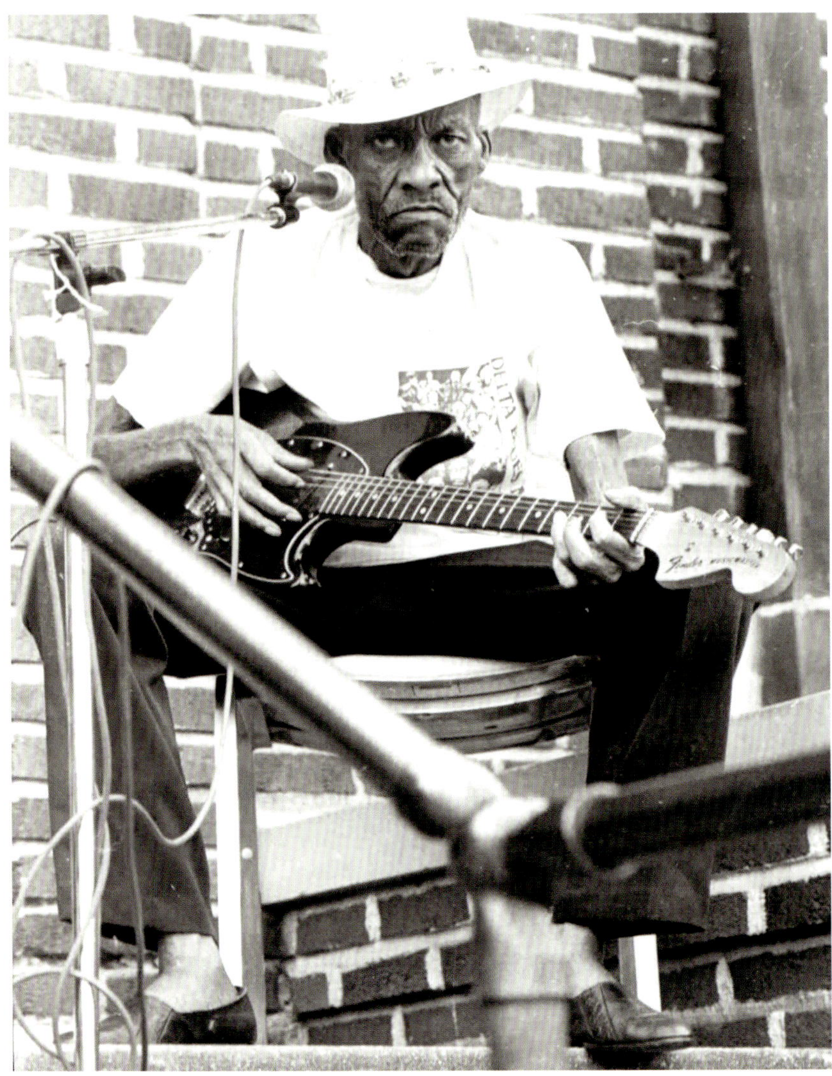

▲ Famed blues guitarist James "Son" Thomas of Leland, who once played in the White House, gives one of his last public performances outside the Delta Blues Museum in 1992.

◄ A decade later another student education fund drummer keeps the beat going in the Delta Blues Museum's present historic freight depot location. The after-school program was awarded a 2013 National Medal for Museum and Library Services by First Lady Michelle Obama, and the DBM Band earned a standing ovation in the White House following its finale concert.

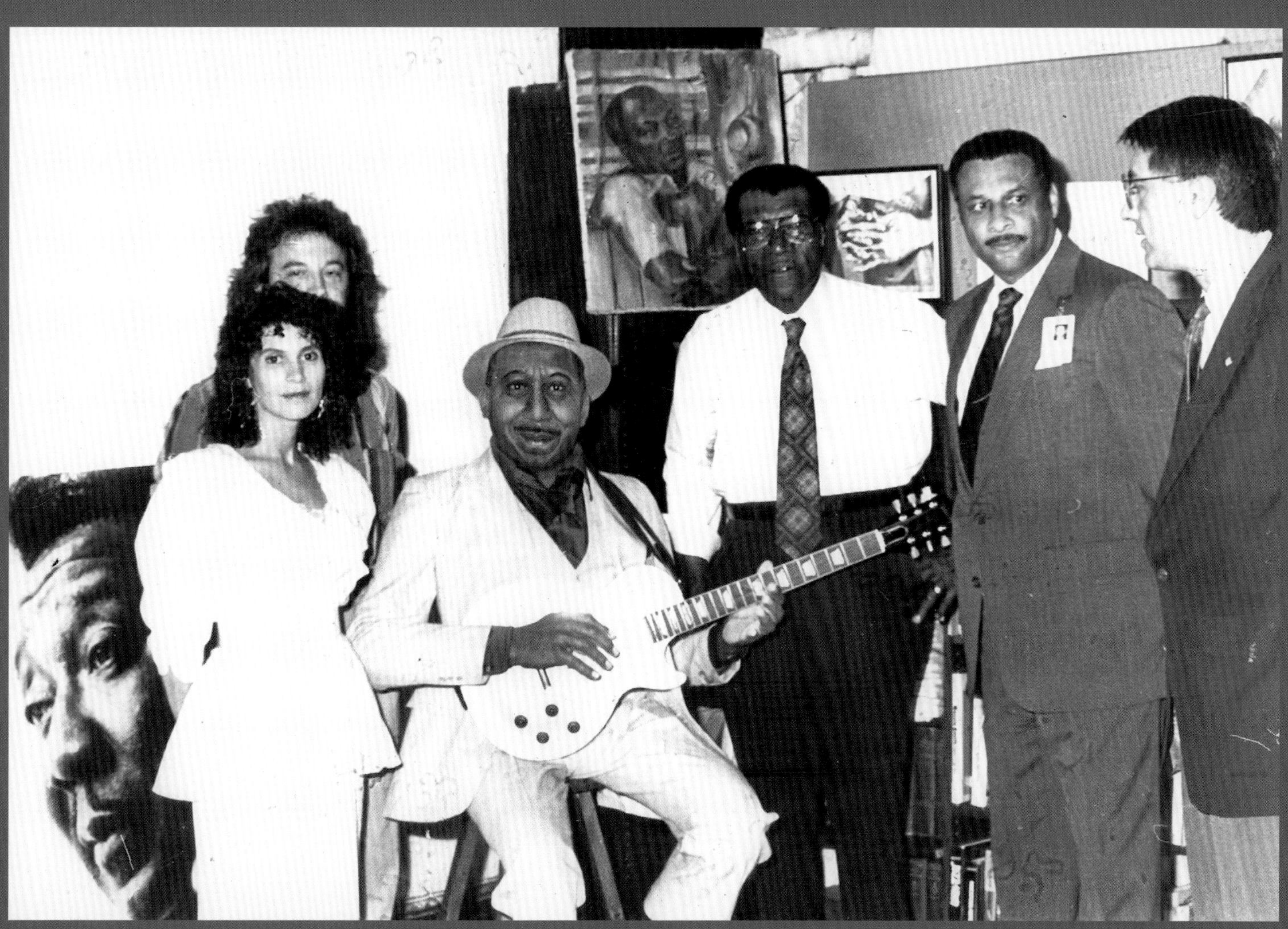

In 1990 Ray and Mary Daub of Wilmington, Delaware, donate a five-foot eleven-inch, life-sized wax sculpture of Muddy Waters to the Delta Blues Museum, and it becomes a major tourism attraction. Accepting the sculpture are Sid Graves, museum director, Clarksdale mayor Henry Espy, and Early Wright of WROX radio.

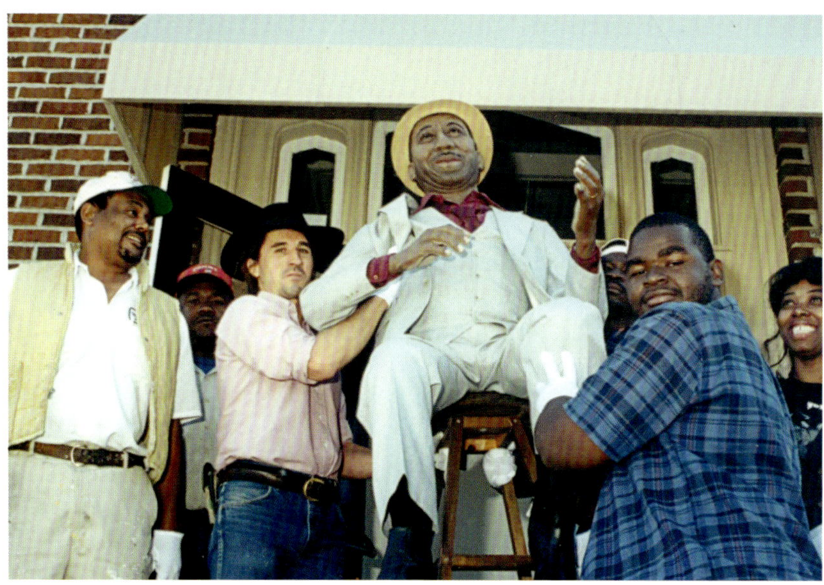

life-sized wax sculpture they created of Muddy Waters. It wears the musician's own clothes, and it became an instant tourist attraction.

The museum's freight depot location on the railroad tracks was renovated, and the museum has continued to be a vibrant part of the community. Partnering often with other entities, the museum has sponsored exhibits and receptions for photographers, artists, and entertainers, including Acoustic Africa, renowned quilter Gwen Magee, Founders Day programs for Coahoma Community College, retirement celebrations (including a memorable event for Dr. Vivian Presley, retiring president of CCC), and most recently a successful workshop instructing area educators how to teach blues in the schools.

Under the direction of Shelley Ritter, the museum has grown significantly and enjoys a handsome new two-story addition with a smooth-riding elevator and no problems. First Lady Michelle Obama awarded the museum's after-school program a 2013 National Medal for Museum and Library Services, and the Delta Blues Museum Band earned a standing ovation in the White House after its finale concert.

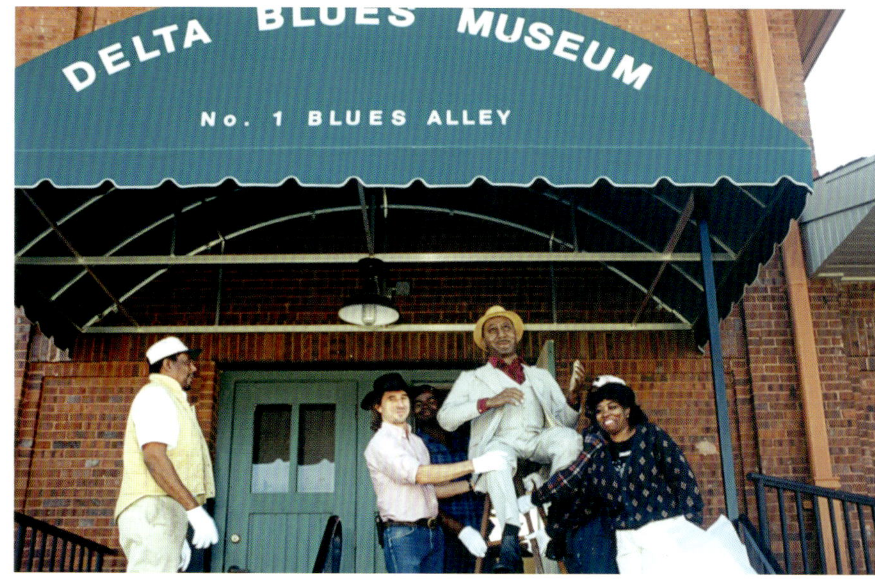

▲ Mission accomplished! Muddy survives a short ride down Delta Avenue and arrives beneath the new Delta Blues Museum canopy. Inside the museum, the sculpture is featured inside the cypress log cabin from Stovall Plantation where he lived with his grandmother.

◄ Very, very gingerly, John Ruskey, Blues Museum curator (in black hat), Maie Smith (right), city workers, and museum staffers ease Muddy beneath the second-floor canopy of Carnegie Public Library into the new Delta Blues Museum on Blues Alley.

► Blending architecturally with the Delta Blues Museum's historic railroad design, the new addition provides two stories of airy, much-needed space for exhibits, receptions, and educational workshops.

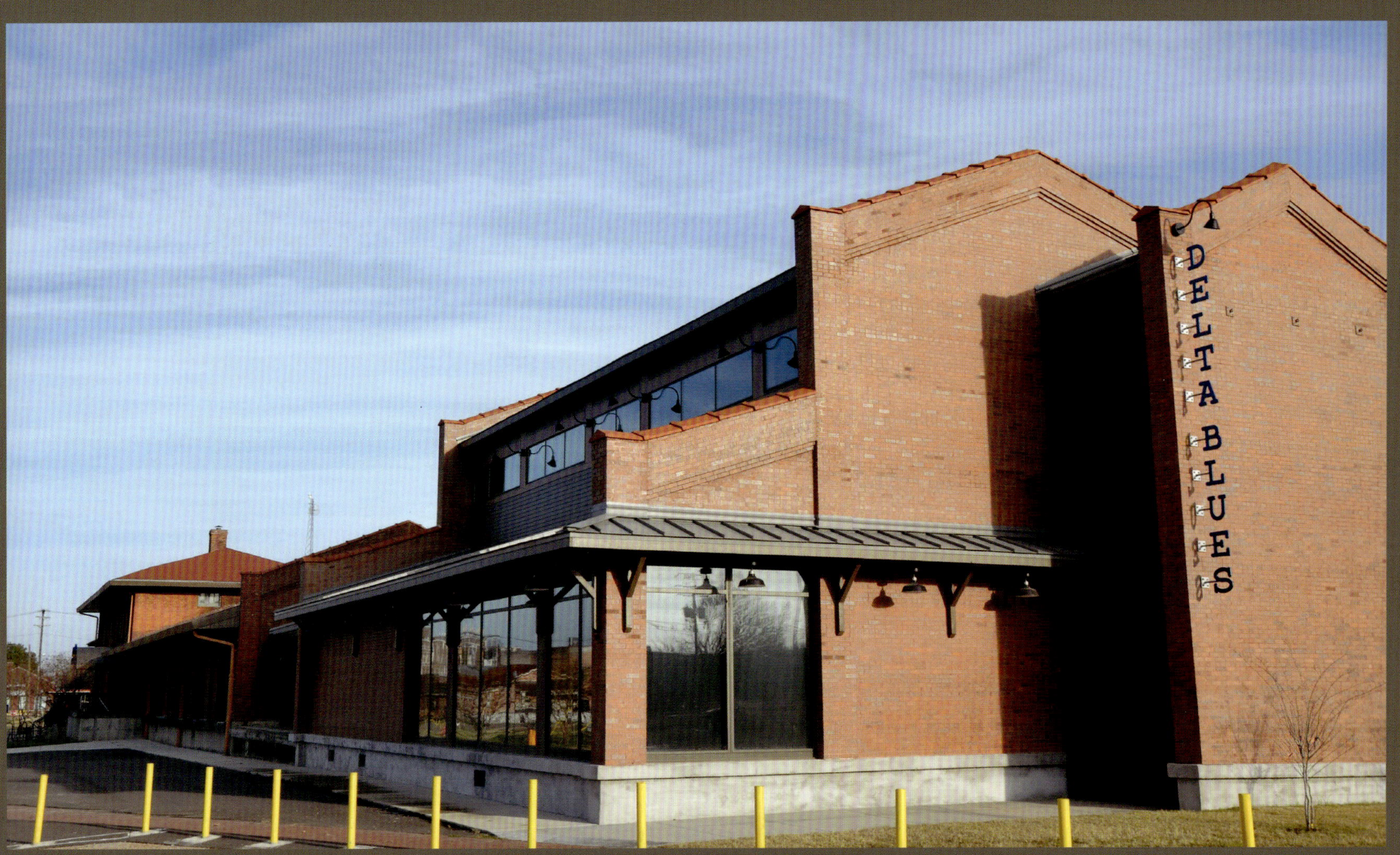
DELTA BLUES

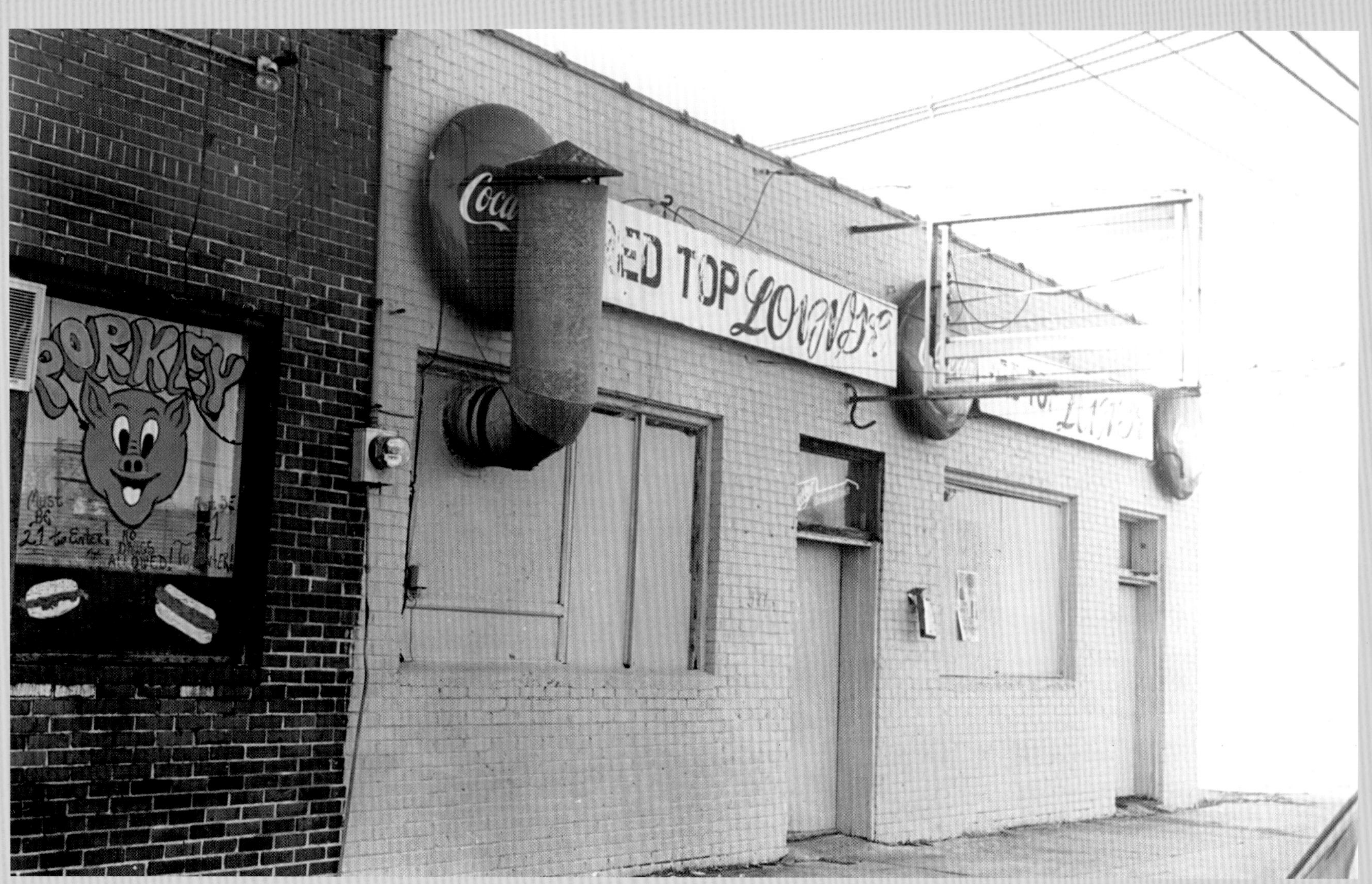

PORKEY
Must
B6
21 To Enter
NO DRUGS ALLOWED To Enter
Coca
ED TOP LOUNGE

1

JUKE JOINTS

SMITTY'S RED TOP LOUNGE

The Jelly Roll Kings posed for the cover of their first album outside Smitty's Red Top Lounge on Yazoo, across the railroad tracks from the Blues Museum. Since then the oversize Coke caps on the sign have been either sold or stolen. A semi-open building occupied the corner where mechanics worked on cars, and where such guys as C. V. Veal and a "chairman of the board" sat in cane back chairs every afternoon "tending to business." On weekends Oscar parked his hot-tamale truck on the curb, plugged his appliances into a custom electrical connection on the light pole, and started cooking. Covered with a tarp in bad weather, the entry was a cozy spot to sit and visit when it rained or became cold. It was also handy for hungry blues fans leaving late-night clubs.

After my first excursion into Smitty's, I became a regular, following the Wesley Jefferson Band with its two lead guitarists: Michael James and Super Chikan Johnson; the Big Jack Johnson

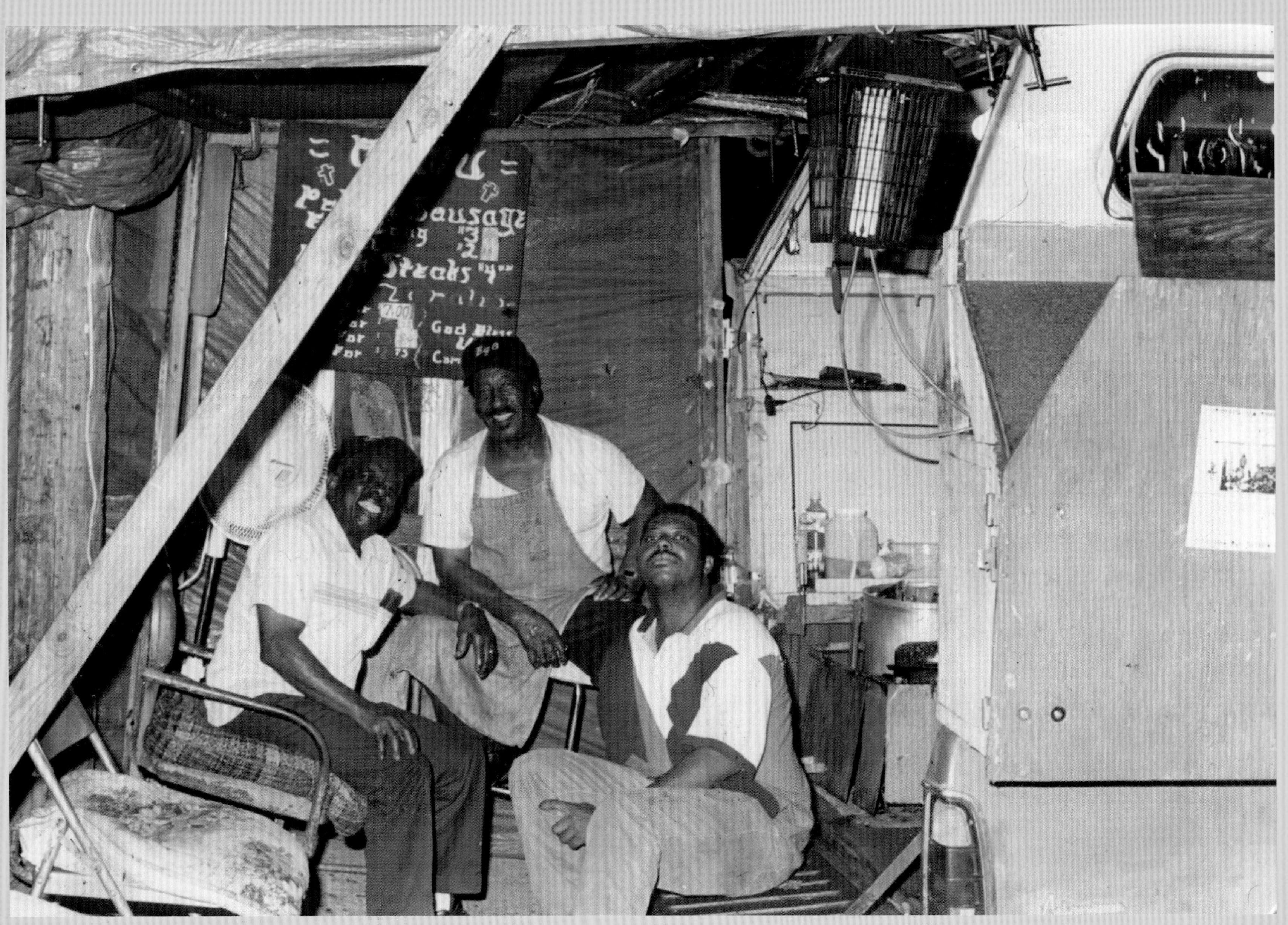
Sausage
Steaks "4"
God Bless

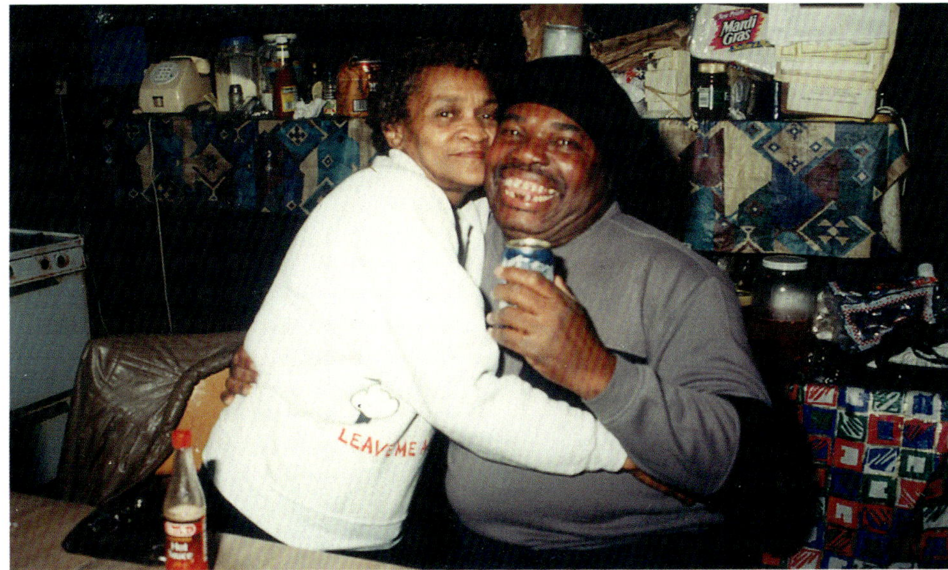

Band, Arthneice Jones, and Robert "Bilbo" Walker in other clubs and juke joints in Clarksdale, Bobo, Shelby, Tutwiler, and Winstonville.

At the time the Red Top was run by James Alford and his helper, Bertha, who occasionally prepared catfish or one-dish meals to sell. No one paid much attention to me—I became part of the woodwork and blues scene—except for an elegantly dressed lady and her brother, both talented ballroom dancers, who always welcomed and invited me to join them on the dance floor, which I did. C. W. Moore, who worked for the County Road Department, and his wife, Bertel, later took over management of the club. They called it C. W.'s which could be confusing, since another C. W. had a business of the same name in Winstonville. We stopped there once with a tour group for supper and ran right into a sign advertising room rates by the hour—which reminded me of an earlier conversation with Mrs. Hill about Clarksdale's curfew during the civil rights era.

She said before Hezekiah Patton's famous Harlem Inn in Winstonville burned down, he booked big-name bands on their way to gigs in Memphis or New Orleans. When their shows were over, it was too late to drive home legally to Clarksdale, so local bands were booked to play till the sun came up and curfew was lifted.

I once escorted the exuberant Swedish vocalist Sven Jetterburg into C. W.'s Clarksdale club when he came to town looking for live music on a weeknight. He stuffed coins into the jukebox, punched in numbers, sat down at a table surrounded by locals, and sang at the top of his lungs.

RIVERMOUNT LOUNGE

Melville Tillis never drank alcohol, but he ran a fine bar with a large dance floor inside his Rivermount Lounge on Sunflower. The Sunflower Blues Association often met there, and I frequently stopped to ask Tillis his opinion about local issues.

When friends from Norway, including a celebrity guitarist, came to town and wanted to visit a blues club, we went to the Rivermount. A large reunion of the Viking Motorcycle Club was in progress, and their members—all friendly African American bikers wearing numbered and registered Viking T-shirts—invited us to join them in line dancing. We did, and the party was progressing in great fashion. Knut,

▲

Bertel and C. W. Moore, who worked for the county road department and also ran the Red Top for a while, celebrate their wedding anniversary there.

◀

On weekends in Clarksdale's New World District, Oscar Renfro parks his hot-tamale truck on the curb of Fourth and Yazoo Streets, plugs his appliances into a custom electrical connection on the light pole, and starts cooking. Covered with a tarp in bad weather, it's a cozy spot to visit for bluesman C. V. Veal (left), Oscar (center), and a neighbor. It's also handy for hungry blues fans leaving late-night clubs.

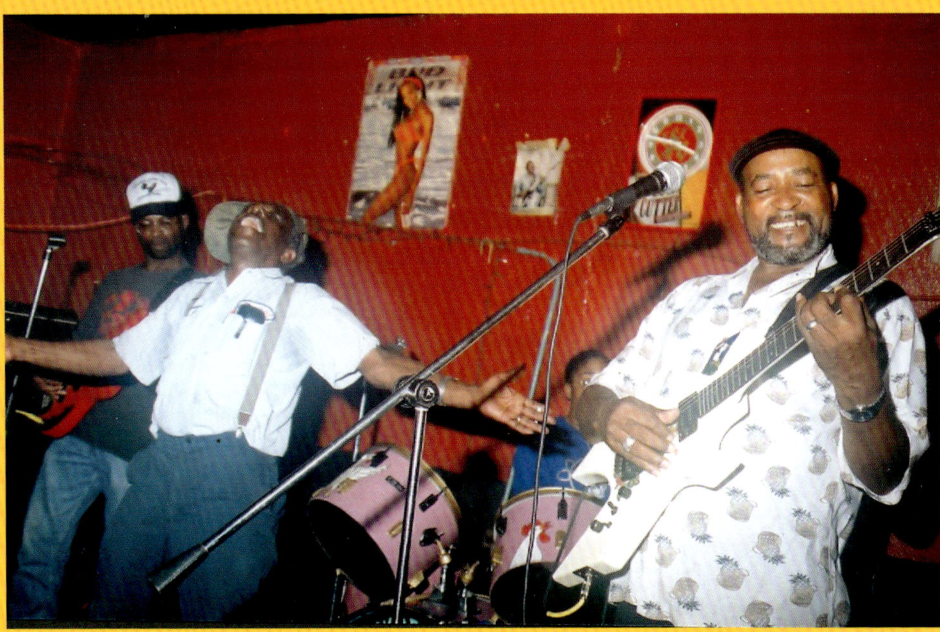

Weekends at the Red Top are lively when gravel-throated drummer C. V. Veal (center) can be coaxed to sing onstage with guitarists Shine Turner (left) and Super Chikan Johnson.

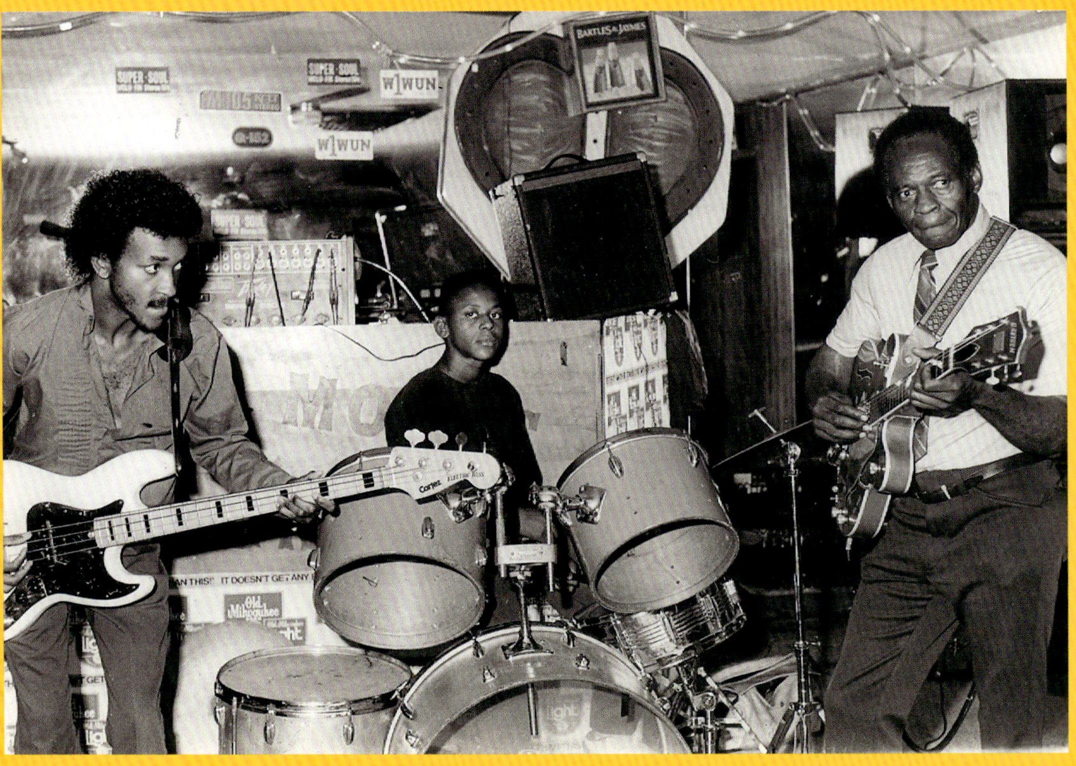

A favorite hangout and venue for visiting celebrities Clayton Love, Little Milton, and Ike Turner, the Rivermount is a popular venue also for local musicians, including members of the Stone Gas Band (from left) bassist Harvel Thomas, drummer Deon Thomas, and Mr. Johnnie Billington.

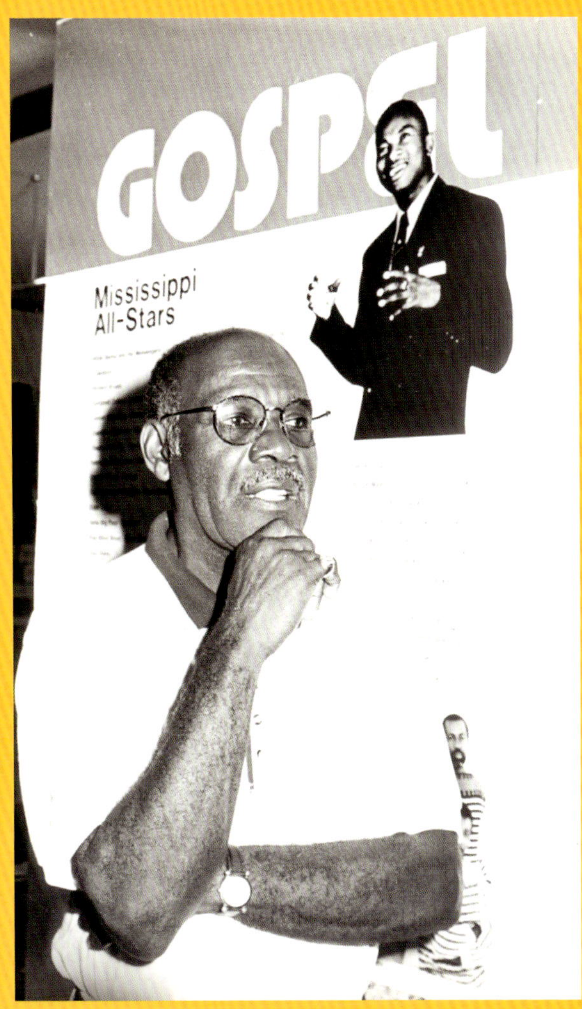

Music historian/educator/coach, longtime Public Utilities Commission chairman, and Sunflower River Festival cochairman Melville Tillis never drank alcohol but ran a fine bar with a large dancefloor inside his Rivermount Lounge. Growing up he played trumpet in local bands, and when introduced later as Ike Turner's trumpet player, he quickly made this correction: "Ike Turner played in *our* band."

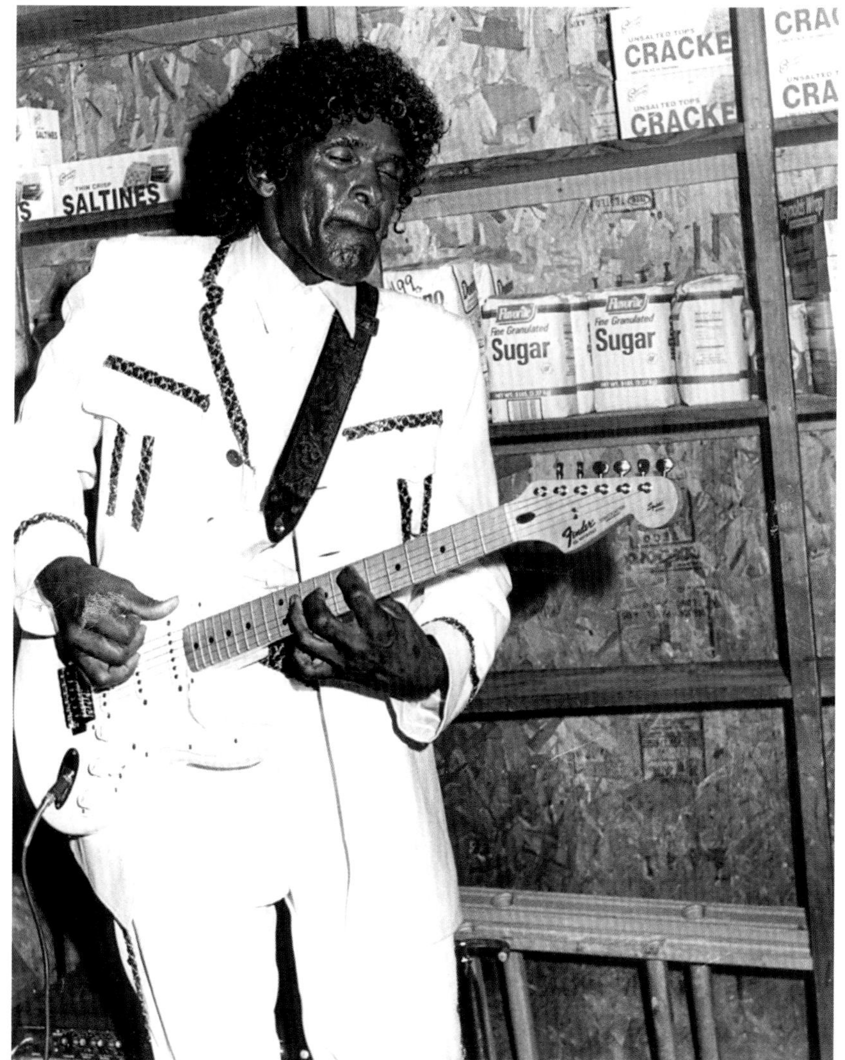

my journalist friend, intrigued by their "Viking" connection, finally convinced a biker wife to let him have a shirt if he swore to wear it only overseas, back in Norway. Knut disappeared for a bit. Next we heard a loud "Aha!" from the men's restroom. The door was thrown open to reveal a resplendent Knut, feeling absolutely no pain but wearing the forbidden Viking shirt. All hell broke loose! With the Viking Motorcycle Club on our heels, we slammed Knut through the front door into my car and screeched down back streets to lie low inside an industrial neighborhood hangout called The Rose.

My great friend Roger Barnes, pressman in charge of the newspaper's printing press and almost everything else, had introduced me to The Rose years earlier when he hosted a fabulous buffet celebrating his birthday during the King Biscuit Festival. The Rose was a "guy" or "Cheers" kind of place. Owned by Franklin Wade, it had the best jukebox in Clarksdale, packed with blues and soul, and we danced to Marvin Sease's "Hittin' and Runnin'," watched sports, and chilled out from time to time with the Rose "brothers" I was proud to know. It also was the site of a memorable dinner, with Mrs. Roby cooking a bear roast.

THE BOBO GROCERY

The Bobo Grocery in Bobo, Mississippi, several miles south of Clarksdale on Highway 61, was a favorite gathering place when Robert "Bilbo" Walker came home from Bakersfield, California. To keep up with his crazy Chuck Berry–style antics, we danced around shelves of paper towels, fly swatters, jars of pickles, and coolers filled with beer

▲

The Bobo Grocery in Bobo, Mississippi, several miles south of Clarksdale on Highway 61, was a favorite gathering place when Robert "Bilbo" Walker came home from Bakersfield, California.

▶

The Bobo Grocery stocked everything from fly spray to Clabber Girl baking powder.

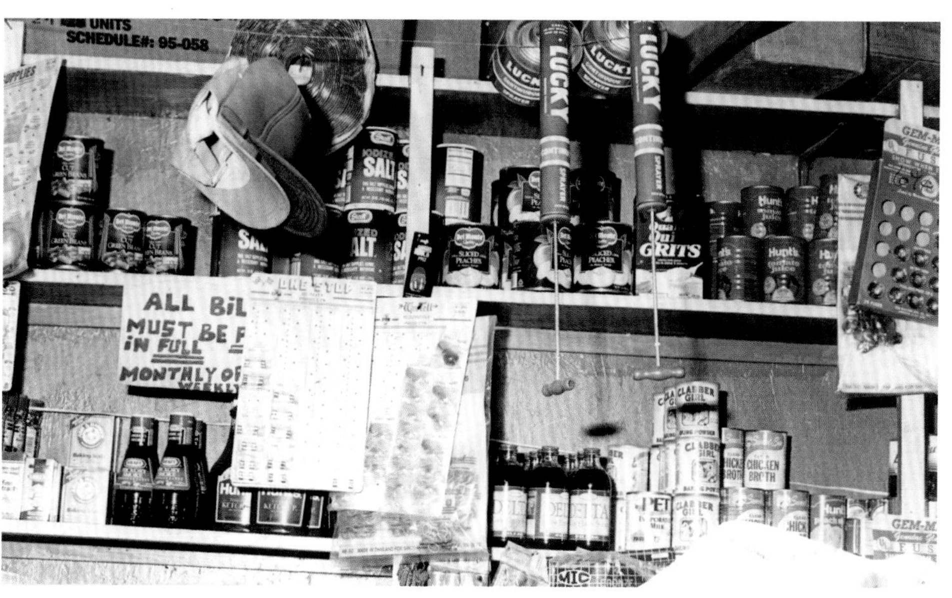

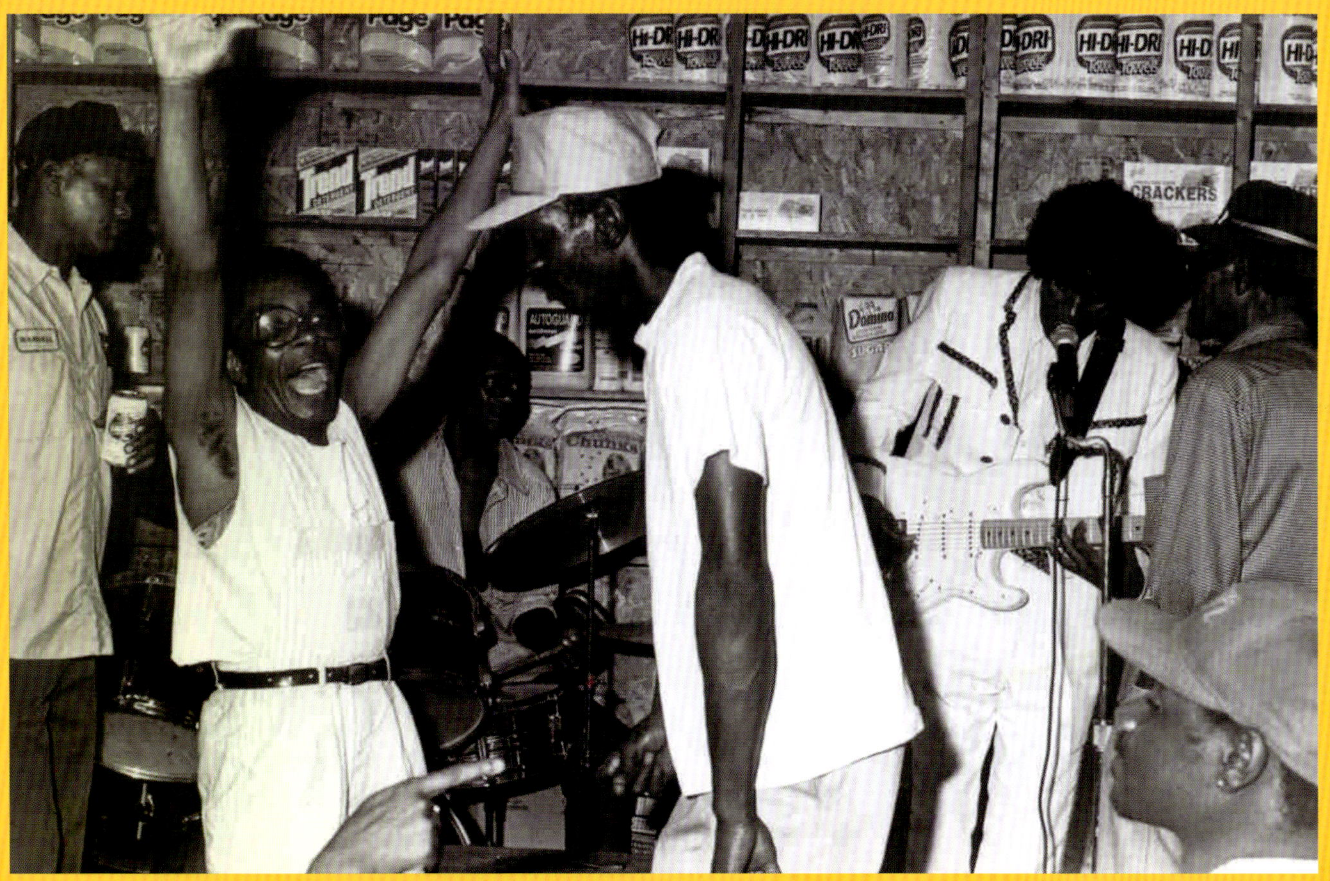

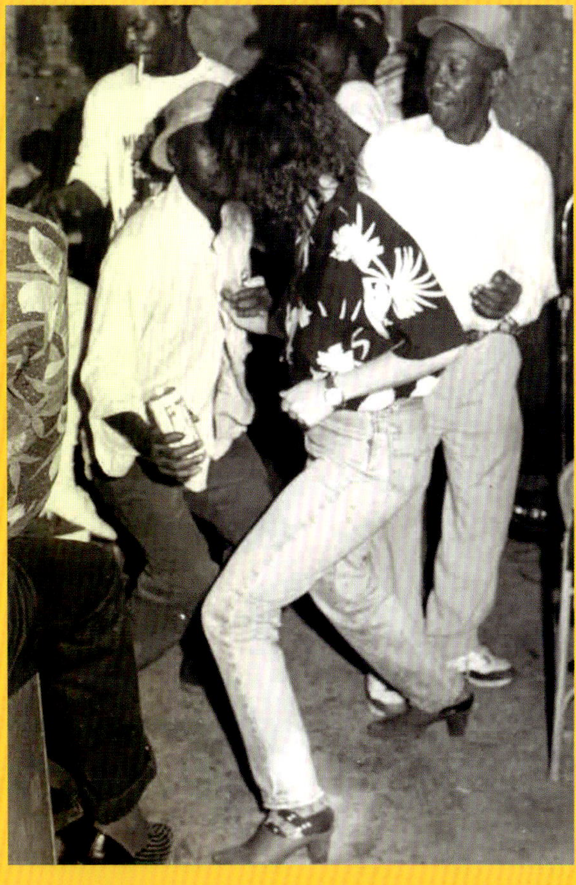

▲ To keep up with Robert Walker's crazy Chuck Berry–style antics, we danced around shelves of paper towels, fly swatters, jars of pickles, and coolers filled with beer and orange sodas.

◄ The Bobo Grocery was a friendly location for both races when celebrating birthdays and anniversaries and became a famous one when the Jelly Roll Kings were filmed here for *River of Song*, a PBS documentary sponsored by the Smithsonian Institution.

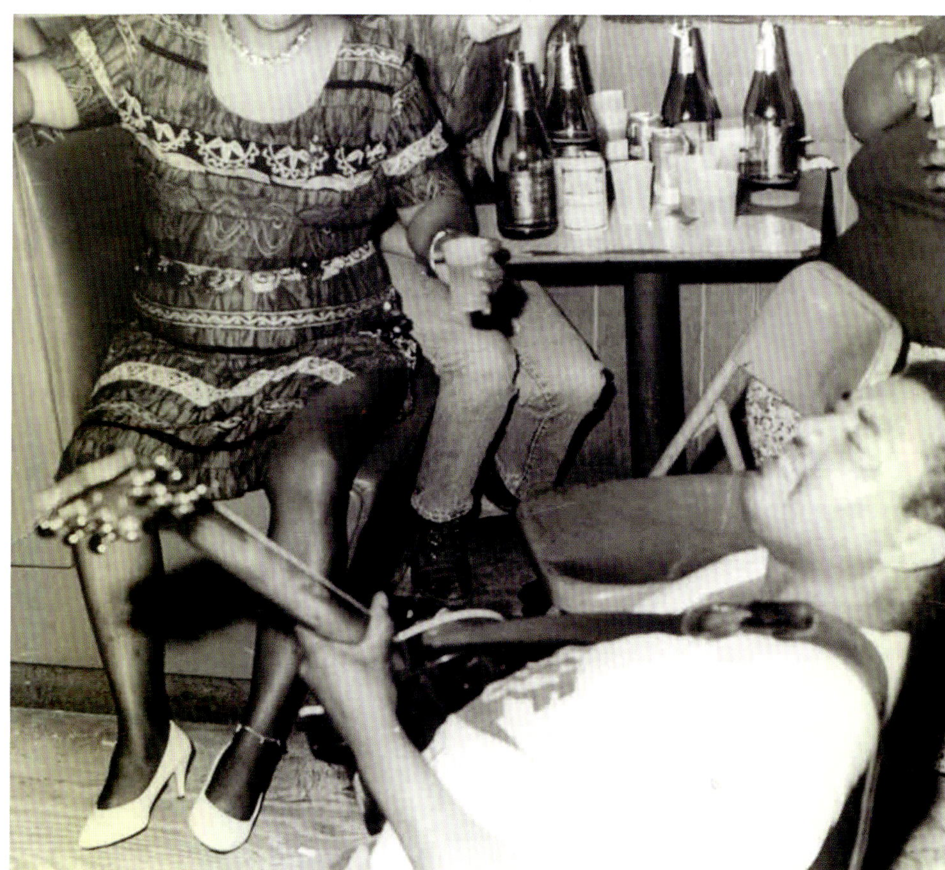

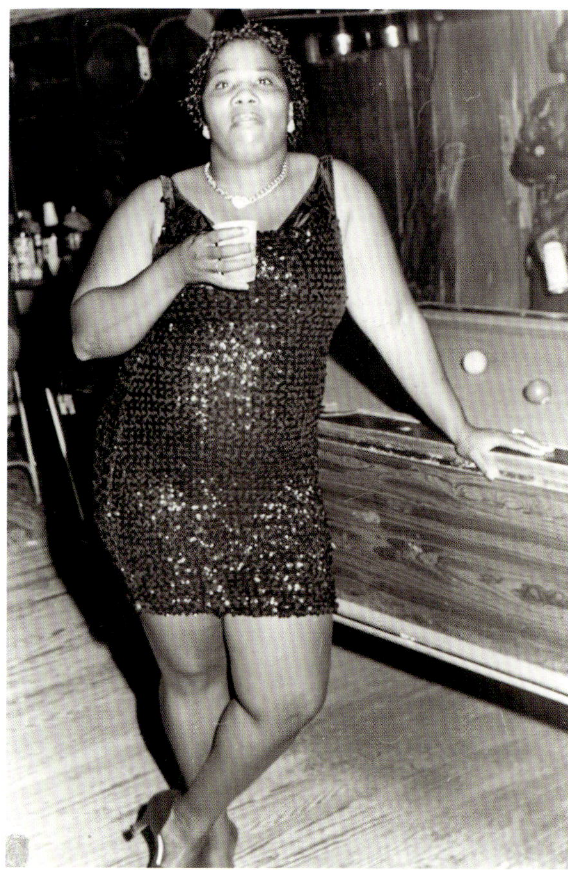

and orange sodas. It was a friendly location for both races celebrating birthdays and anniversaries. It became a very famous one when the Jelly Roll Kings were filmed there for *River of Song*, a PBS documentary series sponsored by the Smithsonian Institution. Unfortunately, misfortune hounded the Bobo Grocery. It burned, was rebuilt, and became deserted after a homicide was committed there.

THE DEW DROP INN

One long Delta summer and fall, the Wesley Jefferson Band played every Sunday night in Shelby at the Dew Drop Inn. When we began going there, the club was so small we sat in booths with long-eared Playboy bunnies painted on the walls, and we threaded around amps, drum sets, and cables to dance. Mama Rene and Big E ran a tight ship and brooked no foolishness or raucous behavior; I remember a woman involved in a heated argument being fast-exited through the front screen door by E. The club became so popular they expanded it, almost doubling its size. The dance floor stayed busy with regulars from Shelby, Clarksdale (including Super Chikan's sister, Christine), and visitors from abroad introducing themselves and dancing.

▲

One of the Wesley Jefferson Band's two super-talented guitarists, Michael James plays from the floor of the Dew Drop Inn in Shelby.

▶

One long Delta summer and fall, the Wesley Jefferson Band played every Sunday night at the Dew Drop Inn, and Priscilla, all dressed up for dancing, was one of the regulars welcoming everyone to Shelby.

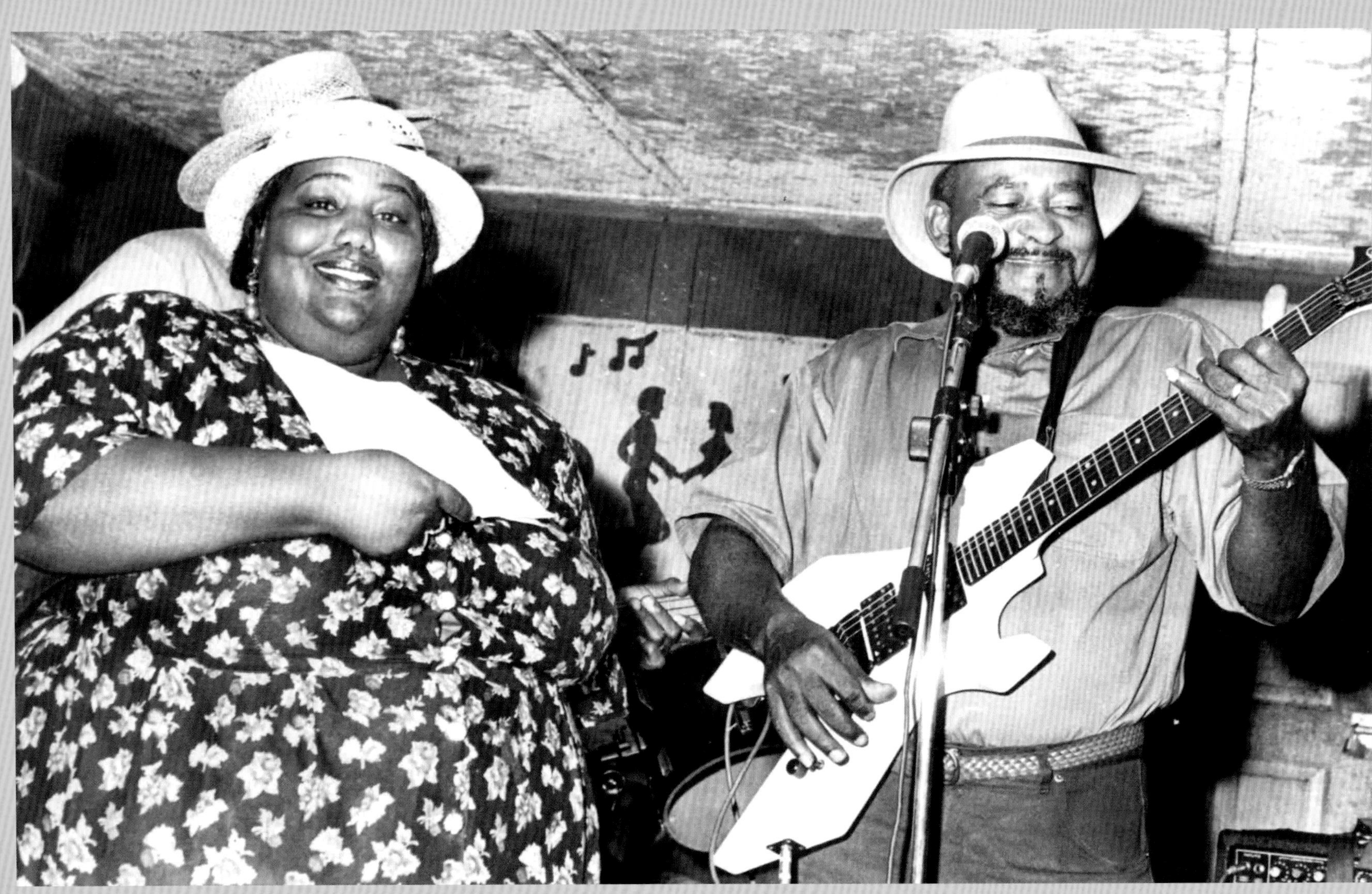

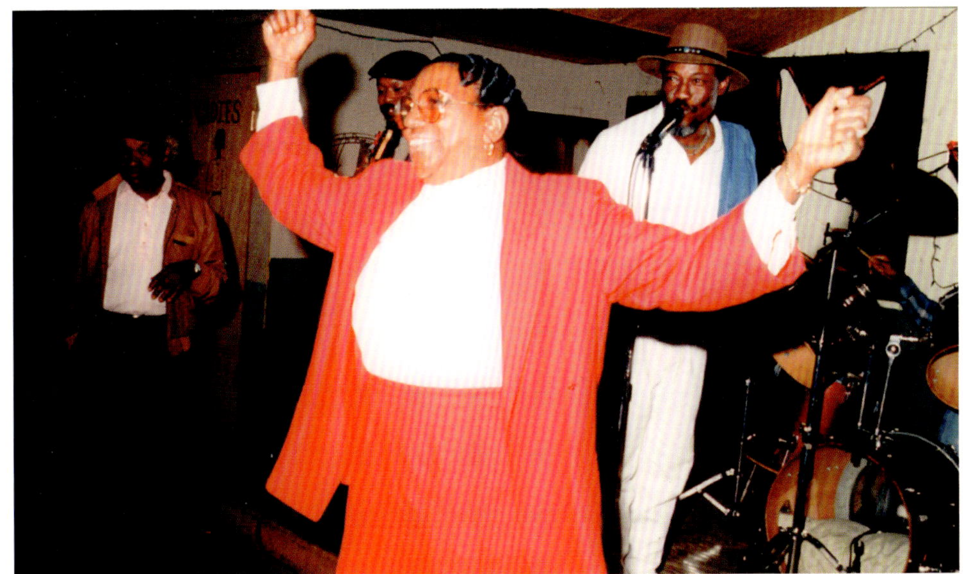

One Sunday night John Ruskey, who played keyboard for the band, planned to celebrate his birthday at the Dew Drop. I was determined not to miss the party, although I had spent the day photographing celebrity chefs preparing multiple courses for a posh James Beard dinner at KC's in Cleveland. Each course was accompanied by a special wine from the Robert Mondavi vineyard. Since I was seated with the Mondavi vintners, I decided it would be discourteous not to sample a few. Fortunately, the distance from Cleveland to Shelby is short. My guardian angel was driving when Shelby's constable pulled me over outside the Dew Drop. Mama Rene rushed out chastising the lawman: "Leave that lady alone; I've known her for years, and she never drinks anything but Diet Coke." This was true. But not this night. My friends took me inside the Dew Drop, took care of me, and drove me home. Weeks later, however, true misfortune struck. Wesley Jefferson suffered horrendous injuries in an accident driving the band van back to Clarksdale. His recovery was miraculous, but the accident closed a rare chapter in Mississippi Delta blues.

MARGARET'S BLUE DIAMOND

However, Delta blues has multiple venues, and for years Margaret's Blue Diamond in Clarksdale was a classic. Facing the railroad tracks on Tallahatchie, Margaret's was a favorite Saturday-night place to party, drink beer or Crown and Coke, listen to music, and dance with friends or anyone or no one but yourself. The club welcomed and invited visitors to share tables. Margaret's was regarded as a safe place in the early hours of an evening, although I once witnessed a customer removing a heavy pistol from her bra and plopping it down on our table before moving to the dance floor. Decorating the wall behind the elevated stage was a diamond graphic sparkling with blue sequins. The musicians wore smart outfits, not the flamboyant "pimp-style" stage clothes favored by some visiting European musicians.

Margaret's was the setting for a music video starring Big Jack Johnson, and another time for a segment of Ted Koppel's *Nightline* for ABC television. Later all of us who had been there, including Margaret, watched the video on a big screen at Carnegie Public Library.

Following renovation by new owners, live music was replaced by a jukebox. C. W. and Bertel moved from the old Red Top to manage this location, and the place continued to be popular with a distinctive

▲

Attired in red and dancing with a customer on her birthday, Mama Rene and her husband Big E ran the Dew Drop like a tight ship. No foolishness or raucous behavior, and E once fast-exited an argumentative woman through the front screen door.

◄

Another Wesley Jefferson Band super-guitarist: Super Chikan Johnson calls on his sister Christine to hold the lyrics of one of his original songs at Shelby's Dew Drop Inn.

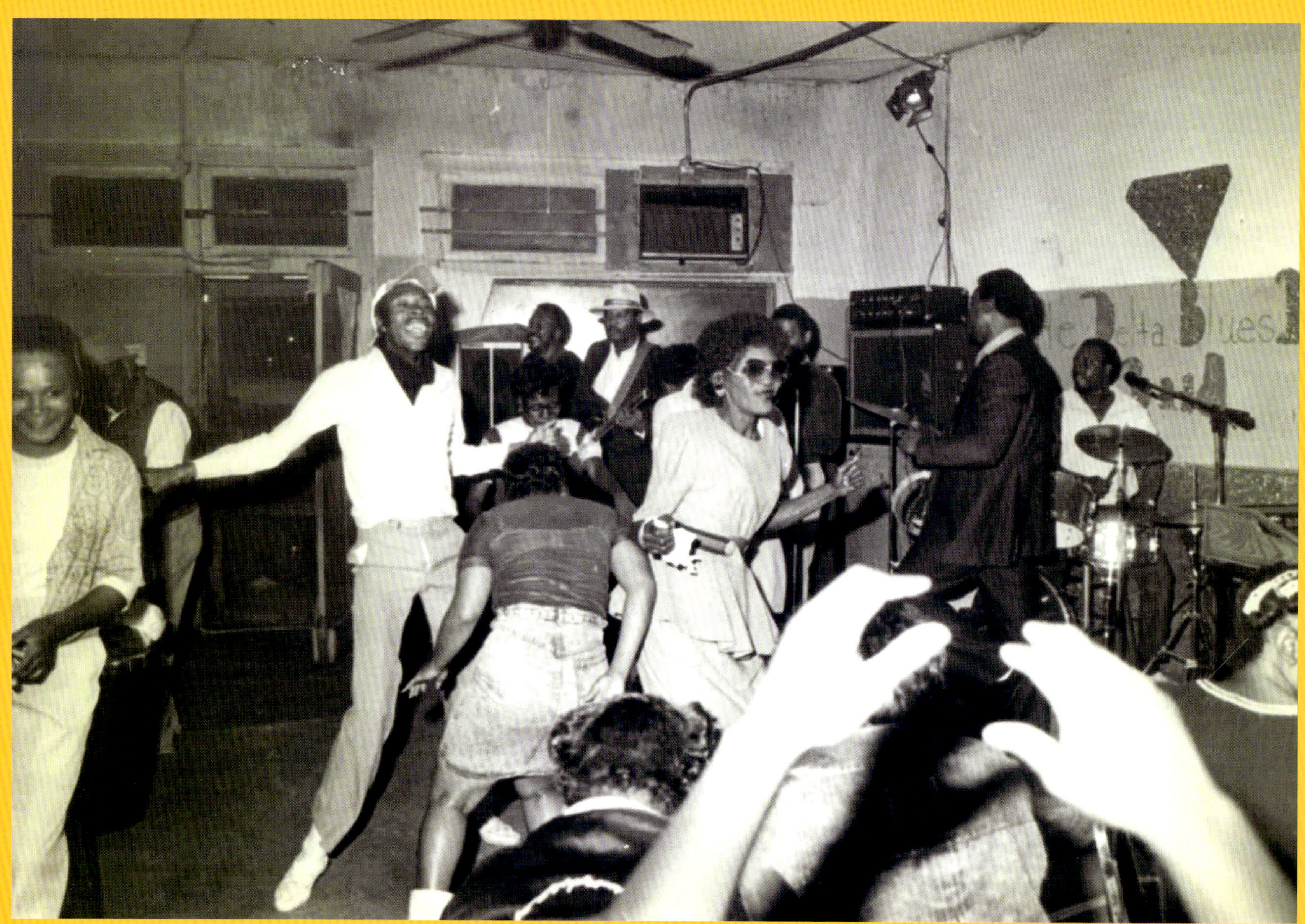

▲ Facing the railroad tracks on Tallahatchie, Margaret's Blue Diamond in Clarksdale was a favorite Saturday night place to party, drink beer or Crown and Coke, listen to music, and dance with friends or anyone or no one but yourself. Among the dancers are Foster "Tater" Wiley (in white) and Margaret (club owner) in sunglasses.

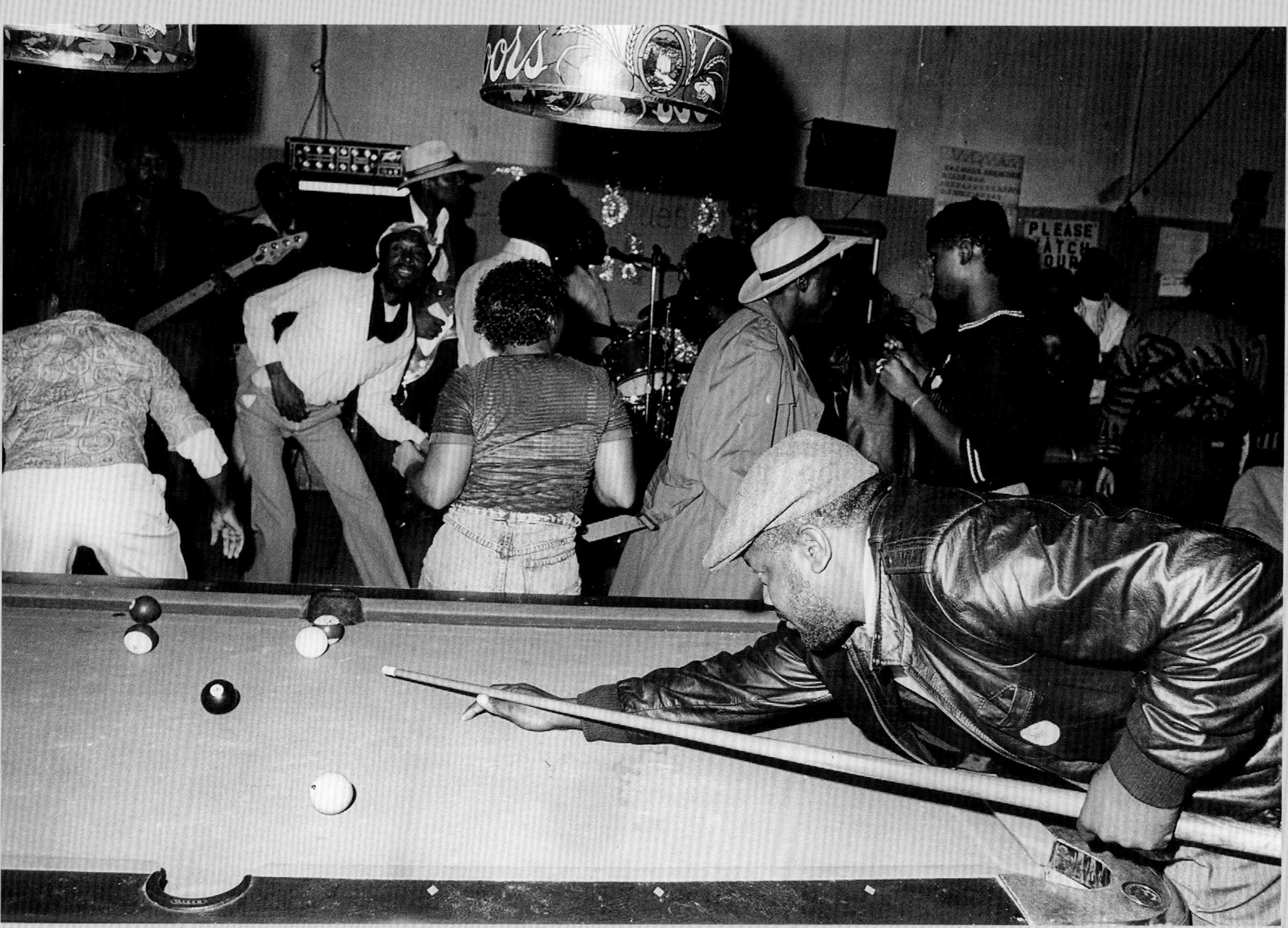

Margaret welcomed and invited visitors to share tables. Once the club was a music video setting, starring Big Jack Johnson, and another time a segment of Ted Koppel's *Nightline* for ABC television was filmed there.

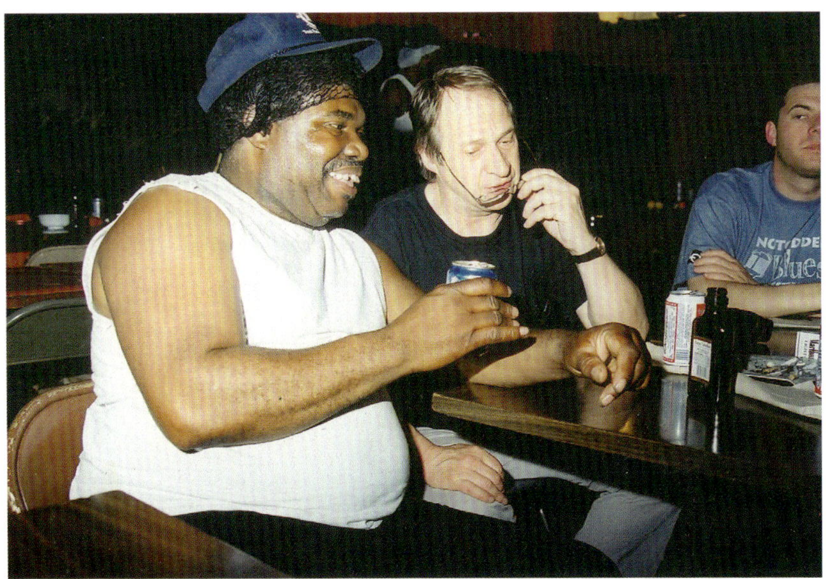

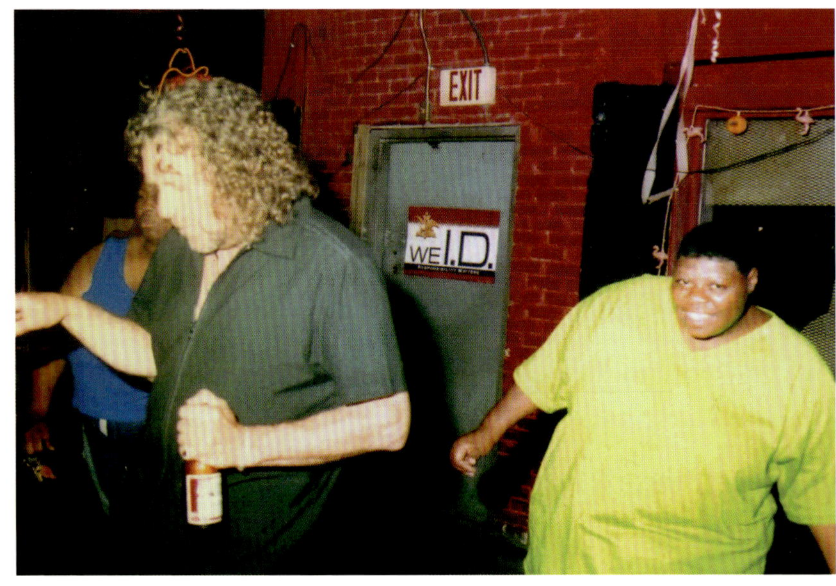

▲ C. W. Moore (left), who moved from the old Red Top and took over Margaret's Blue Diamond, welcomes Norwegian music celebrity Kare Virud and other visitors from Notodden to his club.

▲ No one recognizes or has even heard of Robert Plant, dancing in the crowd one night.

clientele. No one recognized, had a clue about, or had even heard of Robert Plant, who was dancing in the crowd one night.

HOPSON COMMISSARY

Another Delta venue where dancing was fun was the Hopson Commissary, where Ronnie Drew and his son, Marshall, played as did Luther Dickinson and the North Mississippi Allstars, cutting their teeth with Jimbo Mathus. Sometimes they stayed overnight on the semi-second-floor loft. Kenny Neal and Boogaloo Ames, the boogie piano master from Greenville, stamped a memorable evening there together, as did the Wesley Jefferson Band, all decked out in cummerbunds and tuxedos for a video I never viewed.

PO' MONKEY'S AND MORE

Although the Millennium across Delta Avenue from the Ground Zero has changed names several times, few will forget a high-energy show there by Robert "Bilbo" Walker and his dancing daughters.

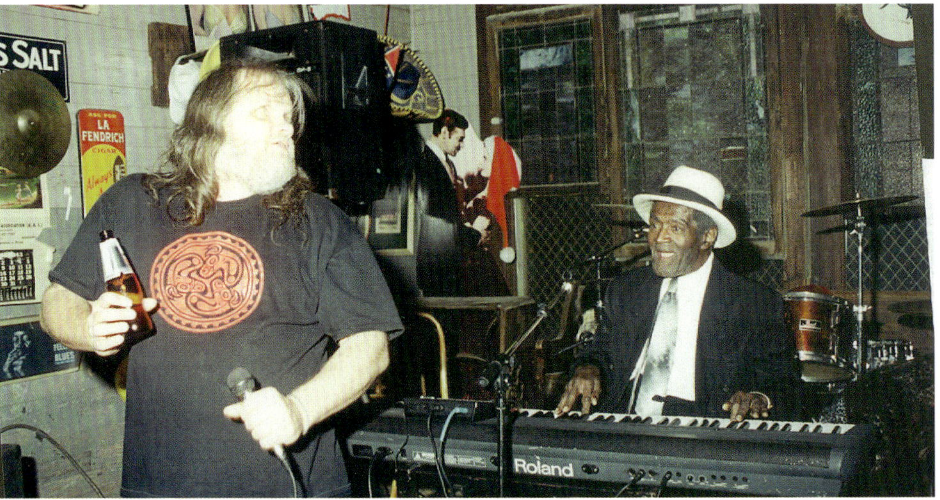

▲ Kenny Neal and Boogaloo Ames, the boogie piano master, stamp a memorable evening together at Hopson Commissary, the renovated historic farm store three miles south of Clarksdale on Highway 49, where the first mechanical cotton picker was perfected and Pinetop Perkins worked as a tractor driver.

▶ Dancing is always fun at Hopson Commissary, where Ronnie Drew and his son Marshall play and Luther Dickinson and the North Mississippi Allstars once cut their teeth together with Jimbo Mathus. The Wesley Jefferson Band, including (from left) Wesley, Super Chikan Johnson, Rip Butler, and Michael James are all decked out in cummerbunds and tuxedos for a video I never viewed.

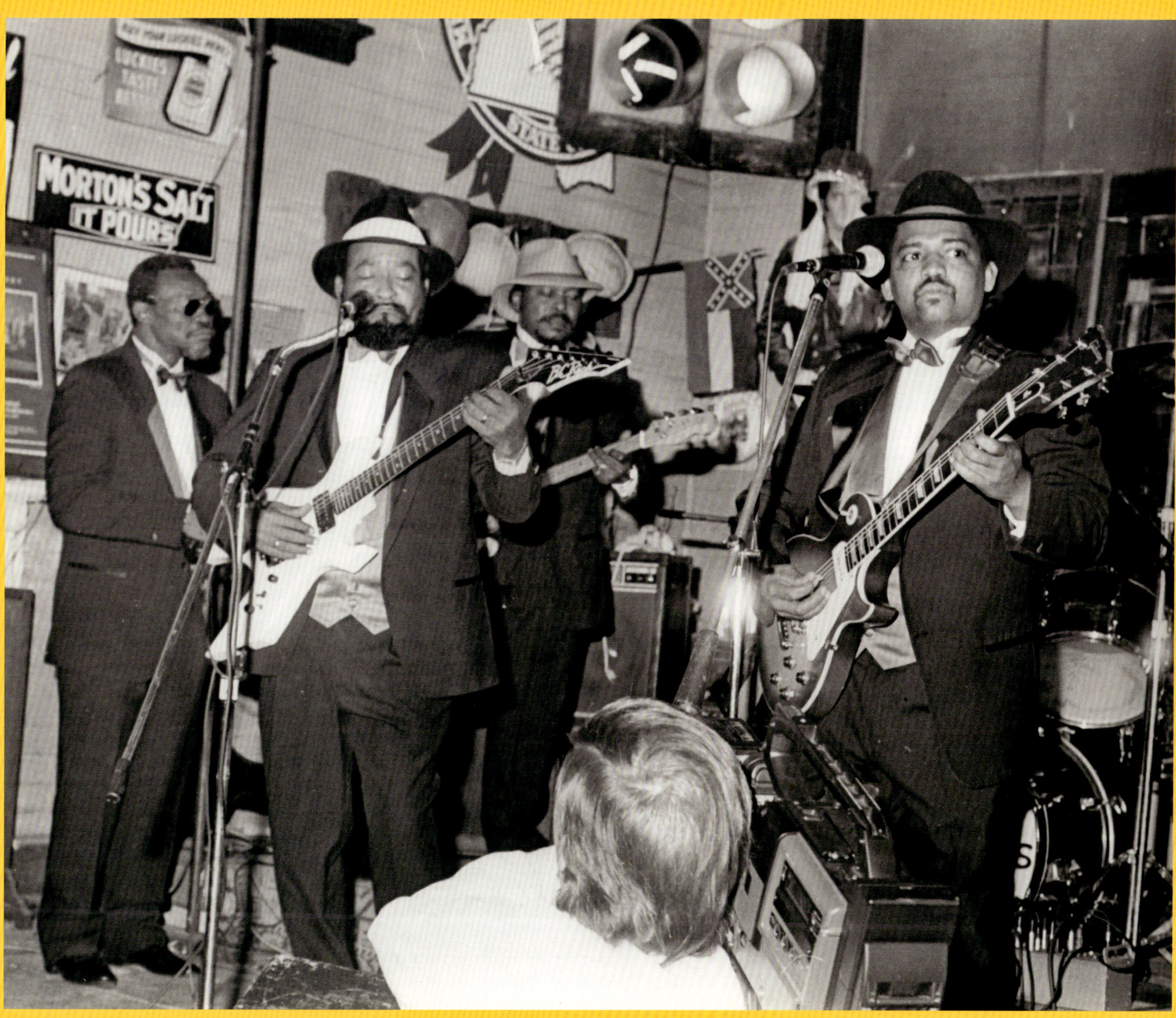
MORTON'S SALT
IT POURS

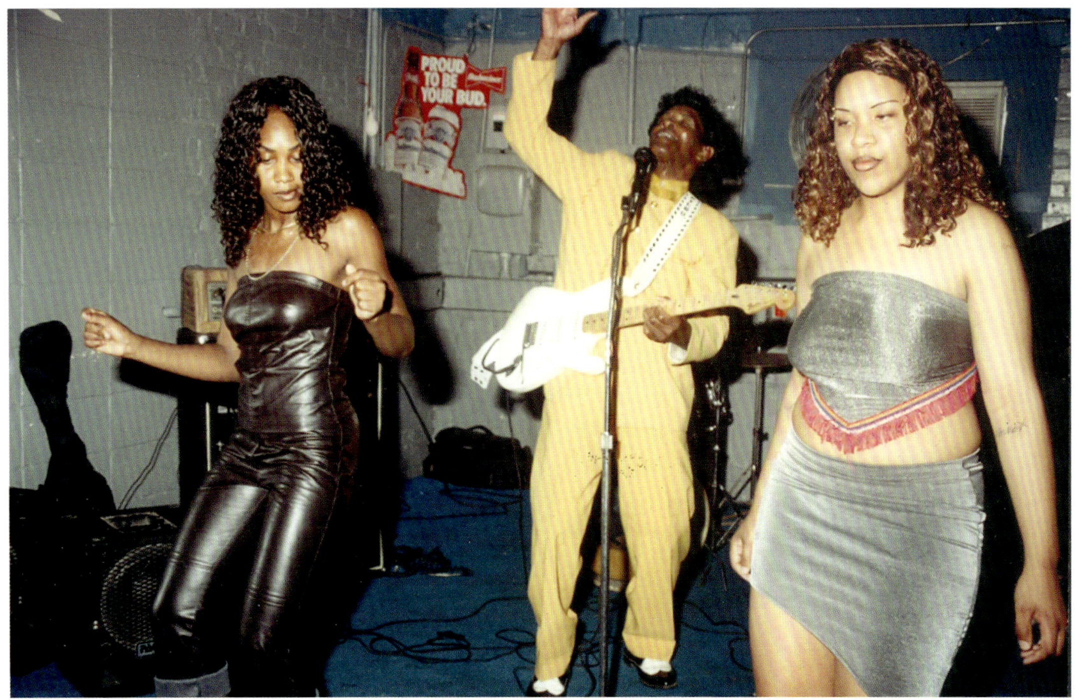

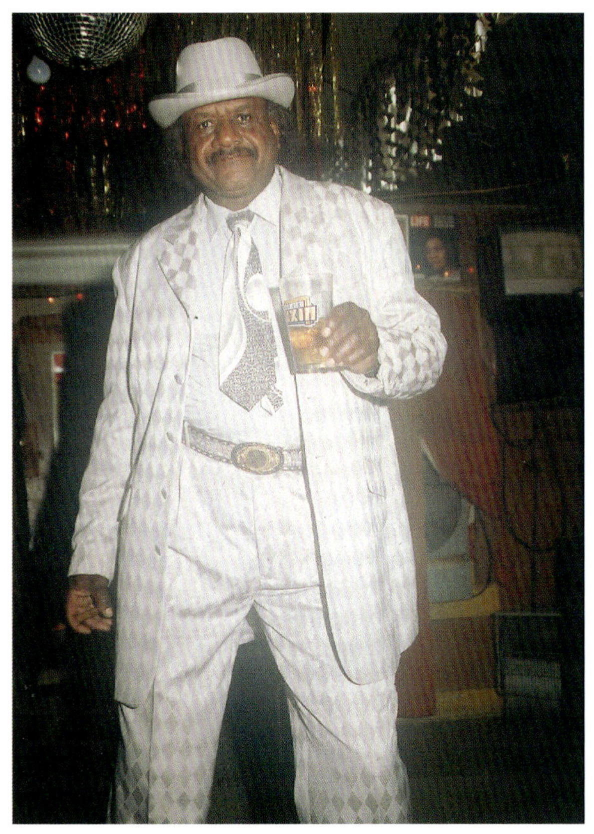

And Willie Seaberry (aka Po' Monkey), proprietor of the country juke joint of the same name near Merigold, welcomed visitors and regulars with a nonstop parade of eye-popping wardrobe changes Monday and Thursday nights. The patina of Po' Monkey's walls is vintage décor aged like fine wine that needs to be experienced to be absorbed. I took a Norwegian couple there, a librarian and a social worker, and heard afterward they were terrified of the place. Something must have been lost in the translation; we shared a table with local residents who were exceedingly friendly. But I doubt any could speak Norwegian.

A slogan in praise of dancing, on the walls of Sarah's Kitchen on Sunflower, was also a key to the personality of its owner. In addition to running a popular blues club, Sarah Moore was a fine chef willing to cook catfish or a full-fledged soul food dinner any time of day. A leaking kitchen roof was only a minor annoyance. Her club took on the personality of a proving ground for fledgling musicians who hoped to be invited to sit in with veteran artists. And dancing indeed was encouraged by Sarah, who resembled Tina Turner when she got all "gussied up."

The Divine Deborah lends elegance to any venue, including a popular blues club in Clarksdale's passenger depot once run by Terry (Big T) Williams. Today the space is the popular restaurant, the Dutch Oven.

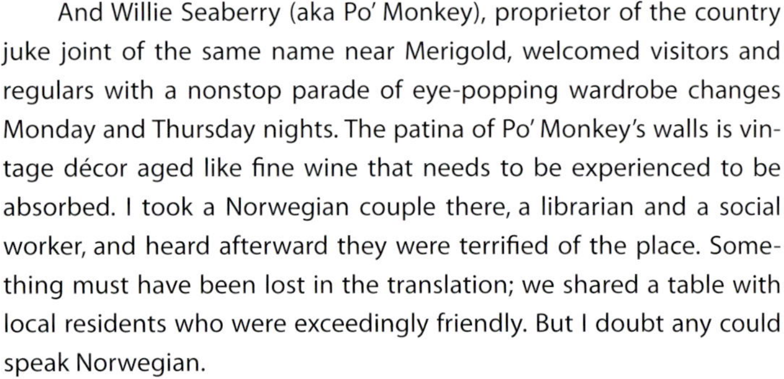

▲ Willie Seaberry (aka Po' Monkey) proprietor of the country juke joint of the same name near Merigold is unforgettable welcoming visitors and regulars with a nonstop parade of wardrobe changes.

◀ Although the Millennium across Delta Avenue from Ground Zero has changed names several times, few will forget a high-energy show there by Robert "Bilbo" Walker and his dancing daughters.

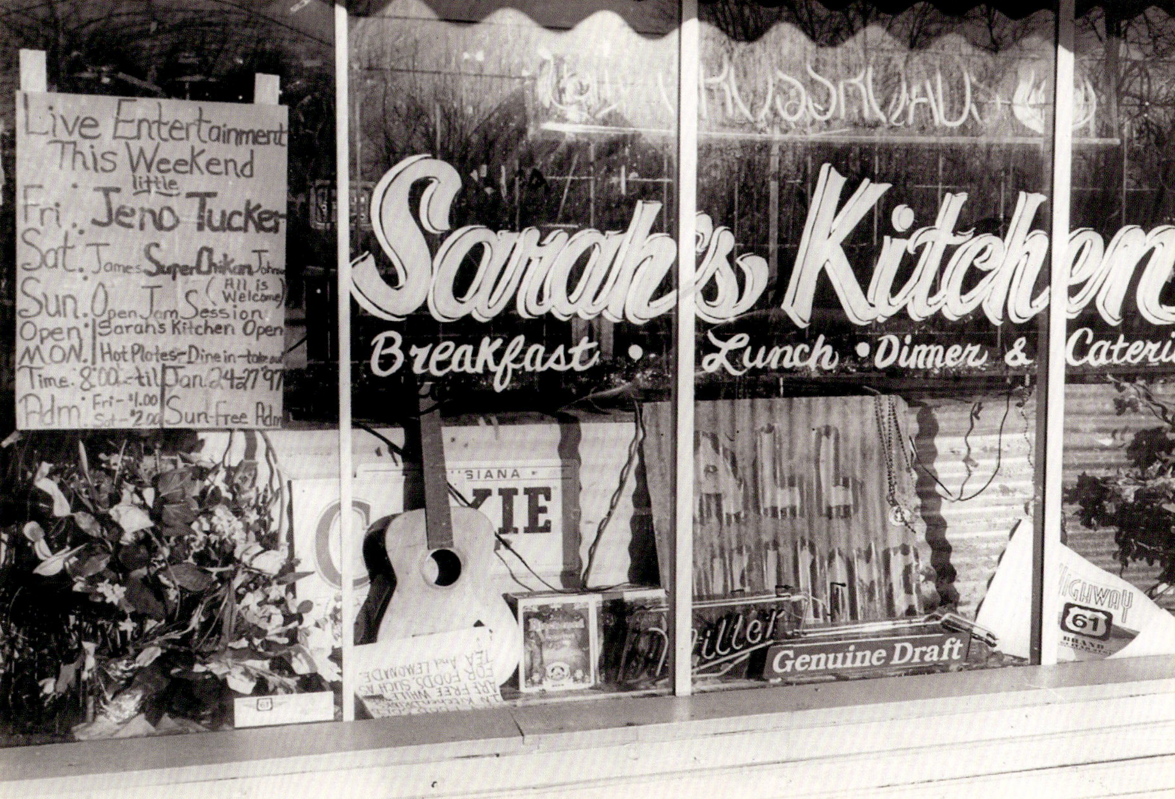

Sarah Moore was a fine chef willing to cook catfish or a full-fledged soul food dinner any time of day and promote local blues musicians, while resembling Tina Turner when she got "all gussied up."

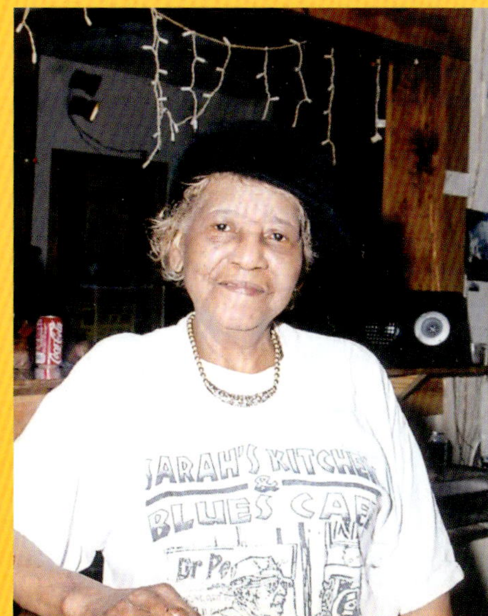

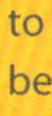

A slogan in praise of dancing, found on the walls of Sarah's Kitchen on Sunflower Avenue, was a key to the personality of its owner and her club that became a proving ground for fledgling musicians.

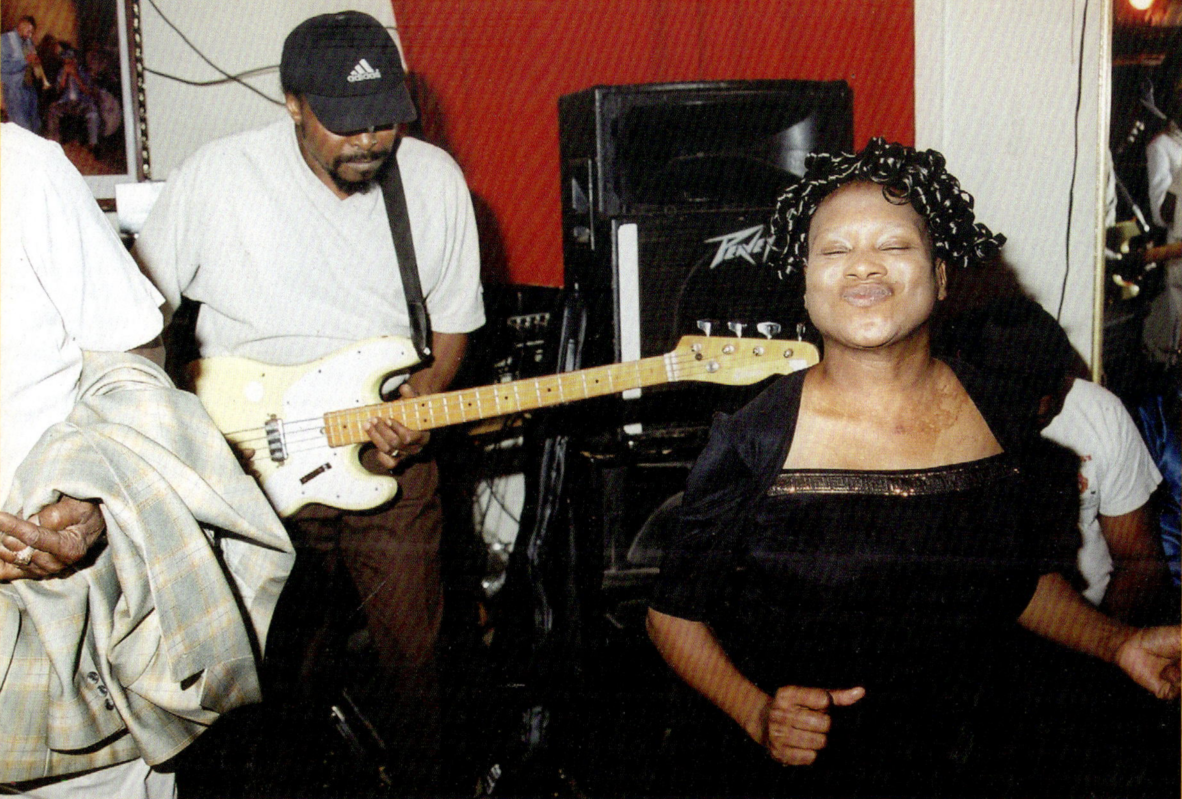

Dancing in the Delta is an art form, and Bobo's Divine Deborah is a winner inside Terry Williams's depot blues club that has become the Dutch Oven Restaurant.

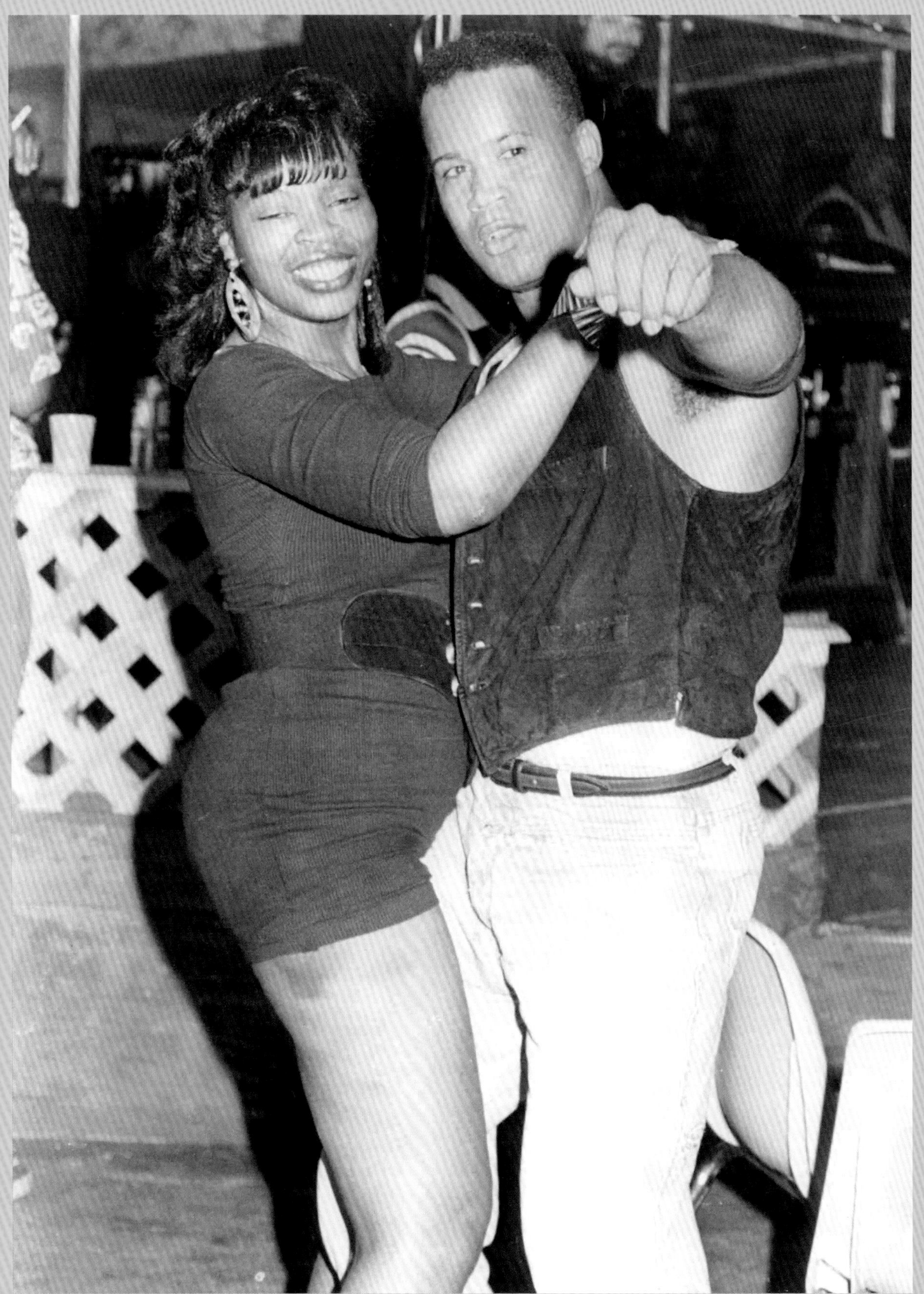

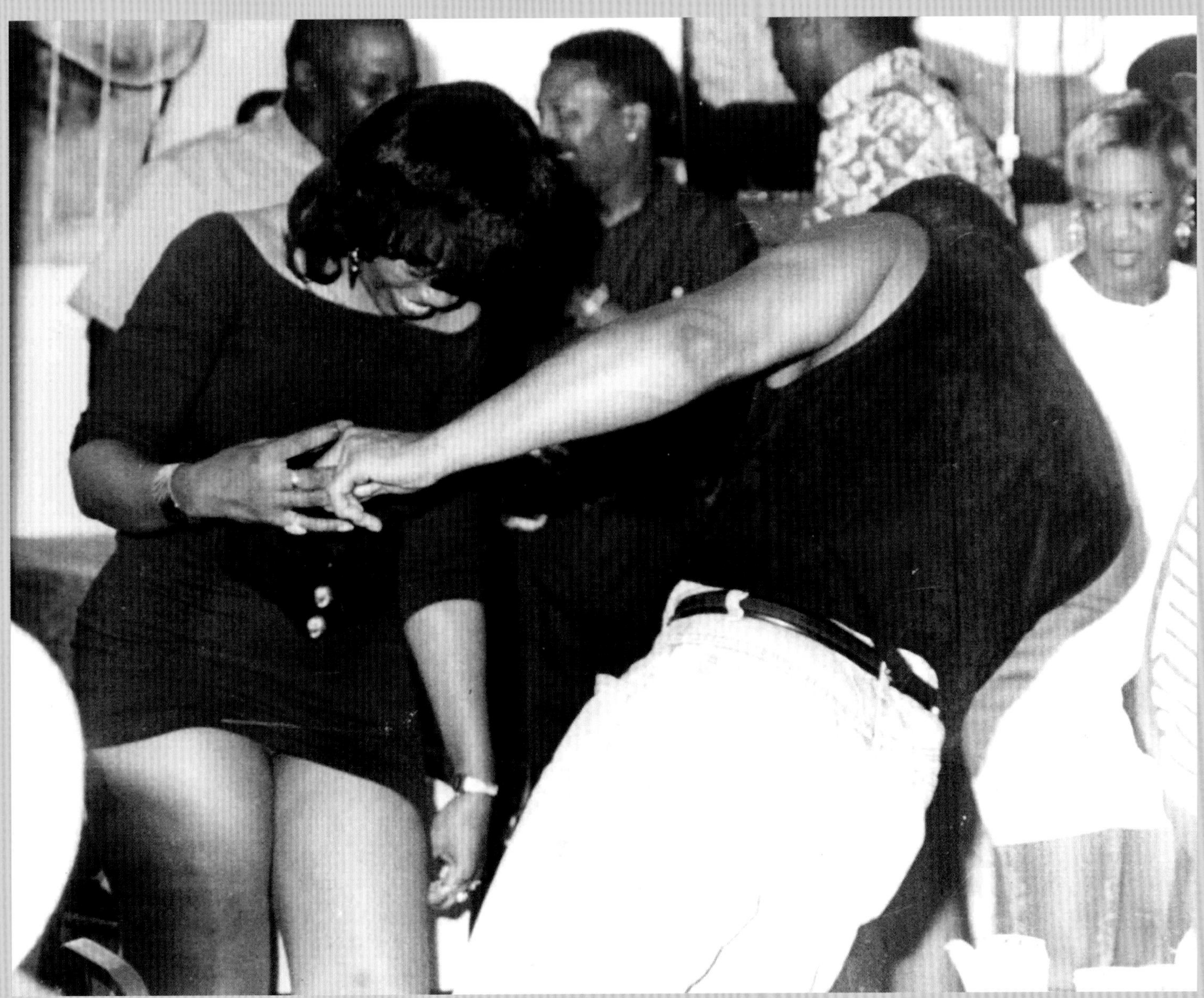

▲

Who can resist a second view of the Steamy
Couple?

◄

All eyes are riveted on the "Steamy Couple"
staging a blistering show on the dancefloor in
Shelby's Windy City Club one holiday weekend.

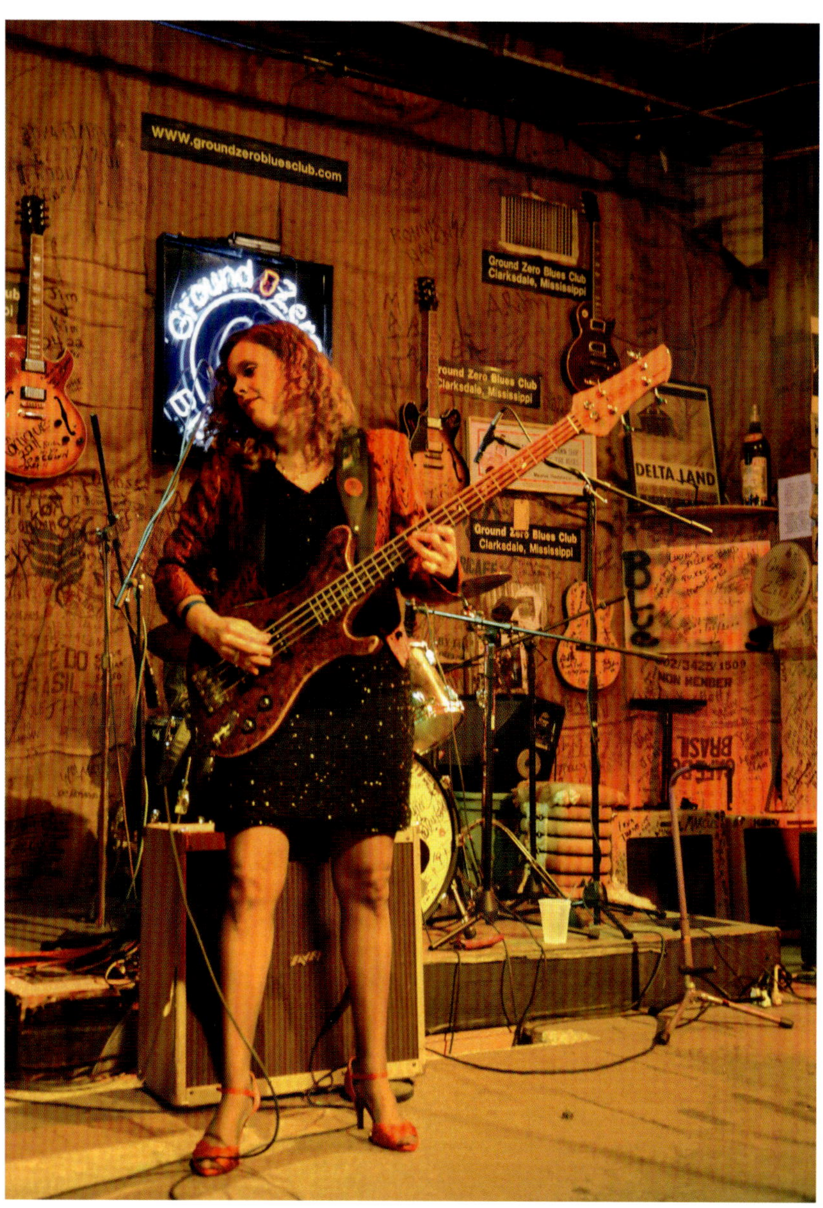

GROUND ZERO BLUES CLUB

Being in Ground Zero Blues Club is so much fun, who cares if it's not an authentic juke joint . . . especially if you dance with Morgan Freeman or Bobby Rush or Deborah. Beautiful blues bassist Heather Crosse heads her own band called Heavy Suga and the Sweet Tones, while Super Chikan Johnson stakes claim as GZBC chief and owns a bronze plaque on the front porch to back it up; virtuoso guitarist Jacqueline Nassar, all grown up now following her debut at age twelve, returns to the stage often when she's in town. Tourists from a zillion places visit

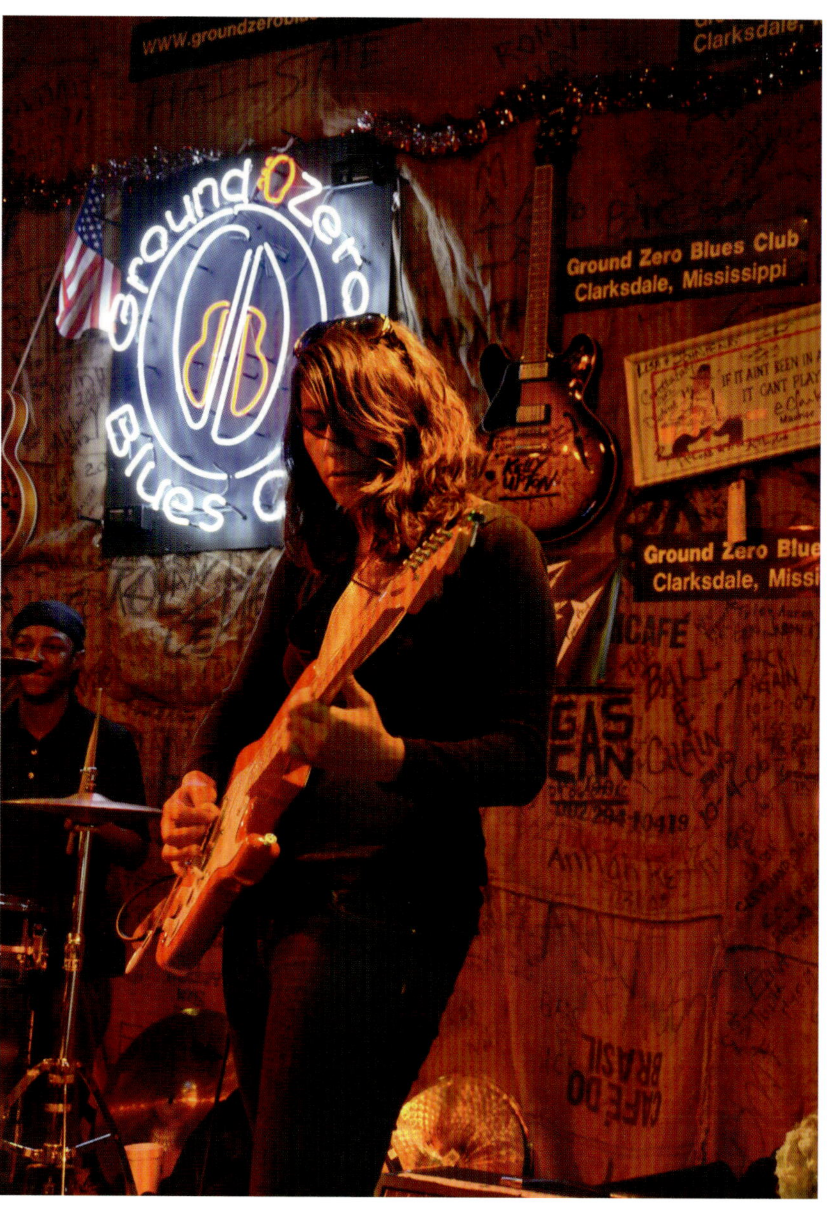

▲ Virtuoso guitarist Jacqueline Nassar, all grown up now following her debut at age twelve, often returns to the Ground Zero Blues Club stage when she's in town.

◄ Beautiful blues bassist Heather Crosse heads her own band, Heavy Suga and the Sweet Tones, performing at Ground Zero Blues Club's Thanksgiving Eve fundraiser for the Sunflower River Blues Festival.

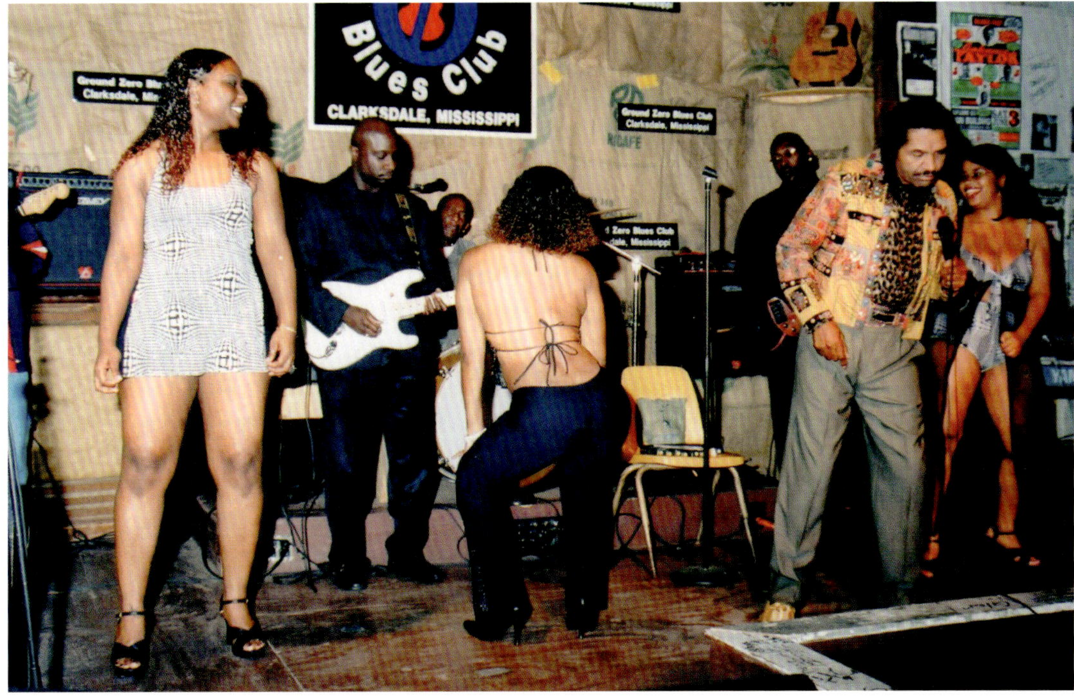

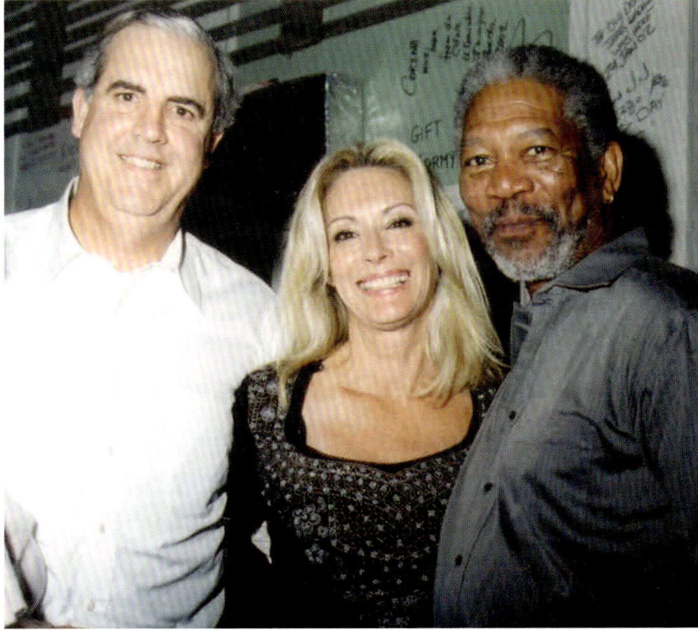

Ground Zero owners Bill Luckett (left) and Morgan
Freeman welcome entertainer Nanette Workman,
a Mississippi native with a celebrity career in
Canada.

Ground Zero each year and leave their names on the walls, tables, and bathroom mirrors. Bikers park their Harleys in the lot, celebrity journalists tape interviews for *60 Minutes*, and it is not surprising that Willie Nelson seems to fit right in. Mayor Bill Luckett welcomes many during lunch, supper, and occasional Morgan Freeman sightings.

RED'S

Decades ago *Esquire* magazine labeled Red's Blues Club at 395 Sunflower Avenue "the best place in America to hear live blues." No other club comes close: "It's the real thing," swear locals, musicians, writers, Blues Foundation purists, and even competitors. If the ceiling leaks occasionally and festival crowds have to sit on the floor to get inside, no one is complaining. Red Paden is in charge; he's become a legend as much as his best friend, Big Jack Johnson.

Red and Big Jack were fishing buddies, and when his late friend was being immortalized with a Blues Trail marker, Red told me stories about watching Jack planting turnip greens for families in the community. Robert Plant listened to music here, and on one cold winter night, Charlie Musselwhite took turns grinding deer meat into venison sausage there with a bunch of good ol' boys in the neighborhood. Red and his club have contributed more to the promotion of Delta blues and blues musicians than any other individual, business, or tourism

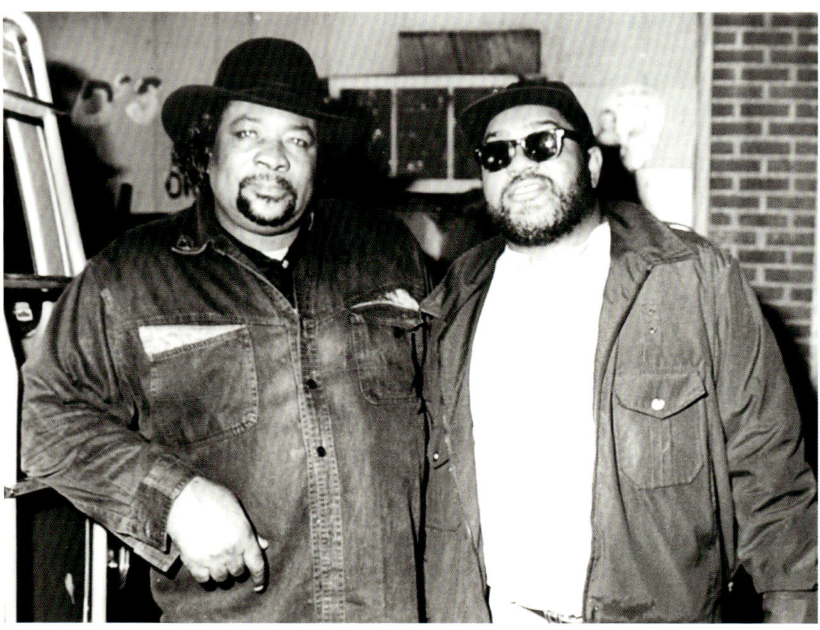

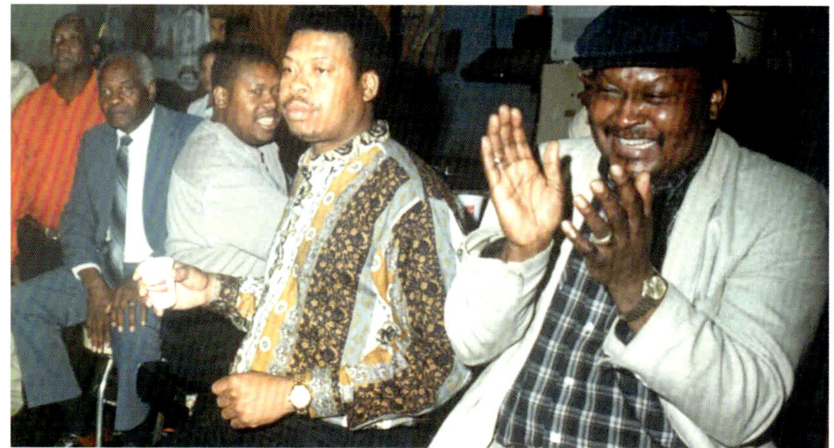

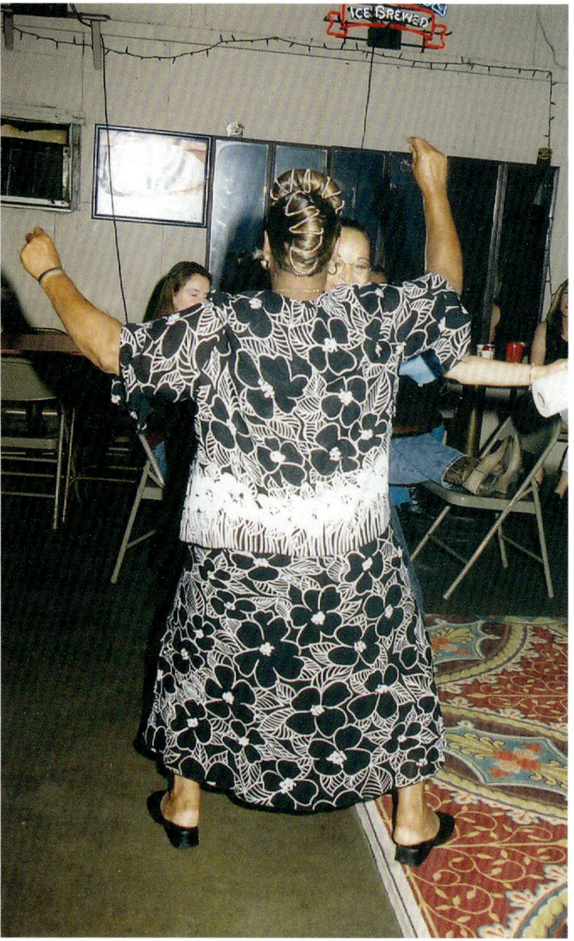

initiative I know anywhere. Loquacious he is not; intimidating he may appear behind dark glasses worn for health concerns, but Red runs "the real deal," welcomes visitors, and has endured decades when blues was not in fashion. Honored with the Blues Foundation's "Keeping the Blues Alive" Award and the Sunflower's Early Wright Award, Red has hosted benefits for ailing and aging musicians and promoted kids just getting started, as well as acoustic masters Robert Belfour, T-Model Ford, and Leo "Bud" Welch, to ripping and running blues bands that rock the walls on Sunflower Avenue. When he was not on tour, Big Jack Johnson played there exclusively. Although few can compete with the dancing elegance of Brenda and Ellis Coleman, everyone loves trying and having fun. Troublemakers in his club, white or black, are rare and are quickly shown the door and quickly forgotten. Red and I were partners recording Delta blues experiences on *Story-Corps* at the Delta Blues Museum following the museum's accolades as a recipient of the 2013 National Medal for Museum and Library Services Award.

Fishing buddies and best friends: renowned bluesman Big Jack Johnson (left) and Red Paden visit outside Red's Blues Club described decades ago by *Esquire* magazine as "the best place in America to hear live blues."

The bar crowd inside Red's is enjoying the show. Through the years Red has promoted acoustic masters T-Model Ford, Robert Belfour, and Leo "Bud" Welch, as well as electric powerhouses like Lucious Spiller.

Who needs a partner? When the music and spirit merge, it's time to dance at Red's.

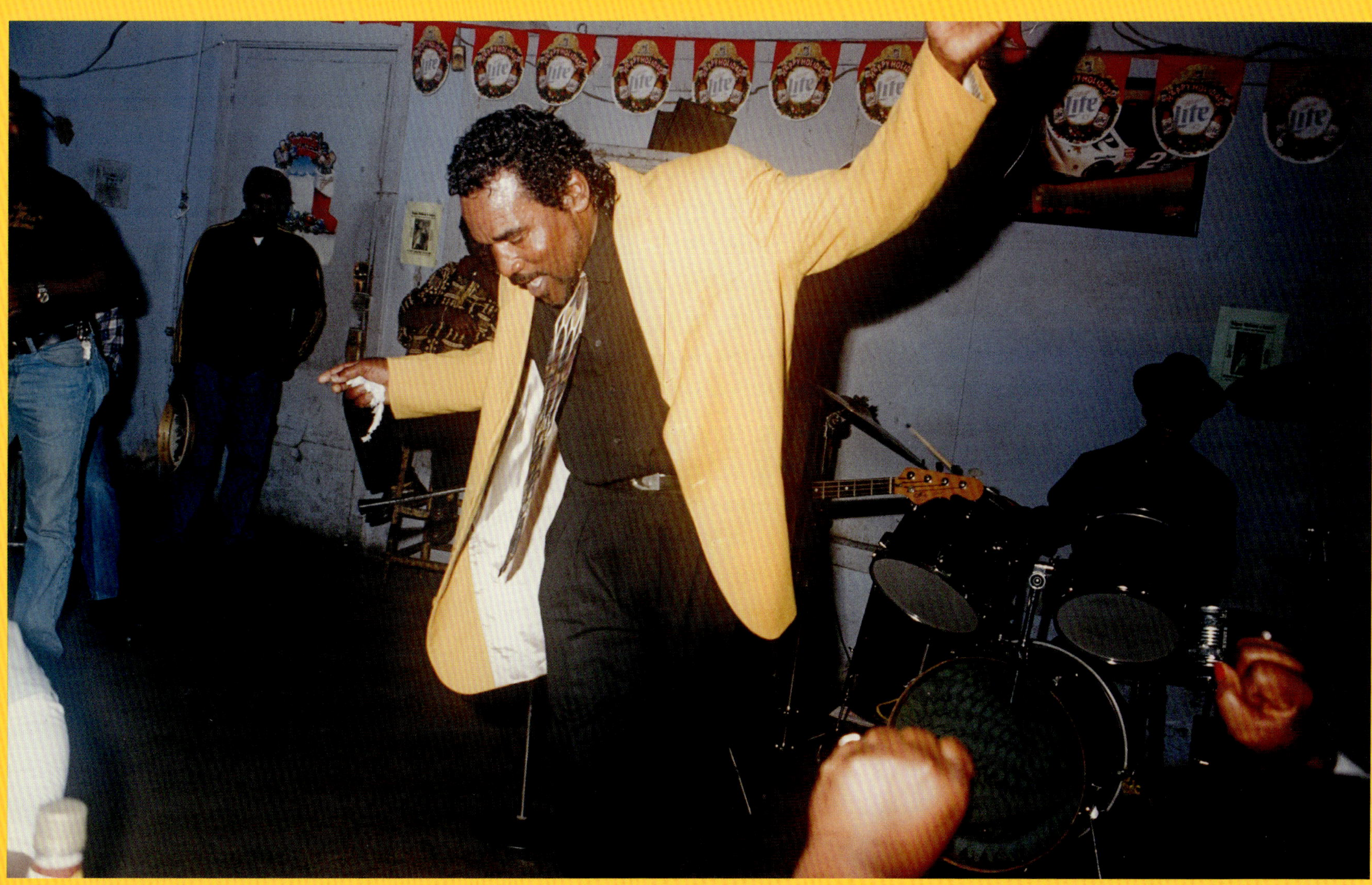

Adding class and dancing elegance on weekends inside Red's Blues Club is Ellis Coleman, Super Chikan's brother. Ellis and his gorgeous wife, Brenda, put *Dancing with the Stars* professionals to shame.

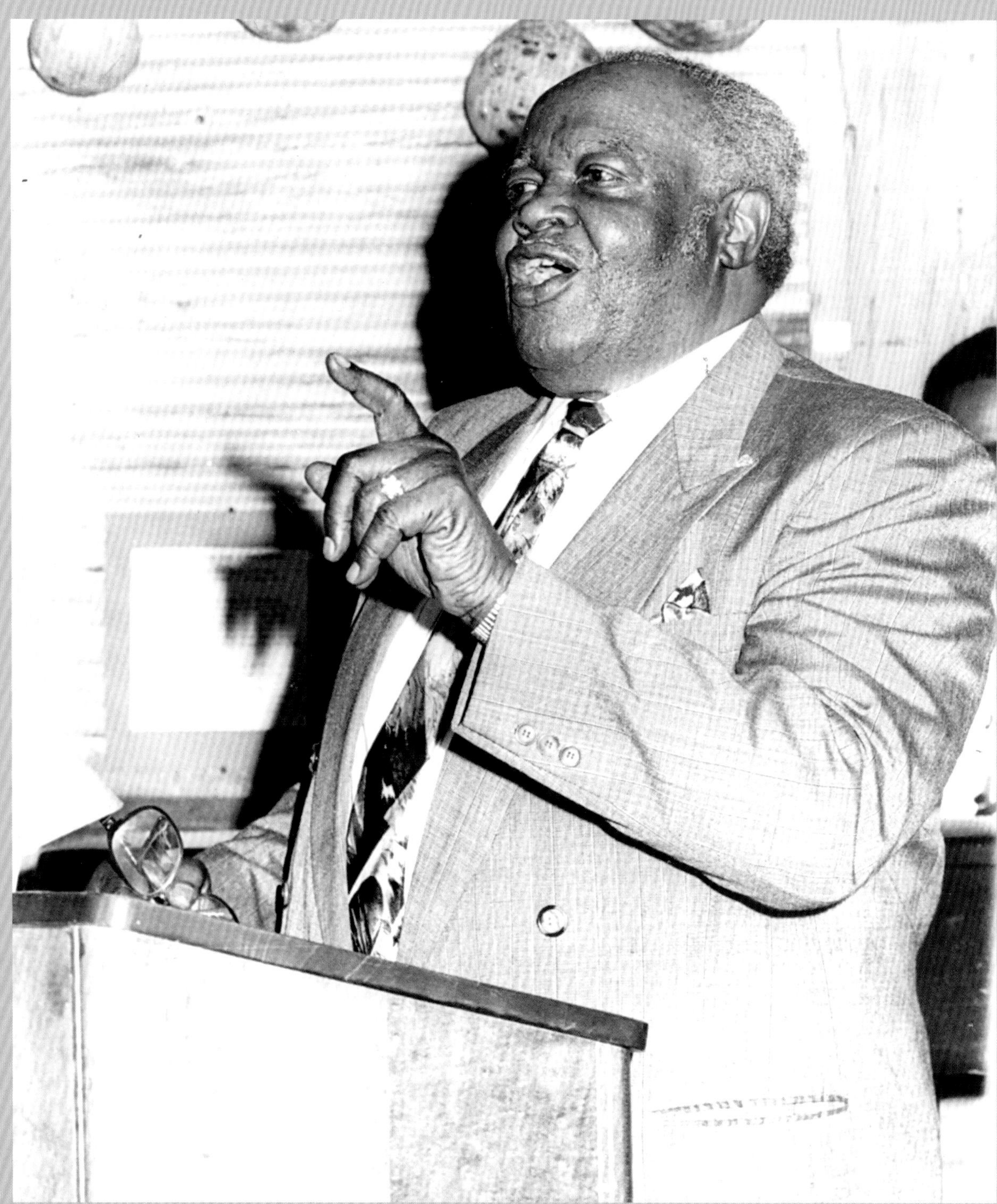

8
GOSPEL

Years ago, when Shirley Fair and I volunteered as tour guides and hopped aboard the first charter buses that came to town, she'd always say, "There's a juke joint or a church on every corner in Clarksdale." That's still about right. Blues music has come into prominence all over the world, with its roots centered in the Mississippi Delta. And the power and influence of gospel music are earth-shattering on Sundays. Listening to the choir of almost any African American church on Sunday morning is an unforgettable experience.

Although the large churches Chapel Hill, First Baptist, Haven Methodist, St. James Temple, New Covenant, and Real Life have exceptional music, even the smallest ones claim voices that rival the angels (or at least Aretha Franklin). And they love welcoming visitors.

The late Reverend Willie Morganfield, pastor of Bell Grove and a first cousin of Muddy Waters, routinely asked me to introduce my visitors at his services; Rev. Marvin K. Myles did the same in Friars Point at Friendship and Liberty Baptist in

The Reverend Willie Morganfield, a first cousin of Muddy Waters, a gospel recording artist, and pastor of Bell Grove M. B. Church, describes visiting Muddy in Chicago, in a talk at the Delta Blues Museum. Outgoing and articulate, he always welcomed visitors to his church and invited them to introduce themselves.

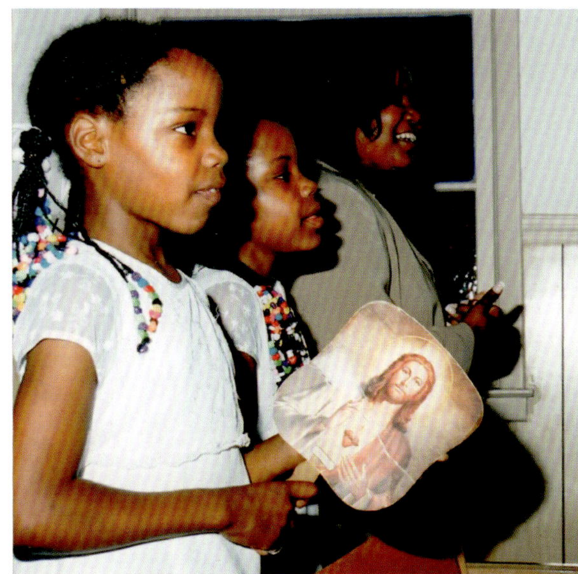

Lyon, where they continue the tradition. A hippie-style bluesman from Canada with blue nail polish on one of his pinky fingers told me he encountered amazing hospitality at St. James Temple Church of God in Christ during Sunday service.

Early Wright once organized gospel concerts featuring Clarksdale's famous native son Sam Cooke, and the Chapel Hill Men's Chorus honored Cooke in a special Sunflower Festival tribute at Ground Zero. In the audience were Cooke's brother E. B. Cooke, his nephew Eric Green, and other family members from Chicago.

The 2015 Sunflower Gospel Fest honored Myra Turner, a cousin of Ike Turner and soloist at Chapel Hill, with its Julius Guy Gospel Heritage Award. Reverend Myles and Johnny Kinnard continue to book a variety of groups from local quartets to Stella Award–winning Lee Williams and Spiritual QCs.

Coahoma Community College's acclaimed concert choir under the direction of Kelvin Towers stages several free concerts each year, travels extensively across the country, and was featured at the Mississippi Humanities Council's annual Awards Banquet in Jackson. Partnering with the Memphis Symphony Chamber Orchestra, CCC's singers annually open the Christmas season in north Mississippi.

To conclude this rambling narrative, I introduce two indomitable women of the Delta I have been fortunate to know. Both are deceased, but their vibrant lives reflect the strength, generosity, and distinctive spirit of the Mississippi Delta.

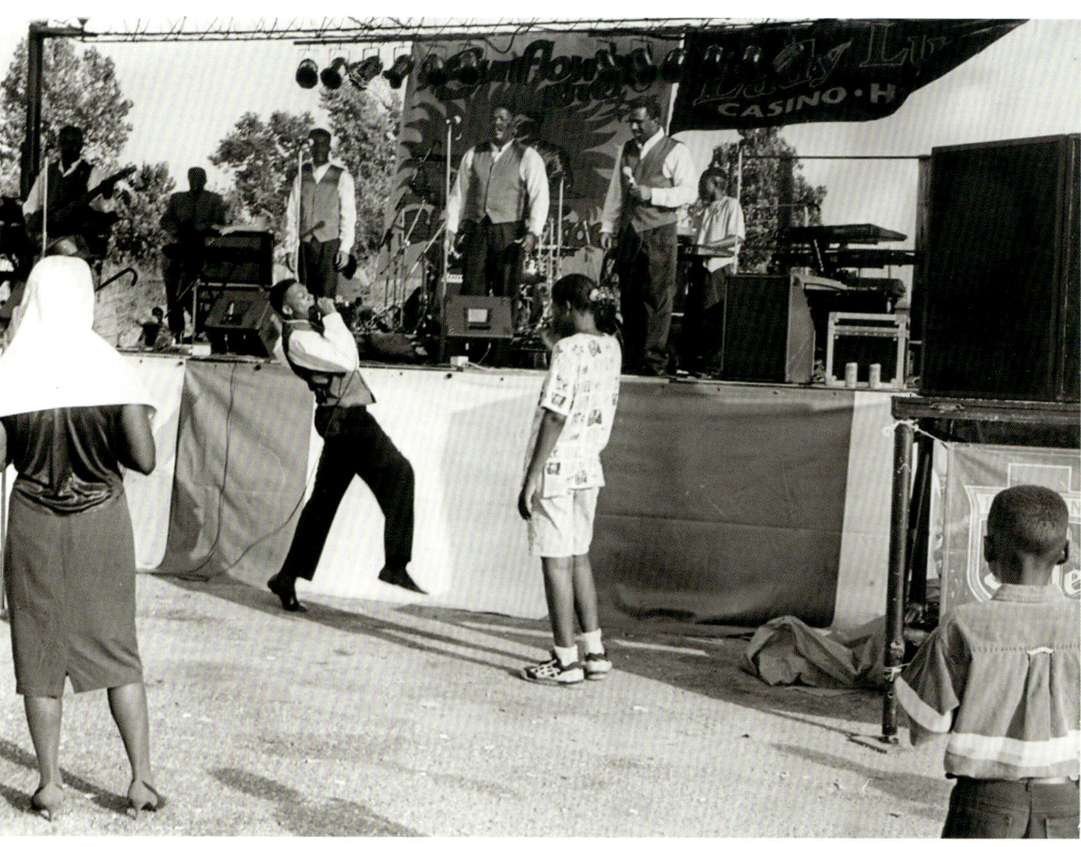

▲ A spirited harmonica player for the Sons of Wonder energizes his audience outside at a Sunflower River Gospel Festival.

◄ Daughters of powerful gospel musicians, the Collins twins listen intently to a concert inside Silent Grove M. B. Church, where soloists were recorded years ago for the Library of Congress.

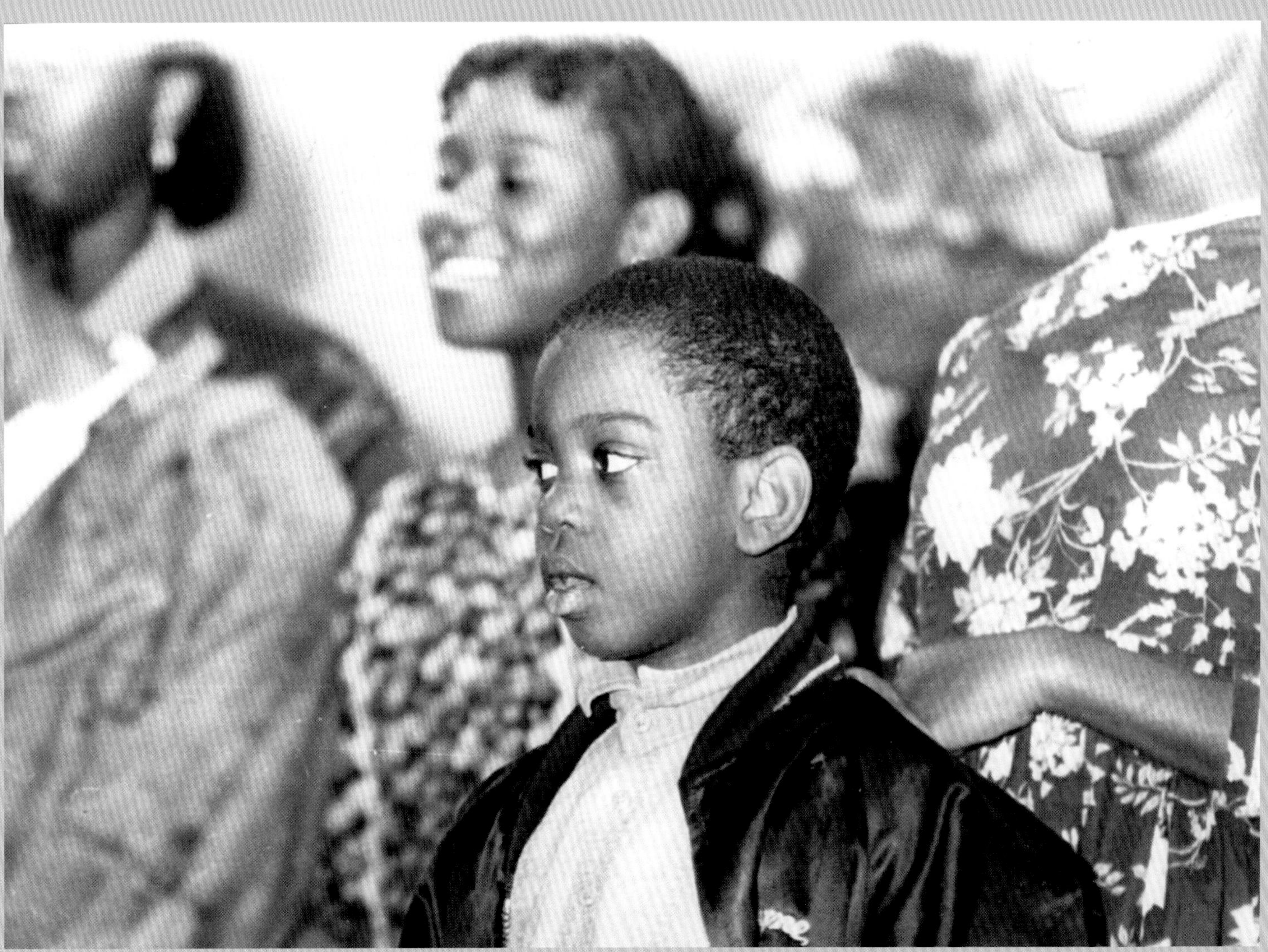

A boy child sings in the Tutwiler Community
Education Center Gospel Choir.

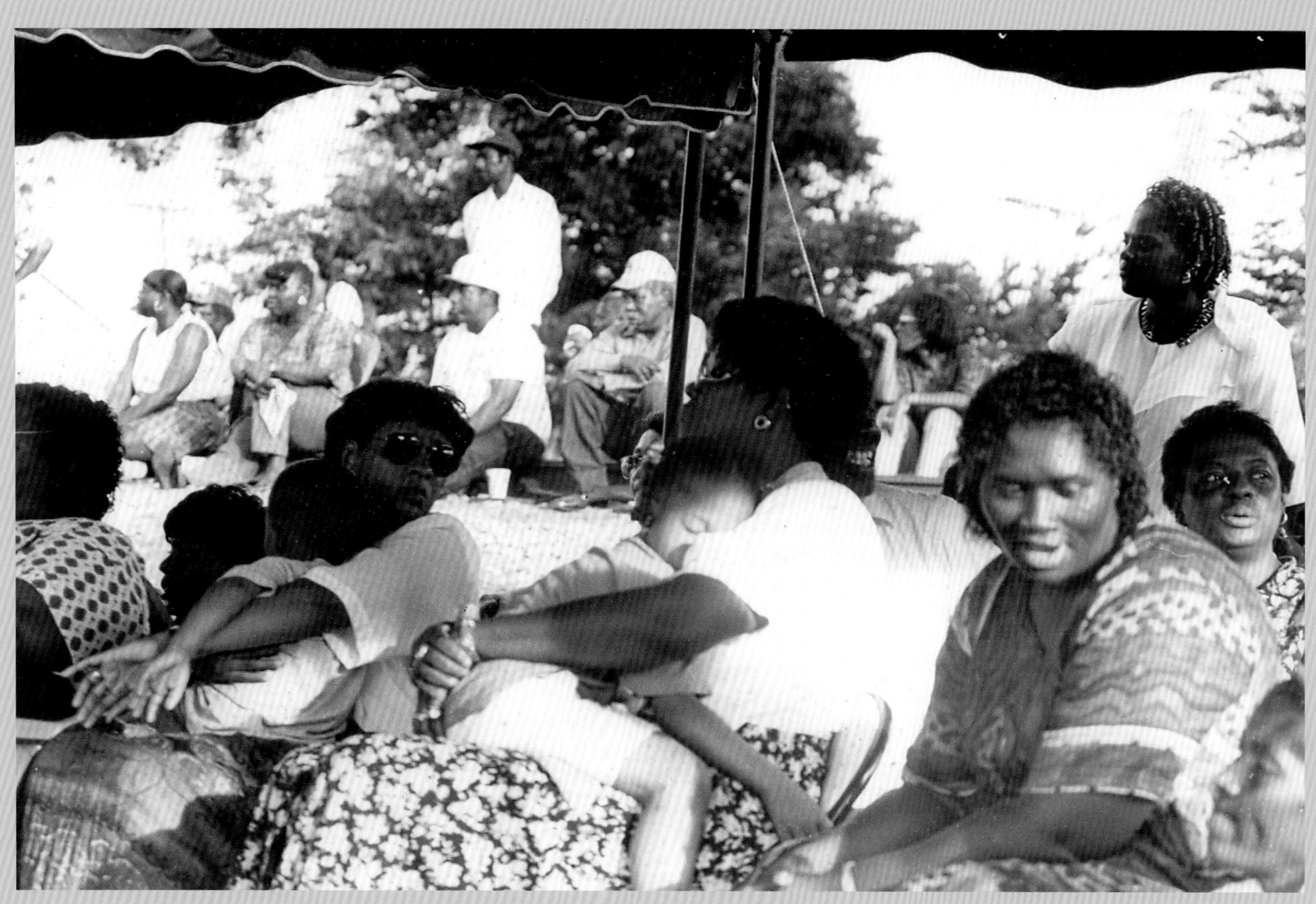

A child sleeps during the outdoor Sunflower Gospel Festival.

In matching outfits, the hat ladies attend all area gospel celebrations front and center.

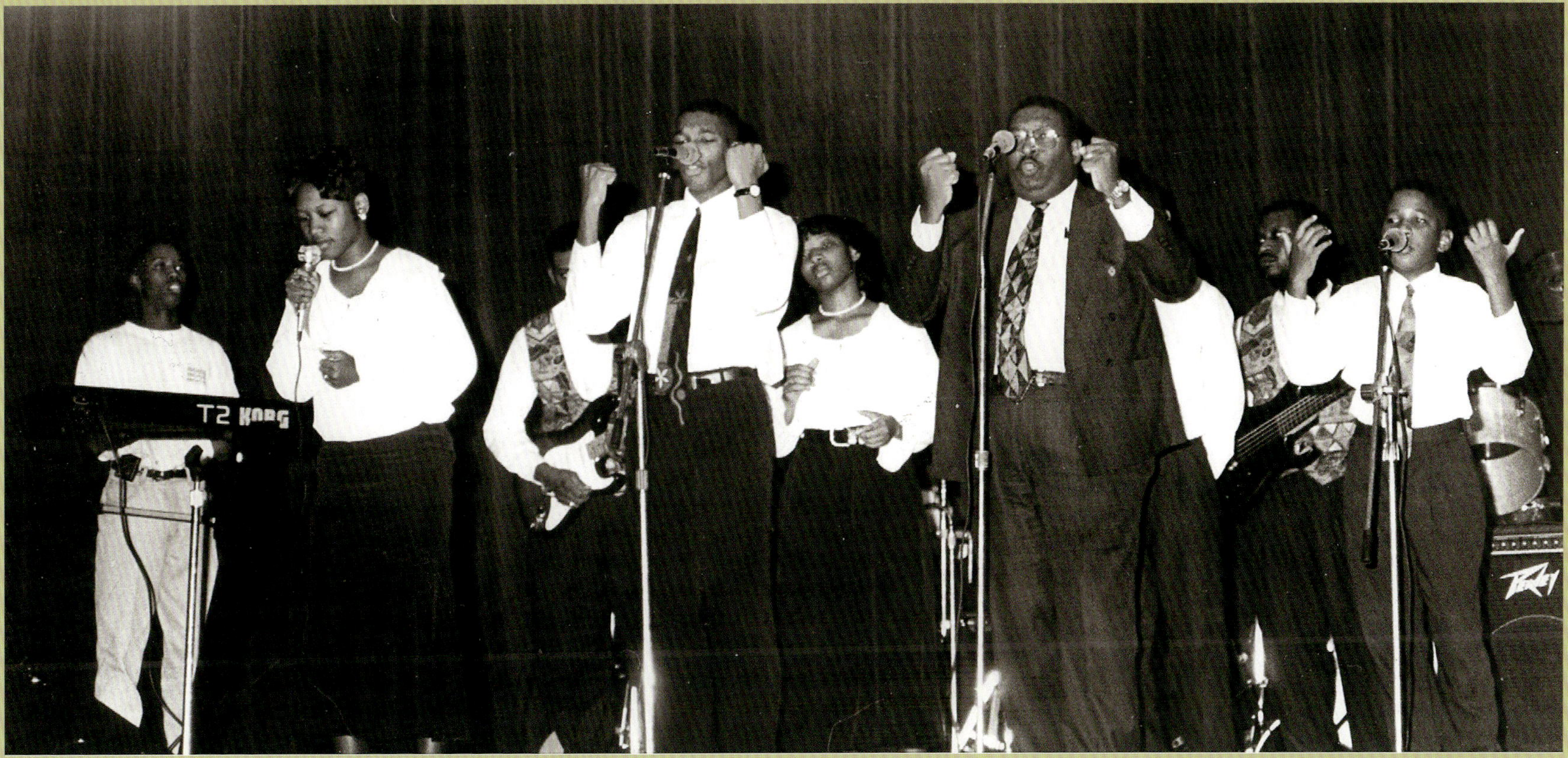

The acclaimed Myles Family—the Rev. Marvin K. Myles, Olivia Myles, and children, former Coahoma County residents when Reverend Myles pastored Friendship M. B. Church in Friars Point and Liberty M. B. Church in Lyon before moving to Kosciusko—stage a powerful gospel concert in the Clarksdale Civic Auditorium.

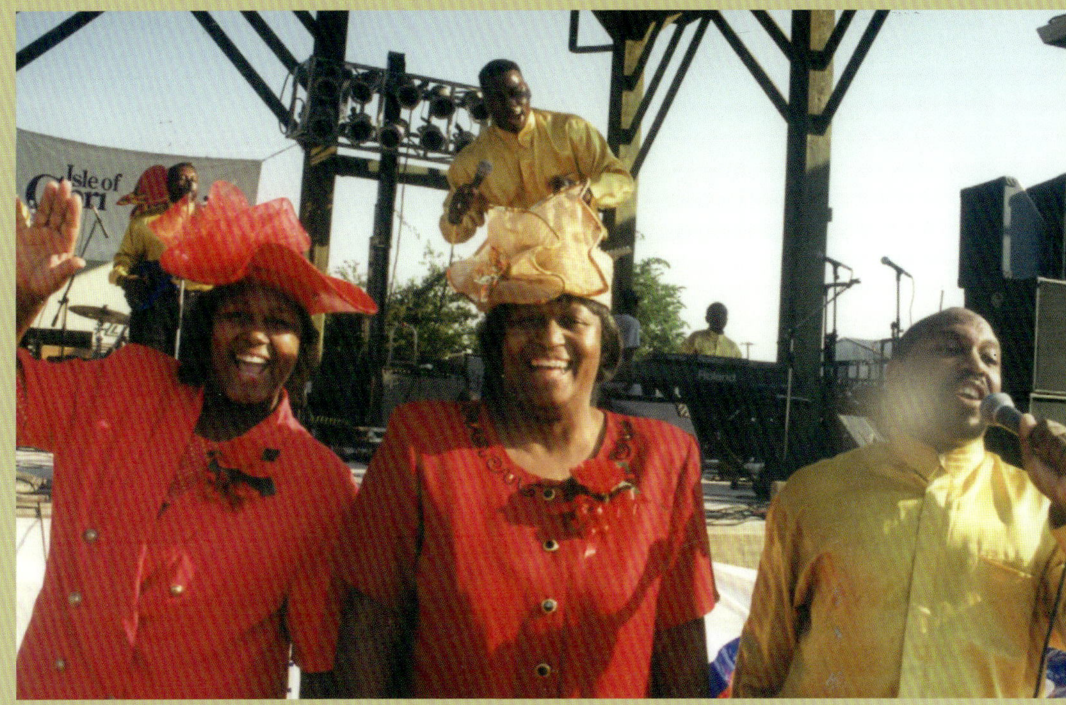

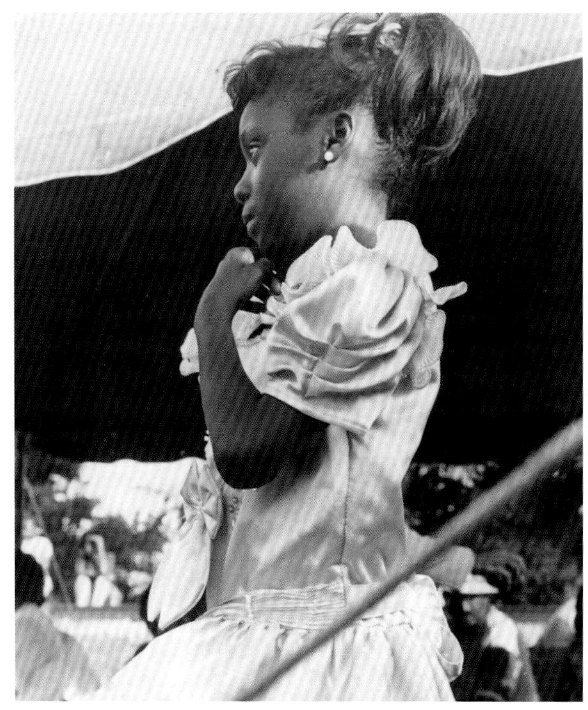

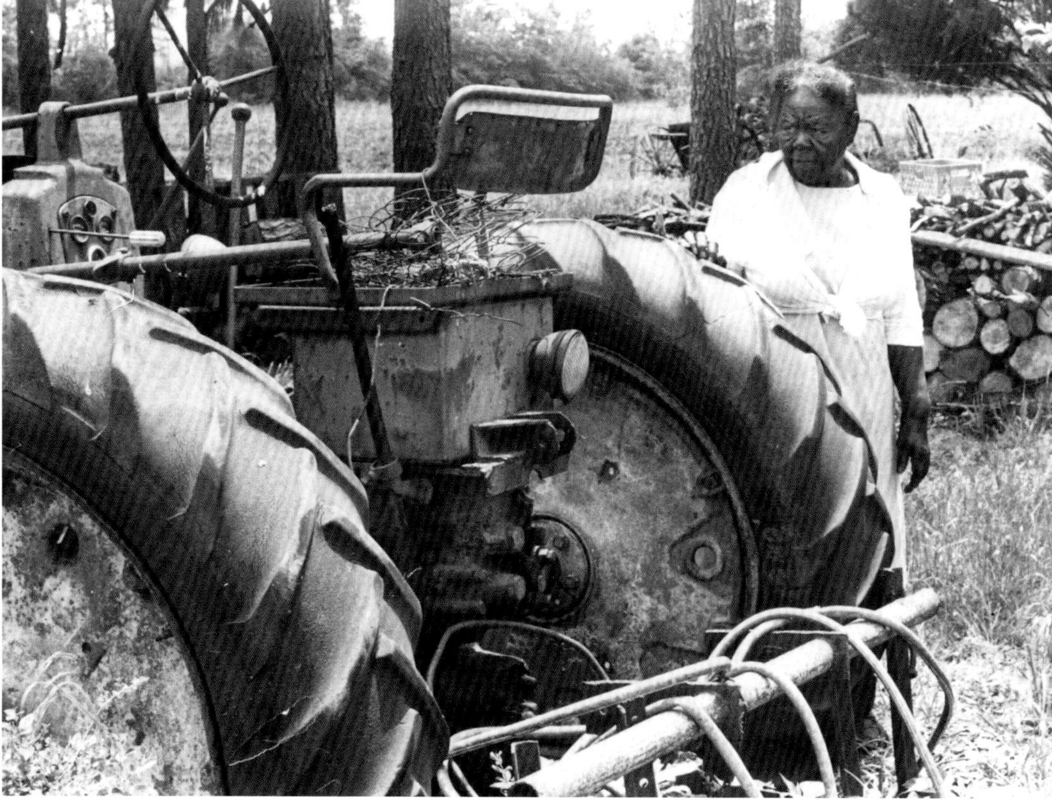

Mrs. Annie Myles, one of eight children, graduated from Rust College and began her forty-four-year teaching career in 1930 in a two-room schoolhouse, New Africa Elementary School, where her husband was principal. Although they had no children of their own, Mrs. Myles farmed, drove a tractor, and raised crops to pay room and board for neighborhood children to move into Clarksdale during the week to attend school and receive a formal education. She retired from teaching in 1974 and was recognized by the Federated Clubs of Mississippi for her instrumental role providing educational opportunities for area children. She died in 2002 at the age of ninety-two.

This photograph of Doris Carr speaks volumes. With hands on her hips, and probably one foot tapping, she is eyeing her celebrity drummer husband, Sam, fiddling around onstage with a guitar instead of readying his drum set for a festival performance. Doris once sang with the Jelly Roll Kings, booked gigs for the trio, and kept phone numbers of Frank Frost's ladies. She telephoned me often with current blues news: updates about the Handy Awards (would Willie "Big Eyes" Smith beat out Sam as top drummer?) and who was booked to play in what festival and when.

Doris and Sam attended many blues gatherings at our house and never failed to thank us afterward with a greeting card mailed

An educator and indomitable Delta woman, Mrs. Annie Myles drove a tractor after school and raised crops to pay room and board for community children to attend school in Clarksdale and receive a formal education.

Dressed in Sunday church clothes, a young girl is enthralled with the music at an outdoor gospel concert.

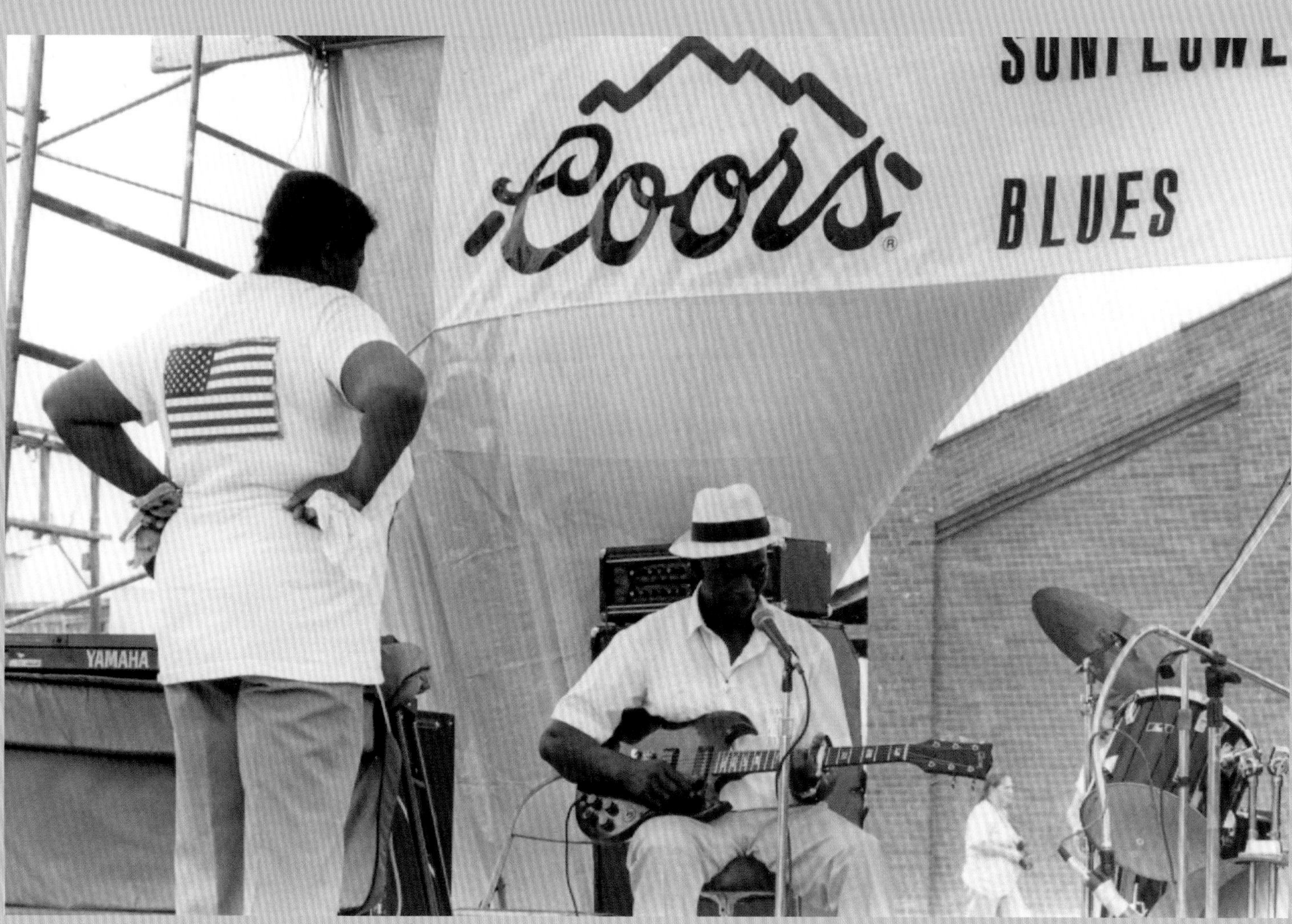

With hands on hips and probably a foot tapping, another indomitably strong Delta woman, Doris Carr, speaks volumes in this photograph while observing her husband Sam Carr onstage swapping his drum set for a guitar.

from Powell Road. She told me matter-of-factly once that several well-known musicians, including Eric Clapton, invited Sam to sit in with them when they played in Memphis.

"But by the time Sam got through with mowing and driving to Memphis, he said, they were already on stage playing, so he just came on home," she said.

Diabetic, Doris lost a limb and was unable to attend Sam's glorious 2007 Mississippi Governor's Award ceremony in Jackson. But her high spirits never diminished, and she wanted to know every detail. After she died, early in November of 2008, Sam was never quite the same. He joined us for Thanksgiving dinner at our house, but his own death followed less than a year later, in September 2009. They were married for more than sixty years. Sam and Doris are resting side by side in Thompson Chapel Cemetery beneath the Mississippi River levee on the way to Helena.

◆ ◆ ◆

During my decades steeped in blues I have learned that those who experience great joys also know great sorrow.

The strident howls from Jimi Hendrix paired with screaming hair dryers in the women's restroom of Seattle's Music Experience Museum will be linked forever to the tragedy of my brother's death. Straining to hear news of Bill's illness on my cell phone in this cacophony is a painful memory I have played over and over in my mind. My sister and I wonder what happened to the youngest in our family. He lingered unconscious for days in hospital and hospice when it became apparent he would not be returning to this world. Years later, the loss is still acute. We never said good-bye. My last words from Bill were written in a silly card urging me to finish this blues book.

When I play those scenes over and over, I am reminded of the great kindness shown to me by young friends in Clarksdale. When I returned home, the weather turned frigid, and the house I love became a prison. The cats and I moved upstairs to stay warm; I caught cold that probably became flu, and went to Dr. Brooks, who gave me an antibiotic drip. However, I was too sick to travel to Chattanooga for Bill's funeral.

My daughter Julia and my niece Sarah came by the house on the way to Chattanooga and discovered that frozen pipes had burst; my basement was flooded with four feet of water. Mara Califf and Shelley Ritter brought homemade soups and other foods every day. Gradually I began to recover and began wanting to recover.

When I have thought about the ending of my book, I realize that I am still in hiding. I had begun to talk about how blues had changed my life, and it did, but I did not tell the whole story: the joys and awakenings that came to me . . . and sorrows that often followed.

When I remember the highs from this period of my life, they are astonishing: standing onstage photographing Robert Plant's concert in Seattle; ordering fresh-squeezed orange juice each morning at the Nacional Hotel in Havana; flying to the moon with Led Zeppelin's "Kashmir" in London; and watching Arthneice Jones on television singing "Annie Mae" in the lobby of the Carlton Hotel in Cannes.

Then one Thanksgiving season while moving my large fig tree back inside the house, I received a phone call ending a relationship with a stranger I thought I knew. Blues music, dancing, and Al Green pulled me through, as well did the words of a gospel song: "I know he didn't bring me this far to leave me."

When my children were small, we loved reading *Winnie the Pooh* and *The Wind in the Willows* . . . I cried the day Owen went to first grade, and the early-afternoon naps and storytelling came to a close. It was a great experience for them to grow up in Tutwiler, and for Laura in Clarksdale. They played kick the can just as I had done, loved cats and dogs, caught lightning bugs in Mason jars. On late-August afternoons, Julia would say, "Mama, the jejews are calling . . . it's time for Owen to be at home."